Disease, Resistance, and Lies

DISEASE, RESISTANCE, AND LIES

The DEMISE of the TRANSATLANTIC SLAVE TRADE to BRAZIL and CUBA

DALE T. GRADEN

LOUISIANA STATE UNIVERSITY PRESS

BATON ROUGE

Published by Louisiana State University Press
Copyright © 2014 by Louisiana State University Press
All rights reserved
Manufactured in the United States of America
LSU Press Paperback Original

Designer: Barbara Neely Bourgoyne
Typeface: Whitman

Library of Congress Cataloging-in-Publication Data
Graden, Dale Torston, 1952–
  Disease, resistance, and lies : the demise of the transatlantic slave trade to Brazil and Cuba /
Dale T. Graden.
     p. cm.
  Includes bibliographical references and index.
  ISBN 978-0-8071-5529-5 (pbk. : alk. paper) — ISBN 978-0-8071-5530-1 (pdf) —
ISBN 978-0-8071-5531-8 (epub) — ISBN 978-0-8071-5532-5 (mobi) 1. Slave trade—Brazil—
History—19th century. 2. Slave trade—Cuba—History—19th century. 3. Slave insurrections—
Brazil—History—19th century. 4. Slave insurrections—Cuba—History—19th century.
5. Slaves—Health and hygiene. 6. Epidemics—History—19th century. I. Title.
  HT1127.G69 2014
  306.3'6209729101034—dc23

                                                                        2013039453

Portions of this text were previously published as:

"An Act 'Even of Public Security': Slave Resistance, Social Tensions, and the End of the
International Slave Trade to Brazil, 1835–1856," *Hispanic American Historical Review* 76, no. 2, 249–
82. Copyright 1996, Duke University Press. Reprinted by permission of the publisher.

"Interpreters, Translators and the Spoken Word in the Trans-Atlantic Slave Trade to Cuba and
Brazil," *Ethnohistory* 58, no. 3, 393–413. Copyright 2011, Duke University Press. Reprinted by
permission of the publisher.

"O envolvimento dos Estados Unidos no comércio transatlântico de escravos para o Brasil,
1840–1858," *Afro-Ásia*, no. 35, 9–35. Copyright 2007, Federal University of Bahia. Reprinted by
permission of the publisher.

"Slave Resistance and the Abolition of the Trans-Atlantic Slave Trade to Brazil in 1850," *História
Unisinos* 14, no. 3, 282–83. Copyright 2007, University Vale do Rio dos Sinos, doi: 10.4013/
htu.2010.143.05. Reprinted by permission of the publisher.

The paper in this book meets the guidelines for permanence and durability of the Committee on
Production Guidelines for Book Longevity of the Council on Library Resources. ∞

For Laura and Luisa

CONTENTS

———— ∞ ————

ACKNOWLEDGMENTS

Dear friends, *caros amigos*, what a journey it has been! I was born in Philadelphia and raised in Rhode Island, attended college in Boston, taught at a high school and attended graduate schools in Connecticut, and for the last two decades have resided in northern Idaho. A vivid memory from my early youth relates to "a message in a bottle." When that bottle washed up on a Rhode Island shore, it set me thinking about faraway places and ocean tides. In many ways, I have been pondering the diverse currents of the Atlantic world ever since.

I have been fortunate to have had the opportunity to read widely. One book that has stayed with me is Kenneth M. Stampp's *The Era of Reconstruction, 1865–1877*, which made an indelible impression in eleventh grade. That small volume sparked a desire to learn more about the history and cultures of the African Americas.

I have also been fortunate to have had some great (and patient!) teachers along the way, including Dale Conly, Richard D. Brown, Francisco A. Scarano, and the late Hugh M. Hamill Jr. and E. Bradford Burns.

Many scholars have shared their time, insights, and good spirits. Thanks to George Reid Andrews, Manuel Barcia, Seymour Drescher, Anani Dzidzienyo, Aisha Finch, Flávio Gomes, Lyman Johnson, Hendrik Kraay, Jane Landers, Leonardo Marques, Paulo Cesar de Oliveira, Eugenio Piñero, Maria Ligia Prado, Ines Quintero, Matthew Restall, James Riordan, David Sheinin, Richard Spence, William Swagerty, Mark Warner, and Dick Wilson. I particularly want to express my appreciation to João Reis and David Eltis, both of whom responded always with *gentileza* to many questions over the years.

Thanks to the anonymous reviewers of the manuscript. Their comments were insightful and helpful.

The Fulbright Commissions of Brazil, Venezuela, and the United States, the Office of Research and Economic Development at the University of Idaho, and the UI Department of History all provided much appreciated funding.

Several individuals helped in the preparation of this manuscript. The maps were created by Christina Brewer, Andrea Villarroel, and Kevin Henry. The vessel lists and graph were constructed by Dirk Van Beek and Jeff Meyers. Eric Wright helped with organizing the endnotes. Many books, articles, and microfilms were found and requested through interlibrary loan by Jesse Thomas and Jennifer O'Laughlin.

I could not ask more of an editor than Alisa Plant at LSU Press. She has been exceptional. Gary Von Euer provided invaluable assistance in the final preparation of the manuscript.

Thanks to the editors of *Afro-Ásia* (Salvador, Brazil), Historia Unisinos (São Leopoldo, Brazil), and *Hispanic American Historical Review* and *Ethnohistory* (both published by Duke University Press) for permission to include materials in this book that were previously published in those journals.

My parents were the offspring of four immigrants who crossed the Atlantic to the United States in the early twentieth century. They created many opportunities for my sister Beth Graden Rom, my brother Gary Graden, and me. They are missed.

This book is dedicated to Laura and Luisa, who have supported me in so many ways.

Disease, Resistance, and Lies

INTRODUCTION

—— ∞ ——

Research on Atlantic history has flourished over the past two decades. With roots in studies published in the 1950s, it has provided multiple prisms to interpret comparative histories.[1] Atlantic historians have sought to make connections among the four continents that surround the Atlantic Ocean. They have also analyzed links within hemispheres, for example between Africa and Europe, and among South America, the Caribbean, and North America. Such research has shed new perspectives on historical transformations, geographic regions, and specific events. Atlantic history has been enhanced through interdisciplinary approaches.[2] Its umbrella enables one to trace the ties that bind international commerce, public health, and social history.

By 1800, the United States, Brazil, and Cuba played major roles in the Atlantic world. In each country, elites gained wealth from the sale of commodities produced by slaves. In the United States, cotton became king. Cotton production in the United States rose from 750 tons in 1790 to 18,300 tons in 1800 to approximately 1 million tons in 1860. Raw cotton represented more than one-half of all U.S. exports by the outbreak of the Civil War in 1861. New England's 472 mills processed hundreds of millions of pounds of cotton from 1830 to 1860. England's 2,650 cotton factories received more than half of all U.S. cotton exports.[3]

In Brazil, coffee replaced sugar as its primary export. Although sugar exports increased from 20,000 tons in 1800 to 120,000 tons in 1850, profits were low. The value of sugar to the economy doubled between 1820 and 1870, considered to be a slow rate of growth. Between 1820 and 1835, the output of coffee jumped from 14,300 tons per year to 66,000 tons per year. This placed Brazil ahead of competitors producing coffee in Jamaica, Cuba, and Java.[4] The value of exports increased significantly, from 7 million pounds sterling in the 1820s to 50 million in the 1850s to 113 million in the 1870s. By mid-century, coffee represented one-half of all exports from Brazil.[5]

Sugar became king in Cuba. In the words of Professor Louis A. Pérez Jr., "sugar cultivation expanded rapidly during the first half of the nineteenth century, and its expansion heralded the transformation of all of Cuba."[6] Between 1839 and 1868, Cuba's share of the world market almost doubled, increasing from 15.8 percent (130,200 tons out of 820,318 tons) to 30 percent (749,000 tons out of 2.5 million tons).[7] Sugar represented 60 percent of total exports from Cuba in 1840 and 74 percent in 1860. During this period, coffee output declined due to two hurricanes, world competition, and a downturn in prices. Coffee exports dropped from 31,250 tons in 1833 to 6,992 tons in 1845 and 1,928 tons in 1867.

The United States was a powerhouse in the Atlantic world of the nineteenth century. Its economy grew rapidly for many reasons, including slave labor, population growth, immigration, the accessibility of natural resources, technological transformation, and entrepreneurship.[8] As a result, trade with Brazil and Cuba widened. By mid-century, the United States received half of Brazil's coffee exports, worth eight million dollars. Brazil purchased flour, lumber, and manufactured goods sent from the United States.[9] The number of U.S. ships arriving in Cuba rose from 150 in 1796 to 1,886 in 1852. The percentage of Cuba's total exports sent to the United State rose from 39 percent in 1850 to 48 percent in 1859, 65 percent in 1865, and 82 percent in 1877.[10] By means of commercial relations, U.S. merchants sought to compete with England for markets and political influence throughout the Americas.

The transatlantic slave trade played a central role in the Atlantic world from the fifteenth century. This traffic has been described as "perhaps the most thoroughly multinational business of the early modern era."[11] Its tentacles reached far and wide. Between 1501 and 1867, traffickers transported some 13 million enslaved Africans to the Americas to satisfy labor demand. Of these, some 10.7 million survived the Middle Passage. Eight million others died on the journey from the interior of Africa or during captivity along the coast of Africa.[12] The United States received less than 4 percent of the total number of Africans brought to the Americas, Cuba 7.4 percent, and Brazil at least 44 percent.[13] Approximately 90 percent of enslaved Africans and creoles (born in the Americas) produced commodities on farms and plantations.[14] The growth of the economies of the United States, Cuba, and Brazil depended on slave labor.[15]

In the first half of the nineteenth century, the transatlantic slave trade differed with regard to the three receiving areas of the United States, Brazil, and Cuba. Based on agreements signed at the Constitutional Convention, the United States outlawed the importation of Africans in 1808. Importations to Brazil continued until 1851, when its imperial government made further disembarkations illegal and enforced this law (known as the Eusébio de Queiroz law and passed in September 1850). During the first half of the nineteenth century, the number of African slaves landing on Brazilian coasts reached levels unprecedented in the long history of that nation. One estimate is that 2.1 million Africans arrived during these five decades, or some 42 percent of the total number transported to Brazil during more than three centuries of the slave trade.[16] In the words of Senator Silveira Martins from the province of Rio Grande do Sul, "Brazil is coffee and coffee is the Negro."[17] In 1867, Cuba became the last nation in the Americas to end the slave trade. As with Brazil, the number of Africans transported to Cuba between 1800 and 1867 reached the highest levels in its history.[18]

Who were the Africans who arrived in Brazil and Cuba? In following the major contours of the transatlantic slave trade in terms of chronology and the numbers of Africans disembarked, this short overview moves from south to north.

From the late sixteenth century to the 1860s, traffickers transported 5 million slaves from West Central Africa to the Americas. This meant that the largest number of slaves forced into the transatlantic Middle Passage departed from the West Central Coast of the continent (45.5 percent). Eltis and Richardson estimate that nearly 2.3 million Africans arrived in the Center South provinces of Brazil from West Central Africa. Another 280,000 Africans were transported from East Central Africa (present-day Mozambique and Tanzania) to Center South Brazil.[19] Hence the Center South provinces (or Southeast) of Brazil received the largest number of African slaves (21.5 percent of the total) of any importing region in the Americas. Its 350-mile coastline was bounded on the north by the town of Macaé (province of Rio de Janeiro) and on the south by Santos (province of São Paulo).

Africans originating in areas of present-day Angola, Congo, Cabinda, Zaire, southern Gabon, and Mozambique departed on slave vessels from the Atlantic ports of Cabinda, Ambriz, Luanda, and Benguela. A bilateral enterprise evolved between Brazil and West Africa from the 1580s to the 1840s. This resulted in a preponderant Bantu presence along the coast and interior of the Brazilian Southeast.[20] The African Diaspora of people and cultures did not move only from east to west across the Atlantic, from Africa to Brazil. As a result of South Atlantic connections, a number of Brazilians and Africans who had gained their freedom in Brazil moved to west central African cities.[21]

Different from other regions such as the Mina Coast further north, where there existed numerous distinct languages, cultures, and ethnic groups, "Central Africa represented a largely linguistically and culturally homogenous region."[22] Given the presence of European and Afro-European traders from the 1480s, a "mixed cultural heritage" emerged. The Portuguese used an assortment of names to identify the origins of these Africans, which included Angola, Benguela, Cabinda, Cassange, Congo, Monjolo, Rebolo, Cabundá, Ganguela, Ambaca, Mondubi (in West Central Africa), and Mozambique, Quilimane, Imhambane, Sena, and Macua (in East Central Africa).[23] Past experiences of West Central Africans enhanced their capacity to resist enslavement in Brazil. In the words of Professor Alison Games, "soldiers from Africa, especially those captured during the protracted civil wars in Kongo and sold into the slave trade, brought with them strategies, ideologies, and communal structures derived from their military backgrounds, and employed them in acts of resistance in the Americas."[24]

Central Africans impressed observers in Brazil by their differences and exoticism less than Africans who arrived from West Africa (such as the Yoruba and Fon people). Authors from the 1890s through the 1970s, including Nina Rodrigues, Edison Carneiro, Ruth Landes, Arthur Ramos, and Roger Bastide, perpetuated a notion of Mina superiority and "religious purity" in contrast to Bantu cultural and spiritual inferiority.[25] A consequence has been that research focusing on the Bantu presence in Brazil lagged in the twentieth century behind that directed toward those Africans who arrived from West Africa. In the past three decades, interest has surged among historians, including Joseph Miller, Mary Karasch, Robert Slenes, Marina de Mello e Souza, Lucilene Reginaldo, Flávio Gomes, David Northrup, John Thornton, Linda Heywood, and James Sweet. These scholars have offered insights on how shared values did much to perpetuate Central African cultural traditions in Brazil and across the Americas.

Situated 750 miles to the northeast of Rio de Janeiro, the Portuguese colony of Bahia (1549–1822), which then became a province of independent Brazil (1822–1889), followed close behind Center South Brazil in the number of African slaves to arrive on its shores. Eltis and Richardson estimate that close to 1.6 million Africans disembarked in the Bay of All Saints at Salvador, on beaches north and south of the city, and on nearby islands such as Itaparica (14.7 percent of the total brought to the Americas).[26] Close to half of the Africans transported to Bahia originated in Central West Africa.[27] Many remained in Salvador and the province of Bahia. Traffickers also sent these Bantu speakers to other provinces, including north to Pernambuco and to gold and diamond mines in the interior provinces of Minas Gerais, Goiás, and Mato Grosso.

A huge influx of African slaves arrived at Bahia from West Africa beginning in the first half of the nineteenth century. The most numerous and influential of these ethnic groups was the Yoruba, who resided in a territory situated in present-day eastern Benin and western Nigeria. Out of an estimated 469,000 Yoruba slaves transported to the Americas between 1800 and 1850, some 291,000, or 62 percent, arrived in Bahia. These slaves departed from the Mina Coast (also often labeled by Europeans "the Slave Coast" and "the Bight of Benin"), which included the port cities of Little Popo, Great Popo, Ouidah, Porto Novo, Badagry, and Lagos. Having forged commercial and cultural ties along the Mina Coast from the eighteenth century, Portuguese and Brazilian traders expanded their operations in the region. Due to conflicts deep in the interior of the Bight of Benin, including an 1804 *jihad* (a Muslim holy war in support of Islam) and continued Yoruba civil wars, increasing numbers of slaves arrived to the coast.[28] As in West Central Africa, an array of Brazilian merchants and traffickers along with freed Africans gained prominence in the cities along the Mina Coast.[29]

The arrival of thousands of Yoruba transformed social life in Bahia from the 1820s. Cosmopolitan in their outlook, many had experience in long-distance trade in Africa. They brought with them established cultural traditions and diverse agricultural skills. Enslaved due to civil conflicts that raged in Yorubaland, some were tenacious warriors. An impressive list of scholars has contributed multiple perspectives on African Bahia, including Pierre Verger, Katia Mattoso, Maria Inês C. de Oliveira, Stuart Schwartz, João José Reis, Lisa Earl Castillo, Maria José Rapassi Mascarenhas, Renato da Silveira, Luis Nicolau Parés, Bert Barickman, and Hendrik Kraay, to note a relatively small number.

In Bahia, the Yoruba became known as Nagô. Many of the Nagô practiced Islam. West Africans of other ethnicities also arrived in Bahia during these years, including Gbe speakers, known as Jeje in Bahia; the Nupe, the Hausa, and the Borno. Many of these Africans also practiced Islam. Professor Joseph C. Miller suggests that "the tone of life under slavery [in Bahia and the Brazilian Northeast] cohered around the Western African backgrounds of the majority of those enslaved there."[30] Havana and Salvador became Yoruba cities in many ways in the first half of the nineteenth century.[31]

As with Brazil, traffickers transported tens of thousands of African slaves to Cuba. The destruction of plantations in Saint-Domingue during the Haitian Revolution (1791–1804) gave impetus to the transformation of the Cuban countryside from small farms to plantations dependent on slave labor.[32] A conservative estimate is that at least 766,000 Africans were disembarked between 1780 and 1867.[33] Cuba "received the greatest mix of African peoples" from different tribes and regions. As a result, the island became home to one of the most diverse African-born populations in the Atlantic world. Purchasers and sellers classified 90 percent of all Africans who arrived in the first half of the nineteenth century into five groups: Carabalí, Congo, Gangá, Lucumí, and Mandinga. In resisting their enslavement, Africans in Cuba showed an impressive capacity to forge pan-African alliances as well as alliances with enslaved creoles and free blacks.

In his classic study *Hampa afrocubana: los negros brujos* (1906), Cuban anthropologist Fernando Ortiz revealed amazement at the richness of the multiethnic world that surrounded him: "I began my investigations but soon realized that I, like most Cubans, was utterly confused. For it was not only the curious phenomenon of Negro Masonry [Abakuá customs brought by Calabarí Africans from southeast Nigeria and northwest Cameroon] that I encountered, but also a most complex mélange of religious survivals of remote cultural origin. All this with a variety of societal origins, languages, music, instruments, dances, songs, traditions, legends, arts, games, and folkways; in other words, I found the whole conglomeration of different African cultures—then virtually unknown to men of science—had been transplanted to Cuba."[34] The former slave Esteban Montejo (born ca. 1860) echoed such perspectives in remembering his childhood in Cuba: "My godfather was named Gin Congo [which meant that he understood himself to be from West Central Africa]. My father's name was Nazario, and he was Lucumí from Oyo [an empire in the northern Yoruba territory of Nigeria of some 150,000 square miles, in power from the

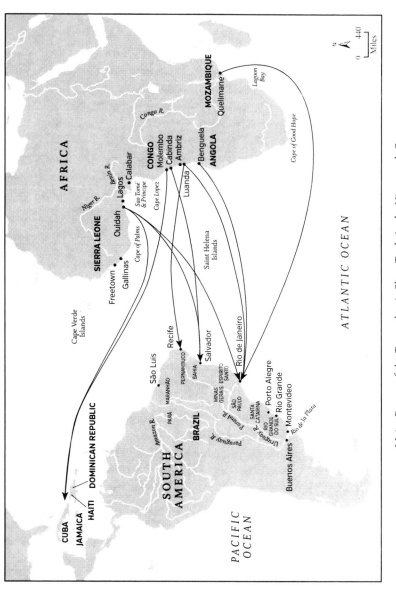

MAP 1. Major Routes of the Transatlantic Slave Trade in the Nineteenth Century

fourteenth century to the 1820s]. . . . The difference between the Congo and
the Lucumí is that the Congo does things, and the Lucumí tells the future.
The Lucumís did not like to work with [sugar] cane, and many ran away. . . .
White man's music has no drum at all. Tasteless."[35] Such insights have inspired
scholars to write detailed analyses of African Cuba since the turn of the twen-
tieth century, including Fernando Ortiz, Manuel Moreno Fraginals, Miguel
Barnet, Pedro Deschamps Chapeaux, María Elena Díaz, Aisnara Perera Día,
Phillip A. Howard, Ada Ferrer, George Brandon, Stephan Palmié, Robert Pa-
quette, Rebecca Scott, Louis A. Pérez Jr., José Luciano Franco, and Manuel
Barcia, among several others.

Given their central role as disembarkation points in the transatlantic slave
trade, the port cities of Rio de Janeiro, Salvador, and Havana became African
cities in the first half of the nineteenth century.[36] Enslaved and free blacks embraced an African lexicon—often distinct from names chosen by Iberians—to
denote locales familiar to them. Examples include the present-day barrio of
Bangu in Rio de Janeiro, derived from the African word *Bangue*, which is a
town near the coast of Cameroon. The term *banguê* was also used by slaves
to describe a mill to store bagasse derived from the crushed stalks of sugarcane. Likewise, the barrio of Calabar, home to an enclave of Calabarí in the
nineteenth century, continues to exist in Salvador. In the case of Havana, no
districts have retained African names. Within the barrio of Jesús María, which
lay outside the walls surrounding the old city of Havana, was a low-lying area
named Manglar (meaning mangrove, most likely of Spanish origin). Manglar
became well known among Africans due to the number of fugitive slaves residing there by the end of the eighteenth century. In the early nineteenth
century, authorities burned it down.[37] Bantu names have survived in other
locales on the island, including Songo, Honsolosongo, and Monitongos.[38] African cultural expression flourished in the religions of Macumba, Candomblé,
and Santería. African mutual aid societies and Catholic brotherhoods provided
succor and fraternity to members. Slaves took off from masters and found refuge in urban and suburban *quilombos* (from the Bantu word *kilombo*, meaning
in Brazil an escaped slave community).

Enslaved and free Africans found employment in the ports and along the
docks. They received and disseminated information throughout the Atlantic
world via the ships that entered, anchored in, and departed from the harbors.
In the words of cultural historian Ivor L. Miller, "among the benefits of having a presence [of Africans of Carabalí origin] on the docks [at Havana] was

communication with sailors who brought news about events throughout the Atlantic world, a privilege that only increased in 1818 when Cuba's ports were open to unrestricted world trade [as occurred in Brazil in 1808]. Black sailors arriving from throughout the Atlantic region, including New York City, Calabar, and Britain, reported on current events, including news of antislavery activity in Brazil, Jamaica, Haiti, and the southern United States. In Havana and Matanzas, the Carabalí and Abakuá were a conduit for these communications."[39] In each of the three cities, port workers became aware of the widening presence of U.S. interests after 1800.

U.S. ships, capital, products, merchants, captains, and crews played an important role in transporting Africans to Brazil and Cuba.[40] While the traffic to the United States remained "legal" through 1807, merchants from Rhode Island transported thousands of slaves to Caribbean islands and different locations in the United States in vessels constructed in the United States. After the prohibition of U.S. involvement in the traffic, U.S. entrepreneurs looked to opportunities offshore. As a result, many ships built in the United States transported African slaves to Brazil and Cuba in the nineteenth century.

Disease, Resistance, and Lies sheds light on two triangles of the transatlantic slave trade in the nineteenth century. The first linked the eastern seaboard of the United States to Africa and Cuba. It emerged in the second half of the eighteenth century and remained in place until the traffic to Cuba ended in 1867. A second triangle, which linked Cuba, Brazil, and Africa, appeared in the 1830s. It continued until the traffic to Brazil was halted in 1851. One vector of the southern triangle was a long-established bilateral trade that linked Brazil and Africa (see maps in next chapter). The southern triangle has received little attention from historians writing about the Atlantic world in the nineteenth century.[41] U.S.-built ships and U.S. capital played a central role in both the northern and southern triangle trades.

British suppression of the transatlantic slave trade had a profound impact on the Atlantic world. In the eighteenth century, England was the largest trafficker in African slaves. From the 1780s, a shift in mentality occurred. A working-class movement coalesced that petitioned Parliament to end British participation in the traffic.[42] Church leaders and activists joined in protests.[43] The expansion of capitalism brought with it values critical of the slave trade.[44] With Parliament's decision to prohibit British involvement in the traffic after 1807, Great Britain made an about-face. It signed treaties with several nations in its quest to end the traffic in African slaves. Prime ministers sent forth the British Naval Squadron to capture slave ships and bring these vessels to international tribunals. Established by treaties signed in 1817, Mixed Commission Courts in England sent judges to Rio de Janeiro, Havana, and Freetown (Sierra Leone) to work in bilateral courts alongside peers representing Portugal (Brazil was independent after 1822) and Spain; these judged ships accused of involvement in the transatlantic slave trade.[45]

A second variable contributing to the demise of the transatlantic slave trade to Brazil and Cuba was infectious disease. Ships carried infections throughout the Atlantic world from the fifteenth century onward.[46] Enslaved Africans forced into the holds of slavers often perished from various sicknesses. Due to insalubrious environments on the coast of Africa, crews of slave ships also died at high rates. From the late eighteenth century, various individuals pointed to the threats to public health posed by the disembarkation of ill Africans on American shores. These included medical personnel, port officials, and common folk. Outbreaks of infections in ports and on land, believed to originate on slave ships, fueled political debates and popular protests over the threats posed by the landing of African slaves in Brazil and Cuba.[47]

A third factor that impacted the transatlantic slave trade was slave resistance. Africans resisted enslavement in every segment of the Middle Passage, during the journey from the interior of Africa, along African coasts, on board slave ships, and after disembarkation in the Americas. Enslaved Africans and their descendants resisted in all sorts of ways.[48] They closely observed British efforts to suppress the traffic along African and American coasts and on the high seas. They witnessed captured ships brought into Brazilian and Cuban ports. They communicated with each other. The actions of African and creole slaves played a role in forcing a halt to the traffic to Brazil and Cuba.

Many documents used in this book are contained in Foreign Office Records of Great Britain Number 84 (Slave Trade Department and Successors: General Correspondence before 1906). These records are a key source for histories focusing on England's efforts to suppress the slave trade to Brazil and Cuba from the 1820s to the late 1860s.[49] Read closely using tools provided from Atlantic histories, British diplomatic correspondence provides helpful descriptions of public health conditions and slave resistance. Many of these documents have never previously been used by a professional historian. This archive facilitates analysis that is, in the words of Dr. Games, "transnational, transregional, oceanic and integrative."[50] Indeed, British and U.S. diplomatic correspondence, along with materials found in national and state archives, sheds light on "strategies of resistance and survival" within the "periphery" of the modern world system in the nineteenth century. As Professor Steve J. Stern has noted, for the colonial period of Latin America, such histories merit close analysis.[51]

Chapter one provides an overview of U.S. involvement in the transatlantic slave trade to Brazil and Cuba. Chapters two and four focus on political discourse and government responses related to the disembarkation of hundreds of ill Africans from slave vessels. Chapters three and five point to the ways in which slave resistance contributed to social tensions and the demise of the slave trade. Chapter six analyzes the role of interpreters and translators in aiding or suppressing the traffic. Examples are noted of blacks speaking in the English language to U.S. and British officials to protest their enslavement. Chapter seven sheds light on the period between 1850 and 1867, the final years of this terrible business.

A short note about a few terms. The terms *free African* (*Africano livre, libre*) and *free black* (*negro livre, libre*) obviously imply that an individual is a free person. He or she could have gained free status based on a law passed in 1831 that assured freedom to any slave who arrived in Brazil after that date, or on a treaty signed in 1835 between Spain and England that outlawed the slave trade to Cuba and anywhere else in the Spanish empire. A free African or a free black could also have been born as a free person to parents in Brazil or Cuba. The terms *freedman* (*liberto*) and *freedwoman* (*liberta*) mean that an individual is a former slave who attained his or her "legal" freedom by whatever means (such as self-purchase). A Liberated African, also known as an *emancipado* in both Brazil and Cuba, alludes to those Africans removed from slave ships captured at sea by the British Squadron (in a few instances seized by vessels from other nations) or "recaptured" from traffickers if found to be "recently landed." When the status of an individual is known, a specific term is employed. Otherwise, the broader, all-encompassing terms *free African* or *free black* are invoked.

1

U.S. INVOLVEMENT IN THE TRANSATLANTIC
SLAVE TRADE TO CUBA AND BRAZIL

———— ∞ ————

Ships built in the United States played an important role in the transatlantic slave trade from Africa to the Americas. With the conclusion of the War of 1812 between the United States and England (1812–15), U.S. merchants and shipbuilders looked to new trading opportunities in an expanding Atlantic economy. One such business was the transatlantic slave trade from Africa to Cuba and Brazil. In spite of the passage of several federal laws to halt U.S. participation in the slave trade (1794, 1807, 1818, and 1820) and British suppression efforts in the wake of England's prohibition of the slave trade in 1807, U.S. capital made significant investments in this offshore enterprise.[1] The transport of Africans to Cuba and Brazil in U.S. ships from the late eighteenth century to the 1860s proved lucrative. Indeed, one-third of all vessels that transported Africans to the Americas after 1810 were constructed in U.S. ports.[2] Key centers of this slave trade network in the United States included Boston; Salem, Massachusetts; Portland, Maine; New York; Baltimore; Charleston, South Carolina; and New Orleans. These ports were closely linked to Havana and Matanzas in Cuba, and Salvador and Rio de Janeiro in Brazil.

UNITED STATES AND CUBA

From the middle of the seventeenth century, merchants in the British North American colonies forged close ties between the eastern seaboard and the Caribbean.[3] Trade flourished as sugar plantations worked by African slaves spread through the British Caribbean in the seventeenth and eighteenth centuries. British North America supplied all sorts of goods to the islands, including bread and flour, rice, beans, wheat, oats, corn, pine, oak and cedar boards, staves and headings, horses and livestock, beef and pork, dried fish, potatoes, onions, fruits, and tobacco. In the period 1768 to 1772, 63 percent of New England's trade was with the Caribbean.[4]

In return, several regions in British North America (after independence, the United States) received molasses for making rum. In 1770, Massachusetts and Rhode Island together imported 3.5 million gallons of molasses that was converted into 2.8 million gallons of rum at seventy distilleries.[5] Rum makers found a ready domestic market as well as high international demand.

Building on its maritime ties to the Caribbean, Rhode Island became deeply involved in the transatlantic slave trade. Between 1725 and 1807, Rhode Island ports (primarily Newport and Bristol) sent 934 vessels to Africa, and these ships transported 106,000 slaves to the Caribbean and North America. By 1807, when federal law deemed the slave trade to the United States illegal, U.S.-owned ships had transported more than 300,000 Africans to the Americas.[6] Historian Jay Coughtry has written that it is "feasible to talk about an American slave trade in the same sense that one can discuss the British or French slave trade."[7] On the west coast of Africa, Rhode Island ships became known as "rum-men," an allusion to the quality and quantity of that drink they carried in their holds. A triangular trade emerged: Rhode Island merchants sent their vessels to the coast of Africa to purchase slaves. These ships transported captives to the Caribbean (also a small number to the U.S. South and the U.S. North), and then the vessels returned to Rhode Island with molasses, sugar, tobacco, and coffee.[8]

Commercial relations with Cuba had been dominated by Spain's *Casa de Contratación* (House of Trade), in existence for nearly three centuries (1503–1790). Founded in Seville and then moved to Cadiz after 1717, the Casa levied a 20 percent tax on all goods imported into Spain. Controlled by a small guild of wealthy merchants, the Casa sought to enhance Spain's mercantile relations throughout its empire. A key component of its success was the convoy system, also known as the West Indies fleet, which set out every year from Seville with destinations of Veracruz, Mexico; Portobelo, Panama; and Cartagena, Colombia. Spanish vessels received an array of goods produced in the viceroyalties of Peru, New Granada, La Plata, and New Spain (including silver, gold, sugar, tobacco, and lumber) to be transported back to Spain. To prepare for the re-

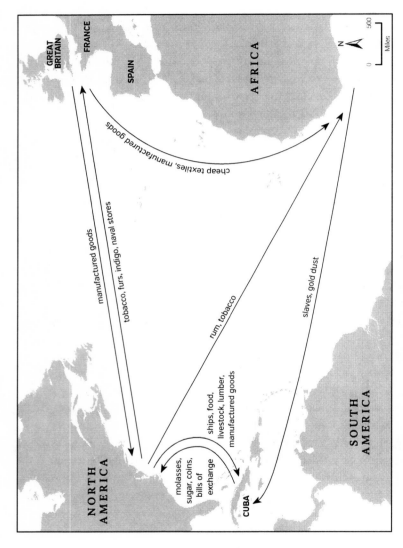

MAP 2. North Atlantic Triangle Trade, 1800

turn voyage at the end of the hurricane season, the convoys met at Havana, which made the city Spanish America's largest port and one of major strategic and economic importance.[9]

Responding to the expansion of commerce throughout the Atlantic world, the Casa de Contratación took great interest in the transatlantic slave trade to Spain's American colonies. By the middle of the sixteenth century, Spain's ships could not satisfy labor demand in its American colonies. In an attempt to regulate and profit from the sale of African captives, the Casa sold exclusive contracts (*asientos*) to merchants and trading companies through a system that remained in existence from 1545 to 1789. In the eighteenth century, the Spanish Crown provided an asiento to the British, which enabled England to control the transport of slaves to all of Spain's American colonies. British traffickers carried some 75,000 Africans to Cuba between 1700 and 1760.[10]

The British occupation of Havana for nine months from June 1762 through February 1763 contributed to the expansion of the Cuban economy. An outcome of England's Seven Years War against France, the takeover enabled the British to open the port of Havana to expanded international trade. The response was immediate. During the British presence of less than a year, traffickers landed some four thousand African slaves on Cuba.[11] In the 1770s, sugar exports from Cuba rose five-fold.[12] The number of sugar mills increased from 174 in 1778 to 308 in 1800 to 534 in 1817.[13] As Spanish and creole planters moved quickly into the burgeoning sugar sector, labor demand rose. As a consequence, slave importations surged.

A dilemma for Spain was how to retain control over its jewel in the Caribbean and at the same time assure a ready supply of African slaves. This was resolved by Spain's allowing all nations to transport slaves to Cuba and the rest of Spanish America after 1788. The docking period allotted for foreign vessels to remain anchored in the harbor of Havana was increased from eight to forty days. The Spanish Crown also authorized Spanish merchants to export commodities from Cuba necessary for slaving voyages. Employing their knowledge of the Atlantic world, North American and Cuban merchants became major participants in transporting African slaves to the island.[14]

Cuba became the nexus of a New England–Caribbean trade network. Commercial data reflect the upsurge in trade between the eastern seaboard and Cuba from the end of the eighteenth century. In 1806, an estimated six hundred ships officially entered Cuba from the United States. They carried primarily provisions grown on farms and basic construction materials (wood and iron goods). Of these vessels, ninety-seven had departed from Philadelphia and ninety from Baltimore. During that same year of 1806, over five hundred U.S.-built ships sailed back to the port cities of New York, Philadelphia, Boston, Baltimore, and Charleston. Among U.S.-built ships that arrived in Cuba, an unknown number were purchased by Spanish and Cuban merchants involved in Atlantic trade ventures. Using an export-led growth model, economist Javier Cuenca Esteban has shown that the widening ties to Cuba in the first decade of the nineteenth century played a decisive role in reducing the international indebtedness of the United States.[15]

Two Rhode Island families gained renown in these endeavors. The Browns of Providence supplied Newport slave vessels with iron products and spermaceti candles from factories they owned. They invested in several slaving ventures, including one by the ship *Sally*. The vessel sailed from Providence in 1764, the same year that the Brown family founded Rhode Island College, later renamed Brown University. *Sally* carried chains, shackles, swivel guns, and small arms, along with a cargo of candles, tobacco, onions, and 17,274 gallons of rum.[16]

In the words of a group of scholars who authored a study entitled *Slavery and Justice*, "the voyage was a disaster in every conceivable sense."[17] When Captain Esek Hopkins of the *Sally* arrived on the windward coast of West Africa (present-day Ivory Coast), he encountered numerous vessels looking to buy slaves, including twenty-four ships from Rhode Island. It took nine months for Hopkins to locate and then purchase 196 Africans. By the time of departure, nineteen of the Africans had died, including several children and a woman who had hanged herself. On the eighth day out to sea, the slaves revolted, forcing the crew to shoot and kill eight and wound several others. During the Middle Passage, sixty-eight Africans succumbed, and another twenty lost their lives soon after the *Sally* reached the island of Antigua. All told, 108 Africans perished in the crossing. As a result, three of the Brown brothers—Nicholas, Joseph, and Moses—withdrew from further investments in slave voyages. They did continue, however, to sell rum from their state-of-the-art distillery along with other goods to Rhode Island merchants involved in the traffic.

The disastrous voyage of the *Sally* did not deter John Brown from continuing in the slave trade. In 1769, Brown joined with two other investors to send a vessel named *Sutton* to Africa in search of slaves. During the next twenty-five years, John Brown invested in at least three other slave voyages. One of his coinvestors was his son-in-law, John Francis.

The American Revolution disrupted the slave trade from Rhode Island. During and soon after the war (1775–87), Rhode Islanders embarked on thirty-three voyages and transported 3,467 Africans to the Caribbean and U.S. South. In the next two decades, Rhode Island's involvement peaked. From 1788 to 1807, Rhode Island merchants sent forth 391 voyages to West Africa, and carried back 44,638 Africans.[18] Bristol, Rhode Island became the predominant slaving port in this period.

A second Rhode Island family who became deeply enmeshed in the slave traffic was the DeWolfs of Bristol. From 1769 to 1820, seven DeWolf brothers were the leading slave traders in the United States.[19] They transported some ten thousand African slaves, primarily to well-known slave marts at Charleston and Havana. The brothers established a multinational enterprise, which by 1830 included rum distilleries in Bristol, textile mills that received cotton picked by slaves in the U.S. South, whaling ships, the Bristol Bank, the Mount Hope Insurance Company, three sugar plantations in Cuba, and properties in Rhode Island, Massachusetts, New York, Kentucky, and Baltimore. The family constructed a warehouse in Bristol using timber and stone imported from Africa as ballast on ships.

James DeWolf (1764–1837) captained several slavers, invested in at least twenty-five slave voyages, and was elected senator from Rhode Island (1821–25).[20] An amendment put forward by DeWolf, which passed the U.S. Senate, forbade the British Squadron (in existence from 1808 to 1870) from searching a vessel sailing under the U.S. flag. This law did much to enable U.S. merchants and ships to participate in the transatlantic slave trade into the 1860s (President Lincoln ended this protection in 1862). By the time of James DeWolf's death in 1837, he was the second wealthiest resident of the United States. The DeWolf mansion, known as Linden Place and constructed in 1810, remains a popular tourist site in the historic district of Bristol. In my youth, I stood on a sidewalk in front of that big house to watch Fourth of July parades.

The mercantile expansion of British North America and the dynamic economy of the United States after it gained independence fueled ship construction. In 1700, Boston and nearby towns built seventy ships a year. This region became the most prominent shipbuilding center in the Americas. By the beginning of the nineteenth century, several Atlantic port cities hummed with activity at shipyards, including Baltimore, Philadelphia, New York, Boston, and towns in Maine (Portland and Brunswick). Shipyards became hubs of economic growth. They provided employment to hundreds of workers, including shipwrights, carpenters, ironworkers, riggers, and sail makers. Coastal enclaves had an effect on infrastructure deep into the interior. Lumbermen felled two thousand trees for a medium-sized ship.[21] With knowledge gained from wide-ranging maritime endeavors in the seventeenth and eighteenth centuries, residents of the Northeast played a major role in the Atlantic world of the nineteenth century.

Ships built in the United States became famous for their quality and capacities at sea. Adapting to changing international conditions, U.S. craftsmen constructed vessels after 1815 capable of carrying larger numbers of Africans for longer distances. Tonnage estimates reflect this transition. Between 1755 and 1769, Rhode Island slavers averaged eighty-three tons in weight. In striking contrast, U.S.-built vessels that carried Africans across the Atlantic from 1845 to 1860 averaged 208 tons, or about a 150 percent increase.[22] Between 1816 and 1830, foreigners purchased at least eighty-seven Chesapeake-built vessels for use in the slave trade.[23] A U.S. consul at Havana wrote in 1834 that "the slavers are all built in the United States. Vessels built for the slave trade come chiefly—perhaps altogether—from Baltimore and New York."[24]

With the signing of an 1835 treaty between Spain and England that "totally and finally abolished [the slave trade] in all parts of the world," British seizures of Spanish slave vessels destined for Cuba increased significantly. U.S. merchants who flew the U.S. flag as protection from British capture immediately filled the lacuna. Observers listed five U.S. vessels involved in the traffic from Havana in 1836; eleven in 1837; nineteen in 1838; and twenty-three in 1839.[25] These vessels commonly sailed directly to the coast of Africa to purchase slaves and then transported them to Cuba.

Of the fifty-nine departures in 1839, twenty-six sailed under the Portuguese flag, twenty-three under the U.S. flag, eight under the Spanish flag, and two under other colors (Oriental, Hamburg). (See Table 1, Appendix.) The *Duquesa de Braganza*, listed as a Portuguese vessel, was in fact the Baltimore clipper *Venus* (hence the twenty-three U.S.-flagged ships). It would appear that all of the U.S.-flagged ships had been built in the United States, and the majority of vessels sailing under other flags had been constructed at other locations. After picking up slaves on the African coast, these ships returned to Cuba, often disembarked the "cargo" at remote locations, and then reentered the port of Havana in ballast.

This is exactly what occurred with the slave ship *Venus*. Constructed at Baltimore in 1838, this "splendid corvette" arrived in the harbor of Havana on August 3 of that year. Captain William Wallace immediately dismissed the eighteen crewmembers listed as citizens of the United States and replaced them with crewmen hired in Havana. Departing twenty days later, the *Venus* most likely stopped at the Cape Verde islands and then continued on to Mozambique on the southeast coast of Africa. There it received 1,120 Africans and returned to Cuba, where it landed 870 survivors at a remote location on the coast. The brig then entered the port of Havana in ballast. In the words of the U.S. consul, "every boatman in the harbor knew before sunset of that day that twenty ounces [of gold had been paid] per head," which amounted to $200,000 in profit (approximately eight million dollars in 2013).[26] The *Venus* landed another 2,831 Africans in Cuba from four other transatlantic voyages during the next two years (456 Africans perished during those voyages).[27]

The significant presence of U.S.-built ships during this period was readily witnessed on the west coast of Africa. In 1844, of twenty-seven captured slave vessels condemned at a Mixed Commission Court at Sierra Leone, ten were U.S.-built and five were constructed in Brazil. None of the other "countries of origin" listed had built more than two slavers.[28] In 1845, of thirty slavers captured by the British Squadron along the coast of West Africa, seventeen were U.S.-built, while eight were constructed in Brazil and five in Spain.[29]

A major reason for the steady increase of U.S. participation in the traffic to Cuba was the opening of new sugar plantations and coffee estates on the island (fifty were owned by U.S. citizens in 1823, valued at three million dollars). Planters cleared some 1,700 acres of forestland annually in the 1790s to plant sugarcane, 3,500 acres each year in the 1810s, and a staggering 13,000 acres annually in the 1840s. Sugar output increased from 55,000 tons in 1820 to 130,200 tons in 1839 to 749,000 tons in 1868. The number of sugar mills doubled from 1,000 in 1827 to 2,000 by 1868.[30]

Technology and expertise from the United States and England contributed to the transformation of Cuba. Engineers built railroads in Havana in the 1830s that later were continued to Matanzas. Installation of telegraph in 1851 connected Havana to Cárdenas and Matanzas. Havana and Matanzas became the most cosmopolitan region in Latin America. The introduction of steam engines on sugar estates enabled output to soar. Expansion of the sugar sector stimulated the collusion of government officials in the slave trade at all levels.[31]

U.S.-built ships and capital facilitated the transatlantic slave trade to Cuba in three ways.[32] The first was to supply African depots. In a deposition before

a U.S. consul in early May 1845, a ship captain from Salem, Massachusetts described his experiences along the west coast of Africa. Captain Gilbert Smith
had sailed the *Sea Eagle* of Boston to Cabinda (present-day Angola) and then
north to Ouidah (also known as Whydah; it is located in the present-day Republic of Benin). Smith encountered factories owned by individuals from the
United States, Brazil, Portugal, and France.

The use of the word *factory*, reflecting the evolution of the Atlantic world,
was derived from the Latin word *facere*, meaning "to do." A factory became
known in medieval Europe as a trading post or commercial-military outpost.
With the expansion of the Portuguese and Spanish empires from the fifteenth
century, the terms *feitoria* (Portuguese) and *factoría* (Spanish) gained notoriety
around the world, from Lima to Goa to Nagasaki. By the nineteenth century,
the English word *factory* took on various meanings. The most famous related
to enterprises that employed workers under a single roof to mass-produce
goods such as shoes and iron goods. On African coasts from Guinea to Angola
to Mozambique, a factory denoted a locale that "produced" slaves and was
managed by a "factor." In the western frontier of the United States, "a series of
'factories' or posts were designed to trade fairly with Indians [this determined
by the Congress in the 1796 Trade and Intercourse Act], supplying them with
high-quality goods in exchange for pelts and hides, until such time that they
gave up the chase for farming." By the first decade of the nineteenth century,
"western" factories had been established at Detroit, Fort Wayne (Indiana),
Fort St. Stephens (Alabama), and Chickasaw Bluffs (Tennessee).[33] The choice
of the word *factory* to describe enterprises from Birmingham, England to Law-
rence, Massachusetts to enclaves on the coasts of Africa and outposts in the
Louisiana Purchase, bespoke a shared aura associated with international trade
as well as modernization on land and sea.

While sailing along the Slave Coast, Captain Smith met up with several U.S.
ships supplying factories with items produced in the United States and Europe, including dry foods, crockery, tobacco, printed cotton cloth, alcohol,
muskets, gunpowder, and iron. Factors sold African slaves along with gold,
wax, ivory, cattle hides, palm oil, gum opal, and spices to purchasers who
visited their enterprises.[34] Factories often provisioned slave ships with fresh
water and shackles. In the words of one crewmember of the *Sea Eagle*, "it was
common for blacks to come out to the slave ships selling fish and fruits, and
it was common for blacks to be working on the small boats which carried the
slaves out to the slave ships."[35]

Smith observed that "the factories are in constant communication with each other. The parties must know each other's business as well as one farmer in New England must know the number of acres of corn his neighbor has planted."[36] Communication was maintained by Africans who could run fifty to sixty miles in a day at a rate of five to seven miles per hour. These athletes were stationed at various points along the African coast. "On the arrival of a vessel at the Congo River, runners immediately start out to Cabinda, about 35 or 40 miles distant, or for [the village of] Obama, situated about fifty miles up the said river, to communicate the intelligence."

Factors commonly signaled captains of slavers to inform them of the most propitious moment to board slaves. One well-known entrepreneur along the coast, a Frenchman named Don Alphonso, entertained British officers from the Africa Squadron (there to suppress the traffic in slaves) at his factory while simultaneously sending messages to a slave vessel waiting to receive slaves twelve miles offshore.[37] Factors sought to bring a certain degree of stability to the volatile business of human trafficking.

Besides provisioning factories, U.S. ships furnished materials employed in slaving ventures. Tender ships carried goods manufactured in the United States or England (shackles, irons, cooking tubs, barrels, and cloth) that would later be transferred to slave ships along the coast of Africa.[38] By sailing under a U.S. flag, the tenders could transport "slave trade equipment" prohibited for other carriers under international treaties.[39] In the words of two astute British observers:

> During the month of September [1836] there arrived in this port [Havana], for sale from the US, four new schooners, we believe two from New York and two from Baltimore, all built at the latter place, viz. the *Anaconda* and the *Viper* and the *Emanuel* and *Dolores expressly constructed and peculiarly fitted* for carrying on the slave trade. The former of these vessels having received on board from the French House of Forcade & Co., a cargo of which, by the Treaty of June 28th, 1835, would have condemned as a slaver any vessel bearing Spanish colors [meaning equipment used in the slave trade], cleared out and sailed under the American flag, the *Anaconda* on the 6th, the *Viper* on the 10th for the Cape de Verde Islands, there to be transferred to a Portuguese subject and to proceed with the flag of that nation to the coast of Africa, upon a slaving enterprise.
>
> The protection which these schooners will receive from the American colors, both as regards their fitting and cargo, will effectually secure them against capture by His Majesty's cruisers until they arrive at the scene of their depreda-

tions. The *Emanuel* and *Dolores* have, we believe, left the Port under the Spanish flag; but we have also to inform you that some time since the brig *Martha* of Portland [Maine], which arrived here from Matanzas [Cuba], took on board in this harbor a cargo which would equally have confiscated as a slaver any Spanish vessel, and sailed direct for the coast of Africa, to deliver it at some of the numerous Factories or dens of infamy established there, in connection with the Slave Traders of Havana.[40]

Such endeavors often took on a multinational character. On March 7, 1837, three ships departed from the port of Havana bound for Africa. One was the U.S. brig *Two Friends*, and the other two the Portuguese schooners *Tratado* and *Olimpia*. *Two Friends* carried "Coast Goods" (cooking tubs, utensils, shackles, water casks, small arms, gunpowder, aguardente, dried beef, manioc flour, and so on) that enabled the Portuguese ships to return to Cuba with slaves on board.[41] In January 1843, the U.S. brig *Angeline* sailed out of Havana with a destination of the Pongas River (present-day Guinea), carrying similar goods to be used by the Spanish slavers *Jacinto* and *Tres de Febrero*.[42]

After fulfilling its supply function, a U.S. tender could be employed to transport mariners back from Africa to Cuba or Brazil. Masters of slave ships sometimes dropped off U.S. sailors when they brought slaves on board. Sailors of other nationalities who refused to join in a slaving voyage found themselves abandoned on inhospitable African shores. In several instances, these men looked to U.S. tenders as a way out of desperate circumstances.

A third insertion into this commerce was the transport of slaves to Cuba and Brazil. The journey of the *St. Salvador* provides evidence of the prominent role of U.S. ships in the slave traffic of the nineteenth century. Captured at anchor at the mouth of the Mani River on January 20, 1820 (also referred to as the Manna or Mano River, present-day border between Sierra Leone and Liberia) by the British cruiser *Myrmidon*, the *St. Salvador* arrived as a prize into the port of Freetown on February 8. The master of the slave vessel Antonio José Alvárez admitted under interrogation that the *St. Salvador* had successfully eluded capture when it had been chased a few days earlier by the *Myrmidon*. During that episode, Alvárez landed twenty-five Africans at Gallinas who had been shackled on board so as to hide evidence of the ship's activities.

Alvárez explained that the ship had been purchased at Baltimore on behalf of a Mr. Martínez, resident at Boa Vista in the Cape Verde Islands. From Maryland the ship sailed to Bristol, Rhode Island where the captain purchased supplies, again on the credit of Mr. Martínez. It journeyed to Boa Vista and then on to the coast of Africa. The crew included thirty-two men, among them ten U.S. citizens, six Portuguese, and sixteen Italians and French. It was armed with eight eighteen-pound cannonades and lots of ammunition. The plan had been to board slaves brought out from the river in canoes and transport them to Havana.[43]

One year later, the Baltimore-built schooner *Anna Maria* arrived at the Bonny River (present-day Nigeria). Its captain immediately commenced to purchase slaves. In late March, HMS *Tartar* captured the slaver. Ship's papers and depositions showed that the *Anna Maria* had departed from St. Jago, Cuba in December 1820. This meant that the ship had departed six months after Spain had implemented a treaty with England prohibiting the further transport of slaves to Spanish possessions. Several individuals had invested in the voyage. These included a Mr. Wright, who had been raised in the United States, and a Mr. Shelton, a U.S. citizen who had previously been U.S. consul at St. Jago. The outward cargo from Cuba consisted of rum, cloth, muskets, powder, and cutlasses.

The mate of the *Anna Maria* turned out to be a British citizen named George Gardner, who had resided in St. Jago for the previous three years with his wife. Gardner had been appointed mate by a Mathew Smith, also known as Mathias Sánchez, who was an American by birth but later naturalized as a Spaniard. Gardner stated that at a former time the *Anna Maria* had been named the *Brutus*. It had departed Cuba under a Spanish flag. The vessel also carried flags from the United States and England as well as a private flag of white with a blue cross. "We had these colors on board in the event of our falling in with privateers, to deceive them and prevent their taking us."[44]

In response to questions, a British captor described the *Anna Maria* as follows:

> The ship was in a horrible state. The tonnage is 180, and yet she had on board nearly 500 living souls. The intense heat and filthy state of the slave rooms, only three feet and a few inches high, must have made the conditions of the poor miserable beings there confined approach nearer suffocation than any other. The conditions were wretched, the Africans confined more loathsomely and more closely than the hogs brought to a morning's market for sale. We were astonished to view the maddening act of self destruction which occurred to some by throwing themselves overboard, prey to the sharks in attendance, rather than endure a continuance of that misery they have only tasted of, or perhaps rather than quit the land dear to them by many unknown ties.[45]

Of an estimated 437 Africans (300 men and boys, 137 women and girls) who departed on the *Anna Maria* at the Bight of Benin, 272 remained alive at the time of capture. Thirty-four more died during the journey from Bonny to Sierra Leone. The 238 survivors who landed at Freetown were declared free by the British-Spanish Mixed Commission Court.

U.S. merchants responded to the many opportunities created by the booming transatlantic slave trade of the first half of the nineteenth century. U.S. entrepreneurs established highly profitable trade companies in Havana, Matanzas, Cienfuegos, Cárdenas, Sugua la Grande, Trinidad, and Santiago de Cuba. These merchant houses communicated far and wide throughout the Atlantic world. They maintained partnerships in Boston, New York, Philadelphia, Baltimore, Charleston, St. Augustine, and New Orleans; Salvador and Rio de Janeiro in Brazil; Cadiz, Spain; and Lisbon, Portugal and were in close contact with factories along the African coast. Long-time U.S. residents of Havana Ferdinand Clark and Charles Drake specialized in the selling or leasing of U.S. ships to traffickers.[46] The U.S. house of George Knight and Company joined forces with notorious traffickers on the island, including Don José Fernández. The latter pursued his business ventures in West Africa through a brother who headed factories at Ouidah and other locales.[47] The U.S. merchant house of Gray, Fernández and Company invested in several voyages, including the brig *Antonio*, which disembarked 203 Africans in December 1820.[48] The firm Menninger (a U.S. citizen) and Johnson (from Nassau) worked closely with renowned trafficker Pedro Forcade through the 1840s.[49] A cadre of U.S. merchant-traffickers took up residence in the city of Matanzas and forged close ties with investors in New York City.[50]

Not only did U.S. merchants in Havana pay close attention to ocean trade, but also to the urban milieu of the city. It was common for men to desert from U.S. ships upon arrival to the city. Frequently left destitute, these sailors found themselves in a precarious condition.

> For a long series of years the desertion of seamen had been so rife in this port, particularly from American vessels, that scarcely one visited it without losing part, sometimes the whole, of her crew. In the service of the three or four hardened miscreants who were at the head of this trade were "Runners," ever on the watch for a straggling sailor, to entice him into a grog shop, as the first step to prevailing on him to desert, or perhaps to kidnapping him if he should prove so extraordinary a character as to resist all allurements. Boats were plying about among the shipping at all hours of the day and night, for the same pur-

pose; and it was but seldom that any vigilance within the power of the master and mate [of the U.S. ship on which the sailor arrived to Cuba] could prove a match for the audacity and activity of those whose sole occupation it was to defeat it. The boarding houses were ever full of seamen; of whom there was a constant circulation going on, through these dens, from the vessels from which they had been stolen, to those which, being ready for sea and without a crew or short-handed, were under the necessity of obtaining their complement, without regard to price or any particular inquiry as to whence the men had come.[51]

Merchants and captains preparing for slave voyages hired the runners to round up a sufficient number of sailors by whatever means. The choice of the word *runner* at Havana likely had ties to the same term used to describe the Africans who carried information by running between factories on the coast of Africa (as described above). The urban runners of Havana, many surely familiar with the coasts of Africa, surveyed the pubs and boardinghouses of the city and brought news back to the merchant houses.

From 1844 to mid-century, slave imports to Cuba declined precipitously. This could be traced to the destruction of several factories and barracoons (from the Spanish word *barracón*, meaning barracks for temporary confinement of slaves or prisoners) on the coast of West Africa by the British Squadron, the use of steamships by the British Squadron to hunt for sailing ships carrying slaves or equipment used for slaving voyages, a Spanish decree of 1842 prohibiting the purchase of foreign ships in Cuban ports and then registering them as Spanish vessels, and a series of slave rebellions culminating in a massive black insurgency in 1844 in Cuba. Natural disasters on the island also played a role. A hurricane in 1844, and severe drought in 1845 followed by another hurricane in 1846, caused a downturn in sugar, coffee, and tobacco output.[52] The resurgence of sugar and coffee production after mid-century combined with access to U.S. vessels caused a spike in slave disembarkations that equaled and then exceeded pre-1844 levels. In response to the turbulent economic and social conditions in Cuba at this interlude, several U.S. merchants shifted their attention to Brazil.

UNITED STATES AND BRAZIL

During the decade of the 1840s, the number of African slaves imported to Brazil reached a peak. U.S. entrepreneurs responded to this demand for labor in Brazil. They sold or leased tens of ships constructed in the United States, in-

cluding the renowned Baltimore schooners, to known Brazilian or Portuguese
traffickers residing in the ports of Rio de Janeiro and Salvador. As with Cuba,
vessels constructed in the United States carried supplies from Brazil to slave
factories on the African coast, provided goods needed for successful slaving
ventures, and transported thousands of Africans to Brazil in their holds. One
observer noted (writing in 1838) that "it is well known that from the different ports of Brazil there are upwards of 160 vessels regularly employed in the
slave trade—that all of these vessels are navigated under the Portuguese flag,
although generally belonging to Brazilian subjects—and that nearly the whole
of them are of North American or other foreign construction."[53] A triangular
trade that connected the coast of Africa, Cuba, and Brazil emerged.[54]

In "Notes on the Subject of the Slave Trade in the Province and City of
Bahia," British diplomat William Gore Ouseley outlined the southern triangle
trade as it related to Bahia:

> A very general course is as follows. A vessel loads at Bahia under the Spanish
> or Portuguese flags (and often the bona fide owners are in fact natives of those
> nations) with tobacco, rum, etc. for the coast of Africa, for which trade Bahia pro-
> duce is preferred. On the African coast the cargo is exchanged for Negroes, with
> whom the vessel often proceeds to the coast of Cuba and there lands them. . . .
>
> Cuba is the island to which the greater number of vessels laden at Bahia
> under foreign colors go, [and] they are nearly all consigned to *Zangroni*, a noted
> slave dealer at Havana. Zangroni's Bills on London are well known in many
> mercantile places and are readily negotiated at Bahia for produce or British dry
> goods (hardware, coarse manufactures, etc.) and most of the Spanish slavers
> thus carry on their business.[55]

Several episodes shed light on the Brazil-Africa-Cuba connections. In January 1831, the ship *Almirante* arrived in the port of Havana in ballast. A British
consul immediately took notice, informing the captain general of Cuba that
this same vessel had been captured off the coast of West Africa two years before with 466 African slaves on board by the British cruiser *Sybille*. Following
condemnation by a Mixed Commission Court at Freetown in March 1829, an
unknown party purchased the vessel at auction and sent it to Havana under
a Brazilian flag. After arrival at Havana, the U.S. merchant house Murdoch,
Storey and Company leased the vessel. When the *Almirante* cleared Havana in
May 1830, obviously destined for another slaving venture to Africa, its well-
known slave captain Juan Bautista Zavala declared its destination to be Salvador in Brazil.[56]

After inquiries and a review of the logbook of the *Almirante*, Captain General Francisco Vives stated that the ship had sailed from Havana to Salvador (May 1830) and then returned directly to Havana (January 1831). He posited that no evidence had been found to implicate the *Almirante* in having disembarked slaves on Cuban shores.[57] British representatives at Havana viewed the denial as just one more fabrication by Spanish officials.

Vessels also sailed from Havana to Africa and then returned to Brazil to disembark slaves. A contract offered to sailors in Havana in early 1838 read that the vessel would sail "from Havana to one or more ports on the Gold Coast of Africa [present-day Ghana] and from thence to Bahia where the voyage ends."[58] Her British Majesty's steam vessel *Prometheus* captured the slave brig *Audaz* near the mouth of the Congo River in September 1844. Letters confiscated from the vessel showed "the connection of the Brazil and Havana slave trade and exhibited some of the operations of the House of Zulueta and Company and others at Havana and Trinidad de Cuba in the traffic."[59] In October 1845, a "suspicious-looking vessel" named the *Angelica* arrived in the port of Havana. As it bore a Venezuelan flag, the captain showed papers that declared the ship had originated in Vera Cruz, Mexico. He claimed the only cargo to be five thousand dollars owned by a German merchant house at Havana. Its appearance raising suspicions, authorities quickly determined the ship to be the U.S. schooner *D.C. Wilson*. The vessel had departed from Havana the previous February with a declared destination of Rio de Janeiro. Instead of heading south it had sailed east to West Africa and then transported slaves to Brazil.[60] After an eight-month journey, the *D.C. Wilson* returned to Havana in ballast.

Traffickers made several attempts to transport slaves from Brazil directly to Cuba. In early 1831, a Brazilian *sumaca* named *Santo Antonio Vencedor* arrived in the port of Havana in ballast, claiming to have sailed from the city of São Luis de Maranhão situated on the northeast coast of Brazil. Consular agents received word that the ship had disembarked slaves on the Cuban coast who had been transported from Brazil "legally" with Brazilian passports. One suggested that traffickers had brought the slaves to Cuba because they could receive higher prices. After a visit of seventeen days, the *Santo Antonio Vencedor* cleared for a return voyage to Salvador da Bahia.[61]

The U.S. consulate at Havana played a key role in the south triangle trade. It was common practice for slave ship captains to appear requesting official papers that would protect against boarding by a cruiser of the British Squadron and potential seizure.[62] As U.S. consul from 1834 to 1840, Nicholas Trist

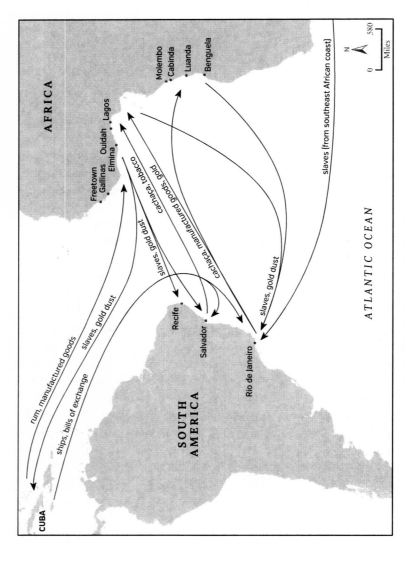

MAP 3. South Atlantic Bilateral and Triangle Trade, 1830–1851

enabled U.S.-built slavers to depart from Havana on supposedly legitimate trading voyages to Africa. To the delight of a powerful bloc of traffickers based in Havana, Trist also took on the responsibilities of consul from Portugal for nearly two years (1838–40). This occurred in the wake of the expulsion of a Portuguese consul who refused to issue documents allowing fictitious transfers of vessels to Portuguese captains.[63] British judge James Kennedy of the British-Spanish Mixed Commission Court (1837–52) lamented that Trist "signed all papers passed to him [from slaver captains]; during 1838, Trist received consular fees [along with bribes] on close to 100 vessels."[64] In a letter published soon after his return to the United States, Trist defended his activities, claiming that he had done nothing to aid enterprises in Havana involved in the slave traffic.[65]

Slave merchants sought to expand the Brazil-Africa-Cuba nexus by planting an ally in the U.S. consulate at Havana. At the age of nineteen years, Peter Crusoe had lots of experience with human traffickers. Born in Gibraltar of British parents, Crusoe spoke English, Spanish, and Portuguese. Few individuals easily conversed and translated in those three languages. After spending three years at the U.S. consulate at Rio de Janeiro, the young man arrived in Havana in February 1838 and commenced employment under the direction of Nicholas Trist. In response to inquiries posed by a British diplomat about questionable activities, Crusoe claimed that he had never aided slave traders through falsification of documents or allowed ships to depart under the U.S. flag.

An investigation carried out by Edward Everett (governor of Massachusetts, U.S. ambassador to England, and president of Harvard University) found Crusoe's statements not credible. Charged by U.S. president Martin Van Buren to analyze the extent of U.S. involvement in the slave trade in Cuba, Everett visited Havana in mid-1840. In a seventy-page letter marked "confidential," Everett accused U.S. representatives, sea captains, and merchant houses in Cuba of active participation in this business. He wrote that numerous clipper ships constructed in Baltimore had played a central role in the traffic to Cuba. Yet officials in that city also had to share the blame. "A ship [alluding to the famed clipper ship *Venus*] being prepared for a piratical expedition was probably as notorious at Baltimore while she was in the stocks as it was at Havana after she had taken in her outward cargo [destined to be traded in West Africa]."[66] Everett learned that the records at the U.S. consulate had disappeared. With regard to accusations by the British of collusion with known traffickers by U.S. officials, Everett wrote:

There was a Mr. Crusoe who worked at the consulate for some time [Crusoe arrived in Havana in February 1838], as a clerk, and who seems to have enjoyed much too large a share of the consul's confidence. He was in charge of the office when the consul was not present. He was born in Gibraltar, came to Havana some years previous from Rio, where he had been employed in the American consulate. This circumstance, together with his acquaintance with foreign languages and somewhat pleasing manners, appears to have been his recommendation to the consul at Havana for a similar employment there. He was taken into the office on a small salary, and had no other visible resources. But it was soon apparent that he must have [had] some ways and means unknown to the public. I was informed by the acting consul, Mr. [John] Morland, a gentleman of undoubted veracity and honor, that Crusoe's pay as clerk would not have defrayed the expenses of his dress, and that he was a person of disrepute and extravagant habits. These circumstances naturally led to the suspicion that he might procure supplies of money from the slave traders by employing his position in the office to facilitate in some way their operations. Representations, as I understand, were made to the Consul [Trist] upon this subject, but without the effect of shaking his confidence in the individual alluded to; which continued unimpaired up to the last moment of the consul's stay in the island, as was apparent from the fact that he had made arrangements for giving Mr. Crusoe the whole charge of the Consulate during his absence. Writer [Everett] confirms that Crusoe's character which was made upon me by his conversation and deportment corresponded with the accounts that I have heard of him and satisfied me that he was a person who ought not to be trusted. Writer suggests that the forms [to allow departure from the port of Havana], signed by the consul, were for use at the office, and were sold by Crusoe to the Portuguese slave traders to be employed by them in authenticating papers as occasion might require.[67]

In early 1840, President Van Buren recalled Trist to Washington to respond to accusations. Trist's departure in no way deterred the traffickers at Havana. In 1840, U.S. merchant Charles Tyng took over the responsibility of signing consular documents that allowed U.S. slave ships to depart Havana with a destination of Africa. These included the *Hudson*, *Plant*, *Lone*, *Seminole*, and *Kite*.[68] Three years later, on July 11, 1843, Tyng dispatched the U.S. ship *Boston* to Rio de Janeiro. Observers wrote that given "Tyng's long connections with the slave dealers, the *Boston* was probably intended for the slave trade."[69]

The machinations at the U.S. consulate in Havana and of U.S. merchants resident in Cuba and Brazil aided the expansion of the south triangle trade of the 1840s.[70] The financial incentives were enormous. A U.S. consul to Rio de Janeiro at this time estimated a 70 to 100 percent profit margin on slave voyages between Africa and Brazil on U.S.-constructed slave ships.[71] Profits derived from the slave trade in the decades between 1820 and 1860 reached their highest levels in history.

Not all U.S. ships that appeared in Brazilian ports were seaworthy, due to age and a lack of maintenance. They also faced inclement conditions once anchored. A harsh tropical sun made upkeep of ships burdensome. North American captains and crews visiting the port of Rio de Janeiro complained of worms capable of eating through the wood of ship bottoms.[72] In spite of such problems, U.S. ships found a ready market during the 1840s. One reason was that slave traders had facile access to skilled workers. Bahian carpenters at Salvador gained fame for their ability to repair wooden ships and prepare vessels for a slaving voyage (such as installation of temporary slave decks).[73] A second reason was the use of the U.S. flag to impede searches of slave vessels by British cruisers. Hence, investors had a huge incentive to purchase or lease a U.S. ship as a way to attain official U.S. documents that would prevent seizure by British cruisers.

In a deposition before a U.S. consul in Rio de Janeiro on June 11, 1851, U.S. citizen William E. Anderson provided an in-depth description of a recent slave voyage of which he partook.[74] Anderson had been born and raised in the state of Maryland. He was forty years old at the time of the interview, was married, and had a child. He had resided in Rio de Janeiro since 1841.

While frequenting the docks of that city, Anderson met two fellow North Americans named Joshua M. Clapp and Frank Smith. The two had extensive experience in the transport of African slaves and their sale on Brazilian coasts. Born in Salem, New York in 1818, Joshua Clapp spent part of his youth in Vermont. At age fifteen, he journeyed on the Atlantic on board a U.S. whaling ship. In 1842, Clapp joined an influx of U.S. seamen who ventured to Rio de Janeiro to seek their fortune in the slave trade. Acting as a front man for U.S. merchant James Birckhead and a firm run by Joseph Maxwell (British) and John S. Wright (U.S.), Clapp purchased at least eight U.S. vessels (*Camilla, Ceres, Whig, Tenobia, Globe, Henrietta, France,* and *Flora*) that subsequently participated in the traffic of African slaves. He also sailed on the U.S.-owned tender brig *Gannecliffe* to West Africa and was captain of the U.S.-built and -owned slaver named *Panther*. The latter was captured by a U.S. cruiser off West Africa in December 1845, sent to Charleston, and condemned.[75] Undeterred by the mounting pressures and dangers posed by the British-led campaign to suppress the slave trade to Brazil, Clapp continued to cast about for men and ships in Rio de Janeiro to enable him to continue his pursuits.

Anderson agreed to rig the vessels (attaching sails, spars, and masts to the hull) purchased by Joshua Clapp. In 1849, Clapp and Smith invited Anderson to be part of the crew on a voyage to Africa on the U.S.-built ship *Quinsey* from Boston. Claiming to be the owners, Clapp and Smith offered Anderson fifty dollars per month along with assurance of a future payment of a large (undisclosed) sum if the slaving venture proved successful. Anderson agreed to the terms of the deal, and traveled as a passenger. The captain was a U.S. citizen named Thomas Myers.

William Anderson boarded the *Quinsey* on March 17, 1849. He understood that the ship's first destination would be Paranagua, located to the south of Rio de Janeiro. Instead, the captain sailed straight north to the port of Vitoria, Espírito Santo, where the *Quinsey* arrived on March 21 or 22. Crewmembers proceeded to paint the boat, carried out repairs, and took on a large quantity of firewood. It then returned to the city of Rio de Janeiro and arrived on April 4 or 5. There men prepared the vessel to transport slaves, which included taking on lumber for a slave deck, and loading three hundred *pipas* of water, a large quantity of beans, manioc flour, and dried beef, along with pots, pans, two merchant chests, sixty slave irons, and a quantity of bar iron. The *Quinsey* departed for Africa on April 16. While at sea, sailors constructed the slave decks. Weighing 213 tons, the *Quinsey* supposedly had the capacity to carry 1,400 slaves from Africa to Brazil.

On June 4, the crew hoisted a signal to waiting observers near the port of Ambriz on the coast of Angola. A man paddled out to the ship to inform the captain of 1,400 enslaved Africans being held a few miles inland, and that they would be ready to be boarded in a few days. Anderson stated that the captain possessed papers from the U.S. consul in Rio and it was sailing under a U.S. flag.

On June 8, at four p.m., the *Quinsey* commenced taking on slaves. After it had boarded an estimated eight hundred Africans, a British steamer of war appeared, forcing the crew hastily to put back onshore all of the Africans. An English officer visited the next morning, reviewed the U.S. documents provided by the captain, and then departed. The *Quinsey* remained at anchor near Ambriz for a few days, and then departed with plans to receive the slaves at a location sixty miles south of Ambriz eight days later. While sailing along the coast, the *Quinsey* was again visited by a British steamer and subsequently a French cruiser. Captains from both asked why the *Quinsey* lingered along the coast. Returning to Ambriz, the *Quinsey* was visited one more time by an English officer who further inquired about its activities and demanded to see the ship's papers. During none of these visits did the English or French officers request a thorough search of the holds of the *Quinsey*. From late June until the Fourth of July, the *Quinsey* laid at anchor near Ambriz.

An absence of European intruders finally made it possible to take on Africans. In the words of William Anderson, "during the entire day of the fourth [of July] we decorated our ship in honor of the day [Independence Day in the United States] and fired a salute from a four pounder [cannon] which we had on board. At four o'clock on this day [afternoon of the fourth] we again commenced taking on our cargo and within an hour we took on board 746 Negroes, when we slipped our anchor and put to sea."[76]

During that one hour, canoes quickly carried the Africans from beach to ship. The crew cut portholes in the side of the vessel and let out rope ladders to speed up the loading of the slaves.

> The Africans were of all ages from one to thirty years of age; of the total there were from 90 to 100 females, about 150 small boys and the rest were men or full grown boys. From what I could learn on the [African] coast this cargo cost about $18.00 a head. They brought [were sold for] at the place where landed $480.00 a head. They were considered an extra fine lot. On the voyage, men kept below and women and children allowed on the deck. As we did not take on board but a few more than one half of the number for which we had made provisions [746 with space for 1400], we were able to water them well [provide water] and thus landed them in very good condition.[77]

The *Quinsey* returned to Brazil and arrived at a plantation about forty miles north of Campos (located at the mouth of the Paraíba River, in the province, now state, of Rio de Janeiro) on August 1, 1849, and there disembarked the Africans. The crew also deposited at this locale the slave equipment used during the voyage, except the water casks so as not to be caught with evidence associated with the slave trade.

Soon after, Anderson returned to his family in Rio de Janeiro. Like so many other histories of this epoch, the story does not end here.

In November 1849, Clapp and Smith again contacted Anderson to ask if he would join in another transatlantic trip, this time on the ship *France*. Built in the United States, the *France* had recently made a successful slaving voyage to Africa. The vessel had journeyed under a U.S. flag but returned into the port of Rio de Janeiro displaying a Brazilian flag. Anderson agreed to the offer, and departed from Rio de Janeiro on December 17, 1849. The crew of the *France* included several U.S. citizens. The captain of the ship carried papers signed by the U.S. consul in Rio de Janeiro, which Anderson believed was either the bill confirming sale to a Brazilian purchaser or the original sea letter provided previous to the first voyage of the *France* to the coast of Africa.

The *France* sailed to East Central Africa, where it arrived near the town of Quelimane, Mozambique on January 29, 1850. Soon after throwing anchor, the ship was visited by the British cruiser *Pantaloon*. British captain Hyde Parker asked to see the papers of the ship and was informed that none were on board. Early the next morning, he returned and demanded that the hatches of the ship be opened. There he found water casks, wheat flour, large copper pans for cooking, shackles, and a slave deck: "every [equipment] necessary for success in her nefarious undertaking."[78] British sailors immediately took possession of the ship. Anderson accompanied the *France* to the Cape of Good Hope. During an interrogation before British commissioners at Cape Town, Anderson admitted to having thrown overboard all of the documents related to the voyage. Claiming to be the captain of the *France*, Anderson stated that the ship was owned by eight individuals of "high station" in Rio de Janeiro. He was tried for complicity in the slave trade before a Mixed Commission Court, and the ship was condemned and destroyed.[79]

William Anderson returned to Rio de Janeiro on June 17, 1850. Making inquiries, he heard Joshua Clapp remained present in the city and that Frank Smith had left for California. At a deposition one year later in June 1851, Anderson understood that Clapp also had returned to the United States.[80] Hoping to prosecute Smith and Clapp for their illegal activities, the U.S. consul sent letters to U.S. officials informing them that both Clapp and Smith could easily be found in Philadelphia. Anderson's deposition is one of tens of interviews carried out by U.S. consular officials in the 1840s, during which traffickers recounted the travels of U.S. ships along the coasts of Africa, strategies to embark slaves quickly and to evade British cruisers, the Middle Passage, and the landings of Africans on Brazilian coasts.[81]

Not all U.S. captains had an interest in transporting large numbers of Africans. In some journeys, U.S. ships carried six to ten slaves on board. The Africans were provided false passports that categorized them as "freemen" and "passengers." In two instances, U.S. consul at Rio de Janeiro George Slacum received information that led him to believe that "passengers" were in fact slaves. When he attempted to speak directly with the recently arrived Africans, Slacum realized he had a problem, given his incapacity to converse in their languages. Captain Ezra Foster from Beverly, Massachusetts informed Slocum that willing purchasers at Rio de Janeiro paid one hundred dollars for each African that Foster conveyed to the city.[82]

The contributions of U.S. diplomats in forcing an end to the transatlantic slave trade to Brazil merit close scrutiny. Several U.S. consular officials stationed in Rio de Janeiro and Salvador during the 1840s sought to disrupt this infamous commerce. These officials recognized the pervasive presence of U.S. merchants and ships in the transatlantic slave trade to Brazil. In the words of Henry A. Wise, U.S. minister to Brazil (1844–47), "I venture to affirm [writing in 1844] that not a vessel of the United States is sold in Brazil to be delivered at a port in Africa, without the United States captain and crew, if not owners and consignees, willfully and knowingly aiding and abetting that traffic."[83] Scorned by traffickers in Brazil, Wise responded:

> Why, [do] I an American slave holder, manifest such extraordinary zeal on this subject? The only answer I shall deign to give is that the fact of my being a slave holder is itself a pledge and guarantee that I am no *fanatic*, foolishly and wickedly bent upon running amuck against any lawful property or trade; and that I find the same old interest [U.S. merchants resident in the U.S. North] at work here and now, to fasten American slavery on Brazil, which in our early history fastened its condition of a slave state on Virginia. Vessels and capital from precisely the same quarter [U.S. North] bring the slaves to this country in this age which carried them to that country, the United States, in times past. The very land in the old [England] and in the new world [U.S. North], where world's conventions are held, and whence abolition petitions flow, are the lands where there are manufacturers of goods "fit for the Coast" [Africa] and where there are owners of vessels to be "chartered and sold deliverable on the coast of Africa."[84]

U.S. consuls stationed in Rio de Janeiro during the 1840s kept detailed records of ship departures and arrivals. Born in Exeter, New Hampshire, George W. Gordon had worked at an import firm in Boston and held public offices (1830–43) previous to his appointment to the consular post in Brazil (1843–46). In September 1845, Gordon listed 64 U.S. vessels that had been sold in the port of Rio de Janeiro since January 1840, of which 34 were reported to have been employed in the slave trade.[85]

A former district attorney for the state of Maine (1843–45), Gorham Parks knew well the design of slaving vessels constructed in New England and the obfuscations of merchants, captains, and crews with links to the traffic. Appointed U.S. consul to Rio de Janeiro (1845–49) during the height of slave importations to Brazil, Parks condemned the involvement of U.S. ships in traffic. At the bottom of his list of vessels departing the port between 1844 and 1849 (Table 2, Appendix), Parks wrote: "Of these ships [a total of ninety-three], all except five have been sold or delivered on the coast of Africa and have been engaged in bringing over slaves and many of them have been captured with the slaves on board."

Based on the calculations of Gordon and Parks, at least 110 U.S. ships that departed from the port of Rio de Janeiro between January 1840 and September 1849 transported African slaves to Brazil. Tens of other U.S. vessels departed from Rio de Janeiro during this period as auxiliary tender ships.

George Gordon proved to be one of the most tenacious and effective U.S. consuls stationed anywhere in the Atlantic basin. During his stay in Rio de Janeiro, he caused the arrest of four U.S. ship captains along with thirty other persons (officers and crewmembers), accusing them of abetting the slave trade. Two of the captains, J.S. Pendleton of the U.S. brig *Montevideo* and Cyrus Libby of the U.S. brig *Porpoise*, were tried in courts in the United States but escaped conviction. Gordon's action provoked the wrath of powerful individuals in the city of Rio de Janeiro connected to the slave trade. Believing that his letters were being opened, Gordon wrote that "the most strenuous efforts are being made by parties in this place to procure my removal from office; that those thus engaged whatever may be their representations, are persons connected with American [U.S.] vessels engaged in the African slave trade, and who are annoyed by the course I have felt it my duty to pursue in regard to that traffic."[86]

As in Cuba, a few U.S. consuls facilitated and profited from the slave trade. On May 4, 1845, a diplomatic pouch sent by the U.S. consul in Rio de Janeiro arrived in Salvador on board the steamship *Imperatriz*. It included a message directed to U.S. consul Alexander Tyler that accused the U.S. citizens Jacob Woodbury and Thomas Duling of having captained the *Albert* of Boston and the *Washington's Barge* of Philadelphia to Africa to procure slaves. After Duling sold the *Washington's Barge* to purchasers on the African coast, he and the ship's crew returned to Bahia on board the tender vessel *Albert*. The plan was for the *Washington's Barge* to transport several hundred slaves to Bahia. Acting on the information he received, Tyler called for the arrest of Woodbury and Duling.

The following day, Duling boarded the *Imperatriz*. After arrival up the coast at Recife, he planned to transfer to a larger ship that would take him to Philadelphia. Moments before his setting out, Bahian police appeared and forced Duling off the *Imperatriz*. "They conducted [him] as a prisoner through the city first to the residence of the consul, who was absent, then to the house of the officer who arrested him, and then to the police office, where he was informed that he was not a prisoner but merely prevented from leaving Bahia at the particular request of the American consul [Alexander Tyler]." Police also detained Captain Woodbury along with the entire crew of the *Albert*. In the words of John Gilmer, a U.S. businessman residing in Salvador, "In this disgraceful manner were two respectable American citizens at the mere whim and caprice of Mr. Tyler, conducted through the most public street of this city in open day, and in the presence of a great number of spectators, native and foreign, to the common prison at the Dockyard, where vagrants only are generally sent."[87]

It did not take long for the two U.S. captains and the crew of the *Albert* to get out of jail. On May 7, Chief of Police João Joaquim da Silva ordered the group released from detention. Duling exited Salvador on May 11, while it appears that Woodbury lingered in the city without concern of arrest. Gilmer and friends (U.S. citizens George Carey, W.T. Harris, George Dunham, and Joseph Ray) complained about U.S. consul Tyler to officials in Washington, D.C. Gilmer emphasized (on behalf of the group) that "in making these observations [critical of Tyler] we beg to observe that we consider them due to the character of our injured countrymen and not from any wish to afford facilities to the continuance of the slave trade, which we sincerely detest, and regret that more extensive powers have not been granted by legislative enactment to our government, for its effectual suppression, so far as the honor of our flag is concerned."[88]

A man with a murky past, Gilmer had maintained close ties with known traffickers in Salvador and in Rio de Janeiro, including the U.S. merchant house Maxwell Wright and Company. In late 1844 at the U.S. consulate in Rio de Janeiro, a U.S. sailor named Charles Bigelow deposed that John Gilmer had knowingly sold the U.S. brig *Gloria* in Salvador for use as a slave ship. The U.S. consul forwarded the statements gleaned from Bigelow to the U.S. secretary of state. To the dismay of Gilmer, the *Boston Daily Atlas* included the accusations in an article published on April 20, 1845. In response, Gilmer lashed out at U.S. representatives in Rio de Janeiro, denying any illegal activities.[89] During the latter half of the 1840s, it appears that Gilmer continued to abet the slave trade to Salvador while denying complicity. Gilmer's corrupt activities surely contributed to the recall of Alexander Tyler from the consul in Salvador in 1848. Two years later, John S. Gilmer gained appointment as the U.S. consul at Salvador, where he remained until early 1862.

In a telling episode in 1852, Gilmer became enmeshed in a controversy related to the possessions left by a deceased U.S. citizen. W.J. Harris had engaged in the slave trade to Bahia for "several years." His dealings enabled him to put aside a fortune worth sixty thousand dollars (over two million dollars in 2013). Gilmer hoped to be the administrator for the estate, but officials in Salvador took control over all of Harris's goods. In an attempt to impede interference, Gilmer placed the seal of the consulate of the United States on several items. Police ordered him to remove the seals, which he did under protest. Harris's estate was sold, in the words of a U.S. official, "at a kind of mock auction, at a shameful sacrifice. In fact, the entire transaction was a complete swindle." Gilmer tried desperately to keep a young slave girl owned previously by Harris, but police officers took her away and included her among the items of property to be auctioned. Heirs to the Harris fortune, residents of New York City, inherited nothing. Gilmer complained to the consulate in Rio de Janeiro and to the State Department in Washington, D.C. that he had been treated unjustly. It appears that no one responded to his letters, and the issue was dropped.[90]

A FINAL COMMENT

The transatlantic slave trade of the first half of the nineteenth century flourished partially due to the involvement of U.S. merchants and the capital of U.S. investors. U.S. shipyards constructed vessels specially designed for speed and agility that aided traffickers to board slaves swiftly on the African coast and to flee from British cruisers. U.S. citizens sold and rented U.S. ships to interested parties in Brazilian and Cuban ports, including renowned Rio de Janeiro traffickers Manuel Pinto da Fonseca and José Bernardino de Sá and Havana traffickers Pedro Forcade, José Mazorra, Joaquim Andreu, Juan Fernández, and Julien Zulueta. In the case of Pedro Blanco, in the wake of the British Squadron's destruction of a slave factory he controlled at Gallinas (just north of the present-day border of Sierra Leone and Liberia) in 1842, the Spaniard resumed his business of purchasing and selling Africans at Havana after a voyage from Freetown to Cuba on the U.S.-built schooner *Hugh Boyle* (later named *Galiana*).[91]

Eric Anderson estimates that at least 430 U.S. ships made 545 slaving voyages to the Americas in the period of 1815–50, the majority to Cuba and Brazil.[92] The peak was during the years 1835–50, with 276 U.S. voyages, or an average of 17.25 voyages a year.[93] I estimate that traffickers purchased or leased another two hundred U.S.-built ships for the transport of slaves to Cuba in the period 1850–67. Historian Leonardo Marques estimates 2,010 slave voyages in vessels constructed in the United States between 1831 and 1860.[94] If we divide by three, this being the average number of voyages per ship, we get 670 vessels for this period. Based on all these calculations, a conservative estimate is that from 1815 to 1860 some 800 to 1,000 U.S.-built vessels were involved in the illegal transport of Africans to Brazil and Cuba. These vessels transported over one million African slaves to Brazil and Cuba during these years. Construction of ships in the United States, the sale and leasing of U.S. vessels to known slave traders, the provision of U.S.-produced goods to factories located on the coast of Africa, and each successful slave voyage brought an income, sometimes a huge profit, to the many individuals involved.

2

INFECTIONS IN CUBA

———— ∞ ————

Slave ships carried infection around the Atlantic world. Thousands of enslaved Africans perished from these diseases. The arrival of ill Africans to Cuba caused great distress among inhabitants and officials on the island. The spread of epidemics provoked public protest and medical debate about the threats posed by the transatlantic slave trade.

THE COASTS OF AFRICA

An outgoing voyage from Cuba to Africa could take from one month to several months. Slavers arrived in African waters as quickly as possible so as to deposit perishable goods. Depending on various factors, including the availability of slaves, a slave vessel anchored in one location or sailed along the coast to make contact with factories or intermediaries. With multiple dangers lurking along African coasts, slave merchants sought efficiency in their business dealings. Captains desired swift departure from Africa so as not to be detected by British cruisers and not lose crew and enslaved Africans to sickness.

Tropical diseases posed major problems for captains and crews. Sailors commonly picked up sickness to which they had no immunity, especially during the rainy seasons. Dysentery, malaria, smallpox, yellow fever, typhus, typhoid fever, dengue fever, and eye infections often spread on board slave ships. Given that insects transmitted diseases such as malaria and yellow fever, the incidence of outbreaks decreased during the dry season.[1] Hence merchants and captains commonly planned for ships to arrive in Africa north of the equator between October and April or south of the equator between May and October.

If a ship lost members of a crew, the captain looked for replacements. Euro-Americans seeking work could often be found at factories. These included sailors abandoned onshore from slave ships, survivors of wrecks, or the crews of captured slavers. Captains also employed Africans to partake of slave voyages. Africans held special appeal, as they were often immune to local diseases and possessed knowledge of the coast, nautical abilities, and language skills.

AN AFRICAN MIDDLE PASSAGE

Enslaved Africans arrived on African coasts walking overland or riding on canoes that traveled down rivers from the interior. These journeys could take days or weeks.[2] After arrival near the coast, traffickers kept Africans at barracoons or out in the open at hidden locales. There they lingered until the arrival of slave vessels from Europe, North America, Brazil, and Cuba. Captives endured unsanitary conditions during this waiting period. Epidemics often broke out, killing Africans before embarkation. Once they were at sea, the filthy environment inside the hold of a slaver and contaminated water contributed to the spread of sickness.[3]

Suppression of the slave trade by the British Navy resulted in the capture of close to two thousand transatlantic slave vessels. Interceptions reached their peak in 1847 and 1848.[4] After seizure of a slave vessel off Africa, British cruisers most often transported the prize to Freetown, Sierra Leone. Of 174,000 Africans recaptured by the British Squadron between 1808 and 1866, some 66,745 were processed at the Mixed Commission Courts at Freetown.[5] Although the time between interception and arrival at Freetown was shorter in duration than the voyage across the Atlantic Ocean to the Americas, the events and conditions experienced en route can be described as an African Middle Passage.

Captures were often violent affairs. On April 1, 1830, sailors from HMS *Black Joke* boarded the Spanish schooner *Manzanares* after a chase of twelve hours off the coast of Liberia. Owned by Francisco Muente of Havana, the *Manzanares*, with plans to return to Havana, had taken on board 354 slaves. Soon after the British took possession of the schooner, the captives revolted. In the fight that followed, British sailors wounded several Africans with their swords, three of whom lost limbs. One British officer was seriously injured.

The Africans believed the British captors to be pirates desirous of keeping them enslaved. Upon arrival at Freetown, the colony's surgeon general determined that forty of the Africans suffered from dysentery and a few others from ophthalmia (inflammation of the eye), these infections being caused by the "crowded, unclean and unhealthy state" of the *Manzanares*.[6]

Five months later, on September 7, HMS *Primrose* captured the notorious slaver *Veloz Passagera* with 556 Africans on board. The ship departed Havana on August 21, 1828, and arrived on the coast of Africa the following November 7. For almost two years, the *Veloz Passagera* sailed near Ouidah and to and from the islands of São Tomé. During this interlude, sailors from British cruisers boarded and investigated the vessel seven times without finding sufficient evidence to seize it. When seized, the *Veloz Passagera* had been at sea four days since leaving the coast. The Spanish captain Antonio de la Vega purchased the Africans from the famed Brazilian trafficker Francisco Félix de Souza (known as "Chacha") near Ouidah and planned to transport them to Havana.[7]

As with the *Manzanares*, a battle erupted at the time of capture. In this episode, the *Primrose* shot cannonballs directly into the side of the *Veloz Passagera*. Several of the Spanish crew died, along with five African slaves who had been forced to take up arms against the British. Three English sailors on the *Primrose* died during the fight, and twelve were wounded. The British captors put a group of the Spanish crew from the *Veloz Passagera* on a boat with provisions and allowed them to row to shore. The remaining twenty-two sailors along with the wounded captain were transported to Freetown and imprisoned. Lieutenant Governor Findlay determined that these men should be sent to London for adjudication.

During the voyage to Freetown, sixteen Africans died and another five died soon after arrival in the port. The surgeon general determined that ten of the Africans suffered from dysentery, three were recovering from smallpox, twenty had ulcers, and numerous others were infected with craw-craw (onchocerciasis, skin rash, and eye lesions spread by blackfly and worms). He requested that the Africans be landed as soon as possible to protect their health.[8]

In spite of immunities to tropical diseases, Africans forced into the holds of slavers commonly fell ill soon after setting out from African shores. After a chase of fifty hours in late December 1825, HMS *Brazen* captured the Spanish schooner *Iberia* off Lagos, Nigeria with 423 slaves on board. Captain Wells immediately placed a prize crew on board the *Iberia* and the two ships sailed for Freetown. Upon arrival on January 22, 1826, the surgeon general visited the slave ship. He found "the slaves on board in a very crowded state, and many suffering from dysentery, as well as fifteen cases of smallpox."[9] In a petition to the British-Spanish Mixed Commission Court, he requested that all of the healthy slaves be landed immediately. This petition was granted, and the *Iberia* was placed in quarantine for several days.

In the interrogations that followed, master Andres Insua claimed that he had sailed the *Iberia* from Havana to Accra and then Lagos on a legitimate trading voyage. When supposedly he could wait no longer for promised payments of palm oil and ivory, Insua took slaves on board. He stated that his plan had been to sell the Africans along the coast and purchase material goods to bring back to Cuba. The British captors found a few documents on board, including a passport, a list of crew, and a bill of sale. Insua denied that he had destroyed or thrown overboard ship papers during the chase. Based on the obvious illegality of the voyage, the Mixed Commission Court condemned the *Iberia* and declared the 417 survivors free (5 died soon after arrival at Freetown).[10]

Far more horrific episodes related to health conditions occurred on prizes of the British Squadron. In early August 1829, HMS *Plumper* captured the schooner *Ceres* along the Bight of Biafra (a 370-mile stretch from the outlet of the Niger River to northwest Gabon) with 279 African slaves on board. Between the time of interception and arrival at Freetown, one hundred of the Africans perished. Another 18 died while the *Ceres* lay at anchor in that port, and 33 more after they arrived onshore. In this African Middle Passage 151 (54 percent) of the Africans died. Of the total number (279) who embarked from near the Cameroons River, 192 (69 percent) were children.[11]

According to an investigation carried out at Freetown, "the water that had been taken on to the *Ceres* had been picked up at low water [low tide] in the River Cameroons, hence it was brackish, which caused dysentery among the slaves. This together with most of the slaves being infected with worms led to the unfortunate loss of life."[12]

The *Ceres* had a previous history as a slaver under the name of *Gertrudes*. The vessel had departed from Havana in late 1827 and picked up slaves at Gallinas in early January 1828. A British ship of the Africa Squadron captured the schooner and brought it to Freetown on January 24. The *Gertrudes* was condemned by the British-Spanish Mixed Commission Court, and the 155 Africans on board were emancipated.[13]

The owner of the *Gertrudes* was a Mr. Brockenton. A resident of Freetown known for involvement in the slave trade, Brockenton purchased the *Gertrudes*

at the court-sanctioned auction and sent it to business partners in Rio de Janeiro. A consortium composed of three British merchants named Platt, Mil-
len, and Reid received the schooner and subsequently sold the ship to the
merchant house of José Botelho and Company.[14] The latter sent the vessel back
to Lagos under the name *Ceres*, where it was seized by the British a second
time in August 1829 (as described above).

Africans on board captured vessels arrived in Freetown with numerous af-
flictions. In the voyage of the Brazilian schooner *Mensageira* from the island of
Fernando Po (present-day Bioko off the coast of Cameroon) to Freetown, 109
of 226 Africans died (48 percent). Of these, 43 perished during the journey at
sea, and 66 died soon after being put onshore at Freetown. The surgeon general attributed the death for the majority to dysentery. Health officials at Freetown frequently encountered smallpox, craw-craw, ophthalmia, and malignant
ulcers among recaptured Africans.[15] Witnesses commented on the "extreme
debility," due to bad food and "tedious passage," of hundreds of Africans who
arrived at Freetown."[16]

Examples abound of the high death rate during the African Middle Passage
and among recaptured Africans soon after landing at Freetown. Between October 1829 and February 1830, the British Squadron seized seven slave ships
along the coast of West Africa. During the African Middle Passage to Freetown and soon after landing, 318 of the Africans from those vessels perished
(20 percent).[17] During the year 1857, the British Squadron captured four slave
ships and two smaller launches with 942 enslaved Africans on board. Between
the time of seizure and adjudication by the Vice Admiralty Court at Freetown
(which had replaced the Mixed Commission Courts), 160 of these souls had
perished (17 percent).[18]

One other episode of note is the capture of the *Nightingale*, a huge clipper
ship (998 tons) built at the Hanscom Shipyard at Eliot, Maine (just outside
Portsmouth, New Hampshire) in 1851. Sold to trafficker Francis Bowen in
February 1860, the *Nightingale* departed New York later that summer with
a destination of Rio de Janeiro. Bowen then sailed the vessel to São Tomé
and on to West Central Africa. Although it is not documented in the Trans-
Atlantic Slave Trade Database, one scholar believes that the *Nightingale* transported two thousand African slaves from Cabinda to Cuba sometime in the
second half of 1860. Returning to Cabinda with plans for a second slaving voyage, the *Nightingale* was seized by the U.S. sloop-of-war *Saratoga* on April 21,
1861, with 961 Africans on board. The U.S. prize crew immediately sailed the

Nightingale to Monrovia, Liberia. Between the time of capture and landing at Liberia, 160 (17 percent) of the recaptured Africans died from African fever (yellow fever).[19] From Liberia, the prize crew sailed the *Nightingale* to New York. Because the crew were found guilty of participation in the slave trade, the U.S. Navy auctioned the vessel. Purchased by the U.S. government, it was employed as an armed cruiser for the Union Navy during the U.S. Civil War.

The British received sick Africans at the Kissy Hospital, situated up a river outside of Freetown. Medical personnel at the hospital created a special ward to treat Africans infected with smallpox. In the case of the captured Spanish schooner *Altimara*, the surgeon general at Freetown estimated that three-quarters of the 217 Africans who survived the one-month African Middle Passage (March 27 to April 25, 1830) along the coast of West Africa had been stricken with the contagion. "The survivors were landed at Kissy, precautions were taken by keeping them separate, to prevent the spread of that fatal disease among the inhabitants of the colony."[20] Those with less debilitating infections were housed at a "Liberated African Yard" in Freetown. The colonial government grappled with the threats posed by the spread of infectious diseases until the demise of the transatlantic slave trade.[21] After Liberated Africans regained their health, many settled at towns in the interior of Sierra Leone.

TRANSATLANTIC MIDDLE PASSAGE

During the 366 years of the transatlantic slave trade, traffickers learned from their experiences. As capitalists, they sought to improve efficiency and minimize loss of investments. They determined the optimal size of a slave vessel for a transatlantic voyage to be between 150 and 250 tons and an optimal carrying ratio to be 1.5 to 2.5 slaves per ton. At the height of the traffic from the late eighteenth to the middle of the nineteenth century, European vessels carried an average of between 350 and 450 slaves per voyage.[22]

Over time the loss of African slaves during the Middle Passage between Africa and the Americas decreased. Changes in the provisioning of vessels and medical knowledge contributed to this reduction. By the early nineteenth century, mortality rates reached their lowest level at 10 percent. However, as historian Herbert S. Klein has noted, "this seemingly 'low' rate produces a crude death rate for a healthy economically active population that is truly astronomic in its level."[23] Contagious diseases and infections caused suffering and death on transatlantic slave voyages until the last slavers arrived in Cuba in 1867.

The events surrounding the capture of the Spanish brig *Midas* off the coast of the Bahama islands in late June 1829 shed light on the devastation caused by epidemics. After a battle of thirty-five minutes at midday on June 27, British sailors from H.M. schooner *Monkey* took control of the *Midas* by two p.m. in the afternoon. Of 562 Africans who had been forced onto the *Midas* at the Bonny River, 400 remained alive, 162 having perished from an outbreak of smallpox during the journey across the Atlantic. During the night after the British seized the ship, 31 Africans jumped overboard to their deaths, "a number of them inspired by fright, it was supposed."[24] Although sentinels were placed on the deck of the *Midas*, nine other Africans jumped to their deaths in the following days.

Due to unfavorable winds and a small force on board the *Monkey*, the two vessels remained at anchor off the Bahamas for several days. In the voyage leg to Havana, 69 Africans succumbed to smallpox. Soon after arrival on July 7, ten more fell victim to the outbreak. The 281 survivors were taken to shore and moved to a lazaretto outside of Havana known as El Vedado. Within days, another 28 Africans died. Cuban medical officials described the captives as being in "a dreadful state, so ill and emaciated that it has hitherto been impossible to make out those descriptions of their persons and marks [cuts on the face and body denoting nation and sometimes rank] that are inserted in their certificates of emancipation [meaning the documents confirming liberation by the decree of the Havana Mixed Commission Court]."[25]

Three weeks later the *Fama de Cadiz* (also known as the *Nueva Diana*) sailed into the port of Havana in ballast. The vessel had disembarked some 300 Africans fifty kilometers to the east of Havana near the town Santa Cruz del Norte. A "notorious slave trader and pirate," the *Fama* had been intercepted by a British cruiser on the west coast of Africa previous to its picking up Africans. Because of insufficient evidence of its malicious intentions, the *Fama* had been allowed to continue on its voyage. It proceeded to attack several slave vessels and took on board 980 Africans. Soon after it set sail for Cuba, smallpox and other sickness broke out. Out of a crew of 157, 66 survived. Of the 980 Africans, an estimated 300 arrived at Santa Cruz. A British diplomat observed that "the majority [were] in such a wretched state that her owners have been selling them for as low as 100 dollars. This expedition has been altogether ruinous from the exorbitant wages due to the sailors and the length of time she has been out."[26]

Spanish officials sought to impede the spread of infection from slave ships to residents in Havana, coastal towns, and the interior.[27] Hence, in several instances they refused to allow recaptured Africans to disembark. This is what occurred with the Spanish ship *Negrita*. It was seized on March 29, 1833, by Her Majesty's schooner of war *Nimble* with 195 Africans in its hold, and the two vessels arrived at Havana soon after. The captain general immediately ordered a boarding of the *Negrita* by medical personnel to examine the Africans. Learning that nine of them showed symptoms of sickness, the captain general ordered a total quarantine for twenty-four hours. In spite of being informed that the Africans were "in an almost unprecedented state of good health for a slave vessel," he requested that the *Negrita* be moved out of the harbor and anchored off the north coast of the island. Numerous Africans soon showed symptoms of dysentery. Residents quickly learned of this outbreak and demanded that the Africans not be landed.[28] "Popular commotions" broke out near Matanzas and other locales along the coast to protest against landings of Africans.[29] A contributor to the Havana newspaper *Diario de la Habana* wrote that the "the negroes should not be disembarked on this island, as [their presence] could undermine our public health and add to the [already prevalent] sicknesses which we endure [meaning a cholera epidemic]."[30] Determining the slaver unseaworthy, the captain general hired a "renowned fast-sailing slaver" named *Carolina* to transport the Africans of the *Negrita* to Trinidad.[31] The *Carolina* sailed from Havana on April 20.

Later that year in November 1833, the *Nimble* seized another slave vessel named the *Joaquina* off the Cuban coast with 329 Africans on board. Upon its arrival in Havana, medical inspectors observed that several of the Africans suffered from dysentery. As with what occurred with the *Negrita*, the Africans of the *Joaquina* were sent to Trinidad. Health concerns influenced the decision of the captain general:

> The recent capture of the *Joaquina* by the *Nimble*, has created some similar circumstances [as with the *Negrita*]. Although the situation in terms of health of the city has changed [a cholera epidemic having subsided], nevertheless it appears wise to send the cargo to Trinidad. Such a removal will remove from us the most remote danger as to the public health, for although the consequence of these Negroes being landed may afford at present no absolute foundation for fear, nevertheless the long navigation of the schooner, the weak and delicate state of the negroes, the sudden change of climate and season, may produce in them suspicious diseases sufficient to alarm this population now convalescent.[32]

British suppression efforts resulted in several captured slave ships arriving at Havana. Of 10,390 Africans emancipated by the Anglo-Spanish Court of Mixed Commission at Havana between 1821 and 1845, at least 1,207 were sent to Trinidad.[33] Various motives can be cited for these transfers, including British interest in cheap labor on its Caribbean islands (slavery was abolished in the British Caribbean in 1834) and a desire to keep Liberated Africans out of the hands of Cuban owners. Another reason can be traced to the desire by potential purchasers in Cuba to allow only healthy Africans from captured slave vessels to set foot on the island. In numerous instances, Spanish authorities discussed the threat to public health of landing sick Africans. Given the profits involved, they hoped for speedy recovery so that recaptured Africans could be distributed as "free Africans" to "responsible citizens" on the island.

The arrival of the captured Spanish slaver *Chubasco* sheds light on the strategies of Spanish representatives in Cuba. After it was taken by His Majesty's sloop *Racer*, the two ships entered the port of Havana on April 14, 1835. Based on advice from the Superior Board of Health, Captain General Miguel Tacón (who ruled by martial law from 1834 to 1838) determined that the 253 Africans be landed immediately "at an estate to the leeward of the city, on account of the smallpox prevailing among the negroes. [At that locale the Africans] are to remain insulated with every necessary medical attendance, while the crew should return to this port [Havana] and remain in quarantine at Marimelena, on board the detained vessel for a space of 40 days."[34]

The captain general had a financial stake in allowing the Africans of the *Chubasco* to come onshore. One anonymous resident estimated that Tacón received between 51 and 102 dollars for each female Liberated African and 102 to 170 dollars for every male Liberated African, and accused him of "removing the [traditional and well-known] restriction over both males and females of *domestic* service and extending it to the *rudest services of the field*."[35] The captain general and government bureaucrats had grown accustomed to remuneration derived from sales of Liberated Africans to well-off residents.[36] Cloaked in benevolence, treatment of Liberated Africans in Cuba was often worse than that endured by slaves.

With tensions rising between the British (captains of cruisers, consular representatives, Mixed Commission Court judges) and Spanish authorities over the fate of ill Africans on board captured slave vessels in the 1830s, the English government placed a "receiving ship" named the *Romney* in the harbor

of Havana in 1837. Downplaying this foreign intrusion into the port, the po-
litically astute Tacón characterized the *Romney* as "a floating depot to protect
the safety of the country, [part of the arrangements necessary] to protect the
sanitary and public security of the island."[37]

Anchored in a distant quarantine sector in the east of the harbor known
as Marimelena, the *Romney* offered shelter and respite to Africans recently
arrived on captured slave vessels. Dismasted and with a roof built over it, this
"floating barrack" included a British lieutenant, a detachment of soldiers, and
medical officials among its personnel. Always seeking to drive a wedge between England and Spain, U.S. representative Nicholas Trist called the *Romney* a "fortification and to all practical intents it is the same as if a portion of
the shore had been placed for an unlimited period under the British flag and
British jurisdiction."[38]

Opinion about the transatlantic slave trade to Cuba became closely en-
twined with discourse related to the spread of epidemics. Spanish colonial
authorities required that ships with evidence of infection on board be quar-
antined for various periods (one to forty days). Spanish officials agreed (as
described above) to the British request that the receiving ship *Romney* be anchored in the port of Havana to aid Liberated Africans in recovery from sicknesses. This prophylactic measure was also intended to prevent the spread of
sickness to shore. In several instances Spanish officials agreed to the transfer
of Liberated Africans to other British Caribbean islands. Although portrayed
as enlightened decisions beneficial to the Liberated Africans, a major motive
related to the perceived threats posed to public health in Havana and the island when Liberated Africans were allowed to come onshore.[39]

A CARIBBEAN MIDDLE PASSAGE

British officials did not desire that Africans remain on board the *Romney* for
extended periods. Their preference was to transfer the Africans to British colonies in the Caribbean, where they could be employed as indentured workers.[40]
This occurred with the first two groups of Liberated Africans placed on board
the *Romney*. In mid-December 1837, 254 Africans from the slave ship *Matilda*
recovered on the ship for twelve days. The majority departed on December 31
for Belize. Eighteen who needed more time to convalesce sailed in early February. In the case of the *Sierra del Pilar*, its crew ran this slaver onto a beach in

early June 1839, where it was damaged beyond repair. Her Majesty's schooner *Pickle* rescued the 173 Africans and transported them to Havana. The *Sierra* Africans languished on the *Romney* for seventeen days from June 13 to June 30. The British consul then sent them to Grenada.[41]

The captured Spanish slaver *Jesus Maria* arrived at Havana on Saturday night, January 9, 1841. British sailors from HMS *Ringdove* had found "252 negroes who were very debilitated and crowded on board" the vessel. A small ship of thirty-five tons, this "coast trader" had been employed primarily to ferry potatoes and onions from the Canary Islands to settlements along the shores of West Africa. Four of the enslaved Africans were adult women, the remainder boys and girls, the majority between the ages of ten and fifteen years old. Through an African interpreter named George Elder, British consul David Turnbull learned of "atrocious and revolting crimes" and numerous episodes of rape carried out by the captain and crew during the transatlantic voyage.[42] The British immediately placed the young Africans who showed signs of illness on board the *Romney* "where they could receive better attention and be separated according to their cases in the several wards of the lower decks."[43]

Given the bad health of eight boys and fourteen girls, one of whom was infected with smallpox, officials at Havana refused to receive the Africans, even at a remote lazaretto. Twelve of the young people died within a few days. With coming onshore not an option, the surgeon general requested that the *Jesus Maria* depart as soon as possible for a British colony. The sick Africans who had been placed on the *Romney* were moved back to the *Jesus Maria*. The latter sailed on February 4. The result was that eleven more of the Africans perished during the short trip to Nassau and two others immediately after arrival. Forty to fifty of the Africans were deposited at a hospital at Nassau. The assistant surgeon from the *Romney* picked up dysentery and left Nassau for the return trip to Havana "without any hope of recovery."[44]

Our studies of the transatlantic Middle Passage need to be extended to include African and Caribbean segments. These latter voyages ranged in duration from several days to several weeks. Africans struggled to survive in the putrid depths of slavers. They often became sick from contagions, which spread quickly. Authorities at ports in the Atlantic world where slave vessels anchored (such as Freetown, Havana, Salvador, and Rio de Janeiro) recognized the dangers posed by the presence of ill Africans. From the 1830s, this became an issue closely tied to debates over the future of the transatlantic slave trade.

EPIDEMICS IN CUBA AND RESPONSES TO THE SLAVE TRADE

Cuba was an inhospitable environment in the nineteenth century. Outbreaks of several epidemics caused widespread suffering and death. A lack of medical knowledge about these sicknesses added to the trauma. A few academic observers linked these epidemics to the transatlantic slave trade. A far greater number of inhabitants understood well that disembarkations of ill Africans represented a threat to public health.

From the mid-1790s, the Spanish doctor Francisco Barrera y Domingo criticized the trauma endured by Africans during the Middle Passage to Cuba. Born in Aragon, Spain, Barrera joined the Spanish Royal Navy as a surgeon. He traveled to various locales in the Caribbean before settling in Havana in the early 1780s. Between February 1797 and July 1798, Barrera penned an 894-page tome entitled *Reflexiones Historico Fisico Naturales Medico Quirurgicas* (Historical, Physical, Natural Reflections of a Doctor of Surgery). In *Reflexiones*, Barrera devoted six chapters to the diseases that commonly spread on board slave vessels arriving in Cuba. One of hundreds of medical practitioners who attended to health conditions on sugar plantations around Havana, Barrera wrote another twenty-two chapters that analyzed common maladies among the African slaves, including parasites, inflammations, tumors, nutritional disorders, ulcers, and skin lesions. In *Reflexiones*, Barrera did not hesitate to express political opinions, including his belief that the slave traffic ought to be halted to Cuba due to its deleterious health effects on Africans and others.[45]

After the turn of the century, medical observers continued to express trepidation over the landing of sick Africans on the island. In 1804, the Cuban medical doctor Tomás Romay y Chacón pointed to the high death rate among Africans during the Middle Passage. His efforts influenced officials to vaccinate slaves upon their arrival in Cuba. Four years later, the captain general determined that a select group of medical personnel would take the responsibility of vaccinating all African slaves prior to their being sold in Cuba.[46]

During the 1810s, the medical doctor J.L.F. Madrid investigated several barracoons in Havana where African slaves were held and sold. Madrid observed "a number of dying blacks naked and spread out on wooden planks, many of them reduced to skin and bones, and inhaling an intolerable stench." In a report published in 1817, Dr. Madrid attributed the high incidence of dysentery among recently landed Africans to harsh treatment and a lack of nourishment. Although read by Spanish officials, Madrid's report garnered little response.[47]

In the first half of the nineteenth century, three diseases caused major health problems in Cuba. Owners of estates, medical personnel employed by planters, members of the colonial government, and common folk linked all these infections to the transatlantic slave trade. They included smallpox, yellow fever, and cholera.

Smallpox (*variola*) is transmitted between persons by means of an airborne variola virus. It is most commonly spread through physical contact. Its symptoms include rash and fluid-filled blisters. In most cases the infection leaves scars on the faces of victims. Scientific research posits that smallpox arrived in the Americas with the arrival of Europeans after 1492. With no immunity to this disease and others, native peoples experienced a demographic catastrophe. To fill the lacuna caused by the "American Holocaust," Europeans turned to Africa for cheap labor.[48]

During the Middle Passages, particularly the African and transatlantic segments, thousands of Africans perished in the holds of slave vessels after becoming infected by smallpox. For Africans who survived the voyage from Africa and landed in Cuba, Dr. Romay did everything in his power from 1804 through the 1840s to vaccinate these individuals. In spite of his commitment, many Africans never received a vaccination. The arrival of slave ships in Cuba contributed to numerous outbreaks of smallpox, including those in the years 1803, 1816, 1827, 1836, 1839, 1843, 1852, 1858, 1861, and perhaps 1870.

Yellow fever is a viral infection spread by the bite of a female mosquito (*Aedes aegypti*). The disease is believed to have its origins in West Africa and to have been carried on slave ships across the Atlantic to the Caribbean islands. Its symptoms include pain, nausea, fever, internal hemorrhaging, and in many instances jaundice (hence the name yellow fever). The first recorded outbreak in the Americas occurred in 1647 on the island of Barbados. From there it spread to Guadalupe, St. Kitts, and Puerto Rico, then jumped to the Yucatan Peninsula and over to Cuba. By 1649, one-third of the inhabitants of Havana had died from this first outbreak.

For the next 250 years, yellow fever appeared often on Caribbean islands.[49] A key reason was the ecological revolution that sugar plantations wrought. In the words of historian John Robert McNeill, "armies of slaves hacked down and burned off millions of hectares of forest to plant cane. Their efforts led to multiple ecological changes. Soil erosion accelerated. Wildlife vanished. More importantly from the human point of view, as plantations replaced forests, conditions came to favor the vector of yellow fever. . . . The most crucial development was what replaced the destroyed forests—the spread of plantations. Plantations made excellent *A. aegypti* incubators."[50] To protect their empires and plantations, European monarchs sent troops to the Caribbean. Tens of thousands of these soldiers perished from yellow fever during the frequent wars of the seventeenth and eighteenth centuries in the region.[51]

Given the close trading ties between the Caribbean islands and the United States, ships carried the infection to the eastern seaboard. In 1793 in Philadelphia, some 5,000 residents died, or 10 percent of the city's population. This was followed by major outbreaks of yellow fever in New York City in 1795 (730 dead); Boston, New York City, and Philadelphia in summer 1798 (5,000 dead); Baltimore in 1800 (1,200 dead); New Orleans in summer 1853 (8,000 or more dead); Norfolk, June to October 1855 (2,000 dead); Mississippi Valley, May to October 1878 (132 towns affected, 75,000 cases, 20,000 dead, a cost of over 100 million dollars).[52]

Havana gained fame for its insalubrious conditions, exacerbated by a doubling of the population in just over four decades, from 94,023 in 1827 to 211,696 in 1869.[53] During the nineteenth century, residents experienced at least twenty major outbreaks of yellow fever, including in the years 1818, 1837, 1843, 1849, 1853, and 1857.[54] In the 1857 outbreak, yellow fever caused 37 percent of all deaths in Havana. Of all the diseases that plagued Cuba, yellow fever caused the most deaths and greatest fear.[55] From 1855 to 1879, the disease appeared in Havana just about every month.[56]

African slaves and their descendants showed lower rates of infection by yellow fever than whites residing on the island. This has been attributed to immunities developed while living in tropical Africa, where yellow fever had been prevalent. Based on their experiences, common folk in Havana and in the countryside associated yellow fever outbreaks on land with slave vessels that arrived from Africa.[57]

Cholera is an infection of the small intestine caused by the bacterium *vibrio cholerae,* which is transmitted through human feces. It is primarily spread by the consumption of contaminated water or food. Cholera most often attacks persons who spend time in dirty and crowded environments. Its symptoms are diarrhea and vomiting. During the nineteenth century, tens of millions of people died from this disease. For various reasons, including unsanitary living conditions, far more African slaves and African descendants died from cholera than whites in Cuba and on other Caribbean islands.

Cholera arrived in Cuba in February 1833. Within two months, some 9,000 residents of Havana perished, over 10 percent of the city's population. In the countryside, an estimated 26,000 more succumbed by the time the epidemic subsided in early 1838.[58]

Historian Adrián López-Denis has depicted this tragic episode as a chronicle of death foretold. As cholera spread across Europe, the Superior Board of Health in Havana labored diligently to keep abreast of events and provide information to Cubans about the disease. Composed of elite creoles, its members met in early 1831 to discuss the establishment of a quarantine that would impede transmission of cholera to the island via foreign ships. Late in that year, they learned that the epidemic had appeared in England. Soon after, it spread to France. By June 1832, cholera broke out in Quebec and then quickly made its way into northern New York. In late 1832, Spanish diplomats stationed at Baltimore, Charleston, New York City, and New Orleans affirmed optimistically in correspondence to Captain General Mariano Ricafort that the epidemic had subsided along the east coast. In response, the Superior Board ended the quarantine in January 1833. Within a month, the dreaded epidemic raised its head in Havana.[59]

At this juncture, the creole philosophy professor and magazine editor José Antonio Saco entered the fray with an incendiary essay entitled *Letter Concerning the Cholera Morbus*. Saco accused Cuba's most powerful government official Martínez de Pinillos, also known as the Count of Villanueva, with being responsible for the arrival of cholera on the island due to his decision to end the quarantine. An outspoken critic of the slave trade to Cuba, Saco viewed the arrival of slave vessels with ill Africans on board as the likely origin of the epidemic.

Events in the countryside provide insights into the ways in which free folk viewed slave importations as a threat to public health. In the midst of the cholera epidemic of 1833, Cubans reacted violently to the presence of several hundred Africans held at an estate.

> The affair of Bejucal [twenty-three kilometers south of Havana] has more recently occurred. Slaves from an African trader were conveyed there about six months ago, and deposited in the barracoons of a well known Catalan slave

dealer under powerful private protection. The country people blockaded the place of deposit from the fear of cholera, and the *alcaldes* [municipal magistrates] of that city having taken every precaution to establish the facts of slave importation—[these magistrates] formally and officially denounced the slaves to the superior authority of the island, in order that they [the Africans] might be dealt with according to the royal order of July 2, 1826 [regulations from Spain designed to halt the slave trade]. But as your Lordship will see by the note of his Excellency the Captain General to us, by one of those juggling operations too notorious in the administration of Spanish law, a powerful resident proprietor has obtained the recognition of the validity of his claim to these people [the Africans] as his property."[60]

In spite of an obvious illegal disembarkation of Africans, the captain general once again failed to intervene. Nevertheless, the description provides evidence that inhabitants of the countryside "blockaded the place of deposit from the fear of cholera [being spread]." They viewed with trepidation the health risks posed by the presence of recently arrived Africans in their midst.

In another episode that same year of 1833, country folk attempted to halt a disembarkation of Africans because of their belief that the Africans would quickly pick up cholera and thereby abet the epidemic.

Several weeks ago according to the public belief a considerable cargo of African negroes were landed from a vessel at Vanes [Banes], a small port 8 or 10 leagues to the west of the capital. At first the white country people successfully opposed the landing but the interference of the authorities overcame the difficulties, the slaves were landed and deposited on a property belonging to a number of the commercial firms [merchant houses] engaged in the speculation. Before the sale could be effected, the newcomers on August 13th, aided by some of the resident negroes [suggesting either Africans who had resided in Cuba for an extended period known as *ladinos* or Cuban-born *creole* blacks], broke out into an insurrection, plundered and ravaged about five adjacent estates, and having acquired arms, resisted the attack of a few regular troops, and the district militia, but after a considerable loss of life, order was restored, since which some of the leaders of the insurgents have been tried, some executed and others condemned to work in chains. Notwithstanding the notoriety of these facts, which we believe are not denied even by the importers themselves, Your Lordship will perceive that the Captain General in his response gravely describes the revolt as one of ordinary occurrence—taking no notice of the related laws against slave dealing. The suppression of the truth is publicly said to have cost the importers a very large sum of money.[61]

Although impossible to decipher based on one document, the episode raises the possibility that the recently landed Africans perceived the "white country people" who had attempted to prevent the disembarkation at Banes as potential allies in their revolt.[62]

The cholera-related protests of 1833 and 1834 came to naught. The Spanish authorities, led by Captain General Tacón, clamped down on all expressions of dissent. Notorious for his corrupt activities, Tacón viewed all Cubans as hostile to Spanish imperial interests, and surrounded himself with Spanish-born advisors and military. With Tacón's acquiescence, the Spanish Navy turned a blind eye to the tens of vessels that sailed from Cuba with an obvious destination of Africa and those that returned carrying enslaved Africans.[63]

A second cholera epidemic erupted in Havana in spring 1850 and lingered on the island until 1854. During this interlude, it caused the death of over six thousand residents of Havana and at least eleven thousand others on the island.[64] Cholera returned to Cuba in October 1867, lasted over a year, and took the lives of another five thousand inhabitants.[65]

In spite of the obvious health hazards, traffickers landed thousands of African slaves in Cuba. Many of these ended up for sale at barracoons. Six major barracoons and several smaller ones existed within three miles of Havana by the late 1830s at locales like San Antonio de Chiquito, Recreo de los Amigos, Reforma, and Misericordia, and in the neighborhood of Fort Principe. A major barracoon held a sale of between 1,500 and 2,000 recently arrived Africans.[66] Eight depots existed within the walls of the city of Havana, each of which held 30 to 40 slaves.[67] Private residences often became depots, for example, building number 78 on the Calle del Sol and number 61 on Paseo street. The latter was one of the most frequented avenues in Havana. Potential buyers passed by to look over the Africans. One observer complained that "the unfortunate victims were subjected to the disgusting modes of examination customary at these sales, in the presence of a number of persons congregated as purchasers."[68] Another lamented that "to those places [the depots] people might resort just as freely as to any ordinary store of merchandise in the city, to choose what they wanted."[69]

Focused on profits, participants in the slave trade minimized the risks posed by the arrival of sick Africans. On February 10, 1841, the Baltimore clipper *Venus* disembarked some seven hundred Africans along the coast near the port of Havana.[70] In spite of "all laboring under the attack of smallpox," the Africans appeared for sale two days later at the barracoon San Antonio de

Chiquito.[71] As in other episodes after disembarkations during these months, "the Africans were openly marched to the barracoon, in files, through the highways, conspicuous by their scarred faces, their shaven heads, and their general appearance."[72]

Captain General Tacón took note, and soon banned the sale of recently arrived Africans within the walls of the city of Havana and in the immediate vicinity outside. Although this decree did little to impede continued landings of Africans, it did send a message to traffickers that the colonial government was determined to prevent the spread of epidemics carried to the island by infected Africans. Merchants such as José Mazorra responded by moving their operations to remote properties. This increased costs, made access to purchasers more difficult, and heightened the risk that contagion would spread in the interior of the island.[73]

The spread of sickness from recently landed Africans contributed to condemnation of the slave trade. Lower-class inhabitants did not want to become ill. Residents on a tropical island who knew well the maladies caused by infectious diseases, these folk lived in constant fear of contagion. They viewed *bozal* Africans as real or potential carriers of deathly viruses (a *bozal* is an African slave who has recently landed). Captain General Tacón articulated exactly this perception when he wrote that "the desolating epidemic of the Asiatic cholera morbus and the smallpox are sure to return as often as any negroes arrive from Africa, who commonly are the first victims of those maladies, [this] would [should] suffice for not permitting their debarkation."[74] Creole planters echoed this position in criticizing "traffickers who prosecute a traffic that brings with it disease at present and will infallibly lead in the end to general ruin. . . . The white population of Cuba are becoming daily more open to the truth and the enlightened part of the proprietors of the soil are at length convinced that the real question now is whether it be their interest to entail future destruction on themselves and children for the present gain of a few unprincipled or needy adventures."[75]

A love of present gain superseded reservations about epidemics associated with the slave trade. The steady expansion in agricultural sectors fueled demand for workers. As noted previously, the number of sugar estates nearly tripled between 1825 and mid-century. Although coffee estates decreased in number from 2,067 in 1827 to 782 in 1862 (due to hurricane damage, international competition, and low prices for coffee), tobacco farms rose in number in the first half of the century from 5,534 to 9,102, cattle farms from 3,098 to

4,388, and all other farms from 13,947 to 25,292.[76] The loss of 22,000 slaves to cholera during the epidemic that swept the island between 1833 and 1835 and several thousand others between 1850 and 1854 motivated planters further in their quest to find workers to fill the gap.[77] The transatlantic slave trade to Cuba continued at a torrid pace.

OTHER CONTAGIONS

Besides the suffering caused by physical maladies, residents in Cuba pondered other manifestations of infection. One was the huge presence of Africans. The massive influx of Africans from the 1790s transformed the racial and social composition of Cuba. Africans were everywhere, in Havana, in towns and villages, in the countryside. Whites depicted Africans as dirty and "uncivilized monkeys" who were prone to violence. They were "naturally indolent," "savages," and "barbarians" whose habits were "antisocial and retrograde."[78] The hierarchy of the Catholic Church depicted African religious expression as witchcraft.[79] As in the United States, a white elite of Cuba condemned miscegenation as a pollution of pure blood. By mid-century, observers lamented the "Africanization" of the island.[80]

A second vector of infection was the Haitian Revolution (1791–1804). This cataclysmic upheaval created huge problems for slave owners in Cuba. Led by African and creole slaves, the revolution resulted in the creation of the second independent republic in the Americas. One of its leaders was Toussaint Louverture, a former slave whose name became well known among slaves and free blacks in Cuba as a symbol of revolutionary spirit. By imposing fines and jail sentences on traffickers who smuggled slaves from Haiti to Cuba in the 1790s, Captain General Someruelos sought to impede "the contagion" of insurrection from entering the island.[81] For five decades after Haiti's independence, Cuban planters pointed to the dangers associated with the infiltration of "Haitianism."[82]

Events on British Caribbean islands were a third source of tension in Cuba. Merchants feared that news of slave revolts in the British colonies of Jamaica in 1776, 1794, 1823, and 1831 (an island that received over one million African slaves, or 246,000 more than were brought to Saint Domingue) and Barbados in 1816 would inspire similar outbreaks in Cuba. British activists fomenting abolitionist discourse throughout the Caribbean added to the alarm. One response was Spanish authorities' prohibition of the disembarkation in Cuba of Africans who had previously landed or resided on other islands in the British Caribbean. Captain generals issued several circulars from 1796 through 1832 ordering traffickers to land only Africans who had arrived directly from Africa.[83]

Several episodes related to the receiving ship *Romney* shed light on official concern over the spread of subversive ideas and symbols. Upon its arrival in the port of Havana in September 1837, the British consul hired fifteen free "African negroes" from the British Second West India Regiment stationed at Nassau to reside on the vessel. It was a logical choice, in that these African sailors had survived the transatlantic crossing and remained healthy during their residence in the Caribbean. A few of these Royal Navy personnel proved to be adept interpreters of African languages, and they provided assistance to Liberated Africans transferred from captured slave vessels to the *Romney*.

The presence of free African sailors on board the *Romney* created a scandal. In a letter from the Society for Progress of Agriculture and Commerce (*Junta de Fomento de Agricultura y Comercio de Cuba*), influential residents condemned this spectacle. "For a long time past, a dismasted ship of the Line [has been] stationed in a prominent part of the Bay, manned by emancipated Negroes, dressed in the uniform of the Royal Navy of Great Britain, to which vessel the slaves of both sexes have easy access."[84] Captain General Tacón echoed this position: "this novelty is contrary to the laws of these dominions, to the instructions I have from my government [in Spain], to the particular ordinances of the police security of this island. I am charged not to permit in any manner *the introduction of free negroes under the shadow of whatsoever pretext.*"[85] An edict published by Tacón in 1837 forbade any free person of color of foreign origin from coming onshore.

By late 1839, the detachment stationed on board the *Romney* had increased to thirty-two free Africans from Nassau and Barbados. This continued presence festered with island authorities. Nevertheless, the captain general agreed to allow a small group of these foreigners to land and move about within specific limits near the port. On October 12, 1840, a group of six African Marines along with a white sergeant rowed in from the *Romney*, clambered onto a wharf, and proceeded into the bustling streets. The group split up; one of the sailors met up with a "Negress." A white manager of slaves (known as a *mayoral*) soon approached, told the woman to step away from the Marine, and commenced beating her with a large stick whip. "The soldier interposed to prevent the strokes of the whip, which were distinctly heard on board the *Romney*, when the *mayoral* with the butt end struck the soldier who was not armed with a violent blow to the head."[86]

A boisterous crowd of fifty people gathered. When fellow African sailors from the *Romney* arrived, police took the wounded man and rest of the group to a deserted house. Soon the entourage of Cubans returned with the Africans to the wharf with plans to send them back to the *Romney*. Instead, the Royal Marines were placed under arrest. In response to the commotion, Lieutenant Fitzgerald of the *Romney* arrived at the dock and demanded that the soldiers be freed. After tense negotiations, the district mayor (*alcalde*) allowed the sailors to return to the *Romney* and the wounded African to be treated.[87] The episode reflected the trepidation of Spanish authorities with regards to "agglomerations" of free blacks resident in Havana and their contact with black sailors and soldiers (many of them freed Africans) in the employ of the British.[88] They believed that such interactions spawned attitudes critical of colonial representatives and policies, which indeed appears to have occurred.

To resolve this matter, the captain general demanded that the African Royal Marines be replaced with a smaller detachment composed of white sailors. This transition occurred in December 1842 when HMS *Spartan* arrived with a contingent of fourteen white soldiers to be posted on the *Romney*.[89] Their responsibilities proved to be minimal: for four years between 1841 and 1845, the captain general made sure not to allow any Liberated Africans to be placed on board the *Romney*. In December 1845, the British consul sold the *Romney* to the Spanish government for ten thousand dollars in gold. For the elite of Cuba, the sale ended the multiple "infections" linked to the presence of the receiving ship *Romney* in the harbor of Havana.

By 1846, the population of Cuba included 426,000 whites, 149,000 free colored, and 324,000 slaves. This composition caused well-to-do Spanish and creoles to question future race relations on the island. Conservatives became increasingly skeptical about the cooperation and loyalty of free blacks. They believed such individuals capable and willing to incite slave rebellions, as had erupted on the island on numerous occasions from the 1820s to 1844.[90] In the words of representatives to the City Corporation of Havana (*ayuntamiento*) "if the increased number of slaves were in more contact with the free class of people of color, if the difficulties were removed which subordination and isolation of the slaves present, so that commotions might be prepared, full soon would confirm the experience of Cuba, as has confirmed it that of San

Domingo [Haiti], the presage of that in these islands the black race would ex-terminate the white, which at its time would prevail on the continent [Central and South America]."[91]

Officials on the island implemented a series of repressive measures to stem such fears. The Spanish Crown ordered heightened vigilance over the activities of black militia troops. In 1841, the captain general ordered that the one all-black town council on the island located at Santiago del Prado be disbanded. From 1842, free blacks could no longer carry swords or firearms or be employed as overseers or bookkeepers on plantations.[92] Between 1844 and 1855, the government temporarily banned free black and brown militias (*milicias de pardos e morenos libres*). Foreign blacks and free mulattoes faced expulsion. In 1855, officials forced free blacks and mulattoes to carry identity cards.[93]

The dangers posed by infection did not go unnoticed in Cuba. Residents paid close attention to public health issues. They questioned British motives in stationing free Africans on board the *Romney*. Some suggested that the sole reason for the presence of the "garrison of colored soldiers" on board the *Romney* was to "excite insurrectionary movements."[94] How to assure racial purity among whites also became a topic of great importance. Each of these issues became intertwined with debates over the slave trade.

3

EPIDEMICS AND THE END OF THE TRANSATLANTIC
SLAVE TRADE TO BRAZIL IN 1850

In grasping the role of infectious disease in causing the suppression of the slave trade to Brazil, it is wise to place the yellow fever epidemic of 1849 in historical context. The story begins well before that turbulent year. Inhabitants throughout the empire had much experience with contagion brought to Brazilian shores via slave ships.

Tens of slave vessels arrived at Brazil in the first half of the nineteenth century carrying infected Africans and crews. In late 1836, traffickers forced 855 Africans onto the Portuguese brig *Leão* at Quelimane on the coast of Mozambique. Once it was at sea, smallpox appeared and sailors threw 30 ill captives overboard. Soon after, measles ripped through the ship, causing the death of 253 Africans, along with members of the crew. The *Leão* disembarked the surviving slaves, numbering 572, at the island of Marambaya to the south of the port of Rio de Janeiro. Many were "in so miserable a state that the greater number could not walk but were carried on shore."[1]

As interceptions of slave vessels by the British Squadron rose in number during the 1840s, some observers argued that conditions endured by Africans in the holds of numerous slave vessels worsened. British consul John Howden lamented that "the horrors [of the Middle Passage] appear to increase in exact proportion to the stringency of the means used for the suppression of the traffic."[2] The prevailing strategy for captains became to load as many Africans as quickly as possible and then hope that the ship could arrive in Brazil without capture, a revolt, or the outbreak of an epidemic.

Seizures of slave ships posed major health risks for British sailors. Prize crews who sailed captured vessels "suffered from direct exposure to the slaves, in [becoming infected by] small pox and the cutaneous disease commonly known as craw-craw [onchocerciacis], which is a species of irritant itch contracted by the seamen in prizes [captured slave ships] to a greater or less degree, and which without treatment often degenerate into foul ulcers." Others came down with "dysentery, hemorrhage, ulcers, rheumatism, fever and inflammation of lungs, mucous catarrh [blockage of airways as with a cold or pneumonia] with severe cough, inflammation and adema [meaning edema or swelling] of the leg."[3]

After arrival in a Brazilian port, British sailors stayed on board a captured vessel to prevent attempts to steal the slaves and ship. As a result, the possibility of their becoming ill increased. Writing at Rio de Janeiro in 1839, British consul William Gore Ouseley bemoaned that "Problems [have been] caused by delay of the imperial authorities [of Brazil] with regards to the captured slavers *Feliz* and *Diligente* [slave vessels seized off Brazil by HMS *Wizard* and *Electra*]. [We face] extreme difficulties attending [to] the custody of the vessels due to the risk of infectious diseases already too fatally felt here."[4] With an average delay of fifty-two days to remove Africans from prizes brought into the port due to bureaucratic red tape (at the Mixed Commission Court and with ministries of the imperial government), British officials faced a crisis.[5]

As at Havana, the English responded to this situation by placing a hospital ship in the harbor of Rio de Janeiro. A temporary "hulk" took Africans on board from April 1839 to April 1840, and was then replaced by HMS *Crescent* as the official receiving vessel. The *Crescent* played a far more important role than did the *Romney* in Havana. During its fourteen years anchored at Rio de Janeiro (1840–54), the *Crescent* admitted hundreds of Africans from captured slavers. Medical personnel labored diligently to provide assistance. This included close attention to the nutritional needs of the most debilitated.[6] Suppliers in the city sent fresh supplies to the *Crescent* whenever necessary, including *farinha* (manioc flour), jerked beef, fresh beef, beans, vegetables, and fresh water, along with fuel for cooking.[7]

Traffickers commonly moved disembarked Africans to houses or depots where they could be displayed to purchasers. One journalist writing in July 1848 told of conditions in Rio de Janeiro as follows:

The scandalous traffic is carried on even in the center of the city on a large scale. We should not be victims of so many pestilential emanations by the accumulation of thousands of those unfortunates [recently arrived African slaves] in different points [urban depots], as well in the suburbs as in the capital itself. Those focuses of infection are one of the real causes of the diseases which our sleepy headed Imperial Academists pompously term *reigning* and *endemic*. Let that nuisance to be removed to a distance, let those infected Lazarettos [quarantine stations] be duly inspected, let the attention of the authorities be called to the filthiness of those disgusting depots of human flesh, frequently the prey of anticipated putrefaction brought on by hideous diseases. And the pestilential smallpox, the severe and purulent ophthalmias, the pernicious etceteras, will disappear from the healthy soil of Santa Cruz.

When this kind of traffic was formerly permitted, and honest merchants sought to make their fortunes by it, the depots for the blacks were kept clean, there were health officers charged with keeping a watch to prevent dangerous accumulations, not only over those arriving in a sickly state, but also over the healthy. Nowadays everything is permitted or tolerated, the traffic may be carried on, that is winked at, and the result thereof is the great immorality proceeding from the purposed disrespect for and continued disobedience of the laws. Thousands of *negros boçais* [recently arrived African slaves] are allowed to be scattered throughout the empire, but no one considers it his bounden duty to bear in view the innumerable disasters resulting from so licentious a course.[8]

Another resident wrote that it was "impossible to walk through the streets of this capital [of Rio de Janeiro] without remarking [encountering] the infinite number of slaves afflicted with chronick ophthalmia [which causes blindness or death], or with limbs crippled from unnatural confinement [in the holds of slave vessels]."[9]

From the 1820s through the 1850s the arrival of sick African slaves provoked dread all along the Brazilian coast. In a report to the Legislative Assembly in Rio de Janeiro in June 1833, the minister of marine wrote that the most efficient way to halt slave disembarkations was to arm numerous small vessels that could carry out patrols. This would be a "sort of *Cordon Sanitaire* which may prevent the access to our shores of those swarms of Africans that are continually poured forth in so abominable a traffic."[10] In one of eight major eruptions of smallpox epidemics to break out in the city of Rio de Janeiro between 1825 and mid-century, an outbreak occurred in 1837 and continued into outlying regions. In the words of the British consuls Hesketh and Grigg, "the previous cargoes of [enslaved African] Negroes, deposited in this vicinity, have undergone great mortality from the smallpox, which, in several cases, has reached the free population of this city and its environs." Numerous inhabitants asserted that the upsurge of measles and ophthalmia could be traced to slave importations. Not surprisingly, this perception caused widespread alarm.[11]

A smallpox epidemic spread quickly from the port of Recife into the interior of the province of Pernambuco in late 1840. British vice-consul Joshua Goring, writing on behalf of an incapacitated head consul, claimed that Africans who had been brought onshore from three vessels (named the *União*, *Andorinha*, and *San José*) at first sight had been considered "generally healthy. However, since their arrival in the interior the smallpox has been rife and spread its pestilential venom even [back] into this city, [which is] a condign punishment upon the nefarious abettors of such an iniquitous traffic."[12] Planters in Pernambuco complained that on numerous occasions infections broke out soon after their purchase of recently arrived Africans. As a result, "smallpox, ophthalmia, and other contagious diseases have been introduced among heretofore healthy laborers, which have carried off more than they had paid and purchased."[13]

Such experiences translated into harsh criticism of the slave traffic. A letter penned by an "inhabitant of Recife" depicts the dire consequences wreaked upon that city as a result of the arrival of infected Africans, as well as his hope that the importations would be terminated.

> In days yore our Pernambuco enjoyed one of the most salubrious climates in Brazil, several maladies not even known here. It is now otherwise, and this is in a great measure owing to the importation and accumulation of Africans in this capital. Anciently the vessels that brought the unfortunate blacks performed Quarantine [often a seven-day waiting period to be sure that there was no infection on board] and the slaves prior to being disposed of went to reside for some time in a kind of depot [lazaretto] at the village of Santo Amaro, a spot at once airy and distant from places inhabited. Such is not the case in the present day. The wretched Africans [are] crowded together in vessels where they are systematically treated with barbarity, infected with pestilence and ill of the scurvy, in consequence of the deteriorated mephitic [foul-smelling] atmosphere in the ship holds and the worst kinds of sustenance wherewith the feeble flame of life is fed; walking skeletons, mummies half alive they are transferred from the holds of ships to depots, shops, houses, etc., etc., and expiring by dozens in these hidden retreats and as if these foci of infection and pestilence were not sufficient, large lots of these putrid bodies are cast into the river!

And this is suffered, is tolerated, this passes in the heart of a populous city? Are there no measures taken? What is the police about? Alas! All its efforts are and will be thrown away. The honorable merchants of human flesh are above the laws whose guardians cannot even with the best intentions, prevail against men upheld by perchance the most elevated personages in the country. Never mind, let us have the plague, let people perish here in vast numbers, the traffic must go on, for, if it does not, by what hands is the sugar cane to be reared and sugar to be made? All the world are unanimous in confessing that slavery is a soil fertile in immorality, but what of that? Is it not indisputable that without Africans no agriculture is practicable in Brazil? The African race descends from Ham, the cursed son of Noah, and when the Almighty created them, he did so only in order to [send them to] their thralldom in Brazil. Gentlemen, let us pray the Creator to have mercy on us! But make no account of the human species being doomed to misery; do not mind the infection of the country; take no notice of the inhabitants growing more and more wicked provided that half a dozen of ambitious men—men but yesterday clothed in tatters and poor—may today acquire the possession of magnificent country seats, roll about in splendid equipages, etc., etc., thanks to the traffic in human flesh.[14]

Echoing such a lamentation, the Public Health Council of Pernambuco (*Conselho Geral de Salubridade Pública*, established in 1845) denounced the slave traffic as "the greatest sources of disease."[15]

As in the port cities of Rio de Janeiro and Recife, inhabitants of Salvador and the interior of Bahia had long known that landing sick Africans posed grave health risks. Africans disembarked at Bahia sickened by smallpox, scurvy (a disease caused by lack of vitamin C resulting in weakness, anemia, and gum and skin infections), chicken pox, scabies (*Sarcoptes scabiei*, a skin disease spread by a small species of mite), measles, eye infections, and diphtheria (an acute infectious disease spread by the bacterium *Corynebacterium diphtheriae*). Observing the annual arrival of more than twenty slave ships into the port of Salvador at the end of the eighteenth century, professor of Greek Luiz dos Santos Vilhena denounced *tumbeiros* (slave vessels) as the main source of infectious disease in Salvador.[16] Cognizant of this threat to public health, residents complained to the governor of Bahia about the transmission of sickness from the slave vessels to residents on land. In response, officials established a quarantine station for recently arrived Africans and crews at the Ponta do Monserrat in the Bay of All Saints.[17]

In early 1847, an epidemic swept through Salvador described as the "African fever." African fever was a term used to describe a strain of yellow fever common along the west coast of Africa. Although few persons died from this outbreak, several observers traced its origins to the disembarkations of Africans. In the words of the British consul: "An epidemic has prevailed here since the month of February last [1847], which has affected almost the whole of the population. It is said by medical men to have all the symptoms of the African fever, though in a milder degree, as there is hardly a single instance of its having proved fatal. An opinion prevails that this fever has been brought here by newly imported slaves."[18]

THE *BELLA MIQUELINA* AFFAIR OF 1848 IN THE
BAY OF ALL SAINTS AT SALVADOR

In the early evening dusk of Saturday, April 22, 1848, the British sloop HMS *Grecian* encountered a "suspicious looking brig running under all sail before the wind apparently steering [southward] for Bahia." After a failed attempt to "cut her off" [meaning forcing the unknown brig to slow and allow the *Grecian* to come alongside], the *Grecian* fired a gun as a signal, demanding that the vessel identify itself with a flag. At midnight, members of the crew from the *Grecian* climbed on board what proved to be the Brazilian slave ship *Bella Miquelina*. Inside the hold were 517 Africans. Of these, 350 were male and 67 female. Their ages ranged from two-year-old Ehkusumee (female) to the thirty-six-year-old Yasofar (male). None of the women were over twenty-nine years old.[19]

Having departed from Bahia the previous February 17, the captain of the *Bella Miquelina* declared in the ship manifest submitted to port officials at Salvador the vessel's destination to be the Azores islands. Instead, the brig journeyed to the west coast of Africa in search of slaves. Near Lagos, it picked up Africans and set sail for a return voyage to Brazil. After seizure of the *Bella Miquelina*, Commander Tindal of the *Grecian* placed Lieutenant D'Aguilar in charge.

With the aid of a prize crew placed on board, D'Aguilar sailed the *Bella Miquelina* in the direction of the Bay of All Saints at Salvador. Short of food and water, the *Bella Miquelina* had "no more than the sweepings of the provision room to supply the slaves."[20] The plan was that the *Grecian* would head into the Bay, take on food and water, and return to the *Bella Miquelina*. Bad weather separated the ships, however. As a result, the *Grecian* remained at sea while the *Bella Miquelina* sailed to Salvador, anchoring in the harbor at four p.m. on Saturday, April 29.

News of the arrival of the slave ship circulated quickly throughout the city. That the British had captured the *Bella Miquelina* "caused much excitement among the lower classes and ill-feeling towards the British residents."[21] One reason for such discontent can be traced to resentment over numerous British captures of slaving vessels. Common folk took offense that a Brazilian ship under the command of a British prize crew had entered the port of Salvador. That both the slave ship and the profits from the sale of the Africans had potentially been lost also roiled investors. Through the 1840s, similar agitation erupted in response to vessels captured by the British Squadron in the port cities of São Luis, Recife, Campos, Rio de Janeiro, and Santos.[22]

In the early evening a group of men gathered to discuss a course of action. At first they considered an attack on the house of the British consul. Soon, however, they came up with a more ambitious plan. They decided to row out to the *Bella Miquelina* and take over the ship. Once in control, they would sail the ship out of the harbor and disembark the slaves along the coast or at a well-known landing site on the nearby island of Itaparica.

At 9:30 p.m. on that Saturday night, an armed group of some eighty men embarked on two large *feluccas* (also known as *barques*, or market boats). "Headed by some 8 or 9 white men of the country [suggesting that they were native-born Brazilians]," this gang attempted to board the *Bella Miquelina*. In the words of Lieutenant D'Aguilar, "I opened fire on the boats immediately on discerning their piratical intentions and continued until they retreated, about a quarter of an hour in all." The fighting left three of the Brazilians dead along with several wounded. Among the British prize crew, D'Aguilar received a small head wound and two men were cut by sabers. The evidence suggests that the attackers from the two boats came close to taking over the *Bella Miquelina*. A British diplomat wrote that "had the expedition from the shore succeeded in re-capturing the slaver, there is no doubt but that all the prize-crew would have been murdered, and the vessel carried out of the harbor, with very little chance of ever identifying the perpetrators of the crime."[23] For the rest of the night, the British crew on board the *Bella Miquelina* kept a wary lookout in case of another attack.[24]

The next day, Sunday, April 30, the captain of the Brazilian frigate *Constituição* anchored in the bay made contact with D'Aguilar. He warned that the *Bella Miquelina* remained vulnerable due to the location of its anchorage. Suggesting that the *Bella Miquelina* be positioned close to his vessel as a protective measure, Lieutenant D'Aguilar accepted this invitation and moved the *Bella Miquelina*.

As feared, another attempt to take over the *Bella Miquelina* occurred at 7:30 p.m. that Sunday evening. "A large felucca full of men bore down upon us [the *Bella*] and after being hailed repeatedly in English and Portuguese did not alter her course but came within half pistol shot of our bows, when I [Lieutenant D'Aguilar] ordered a shot to be fired over her and to be hailed again. She did not answer and still continued to run with the intention of boarding us. I fired into her with all my musketry and continued doing so until she cleared off and stood in for the land under Fort Gamboa."[25] After another long night of watching and waiting by the prize crew on board the *Bella Miquelina*, the dawn of Monday, May 1 arrived. A few hours later, the *Grecian* sailed into the port under the command of L.S. Tindal and anchored next to the *Bella Miquelina*.

On Monday evening, Commander Tindal went onshore to discuss the situation with British consul Edmund Porter. The latter had been in constant contact with city and provincial officials. Tindal and Porter pondered how best to proceed with regards to the *Bella Miquelina*. Vice governor of Bahia Manuel Messias de Leão expressed outrage over these incidents and called for an inquiry. He requested that the English sailors wounded in the first attack on the *Bella Miquelina* appear at the courthouse in Salvador to provide depositions about what had occurred. Neither Commander Tindal nor Consul Porter considered this wise, due to the likelihood of violent confrontations in the streets of the city. Hence, an interview was scheduled for Wednesday, May 3, at 11 a.m. on board the *Grecian*. This did not occur for some reason. The *Grecian* and the *Bella Miquelina* sailed that afternoon of May 3 bound for Rio de Janeiro.

In a letter written in the midst of the *Bella Mequelina* affair, the vice governor expressed concern about the health threat posed to residents of Salvador if the *Bella Miquelina* lingered in the port. On Monday, May 1, he called for an immediate departure: "[I am writing] in response to the letter of yesterday, describing the *Bella*, captured with a cargo of Africans made slaves. We recognize the enormity of this atrocious act, and have issued the appropriate orders to apprehend those persons who perpetrated this deed. Finally in behalf of public salubrity [health] which is necessary since there is a risk incurred by keeping anchored in a port a vessel loaded with so large a number of individuals affected with diseases inevitable in consequence of the barbarous manner in which they are brought over, it is requisite that you should take such steps as will cause the immediate departure of the said *polacca* [brig] from this port."[26]

Why would the vice governor of Bahia have been so concerned about public health? One reason had to do with the outbreak of African fever the previous year, which had spread throughout the city of Salvador. Leão was also aware of desperate health conditions in Rio de Janeiro attributed to slave importations. Unlike at Rio de Janeiro or Havana, there was no hospital ship present in the Bay of All Saints to receive Liberated Africans. If the *Bella Miquelina* remained for an extended period, a decision would have to be made to bring the infected Africans onshore for medical care. This is exactly what the vice governor and inhabitants did not want.

THE YELLOW FEVER EPIDEMIC OF 1849

By the time yellow fever invaded Bahia in October 1849, Brazilians of all backgrounds had witnessed firsthand the spread of infectious diseases caused by the disembarkations of thousands of sickly Africans. What exactly occurred when the epidemic commenced in October 1849? How did this yellow fever epidemic, one in a long history of infections in Brazil, shape the worldview and decisions of high-ranking politicians and imperial officials?

A prevalent interpretation points to a U.S. ship as conveying the yellow fever epidemic to Brazil. On September 29, 1849, the U.S.-built clipper brig *Brazil* entered the port of Salvador. Its captain asserted to port officials that the vessel had sailed from New Orleans directly to Salvador. In fact, the *Brazil* had previously landed African slaves on the Brazilian coast on two occasions, visited the port of Havana, and then continued on to Bahia. One of numerous vessels involved in the southern triangle slave trade, the *Brazil* journeyed to Salvador because the merchant house Joaquim Pereira Morinho and Company had leased the ship to engage in the traffic in slaves.[27] Given that an outbreak of yellow fever had caused the port and city of Havana to be "decidedly sickly" by June 1849, the October outbreak of yellow fever in Salvador likely had its origins in Cuba.[28]

The captain of the *Brazil* also lied in claiming no one on board the brig had taken ill previous to entry into the Bay of All Saints. In fact, two crewmembers had died during the voyage from Havana to Salvador. The overseer of the port of Salvador allowed the *Brazil* to anchor among other merchant vessels without an inspection. Three days later, a letter appeared in a Bahian newspaper asking how the *Brazil* had been permitted to enter the Bay of All Saints without quarantine when this measure had been required of all vessels that arrived from Europe to protect against the spread of cholera.[29]

Taking leave of the *Brazil*, its captain made his way to a boardinghouse in the city. Soon after his stay, two patrons at that inn became ill, one of whom died. Spanish passengers from the *Brazil* rented rooms in the neighborhood of Santa Barbara in Salvador. Three weeks later, residents of that barrio came down with the fever.[30] The U.S. consul in Salvador Thomas Turner visited the *Brazil* to investigate accusations that this U.S. ship had transported slaves. Within days, he succumbed to yellow fever, likely caused by his boarding the *Brazil*.[31] By November 20, two deaths were reported on the Swedish ship *Scandia* anchored close to the *Brazil*. Soon after, the majority of the crew of the *Scandia* died from yellow fever. In mid-December, sailors on just about every ship anchored in the Bay of All Saints had taken ill. By March 1850, on five British vessels where the epidemic had erupted, nearly one-third of the infected sailors perished (70 of 223 cases).[32] Given that yellow fever is transmitted by mosquitoes, ships anchored near the *Brazil* easily received the contagion. The epidemic swept "like wildfire" into the city of Salvador and then dispersed to villages ten to twelve leagues (thirty to thirty-six miles) into the interior of the province of Bahia.[33]

The contagion caused havoc in Bahia, infecting an estimated 100,000 persons and causing the death of some 3,000 inhabitants before it subsided in April 1850.[34] Yellow fever persisted in the province for the next three years, becoming once again a major public health issue in Salvador between October 1852 and June 1853.[35] The British medical doctor John Paterson wrote that "among the native Brazilians and those long resident in a tropical climate, it [the yellow fever] was comparatively speaking a very mild disease, fatal certainly in [not more than] one percent. Among the African blacks, it was still milder. The native colored population [became infected] as numerously but perhaps less severely than the whites."[36] As in Cuba, light-skinned residents with no previous exposure to yellow fever suffered most severely.

The fiction that the *Brazil* had sailed from New Orleans can be traced to the governor of Bahia Francisco Gonçalves Martins. For at least five months after the arrival of the *Brazil*, Martins steadfastly claimed that the ship had sailed directly from Louisiana to Bahia and that the origins of the yellow fever epidemic in Salvador could be traced to the city of New Orleans. It is likely that Martins lied about the journey of the *Brazil* to divert attention from evidence that attributed the cause of the contagion to recently arrived Africans who had been transported to Bahia from Africa. It would appear that Martins had benefited financially from the slave trade to Bahia, another motive for claiming that the *Brazil* had sailed from Louisiana and was not involved in the traffic. One journalist commented on Martins' statements: "It is useless for Senhor Francisco Gonçalves Martins, president of Bahia, to endeavor to make us believe that fevers are not the product, and did not come from the coast of Africa, but from the United States in the vessel so and so [Brazil] which His Excellency has mentioned a dozen times in his official dispatches, but in vain. Because the general belief points to Africa, and holds Senhor Gonçalves Martins as suspected in this business, not only because he is the intimate friend of the principal slave dealers of Bahia, but also there are not wanting people who attribute to him directly participating in the pecuniary profits of the traffic."[37]

Lots of common folk understood that the disembarkations of Africans from slave ships had caused an array of infections in late 1849. This included inhabitants along the coast, port workers, and sailors. The same journalist as above articulated this perception:

> In Bahia in October and November last several cargoes of blacks [African slaves] arrived [on various ships] and both the cargo and the crews of the vessels were horribly afflicted with the maladies of the coast [of Africa], especially fevers. Only yesterday in the presence of two deputies an individual from the province of Sergipe related to us that a countryman of his [after] having purchased at Bahia [the city of Salvador] eighty negroes in the month of November [1849], the whole of them died during the first three days of the voyage, that is before they arrived at Inhambupe [interior of the province of Bahia, located seventy-three miles north of Salvador, and forty-seven miles from the coast]. The scourge still continues in Rio [in April 1850]. The opinion of the learned men and able physicians is that the yellow fever and other maladies, such as ophthalmia, contagious dysentery, swelling of the glands, measles, scarlet fever, smallpox, are imported from the coast of Africa. It is also certain that in the beginning of this year not a few vessels arrived [at Rio] from the coast of Africa which brought more fevers than blacks.[38]

Yellow fever caused death and suffering in towns and countryside from Pernambuco in the Northeast to Santa Catarina in the South. The fever dispersed quickly from barracoons situated along the coast. In Pernambuco, an estimated 30,000 inhabitants became ill, of whom 2,000 perished by March 1850.[39] In the province of Rio de Janeiro, the epidemic spread from locales of disembarkation at Macahé, Rio das Ostras, Cape Frio, and Manguinhos.[40] The epidemic proved severe in the city of Rio de Janeiro.[41] Some 100,000 residents came down with yellow fever; estimates of the number of dead in the city ranged from 4,000 to 15,000.[42] Commentators in Rio de Janeiro were quick to place the blame on several vessels that had visited Salvador and then touched at locales along the Brazilian coast.[43] Others pointed to the arrival in January 1850 of slave ships directly from Africa "contaminated with fever." Crewmembers and African slaves who attempted to recover in private homes helped spread the epidemic.[44]

One observer in the city of Rio de Janeiro (early 1850) shared the belief held by many that the yellow fever epidemic could be linked to slave importations:

> If the government had listened to us some time ago we are certain that these locuses of epidemic diseases, the deposits of Africans, would no longer exist, and would no longer carry into the heart of society the ravages which it alone has produced.
>
> If the government were not so weak as to allow the traffickers in slaves to treat the laws under foot and to carry on the slave trade it is certain that this pest would not exist, and this *African fever* would not have come here to desolate as it has desolated our families.
>
> Danger of insurrection [exists], when these Africans hear the cry of freedom spread amongst these slaves by the ambitious in Brazil or by the malicious foreign enemy who may approach our shores. These imported Africans are an internal enemy.[45]

THE COUNCIL OF HEALTH IN BAHIA

In response to public pressures, Bahian governor Martins convened a Council of Health in Salvador to investigate the epidemic in early December 1849. Composed of a group of medical personnel, the Council professed that individuals who had come down with the yellow fever were predisposed to getting sick. Suggested remedies included consumption of easily digested foods and abstention from wine and alcohol. The Council called for "the cessation of knolling [ringing] of the Church bells which [by] infusing in the patients the idea of death greatly increase their malady [!!]." The 1849 Council posited that the contagion "is aggravated by the overflowing of the rivers, by the filth of the city, bad directions [in the flow] of the public sewers, the burial of the dead in the churches and from the absolute want of a medical police, to which must be added the terror that always accompanies a population on the appearance of an epidemic, a terror that has been increased by imprudent writing and as it were purposely exaggerated by some newspapers in this city." Once again,

officials directed part of the blame at those *imprudent journalists*! Given that
the Council reported what Martins wanted to hear, no one alluded to slave
disembarkations as being responsible for the epidemic.[46]

In spite of lack of public comment by the 1849 Council, Martins understood fully that the yellow fever epidemic could be traced to the slave traffic.
Throughout that year, slaves had been sold at several depots in the center of
Salvador. Although the chief of police threatened in April to confiscate the
slaves on display at these depots if they were not moved outside the city, this
did not occur.[47] After being apprised of the situation by medical personnel,
British consul Porter met with Martins in December 1849. He wrote: "On my
representing to the president of the province that the landing and introducing
into the midst of the dense population of this city eight to ten thousand slaves
annually, many in a state of disease, might possibly account for the malignant fever at the present moment decimating the white inhabitants, secret orders were given [by Martins] for the immediate removal of the depots of new
blacks to the other side of the bay, although the existing law in Brazil [1831
law] enacts that all new slaves be seized and forthwith emancipated."[48] This
policy remained in place until the epidemic had passed in the middle of 1850.
Martins did nothing when traffickers moved the depots back to the center of
Salvador.[49]

The Council of Health reconvened in June 1853. It reiterated many of the
statements posited three and a half years before, including the need to clean
up "dunghills" present near the Custom House and the Post Office. The members of the 1853 Council called for a prohibition of tossing dirty water and
other matter out of windows into narrow streets, particularly in the lower
part of the city by the port, as such materials might form "new focuses of
infection." They requested that the public slaughterhouse be moved to a sub-
urb, and reiterated the notion that church bells being rung to commemorate
death had a detrimental impact on the well-being of the living. The Council
urged that vents allow for the free circulation of air in the holds of ships. "If
its passage is prevented without a gradual and disseminating renewal, it [con-
tagious air] accumulates and when the hatches are removed it comes out in
such abundance that very often it infects the persons on board."[50] Certainly
the thousands of Africans in Bahia who had survived the Middle Passage knew
well the suffering caused by a lack of ventilation in the depths of slave vessels.

A member of the 1849 Council participated in the 1853 gathering. Salustiano Fereira Souto praised Governor Martins for implementing remedial

measures proposed by the 1849 Council. Souto maintained that the epidemic had spread due to an inadequate response by public health officials. He also suggested its dispersion could be traced to "the fear inspired by quacks and empiricks [charlatans], who from sordid love of gain tried to impose on the credulity of the people."[51]

Not surprisingly, Souto added commentary related to slave disembarkations in his analysis of mid-1853. He posited that "great weight ought to be given to the recommendation of removing from the center of the population the focuses of the plague which all know exist amongst us owing to the barbarous and immoral traffic in slaves imported into this city by men who for their own interest sacrifice all human personality against law, against the rules of medicine and religion, and which slaves are huddled together in lots or straightened warehouses in complete oblivion of hygienic measures." Did Souto link the yellow fever epidemic to the slave trade based on personal observation and what he had recently learned? Perhaps. More likely, however, is that Souto recognized from late 1849 or before that ill slaves arriving on Bahian shores carried infection into Salvador and the countryside.

Due to pressures exerted by Martins and the powerful slave trade bloc of Salvador, no mention was made about the slave traffic at the 1849 meeting of the Council. By 1853 the political milieu had changed drastically. On the positive side, the imperial government had been successful in halting slave importations to the empire during this interlude. The stark reality, however, was that Brazilians of all backgrounds continued to face dire threats posed by contagions. Martins and allies such as Souto sought to reshape the historical record so as to erase evidence and memory of their role in causing the yellow fever epidemic. At this late date, Martins continued to malign foreign trade and naval vessels arriving in Brazilian ports as being the source of infections. As minister of empire (foreign affairs), he wrote a telling letter to the president of the Board of Health in Rio de Janeiro:

> Complaints have been received of certain boarding houses near the landing places in this city [Rio], into which sailors from on board Men [Ships] of War and merchant vessels were received, who giving themselves up to all sorts of revelries, therein become infected with yellow fever, to which they fall victim in consequence of those excesses, and also the apparent localization of the disease in those houses, the following being particularly pointed out, among others: The Neptune Hotel in the Rua da Misericordia; a house of entertainment kept by a Frenchman called Jack opposite the Neptune; the California Hotel in the

Rua Fresca; a public house with the signboard "The Flag of all Nations"; The New York House in the Becco do Cotovello and others. These houses should immediately be visited with the assistance of the police, and in case it should be found that the continued existence of those houses, as lodging and boarding houses would be prejudicial, you will cause them to be immediately closed; and will not permit them to be reopened until after all the necessary cleansings and purifications have been done satisfactory to the Board and when they are wholesome. The heads of such establishments need to perform these salutary measures, and all of this needs to be communicated with the police authorities in order that they may see to the performance of these heads of establishments. God preserve you.[52]

ACADEMIC COMMENT

From the late eighteenth century, diverse observers had associated the transatlantic slave trade with outbreaks of infection among resident slave and free populations in the Americas. These included intellectuals and medical personnel. The French abolitionist Lecointe-Marsillac wrote about the slave trade as a factor in the spread of contagion in a book published in 1789. Chapters included the titles "Treatment of sea-sick Negroes," "Mortality of slaves at sea," and "Causes of the depopulation and the mortality of Negroes." Lecointe-Marsillac noted that conditions were so bad in the depths of slave ships that surgeons dreaded treating slaves, for "they themselves fear breathing the pestilential air." One historian writes that "on the eve of the French Revolution, abolitionist writers in France insisted that the slave trade itself was the source of health problems among blacks."[53] As noted in chapter two, the Spanish doctor Francisco Barrera y Domingo criticized the trauma endured by Africans during the Middle Passage to Cuba in the 1790s.

In a study of public health in Rio de Janeiro published in 1808, the medical doctor Manuel Vieira da Silva pointed to ties between the transatlantic slave trade to Brazil and the spread of epidemics. Silva emphasized the need to establish lazarettos outside the city where medical personnel could evaluate the infirmities of recently landed Africans. The doctor called for an immediate decrease in the traffic for reasons of both public health and the health of the African slaves.[54]

Da Silva's book was followed by several treatises published in Brazil over the next four decades by medical personnel concerned about insalubrious conditions and infirmities of slaves. All of these authors pointed to the deleterious health effects of slave disembarkations; all called for an end of the traffic to Brazil. One of the best-known of this group was Jean Baptiste Alban Imbert, who published the *Manual do fazendeiro ou tratado doméstico sobre as enfermidades dos negros* (*The Planter's Manual or Domestic Treatment of the Infirmities of Negros*) in 1834. In that well-known book, Imbert argued that "the civilized peoples of the universe have generally recognized the human necessity of putting an end to that abominable and odious traffic, known as the commerce in slaves, which during many centuries has taken slaves from the part of the world where nature brought to birth the negro race, who are called African."[55] Others included José Martins da Cruz Jobim, David Gomes Jardim, and José Rodrigues de Lima Duarte in Rio de Janeiro; Otto Wucherer in Salvador; and Pedro Dornellas Pessoa in Recife.[56]

In 1815, the British doctor William Pym published *Observations Upon the Bulam Fever*, the first scholarly analysis of yellow fever.[57] Based on investigations on the islands of Martinique and Guadalupe, where sixteen thousand British troops perished due to yellow fever, Pym emphasized the highly contagious nature of the disease. Although Pym did not argue specifically that the origins of epidemic in the Americas could be traced to the slave trade, he did allude to the "African fever" prevalent along the coast of Africa and the well-known fact that yellow fever followed shipping lanes. In 1848, Pym published a second edition of the book with minor revisions entitled *Observations on Bulam, Vomito-negro, or Yellow Fever*.[58] One addition to the second edition was Pym's assertion that there existed two variants of the yellow fever. The "Africa Fever" present along the west coast of Africa was remittent and not contagious (this due to long-term exposure to yellow fever among Africans resident in the region), while the disease known in the Americas often proved to be highly contagious.

From the 1820s to the early 1850s, the French medical doctor M.F.M. Audouard expounded on a connection between yellow fever and the slave trade. Audouard observed that outbreaks of yellow fever diminished in the United States after the slave trade had been halted in 1808. He also analyzed health conditions in the French and Spanish Caribbean islands in the 1830s, suggesting that the steady disembarkations in the latter were responsible for the numerous outbreaks of the epidemic.[59] Such information was disseminated by word of mouth and in book form throughout the Atlantic world.[60]

Several medical personnel grappled with the origins of the yellow fever epidemic and its transmission. Although failing to identify the mosquito as the agent of transmission (this did not occur until the discovery by the Cuban scientist Carlos Finlay in 1881), they did recognize to varying degrees that ships, filth, moisture, and climate all played a role in spreading the infection. It did not take much for these learned individuals to consider the possibility that the squalid innards of slave vessels and arrival of sickly Africans contributed to outbreaks of yellow fever in Brazilian ports and on land. These individuals included Salustiano Fereira Souto (noted above); his "illustrious teachers" A.P. Cabral and V.F. de Magalhaes; the British medical doctors John Paterson and Alexander Paterson at Bahia; Doctors Paton, May, and Arckbuckle at Pernambuco; and Doctors Lee, Pennell, and Cockranat along with the German medical doctor Lallement, all at Rio de Janeiro.[61] The commentary of these men received close attention from cabinet ministers, senators, and representatives from late 1849, when the epidemic commenced, through the months that followed in 1850.

POLITICAL DISCOURSE OF 1850

It is difficult to measure or quantify the severity of threat posed by infectious disease at a particular moment and the extent to which this impacted government legislation in Brazil. One study affirms that contagion played no role in the cabinet's decision to halt the landing of slaves in Brazil in January 1850. Professor Jeffrey Needell has written that "there are some historians who argue that the slave trade was ended in 1850 partly because it was associated with the transmission of yellow fever. Such an argument is interesting, but suggests a poor grasp of the facts about the epidemic, their appreciation at the time, and the political realities of the era."[62]

That the yellow fever epidemic did not enter cabinet discussions in late 1849 and early 1850 to outlaw the slave trade in no way means that it was not a topic of consideration. High-ranking officials in the imperial government were aware of the outbreaks and the ensuing public health crisis in several Brazilian ports. Like Francisco Martins, several of these men had long-term personal involvement in the slave traffic.[63] They had every incentive not to comment on a raging epidemic caused by infected Africans disembarked from the holds of *negreiros*.

At least three Brazilian senators did comment on the ties between yellow fever and the African slave trade in 1850. The senator from Rio Grande, do Sul Cândido Batista de Oliveira, stated in May that "the epidemic that at present afflicts this capital, and that has snuffed out not a few lives all along the coast of the empire is in truth a deplorable catastrophe. But this same epidemic has brought with it two great benefits to Brazil. The first is that it has forced the transfer of cemeteries to locales outside of towns and cities. And the second is the conviction that has begun to be manifest and recognized by the population of the need to impose a barrier against the traffic in Africans. This conviction, Mr. President, is born of the opinion, which I share, that this horrific epidemic was a fatal gift brought to us in slave ships."[64] Ten days later Senator Antônio Pedro da Costa Ferreira echoed this opinion, as did the senator from Bahia, Manuel Alves Branco, in September.[65]

Certainly British envoy James Hudson believed contagion played a decisive role in the policy debates at the court in early 1850:

> The Imperial government probably thought that with an overwhelming majority in the Houses of the Brazilian legislature they could direct and carry at their pleasure such measures as they thought proper with regard to the slave trade: this was a greater error than even their contempt of the opposition. Public opinion in Brazil had arrived at the conclusion that the yellow fever—which had decimated their white population, while it appeared scarcely to affect the colored races—had been imported from Africa in slave ships. *The apathy (probably resulting from ignorance) of the government with regard to that epidemic had disgusted a respectable portion of the Brazilian people, and a feeling existed, and exists, among many of the supporters in Parliament of the present Cabinet, that it is necessary to put down the slave trade in order to cut off the source of the African fevers and diseases.* This feeling was evinced (as our Lordship will subsequently see in this dispatch) upon the occasion of the Chamber of Deputies debating in secret session a bill for the suppression of the slave trade. The position of the Brazilian cabinet was not, therefore, so strong as its numbers supposed.[66]

In mid-1850, two powerful politicians passed away, victims of yellow fever. Senator from Pernambuco José Carlos Pereira de Almeida Torres, the viscount of Macahé, died on April 25. He had been a close ally of the slave trade, a man who attempted to coerce his daughter into marrying the famed trafficker based in the city of Rio de Janeiro Manoel Pinto de Fonseca. The second was senator from Minas Gerais Bernardo Pereira de Vasconcelos, who died on May 1. Although the deaths seem to have passed unnoticed in the Senate, several parties took close note. James Hudson remarked:

> Vasconcelos was endowed with talents of high order, with untiring industry; thirsting for information; of unflinching determination; a wonderfully retentive

memory; thoroughly conversant with the history and resources of his country. His eminently great qualities were a curse to Brazil and to humanity. He knew that Brazil required labor and he affected to believe that the importation of slaves could alone supply it. He was the persevering—untiring—audacious supporter of slavery in every shape and every form.

In politics he was a thorough despot, and ruled the present Brazilian cabinet with a rod of iron. His hatred [directed] to Her Majesty's government for their efforts in the suppression of the slave trade was intense and unquenchable, and I consider him as having been of late years one of the bitterest enemies whom Great Britain possessed in Brazil.

His death will remove one of the chiefest obstacles to the suppression of the slave trade in this country.[67]

In September 1850, the imperial government passed the Eusébio de Queiroz law, which made the slave trade illegal. For various reasons, including their own survival and the physical well-being of Brazil's free inhabitants, Brazilian officials enforced the new legislation.

4

SLAVE RESISTANCE AND DEBATES OVER THE
SLAVE TRADE TO CUBA, 1790s-1840s

———— ∞ ————

A major field of study is slave resistance in the Americas and the Atlantic world. During the "Age of Revolutions" (1750–1850), slaves resisted enslavement in numerous ways. Examples included rebellion, assassination of masters and overseers, flight, suicide, and infanticide. More subtle and less confrontational day-to-day resistance included theft, lying, work slowdowns, insolence, insubordination, laziness, and feigned illness.[1] Slave resistance played an integral role in the century-long process of international abolition (1770s to 1888).[2] This chapter discusses ways in which resistance by slaves and free blacks in the first half of the nineteenth century inspired opposition to the transatlantic slave trade to Cuba.

A RASH OF REVOLTS

Historian Manuel Barcia has written that between 1795 and 1844, Cuba experienced the "longest cycle of slave revolts ever witnessed in the Americas."[3] He estimates that sixty slave plots and revolts occurred during this period, most of them African-led.[4] This cycle can be broken into three periods. The first is from the mid-1790s through the early 1820s. The second is between the Great African Slave Revolt of 1825 through major uprisings in late 1843. The third comprises the Escalera insurgency of 1843–44 and its immediate aftermath.

In the fall of 1794, "Havana was consumed by fear" over rumors of an impending insurrection in the city led by slaves believed to have been influenced by the revolution that had exploded on the nearby island of Saint-Domingue (the western part of Hispaniola that became Haiti after the conclusion of the revolution). In November, Captain General Luis de las Casas sent a subordinate to investigate a rumor of a planned insurrection on a sugar plantation situated near the city of Matanzas. A few months later, on July 6, 1795, a small contingent of slaves led by "José the Frenchman" rebelled on an estate named Cuatro Compañeros (Four Companions) in the region of Puerto Príncipe (present-day Cienfuegos, located 325 miles to the southeast of Havana). The name suggests that José had previously resided in Saint-Domingue. The group quickly fled to nearby plantations seeking to recruit other slaves. The entourage increased in number to seventeen. It appears that José had plans to attack the town of Puerto Príncipe. On the morning after the revolt, a force composed of whites and slaves captured the fugitives.

The captain general responded with a series of harsh measures. In a proclamation distributed in late February 1796, he ordered that all French-speaking slaves brought to Cuba after August 1790 and all English-speaking slaves introduced after 1794 be expelled from the island. Las Casas emphasized that slaves should be transported to Cuba directly from Africa without touching land anyplace in between.[5] These directives did little to inhibit traffickers from continuing to ferry slaves to Cuba from nearby French and British Caribbean islands in the following years. Several of these "indoctrinated" slaves, suggesting that they had been subverted by French or Haitian revolutionary ideas or British abolitionist thought, led and participated in subsequent insurrections in Cuba.

In June 1798, another revolt broke out in Puerto Príncipe. At the head of this rebellion were Antonio, Fernando, and Pedro Nolasco. All appear to have been Carabalí originally from the Calabar region of West Africa. Other participants included urban creole slaves referred to as "Frenchmen," who most likely had knowledge of the revolution in Haiti. After setting fire to several plantations, the participants fled into the mountains. A search party of twenty whites succeeded in killing several of the escaped slaves and capturing three others. Authorities imposed stiff sentences in the aftermath, including the hanging of the three accused Carabalí leaders.[6]

Weeks later, Spanish officials in the south central coastal city of Trinidad uncovered plans for an insurrection among slaves laboring on nearby sugar plantations. Captured plotters confessed that the slaves planned to kill all of the whites on the estates as well as in Trinidad and then escape to Jamaica, where they would find protection among maroon communities. Evidence suggests that several of the conspiring slaves had come to Cuba from Jamaica and other Caribbean islands. Again, authorities inflicted harsh punishment on the accused.

All sorts of slave resistance continued between mid-1798 and 1810. These included revolts, work stoppages, and the escape of thirty-eight male slaves from a sugar plantation. African and creole slaves participated. In some instances, news of the Haitian Revolution and British pressures to end the transatlantic slave trade inspired leaders to act. In others, Africans with little knowledge of events in other parts of the Caribbean took the lead. Historian Matt D. Childs writes that "the marked increase in revolts during the decades of 1790 and 1800 testifies to a heightened commitment to resistance by Africans in Cuba."[7]

In 1812, the Aponte Rebellion shook Cuba's elite to its core. It was led by a group of free blacks and mulattoes resident in Havana, several of whom had been born on the island (creoles). Aware of the disembarkation of thousands of Africans during the previous two decades, the leaders sought the support of the urban and rural slaves.

Given the upheavals that convulsed Puerto Príncipe from the mid-1790s, planters in that region understood well the dangers created by an expanding slave population. In mid-January 1812, the "opening battle" of the Aponte Rebellion broke out on the outskirts of the city of Puerto Príncipe. Slaves and free blacks rose up on the Najasa plantation, burning the master's house and killing three whites. The insurgents quickly moved to nearby plantations, setting fire to buildings and machinery. By the battle's end, eight whites had died, numerous whites were injured, and several plantations had been burnt or partially destroyed.[8] Local officials reacted swiftly. The governor sentenced 14 of the rebels to death and rounded up 170 slaves and free blacks. Many of those arrested were whipped and imprisoned for one to ten years or banished from the island.

In the wake of the Puerto Príncipe rebellion, fears of insurgencies led by slaves and free blacks mounted throughout the island. In the eastern town of Bayamo, Antonio José informed his owner that fellow slaves were planning a revolt on the night of February 7. During the search of the house of a Bayamo conspirator, police found two Carabalí Africans who had escaped arrest for their participation in the uprising at Puerto Príncipe. This confirmed in the minds of authorities the existence of ties between the two rebellions. Police quickly apprehended numerous slaves and free blacks. The governor requested that five of the leaders be executed, with their body parts to be exhibited at various sites in the city as a statement to anyone plotting future insurrections. In response to the protests by owners, officials reduced the severity of the penalties. The leaders were sent to (Spanish) Florida to serve prison sentences, the free blacks found guilty of involvement in the plot served two-year work sentences on the island, and slaves believed to have joined were returned to their masters with the agreement that they be chained at all times.[9] A thwarted conspiracy at Holguín (located forty-three miles to the northeast of Bayamo) added to the turbulence.

News of events in the eastern end of the island traveled quickly to Havana. Professor Childs affirms that "news, stories, and rumors of a planned uprising circulated widely in Havana during the first two weeks of March 1812."[10] To calm the urban and rural inhabitants, the town council of Havana sent out extra patrols of troops on special alert for signs of slave insurrection.

Similar to the forces in the uprising in Puerto Príncipe and the conspiracy at Bayamo, free blacks and slaves joined together in planning a revolt to occur within and outside Havana. Close contact between city and countryside facilitated interaction among plotters and potential followers. One Congo slave admitted to speaking with an individual he believed to be a leader of the plot on the Day of the Kings (January 6), describing him as "a black man dressed in a military jacket mounted on a horse." Based on bits of information extracted from various persons, judicial officials embarked on a wide-ranging investigation.

Learning that the plot had been discovered, slaves rebelled at the Peñas-Altas sugar plantation on March 14. The insurgents burned the estate and killed one technician, his two children, and two white overseers. They split into three groups and attacked three other nearby plantations. At the Trinidad plantation, the insurgents assassinated five whites, including the overseer and his family. Within hours, military troops and armed militias put down the revolt. The revolutionaries dispersed into the countryside. In the months that followed, officials hunted down most of the rebels and executed them.

Based on statements made during interrogations of accused participants in the plantation uprisings, police went to the residence of the free black José Aponte in Havana. Aponte was an artist, sculptor, carpenter, and skilled artisan. A retired officer of Cuba's militia of color, Aponte practiced the religion of the Lucumí, led the Shangó Tedum cabildo (a mutual aid association based on Yoruba traditions), and was a member of a secret society with origins in Yorubaland known as the Ogboni.[11] Believing Aponte to be a key figure in the movement, police searched the house. There they found a book of paintings or drawings (*libro de pinturas*) done by Aponte. These included portraits of his grandfather and father praising their patriotism; portraits of leaders of the Haitian Revolution, including Toussaint Louverture, Henri Christophe, Jean François, and Jean-Jacques Dessalines; an effigy to George Washington; a battle scene that included two black soldiers holding the severed heads of whites; and maps of streets and military garrisons in Havana.[12] Unfortunately the book has not been found.

A few of the drawings depicted sailing ships in the harbor of Havana. Underneath one Aponte penned the words "a sloop attacking the greed of the dock with death." During an interrogation, Aponte was asked: "How can you content yourself with what you have explained [in the book] about the development of commerce with what is indicated by the drawing . . . when on the dock you see death . . . which indicates destruction of this [commerce], not advancement." Aponte's response: "death only destroyed greed," not commerce.[13]

The drawings likely took inspiration from Aponte's having been witness to the landing of Africans in or near the port of Havana. They also could have alluded to the infections brought by slave ships.[14] At this moment health officials grappled with the many deaths caused by the transatlantic slave trade and the widespread dysentery that plagued Africans housed in the numerous barracoons of Havana.[15] The *libro de pinturas* is Aponte's condemnation of the African slave trade. The compilation revealed that he understood the history of the Caribbean and abolitionist discourse circulating in the Atlantic world. Aponte's statements and the specter that a second Haitian Revolution might occur in Cuba were used by elites in Cuba and Spain to shut down discussion related to any interruption of the slave trade or the abolition of slavery.[16]

José Aponte admitted to being the author of the *libro*. Based on the drawings along with confessions by other plotters, colonial authorities condemned Aponte as having been the leader of an island-wide rebellion. Aponte was hanged on April 9 and his decapitated head put on public display in Havana. Officials hanged 33 slaves and free persons of color found guilty of involvement, whipped 78 others, and sentenced 170 persons to jails situated throughout the Spanish empire.[17] Cuba's elite did not quickly forget José Aponte and the rebellion of which he was a part.

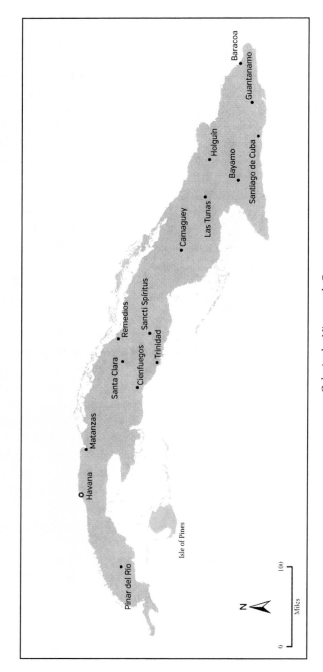

MAP 4. Cuba in the Nineteenth Century

THE GREAT AFRICAN SLAVE REVOLT OF 1825 AND ITS AFTERMATH

The first major slave revolt of the nineteenth century, described as the (
African Slave Revolt of 1825, occurred in the valley of Guamacaro east of the
city of Matanzas. Its leaders sought to kill abusive masters and overseers, take
over land owned by whites they intended to assassinate, and win their freedom. Planning occurred during several months preceding the uprising, including at Sunday drumming and dancing celebrations on estates and at more
remote locations where Africans met to converse.[18] After the revolt, the participants intended to escape from the coffee plantations where they labored with
the hope of residing in a *palenque* (escaped slave community). It appears that
others were prepared to commit suicide. Involving some 201 slaves of differ-
ing African ethnicities and led by several West Africans (Ganga, Lucumí, and
Carabalí), the rebellion was quashed after twelve hours. One participant estimated that in the fighting ten whites died and three were injured, and among
the black rebels forty died. Some of the rebels succeeded in fleeing and caused
disturbances in the region in its immediate aftermath. In retribution, authorities killed several Africans. On September 1, troops executed nine Africans in
Matanzas. Planters took slaves from their properties to the city to witness this
event. All nine were decapitated and their heads placed on display in public
locales, including on plantations where Africans had joined the movement.

African-led revolts convulsed Cuba for the next two decades. In January 1827, fifty-seven slaves assassinated an overseer and administrator of a
coffee estate. For a week the slaves attacked personnel at nearby plantations.
During the search for the rebels, militia troops killed five. Distraught over
their situation, eighteen slaves committed suicide by hanging themselves.[19]
In September 1832, seventeen recently landed Lucumí attempted to assassinate the overseer at a sugar plantation near Havana and fled into the forest
nearby. In July 1833, forty Liberated Africans residing near Havana joined in a
revolt. City officials arrested five free blacks in its aftermath, believing them to
have been involved.[20] Weeks later, 330 slaves, who worked at the coffee estate
named Salvador situated ten leagues to the west of Havana, rose up in a huge
rebellion (as described in chapter two). The majority of participants being
Lucumí, the slaves beat drums, sang, and danced to prepare for battle. In the
words of Professor Barcia, "this tumultuous revolt caused irreversible damage
to neighboring plantations and in the town of Banes."[21]

In 1835, enslaved and free Lucumí from rural coffee estates joined in an uprising at the outer wall of Havana. They called for an end to the institution of slavery and the overthrow of the colonial government. Several rebels died in the reprisals that followed.[22] Hermengildo Jáurequi and Juan Nepomuceno Prieto, two free blacks accused of being ringleaders of this "Lucumí Conspiracy," were executed by firing squad.[23] To enhance security, Captain General Tacón added "four strong patrols of horse to the numerous patrols of infantry that perambulate the city and its outskirts [as a way] to prevent and disperse the many suspicious assemblages of men of color on Sundays and other holidays when no work is done."[24]

Insurrections led and supported by African slaves rocked the sugar plantations and coffee estates of western Cuba during the late 1830s. In June 1837, several slaves attacked the whites employed at the La Sonora sugar mill. This occurred in response to harsh treatment inflicted by the overseer. Although no one was killed, authorities subsequently executed three Lucumí leaders of the rebellion. In September, a group of twenty-five Lucumí attacked the overseer and white employees of another sugar estate. One slave died during the confrontation; two others escaped and hanged themselves in a nearby forest.

These revolts provoked great tension throughout Cuba. From the perspective of historian Jonathan Curry-Machado, "by 1840, slave resistance of both an active and passive kind had weakened the control of the creole elite and the Spanish authorities in the countryside; and the white population was becoming increasingly hysterical about the blacks, the British (who were the principal protagonists in the outlawing of the slave trade), and the possibility of an uprising [on the order of the Great African Slave Revolt of 1825]."[25]

Slave revolts continued through the early 1840s. In June and July 1840, Lucumí slaves rebelled on coffee and sugar plantations near Havana. In a first outbreak, an overseer refused to allow a slave named Tranquilino time off to recover from injuries suffered when he fell from a roof. Upon his refusal to work, the overseer whipped Tranquilino. In retribution Tranquilino killed the overseer. With fifty other slaves, Tranquilino descended on the house of the owner and assassinated him. When troops arrived to put down the rebellion, the slaves threw rocks to defend themselves.[26] In response, Captain Sixto Morejón called on his troops to open fire on the Africans.

In October 1841, nineteen Lucumí slaves refused to continue laboring at the construction site of a large building in Havana. These men had recently arrived in Cuba on a slave ship. Having no knowledge of Spanish, the Africans could not comprehend the commands of the overseer and owner. The latter ordered soldiers to attack. The slaves reacted by throwing sticks and rocks. This tragic episode left six Africans dead and seven wounded.[27]

Between March and November 1843, the largest revolts in the history of Cuba broke out near Cárdenas and Matanzas. Lucumí slaves once again played a major role in what is known as the Bemba uprising. An estimated one thousand slaves from four sugar plantations, one coffee estate, and one cattle ranch revolted in late March.[28] The slaves set fire to crops and structures on five plantations, some of them moving "in military order, clad in their festival clothes, with colors flying, and holding leather shields."[29] British officials estimated that between 300 and 450 Africans died and 40 committed suicide. Spanish troops captured 12 and immediately "shot them on the spot and a few perished from hunger while hiding in the forest. The remainder were killed indiscriminately by the military and country people. Of these many no doubt were innocent persons and among the bodies found cut were those of a woman and her infant child dead."[30] In the aftermath, officials from Matanzas followed common practice: they placed the decapitated heads of suspected leaders on spikes in locations where they would be observed by slaves resident on sugar estates near Cárdenas.

During the months that followed, slaves continued to resist. Normally quiescent house slaves exhibited discontent. The escaped slave José Dolares gained fame for a series of attacks on plantations and attempts to free slaves imprisoned after the Bemba uprising.[31] In June, three hundred slaves from the sugar mill Flor de Cuba in the district of Guamacaro joined in an insurrection. In July, forty African slaves who labored at another sugar mill near Corral Falso damaged property and caused terror among owners and overseers on nearby sugar plantations. In August, recently landed African slaves owned by well-known trafficker Don Joaquim Gómez rose up at a sugar plantation located near Bahia Honda. In the words of British observers, this was a "serious insurrection in which three white men and fourteen negroes were killed. These insurrections we believe are a much more frequent occurrence than is generally known, and give a lamentable view of the state of the country."[32] Between September and October, several small slave revolts erupted on plantations in Matanzas.

The last and largest revolt of 1843 occurred in November in the district of Sabanilla near Matanzas. In a rampage perpetrated by an army of more than three hundred Lucumí slaves, the Africans assassinated an overseer and his family, burned down the buildings at four sugar estates, and damaged two others. In putting down the revolt, soldiers killed an estimated one hundred Africans and captured sixty-seven. Tens of others fled to the nearby mountains.[33] Brutal revenge followed.

Documents suggest that the failure of the 1843 rebellions and the harsh punishments inflicted in response did little to diminish the determination of slaves to protest. Less than a month after the Sabanilla revolt, in December 1843, authorities became aware of plans for a wide-ranging insurgency that involved slaves and free blacks. It became known as the Escalera Conspiracy. As a result, "white racial paranoia now began to run out of control."[34] For the next two years (1844–45), soldiers and planters vented their rage on enemies both real and imagined.

THE ESCALERA MOVEMENT

Officials learned more about an extensive plot in the final days of 1843. Called by historians La Escalera Conspiracy (the Ladder Conspiracy), it derived its name from a torture commonly inflicted on slaves in Cuba. They were tied facedown on a ladder and whipped. Tens of accused participants suffered such beatings during an eighteen-month inquisition that followed between the winter of 1843–44 and summer of 1845.

Building on the contributions of several scholars, a recent study places African and creole slaves at the center of the events of 1844.[35] Historian Aisha K. Finch describes La Escalera as "a far-reaching black insurgency" and a "movement that had been several years in the making."[36] By choosing the words *insurgency* and *movement* to replace *conspiracy*, Finch provides evidence of covert preparations for a slave revolution. Indeed, she writes that La Escalera can best be understood as a planned insurrection with origins in the rural slave rebellions that had broken out during the decade preceding it.[37]

Based on several hundred testimonies from slave witnesses taken at tens of locations during the investigations of 1844–45, a remarkable story unfolds of an extensive rebel movement in the western department of Cuba. Those who were involved resided in Havana, Matanzas, Cárdenas, and rural areas near those cities along with the central regions of Villa Clara and Cienfuegos. Professor Finch asserts that "the 1844 trials reveal a world that was meant to be hidden to colonial authorities: of illicit movement within and across plantation borders, clandestine meetings and conversations, underground trade networks between estates, weapons being exchanged, oaths being taken, religious rituals performed, and royal titles being given for an insurgency."[38]

Sugar spread eastward to the fertile soils of the province of Matanzas during the 1830s and 1840s. Between 1839 and 1842, planters constructed some two hundred new sugar mills in the region. With that expansion, the demand for labor escalated. In 1792, 6,216 slaves worked in the region. This number increased to 10,773 in 1817 and 94,374 in 1841, and then decreased slightly to 89,643 by 1862.[39]

This upsurge in the number of slaves contributed to the dramatic demographic transformation of the island. In 1827, 286,942 slaves labored in cities and countryside. By 1846, that number had risen to 323,759. Numerous slaves purchased their freedom. In 1827, free colored numbered 106,484. By 1846, their numbers had risen to 149,226. The white population rose from 311,051 (41 percent of the total) in 1827 to 425,767 (47 percent of the total) in 1846. As such, whites remained a minority of the island's population until after mid-century. For 1862, official estimates show that the number of slaves and free colored in Cuba had decreased to 43 percent of the total population.

Slaves and free blacks who labored on sugar and coffee estates received news from a variety of sources. Black cart drivers who carried sugar from plantations proved to be adroit conduits. Coach drivers transported owners through plantation districts and to urban areas such as Matanzas and Havana. Such mobility facilitated communication among black folk. Domestic slaves also traveled with owners and overheard conversations related to politics and society on the island. As in other plantation regions in the Americas, slaves moved across the countryside clandestinely at night and unimpeded on Sundays. Given the proximity of estates in the region, planters hired creole and African slaves from neighboring plantations, particularly during the busy harvest season. Through such contacts, tens of enslaved and free blacks in rural Matanzas disseminated information related to the impending insurrection during 1843 and the first months of 1844.

Plans of the revolt circulated around the island. Slaves who labored on rural estates traveled to urban areas and conversed with residents. As one example of many, we know that the African slaves Patricio Mandinga and Blas Lucumí journeyed from their plantation on the outskirts of Matanzas to that city's center. There they "interacted with a broad spectrum of black, mulatto and African workers . . . including market vendors, coopers, dock workers, masons, other [fellow] shoemakers, and cart drivers, [all of whom] had some association with the insurgency. In the course of clandestine conversations and meetings, the two obtained precise information about plans for attack,

names of other conspirators, and locations of potential arms."[40] Upon returning to their residence, they convened meetings with fellow slaves to share
what they had learned about the coming rebellion.

Information and strategies related to the rebellion were disseminated from
urban areas such as Havana and Matanzas to the interior of the island. Numerous black overseers and African women received notice and organized
insurgencies at the grass roots. No wonder that Professor Finch describes La
Escalera as an "overlap of multiple circles of resistance, whose very intersec-
tion made a widespread and collective movement possible."[41]

In the cities of Matanzas and Havana, a "vast network of free and enslaved
black rebels" moved forward with designs to destroy the slave regime. Several
of these individuals commonly fared into the countryside and conveyed intelligence to contacts. One such free black interlocutor was José María Mondejar from Matanzas. Mondejar disseminated news related to preparations for
revolution during three years (1841–43) previous to its discovery by plantation
owners and government officials.

Several historians posit that a few hundred creole free blacks and mulattoes aided in planning the Escalera movement.[42] This group desired to end
the slave regime in Cuba and gain independence from Spanish rule. One participant was the Havana-based entrepreneur Juan Rodríguez, also known as
Miguel Flores. He was part of a black bourgeoisie who attained impressive
wealth in the first decades of the nineteenth century. Viewed as a threat to
white elite interests, these well-to-do urban blacks suffered widespread dis-
crimination at the hands of the Spanish colonial government. Mulatto intellectuals joined the movement, including famed poet Gabriel de la Concepción
Valdés (best known as Plácido), who was executed for his supposed involvement in the insurrection.

Influenced by the abolitionist currents that traversed the Atlantic world,
the plotters believed that British consuls David Turnbull and Joseph T. Crawford would provide aid. It appears that at least one of the participants visited
British ships anchored in Cuban waters in hopes of receiving arms.[43] Authorities took notice. Suspecting that black dock foremen at the port of Havana had
acted as intermediaries between foreigners and plotters, authorities executed
several of these men during the repression of 1844.

In the wake of the discovery of plans for a revolution, Africans became a
primary target of investigations and torture. Military Tribunals carried out a
campaign of terror with "frantic cruelty."[44] A central Military Commission,

established in Havana by a royal decree in 1825, determined the composition of roving tribunals that oversaw 70 military trials. At one trial near the city of Matanzas in September 1844 (noted in documents as the eighteenth case or *cuaderno*), prosecutors called for the interrogation of ninety-seven "persons of color" accused of plotting an insurrection in the district of Lagunillas (located on the outskirts of Cienfuegos 160 miles from Havana on the southern coast). Of these ninety-seven persons, thirteen proved incapable of appearing before the court due to being hospitalized. This meant that they had been severely whipped as a way to force a confession of involvement in the insurgency. At no place in this 18th case were the whippings noted.

Of the ninety-seven called before the eighteenth tribunal, forty-two were "natives of Africa," ten were creoles, and the other forty-five "undistinguished" as to their ethnicity. Most likely Africans composed a significant number of the "undistinguished." Of the ninety-seven accused, twenty-eight "were absolved from punishment and discharged, though condemned to the payment of full costs, all the 28 being described as free."[45] Sixty-seven others were sentenced to punishment of varying degrees of severity. The tribunal sentenced two of the leaders to be "shot and gibbeted"; one of them was executed in this manner. The second was a former slave named Meliton Sotolongo, who most likely expired in the hospital from wounds inflicted by whips.

In a 20th tribunal of September 1844, prosecutors requested that ninety individuals be brought before the court for conspiring in the district of Yumuri (located near the city of Matanzas). Of the accused, sixty-two were described as "Africans of different nations," nineteen were creoles, and no distinction was included for the nine remaining. In what appears to have been an oversight by the scribes, the documents relate that, unlike in any of the other military trials, seventeen of the accused died during the proceedings. This suggested that some or all of those seventeen individuals succumbed from beatings carried out to force an admission of guilt. Another eighteen lay in a hospital too ill to be present; this suggests that they also had endured brutal treatment. Prosecutors accused one black man named Adriano Montalvo of having prepared spears from a hardwood known as yaya that grew in the countryside. Montalvo and another man were sentenced to death, and "they were shot accordingly." The judge sentenced sixty-eight of the accused to various punishments. One man of color named Roberto Pak, also known as an "Englishman," was banished from the island.[46]

In legitimizing this inquisition, members of the tribunal declared it necessary "to maintain at all cost the dominion of the laws and respect of the white class, chastising with severity those who departing from their duties, infringe in the very least against those rules."[47] Authorities exhorted that the organizers of the insurrection sought to "constitute in this Island a Republic just like that of Santo Domingo [meaning Haiti], [with the] assassination of all the whites in order to do so."[48]

In numerous instances, officials asked the accused Africans how they had gone about organizing.[49] From the responses, it was evident that strategies of resistance and war with origins in Africa played an integral role in the insurgency of 1844. Examples abound. A fifty-five-year-old African named Teleforo Lucumí who labored at the Luísa sugar mill sold "witchcraft" items to fellow slaves "so that they could fight and do battle."[50] The former slave Juan José Pérez explained that possession of African talismans would aid slaves in any attempt to murder a hated overseer and assist them "to acquire their liberty, and to persuade them that the weapons of the whites will do them no harm in the event that [the slaves] rise up against them."[51] Africans joined in hidden ritual ceremonies, gathered for drumming and dance, and elected kings and queens to lead the insurgency. The arrests and savage whippings inflicted on hundreds if not thousands of Africans accused of involvement in La Escalera reflected the widespread anxiety among colonial officials with regard to the unceasing slave importations.

The trials of 1844 resulted in the execution of 78 people; the sentencing of 328 persons to ten years in prison, 652 to eight years in prison, and 312 to six months in prison; 27 were assigned to public service; 14 received "light sentences"; and 82 were absolved. An estimated 1,300 free blacks were banished permanently from the island, sent to foreign prisons, or forced to emigrate.[52] These numbers do not include slaves whipped at plantations, confined in dungeons on private estates, and tortured by metal chains and shackles that they were forced to wear for months or years after.[53] British consuls James Kennedy and Campbell Dalrymple wrote in mid-1845 that "it is reported, and we cannot disbelieve the general statement, that as many as 10,000 negroes have been subjected to the severest lashing, and that 2,000 have sunk [died] under their sufferings."[54] At the town of Guines, planters gathered an estimated three thousand people, many of them slaves, to witness these hideous spectacles.[55]

Two individuals who surfaced during the Escalera movement had come to official notice nineteen years previously. Interrogated following the Great African Slave Revolt of 1825, the free black Agustín Ximénez gained his release when no evidence could be garnered to prove his participation in that uprising. His luck did not hold in 1844. Accused of being a leader as well as a sorcerer, he was found guilty at the 38th tribunal and thrown into a cell in Matanzas. Aware of his impending execution, Ximénez took his own life by hanging.

A second figure to reappear during 1844 was the African Pedro Gangá. In spite of being accused by several participants that he played a key role in the 1825 revolt, Pedro was let off with a reduced sentence in its wake. This leniency was shown because he had helped to save the life of his owner's wife when rebel slaves had appeared at their plantation. The court required that Pedro wear irons and perform hard labor for an unknown duration. During the Escalera investigations of 1844, seventeen witnesses accused Pedro of being a leader, sorcerer, and arms dealer. Pedro admitted participation but denied being a key figure. A tribunal rejected his defense. Sentenced to death, Pedro Gangá was executed by a firing squad on September 11, 1844.[56]

One other group swept up in the repression during La Escalera was British and North American *maquinistas* (engine operators, engineers). Planters hired these men to maintain steam engines and machinery on sugar estates and railroads. Hence, they came into close contact with slaves in the workplace. From the first uprisings of 1843, authorities suspected these foreigners of being tainted by abolitionist ideas and fomenting slave resistance. In the accusatory words of Captain General Leopoldo O'Donnell, who had been sent to Cuba in late 1843 specifically to put down the slave rebellions, foreigners "schooled in revolutions and many of them in crimes" had purposely disrupted the social order on the island. As a result, the tribunals arrested tens of foreign engineers, only to declare all of them innocent by December 1844.[57] The *maquinistas* represented a tiny fraction of the thousands who suffered in the aftermath of the Escalera insurgency. Nevertheless, their treatment reflected the deep-seated hatreds and phobias inspired by perceived threats from outside Cuba and from within.

CAPTURED SLAVE SHIPS AND LIBERATED AFRICANS

Cuba's elites believed that England played a role in the Escalera movement. Known for its efforts to suppress the transatlantic slave trade and its support for emancipation, the English Crown sent avowed abolitionists Dr. Richard Robert Madden and David Turnbull to Havana as its representatives. Previous to residing at Havana, Madden visited Jamaica (November 1833) as one of six special magistrates to witness the freeing of slaves on August 1, 1834. Madden wrote of his experiences as well as concerns about British policy towards former slaves in *A Twelvemonth Residence in the Island of Jamaica* (1835). As the first superintendent of Liberated Africans and a judge on the Mixed Commission Court at Havana (1836–39), Madden defended the rights of Liberated Africans and criticized the abusive treatment of African slaves in Cuba.[58]

Arriving in August 1840, David Turnbull accepted the position of consul and superintendent of Liberated Africans. Turnbull immediately focused on the treatment of Africans removed from slave vessels seized by the British Squadron. A letter of 1841 from the Society for Progress (*Junta de Fomento*) in Havana alluded to the threat posed by these activists:

> It appears to them [the British] as of little danger, the contagion they spread among our slaves, by means of the correspondence they maintain with the numerous class of Emancipados [Liberated Africans] whom their fervid humanity has not succeeded in transferring to some of their islands [in the British Caribbean] where they would enjoy perfect freedom; they [British representatives] have lately urged the government to pay domiciliary visits to country houses in the vicinity of the city in which they supposed there were negroes recently brought from Africa, giving by the publicity and ostentation of these acts, which are immediately known and understood by the slaves, new ideas of the illegality of their condition and that they have cause [*facultad*] supported by the English to rise against the whites.[59]

The actions of David Turnbull incited widespread protests. He defended England's efforts to suppress the slave trade to Cuba and traveled into the countryside to observe at first hand conditions on sugar plantations. Within two years, the captain general forced the expulsion of Turnbull from the island. Turnbull has gone down in history books as a committed reformer willing to confront the many beneficiaries of the slave trade. What has been overlooked in this story are the many acts of collective and personal resistance shown by Liberated Africans themselves.

By an 1817 Anglo-Spanish treaty, the British and Spanish governments established a British-Spanish Court of Mixed Commission at Havana to judge captured slave ships. Of some 174,000 Africans freed from 1,983 vessels captured by British cruisers from 1808 to 1866 (out of a total of 8,217 slave voyages recorded as sailing during those years), the Havana court (1819–54) emancipated 12,328 Africans. This number does not include another 14,417 Africans taken from slave ships between 1854 and 1866 by Cuban authorities and Spanish naval patrols. This latter group of Africans was absorbed into the island's slave population through the subterfuge of corrupt authorities and hence was not denoted as Liberated Africans.[60]

Why would 12,328 Africans out of the more than 710,000 Africans landed at Cuba between 1800 and 1866 cause such concern? One reason is that these "recaptured" Africans had witnessed firsthand the determined initiatives of the British. As one example of many, on April 17, 1835, the Spanish brig *Marte* sailed into the port of Havana under the direction of a prize crew from H.M. schooner *Skipjack*. During a daylong chase on April 8, the *Skipjack* and the *Marte* exchanged cannon fire. The British vessel suffered no damage, and no one was injured. The crew and Africans on board the *Marte* were not so lucky. A surgeon present on the slave vessel stated that one Spanish sailor and ten Africans died in the battle, and another six Spaniards and nineteen Africans were wounded. Of 600 Africans who had embarked at Luango (present-day Angola), 442 remained alive.[61] Thirty-nine of the Africans perished from smallpox during the next three weeks. On May 8, the Mixed Commission Court condemned the vessel and emancipated the 403 Africans who had survived the Middle Passage and capture.

The episode provides insights into why Liberated Africans piqued such tension among authorities. The Africans on board the *Marte*, along with several hundred other Africans liberated by the court at Havana from captured slave ships, observed the courage of the British captains and sailors. In spite of sailing a "very fine brig pierced for 20 and mounting 8 guns," the crew of the *Marte* could not fend off the attack by the *Skipjack*. Witnesses to the desperation that prevailed on board the *Marte* as it was hunted down by a British cruiser, the Africans never forgot this episode. Surely they shared their experience with blacks both slave and free. News of this encounter spread by means of the same networks that enabled the planning for the insurgency of La Escalera. In his study of the "odious commerce" to Cuba, historian David Murray writes that the increasing number of Africans liberated by the Mixed Commission Court at this juncture "transformed panic into near hysteria" among authorities in Cuba.[62]

Captain General Tacón believed he had to do everything in his power to prevent "agglomerations of blacks," which included Liberated Africans, in Havana. "These already here can hardly be managed and restrained under the precarious authority and vigilance of the white persons who have received them in the way of deposit with the view of instructing them in the tenets of religion, and in some honest occupation, art, or business to prevent them from being guilty of all sorts of crimes and partial insurrections to which they are predisposed by the stupidity and ferocity of their savage character that is ill repressed by the conditions of their distribution."[63] Tacón merely articulated the view shared by many well-to-do Cubans that Liberated Africans were capable of fomenting subversion and resistance among slaves and free blacks.

Liberated Africans in Cuba endured conditions similar to those of slaves. In one study from late 1845, officials estimated some nine hundred Liberated Africans worked as domestic labor, two hundred labored for the Guines Railroad Company, and two hundred were employed in public works, road construction, and hospitals and other public institutions.[64] Observers lamented that the "conditions of these people had become irremediably wretched."[65] Many of these Africans wore tattered clothing, suffered indignities daily, lived in poverty, and died young from infirmities.

Such depictions should not hide the many instances where Liberated Africans reacted to their debasement. Tens fled from their masters. British commissioners Kennedy and Dalrymple encountered (in 1844) "one hundred of these unfortunate persons, conspicuous by their tin-tickets, tied around their necks, all with more or lighter chains, or bolts, round their legs, and a scantiness of clothing deserving of censure. Their crime we believe has been no more than running away from their taskmasters."[66] Liberated Africans who labored on the Cardenas railroad joined in the slave rebellions of 1843.[67] The Military Tribunals that carried out investigations into the Escalera movement accused that same group of involvement in the 1844 insurgency. "The simultaneous risings on different estates made the authorities suspect that they were part of a general conspiracy, although it is just as likely that they [the rebellions] arose from local causes, from the number of new Africans, chiefly Lucumís, recently introduced [meaning bozales recently landed in Cuba], and among the emancipados on the Cardenas railroad, who saw themselves cut off from the hope of that liberty, which they had been led to expect from the government of General Valdés, when so many of their class had been given their liberty."[68] This last sentence alludes to the initiatives taken by Captain General Valdés (March 1841–September 1843) in defense of Liberated Africans and his supposed opposition to the slave trade bloc. The tenure of Leopoldo O'Donnell (October 1843–48), who replaced Valdés, represented a hardening of Spanish

policy towards creoles critical of the slave trade and Englishmen seen as pro-
vocateurs.

Other incidents related to the arrival of seized slave vessels at Havana merit
scrutiny. In several instances, the Mixed Commission Court invited Africans
to describe what had happened previous to and after capture on the high sea.
That the court officials listened to their words through interpreters and scribes
wrote down their statements certainly made a marked impression. Although
the provision of emancipation declared by the Mixed Commission Court most
often proved to be a dead letter, many Liberated Africans understood that they
had attained a legal right to receive their freedom. The arrival of Liberated Africans at the doors of the British consulate to complain of abuse and illegal enslavement demonstrated such comprehension. Two such episodes are noted.

In April 1853, a "Negress" appeared at the British consul. She gave her
name as Maria Florencia de la Paz (obviously a created name imposed by one
of her owners) but stated proudly that she had been born in Africa and "be-
longed to the Carabalí nation." Maria was among 150 Africans disembarked
from a Spanish slave vessel named *El Nacimiento de Isabel Segunda* near Santiago de Cuba in January 1842. Soon after the landing, Maria and her shipmates were "recaptured" under the orders of Cuba's Captain General Valdés.
In the words of British consul Backhouse, "she knew the date [of her arrival]
by bringing another negro who had been part of the 150 [Africans who ar-
rived] and got his paper of freedom which he brought with him." Maria related
that "one segment of her employment history was with a mistress who exacted
from her a half dollar a day to be earned in whatever way it could."[69] The appearance of the second African at her side showed that Maria had kept contact
over an extended period with fellow Africans who had survived the Middle
Passage and settled in Havana. Backhouse did not know how to respond and
asked for advice from the minister of foreign affairs in London.

Six months later, in October 1853, another freed African named Demetrio
Lucumí met with British consul Backhouse. Based on "good authority," Backhouse learned that the African had arrived in Havana on board the captured
slave ship *Negrito* in December 1832.[70] The ship was immediately condemned
by the Mixed Commission Court and Demetrio was liberated. For the next
twenty years he was consigned to various masters and maintained a "good
character." On several occasions he applied for a liberty card from the colonial
government, which he believed would assure him of unimpeded liberty and
independence. These attempts failed.

Demetrio's master was a man named Esutaquio Rebuelta. Owner of twenty-four Liberated Africans, Rebuelta required that each African pay him five *reals fuertes* (eight reals equaled one U.S. dollar) each week from their profits. Rebuelta demanded that the Africans hand over a percentage of income earned on Sundays and holidays, a requirement harsher than that imposed on slaves. When an African employee failed to pay, Rebuelta "sent them to work out of the city as punishment."

A letter penned by British consul Backhouse offers striking insights into Demetrio's world. Demetrio had worked both in Havana and on plantations. His name had been changed "two or three times" by different masters, one of those names being Pablo. Demetrio knew another Pablo who had been a shipmate on the *Negrito* and who at present managed a group of free Africans employed at the Havana railroad station. That entourage included seven fellow Africans who had been liberated from the *Negrito* by the British. Demetrio described another African he remembered from the *Negrito* who worked at the railroad station, but whom he knew only by his "Guinea" name. "This latter man could be recognized by his having lost all the fingers on his left hand, the thumb alone remaining."[71] Demetrio expressed trepidation that if Rebuelta learned of his attempt to gain unfettered freedom, Demetrio would be arrested and sent to a sugar plantation or stone quarry as retribution.

Demetrio believed that he possessed a special status. With the aid of a lawyer, he produced a petition that he presented to the British consul and that he intended to send to the captain general. The document recounted the capture and court proceedings in 1832 (twenty-one years before!) and showed the illegality of Demetrio's continued enslavement and harsh treatment. He remembered well the Middle Passage on board the *Negrito* and several survivors who remained alive and working in Havana. More than two decades after H.M. sloop *Victor* had accompanied the *Negrito* to Havana, Demetrio, similar to Maria Florencia de la Paz, kept up contact with fellow Africans who had been liberated by the Mixed Commission Court at Havana.

From the arrival of the first captured Spanish slaver at the port of Havana in 1822, the appearance of seized vessels caught the attention of slaves and free blacks who labored at the port of Havana and along the coast. They observed slave vessels in quarantine, the removal of ill Africans to lazarettos onshore, and the intrigues of Spanish officials determined to impede recaptured Africans from being absorbed into the free black community. They understood that the anchoring of the receiving ship *Romney* in the bay of Havana (September 1837–December 1845) was intended to prevent Liberated Africans from coming onshore.[72] In the opinion of the learned Cuban historian Fernando Ortiz, the *Romney* was "a bulwark of abolition in the heart of slavery."[73] U.S. officials characterized the presence of the *Romney* in even more dramatic terms: "the establishment of a garrison of colored soldiers under British uniform with the consent of the Spanish government stationed at the port of Havana apparently to look after the 'emancipados' [was] really to excite insurrectionary movements by their presence."[74]

Black folk in Havana witnessed the transfer of Liberated Africans to ships destined for nearby British Caribbean islands (some twelve hundred to Trinidad, nine hundred to the Bahamas, three hundred to Jamaica, and others to Grenada and Honduras).[75] Slaves and free blacks shared all such information.

The majority of Africans freed by the Mixed Commission Court at Havana became slaves of urban and rural masters. Many questioned their condition, believing that they had the right to be free. Acts of defiance by free Africans added to the social tensions caused by the unceasing arrival of thousands of enslaved Africans in Cuba.

CRITICS OF THE SLAVE TRADE

Slave and free black resistance inspired discourse critical of the transatlantic slave trade to the island. A wealthy investor in sugar plantations worked by slaves named Pedro Juan de Erice articulated such a critique in the wake of the Aponte Rebellion of 1812. Commenting on the slave revolts that broke out in the first months of that tumultuous year, he requested aid from the Spanish government to assure the "salvation and security of this important province."[76] Referring to dangers posed by "domestic enemies," another resident from the town of Guanabacoa petitioned Captain General Someruelos to effect the "immediate suppression of the risky trading in slaves" and the abolition of slavery on the island.[77]

The evolution in worldview of Francisco de Arango y Parreño (1763–1837) suggests that slave resistance caused a shift in mentalité regarding the slave trade among reactionary sectors of Cuban society. The most influential member of the Society for Progress and a man who represented the opinion of fellow planters, Arango emphasized the need for African slaves to satisfy labor demands on the island. In 1789, he played a key role in the successful lobbying of the Spanish government to declare open trade in slaves. This meant that foreigners could transport Africans to Cuba without paying duties. To fill the lacuna caused by the halt of exports of sugar and coffee during the revolution on Saint-Domingue, Arango used his influence to assure that slave importations would be immediately increased to Cuba. In the words of historian Dale Tomich, Arango "re-conceptualized slave labor [in Cuba] within the framework of free trade, individual self-interest, efficient management, and systematic technological innovation."[78]

Francisco Arango refused to believe that the thousands of African slaves who rose up in Saint-Domingue had accomplished this feat by their own wits and courage. Instead, like so many other witnesses of that epoch, Arango attributed the Haitian Revolution to the influx of republican ideas that originated in metropolitan France during its revolution of 1789. Confident in the capacity of the planter class to repress all forms of dissent, Arango downplayed the risks posed by the steady increase in slave population in Cuba. Nevertheless, wariness showed through. In a proposal of 1791, Arango wrote that Cuba's elite needed to take precautions to prevent an insurrection comparable to what had occurred in Haiti.[79]

For more than three decades (from 1789 to the early 1820s), Arango endorsed the landing of Africans on Cuba as the most efficient way to develop "colonial agriculture." In 1811, he defended the merits of traffic before the Spanish Cortes in Madrid. In 1816, as a member of the Council of the Indies, Arango rejected a proposal to halt the slave trade.

Then something changed his opinion. Arango suddenly advocated an immediate halt of slave importations. In the words of historian David R. Murray, "[in 1825], at last aware of the evils of the slave trade, he tried to get the Spanish government to wipe it out. . . . Arango y Parreño's conversion, for it was nothing less than that, was remarkable."[80] The Great African Slave Revolt of 1825 had much to do with Arango's reversal. "He [Arango] reported that strict customs regulations alone would not be enough to check it and he offered his co-operation to enforce any [suppression] measures the peninsular government chose to adopt."[81] This was followed by several *comunicaciones* to the Spanish government between 1828 and 1832 in which Arango called for termination of the slave trade to Cuba.[82]

As Arango was an astute observer of Cuba and its place in the Atlantic world, what exactly caused this dramatic shift in opinion? Two reasons are noted. First, Cuba's slave population had risen at a staggering rate. From the first disembarkations of enslaved Africans in 1674 up to 1790, the island received 26,600 African slaves (official estimates). From 1790 to 1825, traffickers landed 270,000 African slaves in Cuba, a tenfold increase.[83] Determined to break the chains of their enslavement, Africans in the hundreds had revolted or escaped from plantations. Arango knew that the costs and difficulties in maintaining control over the slave population had also mounted. The constant arrival of Africans after 1825 would only pose greater risks and feelings of insecurity among an elite faced with unceasing resistance by slaves.

Another reason for Arango's "remarkable conversion" can be traced to his fears of free blacks.[84] As the number of African slaves increased rapidly after 1790, he warned of alliances that would be forged between African slaves and free blacks. Arango believed that whatever their legal status, slaves and free blacks "have more or less the same complaints and the same motivation for living disgusted with us [the whites]." This could "dispose them to destroy the object they attribute to their degradation [meaning the white population]."[85]

One institution that became a focus of Arango's attention was the militias. Established in the sixteenth century, militias defended Cuba from European aggression and pirate attacks. Due to a shortage of potential white recruits, the government of the colony allowed free blacks and mulattoes to enlist in the militias. Appointment offered upward mobility to free men of color. Benefits included special legal rights and a pension. Many carried arms and were trained in fighting skills. Arango wondered if racial solidarity between militia soldiers and slaves would undermine the presumed loyalty of the former to the island's upper class and colonial government. Of particular concern were men who had retired from black and mulatto battalions.[86] In his 1792 treatise, Arango praised the past contributions of black and mulatto militias, but wrote that "we should not risk their use for internal defense."[87]

Exactly two decades later, in 1812 Arango's worst fears came true. A member of a militia, the free black José Aponte, had followed closely the debates concerning black and mulatto battalions on the island. The steady erosion of rights and respect for the militias fueled Aponte's aversion to Spanish policies. In their review of the *libro de pinturas*, judicial investigators found a map showing the location of the house of "Señor Don Franco de Arango." Professor Childs suggests that "if the map had been drawn to plan the rebellion, Arango's house may have been a target for attack because of his labors to expand slavery and his opposition to the militia."[88] Surely Francisco Arango learned of José Aponte's sketches and actions. African-led slave revolts and the Aponte rebellion led by free blacks caused Arango to call for the extinction of the slave traffic.

In spite of big investments in the traffic by Spanish merchants and their political influence on the island, dissent related to the traffic in Africans widened
in the 1830s. A second reform movement coalesced, led by a group of young
intellectuals, including the writer José Antonio Saco (1797–1879) and literary
critic Domingo del Monte (1804–53).

A well-known observer of Cuban society, Saco claimed free labor was superior to slave labor. An advocate of free trade and modernization, Saco expressed the sentiments of a small group of sugar and coffee planters in the
1830s "who realized that the introduction of the steam engine in sugar production foreshadowed the day when the illiterate African slave would be replaced
by a new type of worker: a wage earner, literate, and therefore able to master
the techniques of processing sugar by machinery."[89] Entrepreneurial in their
worldview, these creoles distrusted Spanish imperial policies. They accused
Spain of having no desire to interrupt the slave trade to Cuba. Instead, Spain
sought to increase the slave population so that slaves would vastly outnumber
whites. In this way, Spanish and creole planters and merchants would remain
dependent on Spain to maintain security on the island.[90] Although he did not
seek to abolish the use of slaves on sugar and coffee estates, Saco considered
the steady import of African slaves to be detrimental to the economic development of the island.

Two important events shaped the opinions of José Saco. Like Arango, Saco
had witnessed the widening of slave and free black resistance from the 1790s.
In an article entitled "Análisis Sobre Brasil" published in the journal *Revista
Bimestre Cubana* (Havana, June 1832), Saco reviewed the book *Notices of Brazil
in 1829 and 1830* (1830) by the Irish curate Robert Walsh. Saco did a comparative analysis of Brazilian society and economy with that of Cuba, claiming
Brazil to be Cuba's "most formidable rival." Saco emphasized that the massive
influx of Africans had caused dire problems in Cuba. He described a "miserable national existence" if a slave revolution erupted on the island similar to
what had occurred in Haiti.[91] Saco also alluded to the recent Baptist Revolt in
Jamaica (1831), which contributed to England's decision to abolish slavery in
the British empire three years later.

Second, Saco pointed to the changing racial composition of the island. In
1775, Europeans composed 56 percent of the island's population and Africans,
slave and freed, 44 percent. By 1827, those numbers had reversed. Rejecting
official estimates which he considered unreliable, Saco claimed that the population of color had risen to 500,000 (62.5 percent) in contrast to a white

minority of 300,000 (37.5 percent).[92] Saco did not want Cuba to become "Africanized." Instead, he desired to "whiten" Cuba by ending the slave traffic and attracting light-skinned European immigrants.

A proponent of the interests of the white creole elite of which he was a part, José Saco recognized their political weakness before Spanish bureaucrats and merchants resident in Cuba.[93] He believed that terminating the slave trade would protect the existing slave property and wealth of fellow creoles. Saco naively hoped that the Spanish Crown would intelligently respond to creole dissent by allowing their participation in decision making in Madrid.[94]

Saco paid the price for his critique of Cuban society and Spanish policies. Influential Spaniards viewed Saco's call to end the slave trade as a façade covering creole aspirations for independence from Spain and a creole agenda to abolish slavery. Soon after his arrival as captain general, Miguel Tacón (1834–38) banished Saco from the island. For the next four decades, Saco wrote from Europe about the need for political reform in Cuba and the suppression of the transatlantic slave trade. Using "special laws" embodied in a royal decree (1837), Spanish authorities in Cuba sought to impede Saco's publications from entering the island.

In an 1837 publication entitled "My First Question: The Abolition of the Slave Trade will ruin or set back Cuban Agriculture?" Saco examined three key reasons why conservative creole planters favored continued slave importations.[95] First, they claimed that only African slaves had the capacity to endure the harsh labor conditions on plantations. Second, only African slaves could survive the heat and infirmities of tropical environments. Third, the immigration of free labor would prove to be too costly for planters, hence profits would rapidly diminish.

Saco refuted all of these claims, asserting that whites had the capacity to labor on plantations and withstand tropical climate and sickness. Furthermore, the employment of free white workers had proven to be less expensive than the costs incurred in maintaining slaves. In envisioning a prosperous Cuba built on free labor and free trade, Saco emphasized to readers that international pressures to terminate the transatlantic slave trade would continue to mount. With more Africans arriving in Cuba, the likelihood of insurrections would only escalate. This in turn could lead to a British intervention and further destabilize the island. Saco's conclusion: Cuban planters needed to adapt to these changing circumstances and halt slave importations immediately.[96]

Born in Venezuela and raised in Cuba, Domingo del Monte also became a major figure on the island. Attracted to liberal thought and ideas about free trade, del Monte traveled to Spain and studied law in Madrid. During this period, he made contact with several Peninsula writers who offered strategies for how best to propagate political ideas through literature. Del Monte also resided in the United States, where he read closely the liberal newspaper *El Habanero* (1824–26) founded by the activist priest Félix Varela and the newspaper published by José Antonio Saco titled *El Mensagero Semanal* (1828–31). Upon his return to Havana, del Monte gathered together a group of intellectuals critical of the censorship and policies imposed on Cuba by the Spanish metropole. In the words of historian José María Auilera-Manzano, this Havana-based group "developed an identity project through literature."[97] With the support of Francisco Arango and sugar planters committed to the modernization of the island, del Monte encouraged journalists, novelists, and poets throughout the island to write about topics relevant to Cuban culture and national interests.

Del Monte gained permission to found a Commission of Literature. Through this entity, the del Monte entourage published the journal *Revista Bimestre Cubana* (1831–34). Accused of fomenting support for independence from Spain, the captain general of Cuba forced the closure of the Commission. In response, del Monte convoked *tertulias* (private gatherings) at his residences in Matanzas and Havana, where authors could meet and discuss politics and culture. From these salon congeries, important publications appeared critical of slavery. Writers included the former slave Juan Francisco Manzano, the mixed race poet Plácido, José de la Luz y Cabellero, and José Victoriano Betancourt.[98] In the novel *Romualdo, One among Many*, the novelist Francisco Calcagno conveyed the sentiments of many of del Monte's followers. "We are in the year 1836. Times are changing: today the slave merchants are beginning to be ashamed of their profession. And it will probably not be long before we will be ashamed of owning slaves. For now there's no reason to reproach anyone for what we all practice: we have the obligation of enlightening people and breaking the veil of concern in order to prepare the day of justice and honor. There's no crime in being a master; only in abusing that role."[99]

Del Monte met David Turnbull in 1838 when the latter visited Cuba for the first time. In an anonymous letter penned by del Monte that Turnbull forwarded to the British government (in 1841), del Monte analyzed three key factors enabling the continuation of the slave trade to the island. First, the Spanish Crown was committed to allowing continued importations to prevent the coalescence of an independence movement. Second, del Monte accused captain generals and local governors of corruption, specifically their receiving enormous bribes paid for every African landed. Third, he alluded to the devious actions of the traffickers who also profited from the commerce in Africans. In del Monte's opinion, "Spain had to be convinced of two things: the presence of a large black population would not deter an independence movement nor would the end of the slave trade lead inevitably to independence."[100]

Del Monte called for political reforms, including representative institutions and a free press. Only by changing popular opinion could the slave trade to Cuba be terminated. Although skeptical that European immigration would be the solution to Cuba's labor demand, del Monte joined with fellow creoles in support of white immigration as a way to bring about a peaceful transition to free labor. In this way, white domination of the island could be assured. In the words of David Murray, "[The royal government in] Madrid decreed that Cuba must be Spanish or belong to the Africans."[101] In contrast, del Monte decreed that Cuba could be creole and belong to the whites.

As black insurgency widened in the early 1840s, del Monte became alarmed over what he saw to be a "future ethiopio-Cuban republic."[102] He deemed that the situation was spinning out of control on the island. Showing his racial bias, del Monte pronounced that "the blacks, as might have been expected, threaten the political and social existence of the colony."[103]

Creole allies who had been attracted to del Monte's agenda deserted him. Forced into exile in May 1843, del Monte traveled first to Philadelphia and then to Paris in January 1844.[104] During the Escalera investigations of 1844, the poet Plácido accused del Monte of having drawn him into the movement. The Military Commission called for his return to Cuba to answer questions about his role in planning the insurrection. Not surprisingly, del Monte refused. For the remainder of his life, he remained in Spain, where he wrote several works about Cuba. A year after del Monte's death in 1853, his remains were returned to Cuba and buried at Matanzas.

MEMORIALS CONDEMNING THE SLAVE TRADE

Pleas to end the disembarkation of African slaves in Cuba continued through the early 1840s. Spanish and creole planters sent *memorials* (letters or communiqués) to the captain general of Cuba and the metropolitan government in Spain that emphasized the social costs and turmoil caused by the rising African slave population on the island. Although desirous of a halt to the traffic, none of the signers of these documents favored immediate emancipation. For that to occur at some undetermined moment in the future, former slaves would need time "to learn the habits of voluntary labor and the customs of regular education."[105]

In a first memorial entitled "To the Provisional Regency of the Kingdom" and signed on February 27, 1841, twelve members of the Society for Progress reacted to pro-abolition articles published in Madrid late the previous year.[106] Composed of Spaniards and foreigners, the Society lamented that "the simple idea that the [Spanish] periodicals (which are here abundantly circulated) are allowed in Madrid to discuss so dangerous a question [emancipation], which will reach our free negroes, and in short time the slaves in the cities and country, has been sufficient to inspire Capitalists and Planters with distrust and anxiety as to the future fate of this island, and they think, with reason, that the period has arrived for them to save what they can of their Capitals, and remove them to other countries that offer more stability and protection." Furthermore, "the inhabitants [of Cuba] would prefer any extremity rather than submit to the granting of freedom to the slaves, which measure they consider calculated to result in the loss of the island, to losing their property, to endangering their lives and subjecting them to the power of the Blacks." Predicting a "Catastrophe," the planters affirmed that "there are no forces that could check the excesses of 500,000 slaves [a better estimate is 320,000], naturally indolent and inclined to dissatisfaction, with whom 200,000 free people of color [145,000], would make common cause [against a white population estimated at 415,000]." Emancipation would result in a "war between the races."

The signees claimed that the publications in Madrid had contributed to the volatile conditions on the island. They considered it imperative to impose strict policies to prevent the dissemination of subversive ideas.

In its biased analysis, the memorial portrayed Cuba as a sort of island paradise. Urban slaves labored on the docks, as drivers of carriages, and in "trades of every kind": "The lowest class at Havana, called the populace, composed as it is of African slaves, and free men from the same sources, [possess] an appearance of respectability, contentment and application to work, such as the best institutions have not been able to attain in Paris or in London. [Their] robust appearance and good deportment bespeak possession of advantages unknown to most of the laborers of Europe. A single beggar of any color, or drunkard, or miserable being to excite the compassion of the public is not to be met with in the streets of this city of slaves." Furthermore, female domestic slaves were "more happy" than urban slave workers:

> From them are selected our nurses, towards whom are preserved the same affection as for our mothers; their children are brought up as companions to ours; the servants who wait more immediately upon the person of their master [gain] a certain intelligence, delicacy of behavior and education, proportioned to their constant communication with the best of society. Their deportment and manners are superior to those of the white men in the fields and manufactories, and they would not exchange their mode of life for that of any laborer who has to earn his own living. The habit of being with them from childhood creates a sympathy in the inhabitants of Cuba for the whole race, and it is never heard that a person of delicacy commits an excess in the correction of his servants.

With regard to the thousands of slaves who toiled on the island's plantations, they "often work at a distance from the master [implying welcomed independence], possess a decent dwelling which, according to the ability of the master, ranges between a capacious hut for a family and a room in a commodious building. On the most economical [estate], they receive a daily ration of eight ounces of salt meat, stewed with nutritious roots, which they divide into two meals, one at eleven in the forenoon and the other retiring from their work at sunset. A small piece of land [a subsistence plot] is given them, which they cultivate on Sunday raising grain and green vegetables with which they vary their daily food and they are also permitted to breed pigs and poultry in an enclosure near their dwellings."

The first memorial appealed for an end to slave importations with the stipulation that numerous white European immigrants would be transported to the island. This enterprise would be paid for with government funds and would be under the direction of the Society for Progress. "We [need] a sufficient number of white laborers to reduce the wages so low, as to give them preference for agriculture, on the score of the economy, to the labor of blacks. This would have been, and still is, the only plan by which to abolish entirely the slave trade, without destroying the crops and to prepare gradually whatever improvements the government may in its wisdom dictate, to free us hereafter from the fatal and unavoidable necessity we are now under of harboring a numerous slave population."

In a second undated memorial most likely penned shortly after February 1841, the City Corporation of Havana (*Ayuntamiento*) further expressed disquiet over the prospect of emancipation:

The existence of the white class is that which may and ought to prevent emancipation, and the inhabitants of the island of Cuba who have no blame in that their government permitted and even protected the abominable trade in slaves, have more justice [a greater right] to seek the preservation of their lives than the slave race to demand their liberty. This liberty may in abstract respects be just, but the preservation of the white population is no less just and due, nor ought the local circumstances to be forgotten which render emancipation impossible. In the abstract the liberty of the minor and of the insane is just, but other reasons prevent it, and those who, affecting philanthropy, should declaim against the authority of fathers and guardians, would be as unjust as those who seek for an emancipation for which the slaves are not prepared. Masters would not allow projects for the transition [to free labor], and such transitions would create confusions. . . .

What would be the use that the slaves would make of their liberty? Immersed in an ignorance which they would not lose when declared free, destitute of property, or knowledge, without any stimulus to acquire or accumulate, their sloth and idleness so much the more lamentable as they are the most numerous, and cannot preserve their existence without perpetuating their crimes, without revenging impiously and barbarously, the former loss of their liberty, and without making incompatible their existence with that of their present masters.[107]

In comparing conditions with Europe and nearby Jamaica after emancipation (post-1834), the authors of the Havana memorial posited that the "mild slavery" practiced in Cuba was superior to free labor.

Political economy will be able to demonstrate that those countries are more productive in which labor is performed by free hands, than in those that experience the consequences of domestic slavery; but when compared, not the production of two people of distinct laws and manners, but the labor of a working slave with that of another free living both in the same place, when it is observed that the consumption and expenses of this are less than those of the freeman, it will not be possible to recognize the greater utility of [free] labor enforced by misery and pauperism over the labor exacted by a mild slavery.

This second memorial of 1841 from the City Corporation of Havana condemned the "execrable traffic in Africa." Echoing the position of the Society for Progress, they called on Cuba's government to "carry then into effect the abolition of the traffic, but its clandestine and hateful continuance ought not to produce the total ruin of the island of Cuba." Noting that the expansion of the traffic had contributed to the widening of slave resistance, the memorial warned that "if the increased number of slaves were in more contact with the free class of people of color, if the difficulties [physical separation] were removed which subordination and isolation of the slaves present, so that commotions might be prepared, full soon would confirm the experience of Cuba, as has confirmed that of San Domingo [the Haitian Revolution], the presage of that in these islands the black race would exterminate the white, which at its time [subsequently] would prevail on the continent." It is striking that nearly four decades after the Haitian Revolution, the "specter of Haiti" remained central to elite discourse in Cuba.

As the two memorials of 1841 make clear, white planters and merchants resident in Cuba did not seek emancipation. What they did confirm is that an observer would be "ignorant of the human heart to suppose that the desires to destroy the white population [by slaves] did not exist." Echoing Domingo del Monte, they posited that "those who exaggerate the sufferings of slavery ought to consider that its evils are less than those which would bring extermination to the white class, and that this island would be lost to civilization and commerce, if a degraded and ignorant class [freed slaves] were to preside over its destinies."[108] Internal conditions in Cuba fueled by the actions of slaves and free blacks induced the authors to take a position critical of the slave trade. These men believed that the continuation of the traffic to Cuba would inevitably undermine future stability and security on the island.

Two subsequent memorials continued in this vein. In a letter sent to the captain general in late November 1843, ninety "persons of much respectability" resident at Matanzas alluded to tense conditions witnessed on estates in that region during the previous months.[109]

> The slave race, sir, has already a marked tendency to rise in insurrection; the breakings out of this tendency are the partial movements which occurred in this sole [past] year at Bemba, and lately on the estate Triumverato of this jurisdiction. To the paternal government of your Excellency, it belongs to hear the general cry against a contraband trade, which if it continues, will compromise more every day the political existence of this meritorious Antilles [Cuba], by swelling the number and strengthening the power of that race. . . .
>
> The risings at Bemba, and the Triumvirato, were suffocated in their beginning. But the death of 300 negroes has diminished in a great degree the fortune of the well deserving proprietors. And what is more the innocent victims, immolated by the barbarity of those desperate savages, call from the tomb to prevent the repetition of scenes so horrid and bloody. . . . But, Sir, no measure

will be completely efficacious, while the slave race continues, by means of contraband [slave importations], strengthening itself and receiving new stimulants and ailments. . . .

It does not demand much penetration to know where may extend the consequences of the preponderance of this colored population, slave and free. Happy it were if so near, Haiti did not present an example that horrorizes, in order never to neglect the arriving of the second edition of such a work [a second Haitian Revolution].

It is time, Sir, that should disappear from among us this contraband trade, shame of our civilization, and horrid abyss where are buried all our hopes of security and future well being: Hydra which frightens the capitalists who come to establish themselves, and drives hence, with their fortunes, those who have acquired them, in order to place them where they may enjoy them without fear of danger. To Your Excellency, is reserved so feat a glory. Your Excellency will solidly cement the happiness and tranquility of Cuba, and secure forever to the Crown of Castille its most precious gem, by prosecuting with firmness the contraband trade of African negroes, into effecting its total extinction.

The 1843 Matanzas memorial was handed to Governor Antonio Garcia Oña of Matanzas with the request that it be forwarded to Captain General Leopoldo O'Donnell. Angered by the letter, Oña tore it up in front of the delegation that had delivered it to him. Oña informed them that "the expression of such opinions would not be favorably received by the government."[110]

Undeterred, a planter named Benigno Gener sent a copy of the letter directly to Captain General O'Donnell:

I put in the hands of Your Excellency a faithful copy of a representation addressed to their protectorate authority by merchants, proprietors and occupiers of estates of this city [Matanzas], whose names go at the foots of the copy referred to. The whole idea of the representation was suggested by the present circumstances of the country, or I shall better say by the events lately taken place on the estate Triumvirato, which have followed so nearly no less disastrous ones of Bemba, and Macuriges [region of Matanzas], and have put just and natural excitement in the minds of the white population of this jurisdiction. It was the object of this exposition to Your Excellency to call attention to this state of disquiet and trouble in which we are living. It is shown in it to Your Excellency, as the first and principal cause of these inquietudes the clandestine introduction of African slaves into this island, which in spite of the vigilance of our authorities, continue to effect, to the scandal of the good, a handful of men, in whose hearts there exists no feeling of justice, and who fear neither the commands of

God or the laws of men. With this we proceed supplicating Your Excellency to employ all the resources of your power to provide the remedy, which our painful situation demands. The moment being nigh already of raising to Your Excellency the original, it was taken hold of by the Governor of this city, and all those subscribing it saw themselves deprived, in this manner, of the consolation hope promised them, that the public inquietude should cease, when Your Excellency advised of our danger, should deign to cast a look of compassion on this loyal colony, now to be found in a crisis so full of anguish. The subscriber, a neighbor of this city, whom only animates his loyalty, and love of this country, where he first saw the light, hopes in addressing this document to Your Excellency that you will pardon this liberty which he has taken, in consideration of the purity of his intentions.

God Preserve Your Excellency many years. Matanzas, December 8, 1843, signed Benigno Gener[111]

Planters near Havana followed with a fourth memorial soon after. Directed to O'Donnell, the signees came "with due respect to expound to you the fears, which [Cuba's] present situation inspires [in] them, deeply involved in its tranquility and well being, by the frequent risings [slave rebellions] which occur in our fields. Among us there is already a sufficient number of laborers to cultivate our fields. We do not need for our rural flourishing [well-being] and prosperity new immigrations of Africans, who may compromise us so much." The planters pointed to the examples of French Caribbean islands and the U.S. South, where the enslaved population had increased by "natural reproduction" after slave importations had been halted. "And how sad must not be our anticipations for the future, when we seek to adopt measures, even supposing they may have an unfavorable influence on our wealth? This only will prove how persuaded we are of our total ruin, if an end not be put to the trade in slaves, and if we do not provide with energy for the security of our lands."[112] Aware of the content of this memorial, O'Donnell refused to accept it.

The government did not take lightly the memorials. Merchants and planters involved in the traffic viewed these communiqués as undermining their political influence and putting in jeopardy the spectacular profits derived from the sale of African slaves. As the investigations of the Escalera insurgency widened in 1844, individuals who signed the memorials were swept up in the dragnet. One of them was Benigno Gener, described by British consul Kennedy as "a respectable, wealthy and intelligent landed proprietor, whose real offense evidently is that of having been active in getting up the Memorial against the Slave Trade, as reported last February 20, and afterwards sending it, with a letter, in his own name [letter of December 1843 above], to the Captain General, and allowing the same to be made public here, so as afterwards to reach the newspapers in Spain."[113]

Warned of his impending arrest, Gener fled from the island. Several colleagues believed that "in so doing, he acted prudently to escape the horrors of imprisonment and the mockery of forms of justice; but his flight will of course be now charged on him as a proof of guilt. As if he, whose real interest was the tranquility of the island, and that tranquility as he believed dependent on the suppression of the slave trade, could possibly be engaged in a plot to give up the island to the black population, by the murder of fellow whites, and the destruction of their property! The present implication appears manifestly therefore only an act of revenge, for the part he took in the Memorial against the slave trade, and the conduct of the government."[114]

Others were not so lucky. Based "on a charge by a negro under lash" of abolitionist sympathies, Martínez Serrano was imprisoned on May 1. "A person of property, having an estate with one hundred and thirty negroes, he held several offices of honor and trust in this city. He is a man of the highest character, with a family of eight children, and yet was kept seventy-three days without any communication with them solely on this charge." Asked if he knew the British abolitionist and former commissioner on the island Mr. Trumbul [sic], Serrano denied that he had met or interacted in any way with David Turnbull.

The real motive for the arrest of Serrano related to his criticism of the slave trade and the allure of the wealth he possessed. A member of the Royal Patriotic Society in Havana, an entity composed of some 350 prominent residents, Serrano had penned two Reports critical of the slave trade to Cuba. In one of those, he pointed to "the great danger of allowing slaves to contest their condition [of illegal enslavement] in the courts . . . and they could rely on the sympathies of the formidable mass of liberated persons [free blacks] which already exists, and which would receive reinforcements so much the more effective, as that those who may compose it would preserve more latent those sympathies, more fresh and active the desire of revenge, and all their passions fierce and antisocial."[115] In a second Report, Serrano "had referred, very unwisely, to the 'ounces of gold' which had been paid [to corrupt officials of the colonial government] for the introduction of negroes, in contravention of the laws. This evidently was the real offence for which he has been thus punished."[116]

Tensions fomented by the resistance of slaves and free blacks fueled criticism of the slave trade. As thousands of Africans arrived on Cuban shores, planters faced insurrections and violent confrontations with slaves. Several residents reacted by penning memorials that demanded a halt to slave importations. Most did not seek to abolish the institution of slavery, but rather desired to secure a slave regime that had been profoundly destabilized by the arrivals of rebellious Africans.

IMPORTATIONS CONTINUE

The slave traffic to Cuba flourished in the first years of the 1840s. The British commissioners of the Mixed Commission Court at Havana counted forty-four slaving expeditions in 1840 that landed 14,470 slaves in Cuba; twenty-seven expeditions in 1841 that transported 9,776 slaves; nine expeditions in 1842 that landed an estimated 3,000 Africans; nineteen slaving expeditions that landed 8,000 slaves in 1843; and twenty-one expeditions that disembarked 10,000 Africans in 1844.[117] Evidence of the traffic to and from Cuba in 1843 is presented in Table 3 in the Appendix.

Throughout 1843, traffickers based in Havana sent vessels to Africa, Brazil, and the United States. In July, the well-known trafficker Pedro Blanco sent the U.S. brig *Elsanore* to West Africa in search of a slave cargo. That same month the U.S. trafficker Charles Tyng dispatched the U.S. schooner *Boston* to Rio de Janeiro with the intention that it partake in the traffic. In November, the merchant house controlled by Don Julian Zulueta dispatched the U.S. barque *Chester* to New York City to pick up cargo and then proceed to West Africa.[118] In the first eight months of 1843, observers estimated at least 4,500 Africans were landed near Matanzas. Recently landed Africans joined in the insurrections of that year. Those from the "Lucumí nation, one notorious for its desperate character, played a leading role."[119]

One of the expeditions that landed slaves in Cuba in 1843 (included in Table 3) was the *Constancia*, a brigantine of 242 tons built in New York in 1835–36. Having previously sailed four or five times on slaving voyages under the names of *Voladora* and *Scorpion*, the vessel carried a crew of 44 men armed with cannon, muskets, blunderbusses, and cutlasses.[120] *Constancia* departed West Africa with 563 Africans in four compartments holding girls, women, boys, and men. Fifty-one of the Africans died during the Middle Passage, and two jumped overboard to their death.[121]

Just off the Guamá river on the south coast of Cuba, sailors from the U.S. cruiser *Vincennes* boarded *Constancia* in early March 1843. On deck they encountered three Spanish Custom House officials. After a review of the ship's papers and assurance to the captain that *Constancia* could continue on its voyage, the U.S. lieutenant in charge requested that the hatches be removed. "We saw lower decks filled with negroes, miserably stowed and closely crowded together, but they seemed healthy, well fed and quite clean." In spite of its obvious illegal activity, Lieutenant Mitchell refused to seize the *Constancia*. He wrote that "the traffic is in every way horrid and atrocious, but we (Americans) can never give material aid in its suppression under existing laws. Nothing but resistance would have entitled us to capture this vessel, which would be viewed by every *other* nation as a pirate." Similar to the British having no right to capture vessels flying a U.S. flag (due to U.S. refusal to sign a treaty), this lieutenant followed international law prohibiting the U.S. Squadron from seizing a foreign vessel with slaves on board.[122]

The appointment of General Leopold O'Donnell to replace Gerónimo Valdes as governor general of the island in October 1843 inspired traffickers to expand their operations. As noted above, O'Donnell was seen as sympathetic to investors and the commerce in Africans. Besides the departure of vessels obviously involved in the traffic, "great demand continued for goods and articles suitable for the African market." Cuban rum (aguardiente) increased in price from twelve dollars a pipe up to twenty dollars a pipe in the last quarter of the year. Traffickers submitted "extensive orders" for shackles, casks, and boilers produced at factories in the United States.[123]

In spite of the optimism exhibited by the slave bloc, the traffic entered a depression in 1845. Several factors contributed to this downturn (see the estimates of the number of expeditions and number of African slaves disembarked in Table 4 in the Appendix). One was that the slave resistance exhibited during the previous decade culminating in the Escalera insurgency caused apprehension. Writing from Sierra Leone, British commissioners Michael Melville and James Hook considered it "probable that the list of Spanish vessels [adjudicated at the Mixed Commission Court at Freetown in 1844] would have been even larger than it is but for the temporary depressing effect which the recent disturbances among the slave population of Cuba has had in creating a want of confidence on the part of the slave traders (especially the Portuguese and Brazilians) on this coast and deterring them from making large shipments to the West Indies on speculation."[124] Within Cuba, the slave revolts impacted demand and the price paid for African slaves. In late 1843, prices decreased by one-third from the beginning of the year, with planters paying two hundred dollars each. "A strong declaration of opinion [has been] expressed by the holders of property on the danger to be apprehended from the further introduction of negroes from Africa."[125] In one episode, acting governor of Matanzas Don Fulgencio Salas prohibited some five hundred Africans to come to shore "on account of the unsettled state of the country."[126]

An increased presence and effectiveness of the British Squadron on the coast of West Africa also played a role in disrupting the traffic. The number of captured vessels brought to Sierra Leone and judged in the Mixed Commission Courts rose from seventeen in 1843 to twenty-nine in 1844. British cruisers intercepted several vessels at the Bight of Benin involved in the transport of Africans from Lagos to Bahia. Spanish ships were quick to respond to this interruption by entering that lucrative route.[127] One unfortunate result of the success of the British Squadron along the coast of West Africa was that the number of Africans held in several barracoons rose significantly, "occasioning much disease and mortality from the crowded state of these places and a scarcity of food."[128]

Environmental factors also played a role in the downturn in landings of Africans after 1844. The sugar trade entered into a "general depression" due to an extended drought during that year. The number of sugar boxes exported decreased from 847,000 (approximately 170 tons) in 1844 to 365,912 boxes in 1845. A massive hurricane in October 1844 destroyed hundreds of coffee farms.[129] By the end of the decade, owners transferred some forty thousand slaves out of coffee and into sugar production. All of the above diminished the availability of and demand for African slaves.

One other variable that impacted the traffic to Cuba was the shift of international capital into the slave trade to Brazil. (See Table 4, Appendix.) Several merchant houses in Havana maintained close ties with merchant houses in Brazil. Numerous vessels fitted out in Havana or other locales in Cuba sailed to Africa and returned to Brazil with slaves. Other ships journeyed from Cuba directly to Brazil and then entered into the bilateral traffic from Brazil to Africa and back to Brazil. Writing in mid-1845, the ever wary British commissioners at Cuba James Kennedy and Campbell Dalrymple explained that "it is said that all the slave dealers [in Cuba] have ordered all their cargoes for the present to be taken to the Brazils, [due to] the price of negroes here continuing very low, and the planters being in so very depressed a condition as to afford no prospect of their being bought at remunerating prices. We regret to say that the slave dealers and their friends show no symptoms of any discontinuance of the trade."[130]

U.S. capital quickly adapted to the changing international markets of the mid-1840s. U.S. shipbuilders constructed larger and more efficient ships.[131] U.S. merchants moved money and information around the Atlantic world. U.S. captains and crews willingly joined in slave voyages and offered the U.S. flag as protection against interception. U.S. interests inserted themselves into the traffic to Brazil and played a central role in transporting Africans to that country.[132]

The southern triangle linking Cuba and Brazil with Africa reached its apogee (as described in chapter one) in the 1840s. With the disappearance of the slave trade to Brazil in 1850–51, the northern triangle connecting the United States and Cuba with Africa took precedence once again.[133]

CONCLUSION

External events caused the upper class and their allies in the government of Cuba to ponder the future of the transatlantic slave trade in the first half of the nineteenth century. These included disquiet over the possibility of a second Haitian Revolution in Cuba; prohibition of the slave trade in the British empire (1807) and to the United States (1808); abolitionist decrees distributed during the Latin American independence movements (1810–25); debates in the Spanish Cortes about ending the slave trade to Cuba; major slave revolts in Barbados (1816), Demerara (1823), Jamaica (1823, 1831), and Salvador, Brazil (1835); England's emancipation decree ending slavery in the British Caribbean islands (1834); an expansion of the international abolitionist movement from the 1820s; the arrival of the British Squadron and captured slaving vessels in Cuban ports; and the appearance of British activists in Cuba from the late 1830s. These diverse external pressures took unwelcome local embodiment in one form by the presence of Liberated Africans in Cuba's urban areas and countryside.[134]

Internal conditions in Cuba also played a major role in instigating political debates related to the traffic in Africans to Cuba. Traffickers landed hundreds of sick Africans in Cuba from the end of the eighteenth century until the demise of the slave trade in the late 1860s. Measures such as establishing lazarettos and inoculating recently landed Africans did little to impede the spread of infections. Thousands of inhabitants in cities and countryside became ill and died. Various observers emphasized that a steady stream of disembarkations posed a major threat to public health.

Recalcitrant slaves became a paramount concern for the elite and government. Day-to-day resistance, tens of slave revolts between the early 1790s and 1844, and the Escalera insurgency all had African roots. Escaped slave communities increased in number through the 1820s, 1830s, and 1840s.[135] These events caused significant disruptions for merchants, planters, and colonial officials. The scale of the brutalities inflicted on slaves and free blacks in the repression that followed La Escalera reflected the apprehension of Cuba's white elite. Several scholars have described this moment as a turning point in Cuba's history.[136] In the wake of La Escalera, expeditions of slave ships to Cuba dropped off precipitously.

In spite of all the external and internal pressures that might have brought a close to this business, the traffic resumed full force in the late 1840s and continued until the late 1860s. Short-term profit and greed overrode all inhibitions. Corruption reigned. Cuba's colonial government effectively stifled domestic protests against the slave trade. Soldiers and private militias clamped down on slave resistance. It would take another two decades of struggle to force the final demise of the traffic to Cuba.

5

SLAVE RESISTANCE AND THE SUPPRESSION OF THE SLAVE TRADE TO BRAZIL IN 1850

———— ∞ ————

A debate exists over why the transatlantic slave trade to Brazil ended in 1850. One interpretation focuses on the Brazilian government. This can be described as the "Enlightenment School." Senators, representatives, and provincial governors maintained a close alliance with planters and merchants who produced sugar, coffee, tobacco, cotton, food crops, swine, and cattle. A high priority for these men was social stability. Pedro II and his ministers also paid close attention to international politics, specifically British initiatives to halt the slave trade to Brazil.[1] They adroitly responded to British suppression efforts in the wake of passage of an 1845 declaration in England (the Aberdeen Bill), which allowed the British Squadron to seize Brazilian ships seen to be involved in the transport of slaves.[2] Viewed through this lens, the combined actions of Brazilian statesmen and the British navy brought an end to importations of African slaves.

The Enlightenment School minimizes social pressures from below, specifically slave resistance, as a factor in forcing an end to the traffic. Fifteen years previous to the Eusébio de Queiroz Law, which effectively outlawed the slave trade to Brazil, a slave rebellion broke out in the city of Salvador, Bahia, that came to be known as the Revolt of the Malês (Muslims). The Enlightenment School contends that the revolt proved to be "inconsequential regarding slaveholding in Brazil generally, or in Bahia, at least after 1835."[3] The revolt's minimal impact is confirmed by the fact that there was no disruption in the transport of African slaves to Brazilian shores.

Historians associated with the Enlightenment School believe that memory of that Muslim-led rebellion and the huge influx of African slaves in its wake had little to do with the political decision to halt the traffic in 1850. One writes that "none of them [what the author labels as the 'reactionaries,' this being a group of influential political leaders, including President Francisco Gonçalves Martins, Minister of Foreign Affairs Paulino José Soares de Sousa, and Minister of Justice Eusébio de Queiroz] called for the [transatlantic slave] trade's repression out of fear that slavery itself posed a fatal security risk."[4]

A second perspective on why the slave trade to Brazil ended focuses on resistance by slaves and free blacks. This will be described as the "Subaltern School." One of its proponents is the Bahian historian João José Reis, who has written that "the revolt in Bahia [of 1835] caused apprehension in the north and the south of Brazil, in cities and countryside. Its impact on the rest of the nation was immediate, causing authorities in Rio de Janeiro [at the *Corte*, meaning the ministers who led the empire] and various local authorities [in several provinces] to take actions [to ensure] public security and it reinvigorated the debate over [the continuation] of the international slave traffic [to Brazil] and over the institution of slavery."[5]

This chapter posits that the Malê Revolt made a deep impression on numerous Brazilians, including both elite and common folk. Memory of the revolt combined with other manifestations of slave resistance played a role in shaping imperial politics and decisions from 1848 to 1851. It is a key variable that forced a halt to the transatlantic slave trade to Brazil at mid-century.

THE MALÊ REVOLT, SLAVE RESISTANCE, AND THE THREATS POSED BY IMPORTATION OF AFRICAN SLAVES

As in Cuba, the disembarkation of thousands of African slaves resulted in a cycle of thirty slave revolts and conspiracies in Bahia in the first three decades of the nineteenth century. Insurgencies occurred in Salvador, suburban towns, and interior regions of the province. Hausa and Yoruba Africans from West Africa played leading roles in these events. In the words of Professor Reis, "constant defiance [by African slaves] caused slavery and ethnic relations in Bahia to be especially charged during those years."[6]

In May 1807, hard-line governor João Saldanha da Gama learned of a planned insurrection by Africans resident in Salvador. The plot included setting fire to buildings in the city and seizing ships in the harbor with the goal of returning to Africa. The reaction was fierce. Authorities executed two Hausa Africans accused of being the ringleaders, one a slave and the other a former slave. Eleven other Hausas received 150 lashes in public. Determined to prevent future conspiracies from hatching, Saldanha forbade Africans from meeting together or gathering for festivities in and around Salvador, and prohibited freed Africans (*libertos*) from moving unimpeded within the city and into the Recôncavo (a fertile region outside of Salvador and bordering the Bay of All Saints, some sixty miles in length and thirty miles in breadth, which included numerous sugar plantations).

Two years later, in January 1809, a group of three hundred Hausa *quilombolas* (escaped slaves residing at a quilombo) attacked the town of Nazaré de Farinhas located in the south of the Recôncavo. Troops and local militia quickly put down the revolt and captured eighty-three men and twelve women. Other participants fled and wreaked havoc in the following weeks. Evidence showed that Jeje, Nagô, and Hausa slaves were involved in the siege. In response, provincial authorities imposed further controls over African slaves, for example, outlawing all dances during day or night and instituting stricter evening curfews. These edicts did little to halt the uprisings.

In February 1814, a force of 250 African *quilombolas* who had escaped from Salvador raided the fishing village of Itapuã, situated some twenty-five kilometers north of Salvador. They burned fishing nets and killed several individuals, including a prominent merchant along with male and female slaves who refused to join in the revolt. Composed of Nagô, Hausa, and Africans of other ethnicities, the insurgents shouted "Death to Whites and Mulattoes." From Itapuã, the small army headed in the direction of the Recôncavo, burning down houses and setting fire to plantations. Near the town of Santo Amaro, troops sent by the governor entered battle against the Africans. The former rode horses and fired their guns during the conflagration. The latter fought with bows and arrows, sickles, and hatchets. A few of the Africans rode horses. Within an hour, the soldiers defeated the insurgents. Fifty-eight Africans and fourteen soldiers died in the fighting. Several rebels escaped. As in the previous outbreaks, authorities executed leaders of the uprising and carried out public floggings of captured Africans. In this instance, twenty-three of the insurgents, most likely all of them freedmen, were deported from Brazil to the town of Benguela in Angola.

Less than a month later, Hausas struck again, this time on sugar plantations near the Recôncavo town of Maragogipe. Seeking to keep an appearance of calm, Governor Dom Marcos de Noronha, known as the count of Arcos, downplayed this uprising. Little is known of its outcome. Two years later, in February 1816, African slaves in the towns of Santo Amaro and São Francisco do Conde rebelled. They burned plantations, attacked houses, and killed several whites, as well as slaves who refused to join in the insurgency. Investigations showed that the insurgents had been in contact with slaves who resided on the outskirts of Salvador several miles away. The revolt caused a "state of panic among local landowners, rich and poor."[7] Influential planters demanded that the provincial government do more to ensure tranquility. One proposal required that owners punish any slave caught away from their property without a pass with 150 lashes of a whip. Perhaps due to a tightening of controls over slaves, no major uprisings occurred for the next six years.

During 1822, slaves rebelled three times in Bahia. The first revolt occurred in May at a plantation situated on the island of Itaparica. During the fighting, thirty-two Africans died and eighty were wounded. In a second uprising in September, African-born freedmen and slaves fought against whites and *mestiços* (a Portuguese term meaning mulattoes). In December, an estimated two hundred slaves attacked Brazilian troops stationed near Salvador, this happening in the midst of Brazil's war for independence against Portugal. Brazilian troops captured a large contingent of slave insurgents, fifty-two of whom they executed immediately, while others were flogged.

At least a dozen slave uprisings, slave conspiracies, and military attacks on *quilombos* occurred in the decade that followed. All of these events occurred in the countryside, except for a major uprising in Salvador in 1830. Two episodes are noted. In December 1826, Nagô and Hausa Africans resident at the quilombo known as Urubu (translated as Vulture) fought off slave hunters who laid siege to the enclave. During a brief battle, fifty of these escaped slaves fought with fierce determination and a variety of weapons, including swords and shotguns. The hunters took several prisoners while other *quilombolas* fled into the backcountry. One of the captured Africans was a woman named Zeferina. During interrogations, she stated that the rebels had plans to attack Salvador on Christmas Eve, kill all the white residents, and gain their freedom.

In November 1828, after days of rumors of an impending insurrection, slaves revolted on a sugar plantation near the town of Santo Amaro in the Recôncavo. After killing the overseer and several creole slaves, the Africans set siege to the main house. The owner's wife barely escaped with the help of loyal slaves. The insurgents attempted to burn down several buildings, but a steady rain prevented the fires from spreading. Troops successfully put down the revolt, with one soldier being wounded and numerous insurgents killed. To address the revolts, governor of Bahia José Egydio Gordilho de Barbuda, known as the viscount of Camamú, sent troop reinforcements to patrol the sugar districts permanently. Aware that this policy would only partially halt the unrest, the governor nevertheless hoped that such a presence would prevent a conflagration similar to what had occurred in Haiti. Adding to the turbulence of these months, an unknown party or persons assassinated Governor Barbuda in February 1830.

In the revolt of April 1830 in Salvador, nearly twenty Africans laid siege to three hardware stores located along a road which connected parishes that bordered the port to the upper city. Fought off by the owners, the Africans nevertheless took away fifteen swords and long knives. They proceeded to a nearby depot where they freed several Africans who had recently disembarked from slave vessels. Eighteen of these Africans who refused to go along were executed. The insurgent force, now numbering over one hundred, proceeded to a police station and killed one soldier. Alerted to the outbreak, troop reinforcements soon arrived. After a short battle, the Africans fled. Police and soldiers hunted down the fugitives. Several Africans were lynched and more than fifty beaten to death. The outbreak showed that "the white man's social and political center [Salvador] had quite a capacity to fight back. No matter how paralyzed Bahians may have been by the daring surprise attack from Africans within the city, they also showed themselves to be surprisingly quick and ready for a counterattack. They were also cruel. Future conspirators would have much to think about and plan before they attempted another adventure of that type."[8]

Three points need to be highlighted with regard to the African slave resistance in Bahia between 1807 and 1835. First, it appears that no Brazilian-born creole slaves or free blacks participated in the revolts or plots. Although rumors surfaced of creole involvement in a supposed conspiracy in May 1814, these could have been hatched by planters critical of what they perceived to be the lenient policies of Governor Noronha (count of Arcos). Creole slaves' refusal to join in African-led insurgencies was not unique to Bahia. Indeed, creole slaves commonly exhibited conservative values under the slave regimes of the Americas. Given familial ties and aspirations of gaining emancipation, creole slaves often did not see aligning themselves with rebellious Africans as a wise strategy.[9] The elite of Bahia encouraged such attitudes by coopting free blacks into the city police force, regular Army, and the National Guard.

Second, many of the Yoruba slaves and freedpersons who participated in the revolts in Bahia came from the same region in West Africa as enslaved Yoruba who were transported to Cuba. Traffickers embarked close to one million Yoruba from the Bight of Benin between 1780 and 1850, the majority destined for Bahia and Cuba. Known as Nagô in Bahia and Lucumí in Cuba, their origins could be traced to Yorubaland, a region located in present-day Nigeria, Benin, and Togo. Having been captured and sold as slaves during the civil wars that tore apart the Oyo empire from the 1790s, the Yoruba brought cosmopolitan views, experience as warriors, and diverse skills with them to the Americas.[10] By the 1860s, some ten thousand Yoruba resided in Salvador, representing close to 80 percent of the African-born slave population there.[11]

Last, Islam became influential among the Africans of Bahia. From the beginning of the nineteenth century, traffickers transported a few thousand Muslim Hausa and Yoruba to Bahia. This occurred due to the expansion of Islam into Yorubaland and subsequent fighting that resulted in the enslavement of defeated Muslims. Although a minority among the total slave population in Bahia, Muslim Nagô (Malês) gained renown for their knowledge and leadership skills. Some could read and write in Arabic. They knew about their past in Africa and in Bahia. Although they embraced militant Islam, their religious beliefs inspired them to engage with fellow Africans in hopes of conversion.[12] Muslim Hausa and Nagô participated in at least two of the revolts in Bahia between 1807 and 1830. It was a group of Muslim Nagô who planned the Revolt of the Malês in Salvador, the largest urban slave rebellion in the history of the Americas.

In the early hours of Sunday, January 25, 1835, an estimated six hundred African slaves and freedmen, many in white dress worn by Muslims, ran through the streets of Salvador shouting and shooting guns. One war cry heard from the rebels was "Long Live the Nagôs." They claimed a desire to kill whites, *pardos* (persons of mixed race, mulattoes), and *creoles* (blacks born in Brazil), and for slaves to gain their freedom. The leaders hoped to forge an "African front" that would attract Africans of diverse ethnicities, along with Muslim and non-Muslim, to their cause. Unfortunately, this did not occur. The rebels succeeded in recruiting only a few Africans of other ethnic backgrounds resident in the city, such as Hausa, Tapa, Borno, Gurma, and Jeje.

For four hours, the insurgents fought against a larger force estimated at 1,500 men.[13] This included police, cavalry, National Guard soldiers, and civilians who possessed swords, knives, clubs, and pistols. The revolt failed. At least seventy rebels died, perhaps double that number were wounded. Nine persons who fought to put down the uprising lost their lives.[14]

Among the 292 rebels (176 African slaves, 112 freed Africans, and 4 whose status is not known) arrested in the aftermath of the revolt, 73 percent were Nagô Africans. Given that the Nagô represented 30 percent of all Africans resident in Salvador in 1835, their involvement in the revolt was substantial.[15] Numerous Nagô paying homage to Islam arrived in Bahia in slave ships; other Nagô slaves and former slaves had converted. Perhaps one-fifth (4,400) of the African population of Salvador (22,000) in 1835 were Muslim, a significant portion of these individuals being Nagô.[16] Hence, observers viewed the slave revolt as including a substantial Muslim presence among its leadership and followers.

The revolt inspired dire warnings. Writing a day after the Malê Revolt, a French consul stationed in Salvador commented that "the agglomeration in Bahia of negroes of the Nagô nation places at all moments this province in danger [of slave rebellion] due to the perfect unanimity of language, of desires, of displeasure and hatred that joins these men together in unity, [men who are] intelligent, strong and courageous."[17] One week later, rumors spread of an impending attack on Salvador by a group of "mulattoes and blacks" residing in the Rio Vermelho (Red River) neighborhood a short distance to the north of the city. The governor of the province issued orders to prepare for another uprising. "Bahia seemed to be in a state of siege. The consternation was universal. Natives and foreigners were summoned to arm. Great were the preparations."[18] To protect the house of a U.S. citizen, the captain of the U.S. corvette Erie landed U.S. Marines onshore.[19] Two days later, British residents took solace in the arrival of the warship HMS North Star into the Bay of All Saints.[20]

Bahian authorities were quick to respond. The provincial government sent to Africa at public expense one ship with 150 free Africans on board. Of these, 120 were former slaves who had gained their freedom and were labeled "suspected persons," and the other 30 were Liberated Africans removed from slave vessels captured by the British Squadron and residing in Salvador.[21] Owners purchased licenses to deport 380 African slaves to other provinces of Brazil. Of these, 136 were Nagô. By the first months of 1836, another seven hundred African freedpersons had received passports to allow departure from Bahia. Officials facilitated this emigration by speeding the applications through the bureaucracy.[22]

The Malê revolt added to the disquiet provoked by the huge number of African slaves being transported to Brazil. A journalist writing in the prestigious

Jornal do Comércio in Rio de Janeiro emphasized that the slave trade should be viewed as "an element of discordance and of future perturbations."[23] Less than a month later, another Rio newspaper, *Aurora Fluminense*, included the alarming statement made by the governor of Bahia at the opening of the Bahian Provincial Assembly: "Every slave disembarked on our beaches is a fresh barrel of gunpowder thrown into a mine shaft, the explosion of which is capable of producing horrific results."[24]

In mid-March 1835, representatives to the Provincial Assembly of Rio de Janeiro articulated their concerns in a letter to imperial ministers: "An insurrection of slaves at Bahia appears to menace the total ruin, not merely of that beautiful portion of the Empire, but also of all the other provinces, among which that of Rio de Janeiro cannot fail to be the first to feel the effect of so fatal a cause whether by its vicinity, by the disproportionate number of slaves it employs in its extensive and opulent agriculture, or by the impolitic mixture of free blacks who are preserved amongst us."[25]

At the end of March, British envoy Henry S. Fox wrote that "the terror that is spreading far and wide through Brazil, since the late insurrection of the blacks at Bahia, has rendered the present moment favorable for this government to improve and strengthen the anti-slave trade legislation. The eyes of most men are beginning to be opened, if not to the infamy of slave dealing, at least to the enormous danger of allowing fresh multitudes of Africans, under any condition, to be poured daily into the country."[26] Two months later, Fox continued in this vein: "I have observed with satisfaction that in all documents and declarations proceeding from the authority of the Government, the slave trade now denounced and condemned, not only as was heretofore frequently the language, from motives of abstract benevolence and philanthropy, or out of deference to the wishes of foreign nations, but as a manifest, acknowledged cause of monstrous, practical evil, and of immediate pressing danger to the existence of the white people of Brazil."[27]

In May 1835, the Provincial Assembly of Bahia sent a letter to the General Legislative Assembly of Brazil meeting in Rio de Janeiro. Signed by the governor and archbishop of Bahia along with the first and second secretaries of the assembly, this communiqué called for a halt to the transatlantic slave trade from Africa, and the coastal transport of African slaves previously landed in Argentina and Uruguay to the southern provinces in Brazil. "The illicit importation of millions of barbarians, which with the most shameful scandal, is still practiced in our ports, is doubtless more fatal to our morals, our security and prosperity, than the spirit of insurrection and rebellion [responsible for] the disastrous event on January 25 of the present year [1835]. The incessant recruitment of new Africans augments the number and the audacity of the slaves and freedmen who exist among us."[28] Such concerns continued to be expressed through the 1840s and early 1850s.

In the annual speech to open Bahia's Provincial Assembly in early March 1836, Bahian governor Francisco de Souza Paraiso noted that "signs have been observed and rumors constantly spread by which the public mind, not yet recovered from the Alarms of January 1835, has been considerably disturbed." Paraiso affirmed that the deportations of free Africans during the previous months had caused "the apprehension of immediate insurrection to be less apparent." He also warned that "as long as these barbarians [enslaved and free Africans], our necessary enemies, shall exist among us, they will never desist from their dark designs, notwithstanding they may always find them fruitless and abortive."[29]

It is important to read closely the governor's words. Fifteen months after the Revolt of the Malês, Paraiso remained focused on public insecurity. He requested that African slaves found guilty of participation in the insurrection be expelled from Bahia. And he was distressed about slave importations.

> It is therefore expedient to pay increasing attention to this subject [another slave insurrection], and to adopt every means that may contribute to our safety. Besides which, it appears to me very urgent that some measures should be adopted with respect to such African slaves as may become dangerous and suspected, especially those concerning in the last insurrection [January 1835], and who were found guilty by the Jury, in order that they may not continue to live in the midst of us—and that their owners should be obliged to sell them, to be sent out of the province.
>
> The contraband of slaves [Africans arriving on slave vessels] continues with the same scandal, and hitherto none of the parties, or abettors, of such an abominable and pernicious trade have been punished. Impunity attends almost every sort of crime, sometimes no prosecution at all being instituted, and at others being so conducted that the criminal is not put on his trial, or should he be, he finds ready means of defense, so as to be acquitted by the jury.[30]

As part of the government's response to the Malê Revolt, the Provincial Assembly suspended individual guarantees and allowed police to search homes belonging to free Africans.[31] So began a systematic campaign by police and politicians against all things Muslim, including searches for documents written in Arabic and the confiscation of material goods associated with Islamic religious practices.

Harassment endured for the next two decades in Salvador and other cities. One example among many occurred in Recife in September 1846. Police arrested a free black named Agostinho José Pereira along with six other free blacks. Authorities accused Agostinho, besides abetting escaped slaves and planning an insurrection, of instilling subversive ideas among some three hundred followers during the previous five years. Agostinho admitted in court that he had taught anyone interested to read so that they could interpret the messages of the Bible. He gained renown in Recife and other parts of Brazil as the "Divine Teacher."[32]

Agostinho's presence became a big issue for the city's elite. Throughout the colonial period, Recife had maintained close ties with Salvador. In 1827, rumors spread that escaped slaves resident at a quilombo named Catucá planned to attack Recife.[33] City officials claimed that the *quilombolas* had been inspired by a slave revolt that broke out the previous year in Salvador. In the two decades that followed, authorities became convinced that the nine thousand African slaves present in Recife and its suburbs knew about events in Salvador, including the Revolt of the Malês and the republican upheaval that followed soon after, known as the Sabinada (1837–38). Given that hundreds of African Mina slaves were transported from Salvador to Recife in the 1830s and 1840s, the Africans of Recife most likely had caught wind of these insurgencies. Certainly Agostinho had. During the court proceedings, police showed handwritten pages they had confiscated that became known as the "ABC" document. In it, Agostinho alluded to the Haitian Revolution and wrote that blacks (he used the word *morenos*, which translates as browns or mixed race) would gain control over whites.

Agostinho believed that Christianity could be used as a tool to emancipate slaves and provide for the spiritual liberation of black folk. His followers included both Africans and creoles. Authorities understood well that just over a decade earlier, the African plotters of the Malê Revolt had gained inspiration from a powerful substratum of Islamic religious beliefs. In the words of historian Marcus Carvalho, "authorities always suspected that the blacks of Recife did not act alone . . . but that they maintained connections [to blacks] in other provinces, principally Bahia."[34] These supposed ties included secret societies that had been formed, composed of blacks from the two cities.

Upper- and lower-class whites in Recife showed signs of paranoia for over a

year. In September 1847, a British consul wrote that "persecution of a black religious sect has progressed so considerably that the populace burnt the house
of the Apostle [Agostinho] and would have destroyed him also if he had not
escaped."[35] Distrust of the motives of a black Christian minister, his charisma
among enslaved Africans and free blacks resident in Recife, and the memory
of the Revolt of the Malês all contributed to this attack.

The city of Rio de Janeiro became one of the largest Atlantic African cities
at this juncture.[36] During the eighteenth century, traffickers brought thousands of African slaves to Rio de Janeiro and then transported them to the
mining regions of the interior province of Minas Gerais. They sent several
thousand other recently landed Africans south to the provinces of Santa Catarina and Rio Grande do Sul. From the turn of the nineteenth century, the
expanding coffee regions in the interior of the provinces of Rio de Janeiro and
São Paulo became major receiving areas. By 1849, more than 52,000 African
slaves resided in Rio de Janeiro, which meant that they composed nearly half
of the city's total slave population of 110,602. Of these, 67 percent were Bantu
speakers from West Central Africa, 17 percent from East Central Africa, and 7
percent were Mina.[37]

Africans resident in the city of Rio de Janeiro resisted enslavement in various ways. They worked as domestic help, as cooks, as *ganhadores* and *ganha-
deiras* selling goods in the streets, at docks, and as porters carrying goods and
people around the city. With their savings, some purchased freedom. African
slaves found employment in small boats that plied the harbor, on vessels that
sailed along the coast, and as crewmembers on slave ships.[38] Historian Jaime
Rodrigues estimates that Africans composed 17 percent of the crews of slaving vessels that sailed between Africa and Brazil from 1780 to 1863.[39] This
allowed for personal liberties and provided income that might enable them to
purchase emancipation.

As in Bahia, slaves provoked "daily torment" in Rio de Janeiro. Slaves
commonly took off from their owners. Some stayed away for days and then
returned. Others joined quilombos that proliferated within and around the
city. Rio de Janeiro became a labyrinth of hidden locales where Africans could
find protection. These urban and suburban quilombos riled authorities. In the
words of historian Flávio dos Santos Gomes, "with borders that were seldom
clearly defined, the social spaces created [in Rio de Janeiro] among individual
fugitive slaves, members of quilombos, freedpersons, Africans, creoles and
others enabled solidarities [to coalesce] as well as conflicts."[40]

Several incidents demonstrate the unease that prevailed. The practice of *capoeira* flourished. *Capoeira* was a martial art practiced by Africans based on rapid leg sweeps and physical agility. *Capoeristas* commonly used their feet as weapons. Authorities viewed *capoeira* as a threat to their capacity to maintain order. Groups of *capoeristas* led by slaves and free blacks roamed the streets and terrorized the free population. On various occasions, gang members exhibited their impressive fighting skills against police forces sent to subdue them.[41] Civilian and military police corps and an auxiliary National Guard force of 6,544 patrolled the city of Rio de Janeiro to maintain surveillance and prevent disturbances.[42]

Disquiet also reigned in the countryside. Large numbers of Bantu speakers from West Central Africa (particularly from the north Congo and to the east of Luanda and Benguela) ended up laboring on estates in the interior of the provinces of Rio de Janeiro and São Paulo. Like all Africans of the Diaspora, KiKongo and Kimbundu speakers brought with them languages, religious beliefs, and cultural practices shaped by experiences in their homelands. Once in Brazil, they encountered numerous creole slaves who were the descendants of West Central Africans who had arrived prior to 1800. These creoles possessed values similar to recently landed West Central Africans. Their shared backgrounds impacted strategies of resistance. Distinct from what occurred in Salvador after 1800, where the majority of the adult creoles were neither the offspring nor the descendants of the rapidly increasing Yoruba population, creole slaves resident in the interior of Central South Brazil joined with African-born slaves in challenging masters and undermining the regime that held them in bondage.[43]

Various observers alluded to the multiple threats posed by the massive slave importations to Rio de Janeiro from the early 1830s. A journalist in Rio de Janeiro noted in November 1831:

> Among the benefits which emanated from the last session of the Legislative Body is the law [November 7, 1831] which subjects to rigorous penalties those who carry on the traffic in African slavery, still most scandalously continued in our country, even since its total prohibition [March 13, 1830]. Police and humanity join hands, both require the termination of an abuse which has brought upon Brazil so many evils, which has perpetuated among us habits of sloth and all the vices of absolute rule, in the very bosom of our families, which in time degrades us in the eyes of polished nations, characterizing us as inhuman and barbarous, while it compromises the internal security of the state itself.

We have always lamented the blindness of avarice, at the sight of the eagerness and rage, accompanying these importations from Africa, and heaping gunpowder on the mine dreaded by all, under futile pretences, and have continued
in the vicious circle of laboring on the one hand to civilize the nation and the
other to barbarize it, by the incessantly repeated traffic in these men, born and
brought up in brutishness, and transferred into the very recesses of our dwellings, and placed in immediate contacts without children from the tenderest age.
May heaven grant that the views of the Legislature may be counteracted, that
the good which is aimed at may not in practice remain only a desideratum. That
Legislative prevention may not be defeated by the subterfuges always suggested
by the private interest of speculators, by the corruption of many of our Public
Men and by habits of impunity. It has been said that the penalties of the law are
rigorous, and excessive, but we do not think so.[44]

Outbreaks of slave resistance in Brazil's Center South added to the unease
caused by disembarkations of Africans. In 1833, tens of slaves resident in the
south of the province of Minas Gerais joined in the huge Carrancas insurrection. An estimated 60 percent of the population of Carrancas was enslaved.
Of these slaves, 56 percent were African. The insurgents carried out assassinations on two estates, including nine members of the family of the wealthy
fazendeiro and representative Gabriel Francisco Junqueira. In the harsh retribution that quickly followed, soldiers hanged 16 of the rebels. News of this
event provoked trepidation among planters deep into the bordering provinces
of São Paulo and Rio de Janeiro.[45]

That same year, Minister of Justice Aureliano de Sousa Coutinho warned
coffee planters in the interior of Rio de Janeiro of dangers ahead if slave importations continued unabated. "Owners of the estates will descend into an
abysm as a result of their own actions . . . because after the Africans have become *ladinos* [meaning that they had resided for an extended period in Brazil]
and realize that they are free, they will not desist in their struggle to escape
from captivity that is condemned by the law [of 1831]."[46]

Social pressures both urban and rural in the province of Rio de Janeiro
mounted during the 1830s. Along with slave owners, many free people viewed
the disembarkations of thousands of Africans as a threat both personal and
societal.[47] Inhabitants of the city of Rio de Janeiro doubted that order could be
maintained. Early in 1836, Justice of the Peace Luís da Costa Franco e Almeida
decried "the barbarous Africans . . . who disgracefully continue to increase
among us, and whom nothing will contain short of a healthy terror."[48] His-

torian Thomas Holloway describes the 1830s as a time when "Rio de Janeiro had tens of thousands of slaves chafing at the restrictions of their condition in many ways, from suicide to subtle sabotage to illicit recreation to violent outbursts against the oppressors."[49] Nevertheless, an economic resurgence late in that decade and into the following one helped fuel the demand for huge numbers of enslaved workers.[50]

With the steady rise in slave importations in the first half of the nineteenth century, the number and size of *quilombos* in the interior of the province of Rio de Janeiro rose.[51] The existence of these rural *quilombos* forced owners to pursue various initiatives to impede slave flight and protect themselves. Police patrols sent out to capture *quilombolas* learned quickly that they could seldom find or capture escaped slaves without luck or a large contingent of troops. In a famous incident that occurred in November 1838, some two hundred slaves fled from two coffee plantations located in the parish of Paty do Alferes in the district of Vassouras. An estimated 150 men searched for the escaped slaves and caught up with them at a *quilombo*. In the ensuing battle, the slaves shouted "Kill the *coboclos*! Kill the devils!" (*Coboclos* were persons of mixed white and Indian descent.) The government captured twenty-two prisoners and killed seven of the escaped slaves, while two soldiers died and two were wounded. In the court trial that followed, the judge sentenced the leader of the *quilombo*, known as Manuel Congo, to death.[52] Such episodes, along with highly publicized assassinations of plantation overseers, contributed to the heightened sense of insecurity among whites during this period.[53] Rumors of slave conspiracies abounded in both countryside and city during the 1840s.[54]

A question posed is, if tensions mounted in Bahia and in Rio de Janeiro in the wake of the Malê Revolt, why did the traffic continue? Within days of the Malê insurgency, an estimated thousand enslaved Africans were landed in the immediate vicinity of Salvador.[55] In the years that followed, disembarkations continued at a torrid pace. The numbers are staggering: traffickers landed an estimated 718,000 African slaves on Brazilian coasts from November 7, 1831 (passage of the Brazilian law that made the importation of slaves illegal and declared free any slave imported after that date) until suppression in 1851. Professor Needell writes that "the era between 1838 and 1849 was the era when, contraband or no, the most captives were sold in Brazil on a per annum basis in the whole history of the Atlantic slave trade. How terrified of Africans could the slaveholders have been if they bought them with such eagerness?"[56]

One response would be that planters needed workers to cultivate their crops. Given a dearth of free workers willing to labor on farms and few immigrants arriving from Europe or other locales, planters remained dependent on slaves to produce goods. Capitalists had significant investments in land and machinery. Many planters believed that any interruption of slave importations placed their livelihood in jeopardy.

The merchant-planter elite rejected the proposition that a slave revolt in Salvador quickly snuffed out by the police, or *quilombos* in existence throughout the Center South provinces, ought to derail a steady flow of African slaves. As in other instances since the rise of international capitalism in the fifteenth century, short-term economic benefits marginalized concerns over problems that might surface in the future. Furthermore, traffickers and their allies had the means to pay off diverse individuals (provincial governors, police, judges, juries, residents on the coast, private militias, ship captains and crews, and foreign consuls) to assure no disruption of slave importations.[57]

By the mid-1840s, numerous individuals recognized that British actions, which included the seizure of slave vessels by the British Squadron, might cause a permanent interruption in slave importations to Brazil. This perception added to the urgency exhibited at this juncture to transport as many African slaves as possible to Brazil.

Hence, internal and external variables caused a seemingly insatiable demand for slaves in the fifteen years that followed 1835.

1848 AND ITS IMMEDIATE AFTERMATH

As in Europe, the year 1848 proved to be a tumultuous one in Brazil. Governor of Bahia João de Moura Magalhães spoke for many when he wrote that "I am writing truthfully, providing exact information of what is happening in this province. We need prompt and energetic measures to prevent insurrections by Africans. Everyone still remembers what happened in 1835, [a revolt] that would have produced far greater destruction, if it had not been promptly annihilated."[58] British consul Henry Cowper echoed this view: "A general apprehension exists in the province of Bahia that the extension of the slave trade is hastening the day when that province will fall into the hands of blacks."[59]

From south to north, rebellious slaves destabilized the empire. In the southernmost province of Rio Grande do Sul, where the Bantu made up the majority of the slave population, West African Minas became the focus of attention.[60] Minas had been present in the province since the early nineteenth century. Some arrived from Bahia having been expelled in the wake of the Revolt of the Malês in 1835. As in Salvador and Rio de Janeiro, officials in the capital city Porto Alegre came to view the Mina presence with distrust. Symbolic of their unease, police scribes of that city only began to include the word Nagô in official documents in the wake of the Revolt of the Malês. Suspicious of Muslim slaves and Islamic practices, police carried out wide-ranging investigations. In October 1838, they broke into a building that they labeled the "club of Mina blacks." Finding two books and other manuscripts written in Arabic, they sent part of these materials to the nearby town of Rio Grande for translation. In 1841, the governor of the Rio Grande do Sul sent another packet containing some materials that had been confiscated to Rio de Janeiro to be assured that Nagô were not preparing a revolt in his province.[61]

On February 4, 1848, police in the town of Pelotas learned of plans for a slave uprising to occur the next day. They accused several "free blacks of the Mina nation" as being the "chiefs of the intended uprising." Participants in the conspiracy also supposedly included 1,500 other free blacks "ready to act on the first rising."[62] Investigations uncovered two hundred muskets, two hundred carbines, swords, pistols, and ammunition stored at a farmhouse. Police arrested three hundred slaves from six estates and "severely flogged" several of the accused; ten died from the beatings.[63] As in the Malê revolt in Salvador, information provided by slaves previous to the uprising proved helpful to authorities. A British diplomat present wrote that "the informers of the existence of this conspiracy are three Mina slaves who feeling great friendship for their masters, who had always treated them kindly, confessed the whole plan to them, and thus most providentially prevented the scenes of St. Domingo in this province."[64]

In his description of this episode, British consul Lord Howden wrote:

> The Slaves implicated in this plot are exclusively natives of Mina [on the African coast between Ouidah and present-day Lagos] and come from the North of the Line, to the east of Cape Coast [present-day Ghana, Togo, western Benin]. This race is the same that prepared the nearly successful insurrection of Bahia in 1835; and the slaves belonging to it are entirely and most remarkably different from all other Africans in Brazil both physically and intellectually. These Mina slaves all speak the same language, have organized societies, and elected chiefs wherever they meet in any numbers, are remarkable for their habits of order, their serious and dignified deportment, their economy, their prevision, and their sullen courage; and they are corporeally the finest specimens of the

human race I ever saw. It is said that the inhabitants of the province of Rio de Janeiro, afraid of the slumbering energies of such men, buy them unwillingly; and,
in fact, but comparatively few of this easily distinguished race are to be seen in
the Capital [city of Rio de Janeiro]. I have no doubt but that this is the People
charged by Providence with the dreadful and inevitable retribution of Africa.[65]

Howden's observations suggest that officials in Rio de Janeiro had sent out
of the city enslaved and free Africans who had arrived from Salvador in the
years that followed the 1835 Malê Revolt. This measure was taken to maintain
public security in the city of Rio de Janeiro.[66]

In that same turbulent year of 1848, a major slave conspiracy coalesced on
several coffee plantations in the Valley of Paraíba, which extends from Rio
de Janeiro into São Paulo. The plan had its origins in Bantu spirituality and
knowledge of the suppression of the traffic to Brazil by the British Squadron.

In the "Secret Report of the Select Committee of the Provincial Assembly
of Rio de Janeiro on Secret Societies of Africans in the Province of Rio de Janeiro," the authors wrote that looking "upon the situation in the country, the
very small number of white men in relation with the millions of slaves who
abound in all parts [and] the insufficiency and impropriety of our criminal legislation, the special commission cannot but recognize the impossibility of at
once calming the apprehension of an insurrection of the slaves." The governor
of São Paulo requested that the same report be evaluated by the Legislative
Assembly of that province.

Based on interrogations of jailed slaves and intelligence gleaned by police
officials, the committee pointed to the existence of an extensive African Society that included members in the city of Rio de Janeiro and in the interior
of the province. Such a portrayal was nothing new. In the immediate aftermath of the Malê Revolt, a Special Committee composed of members of the
Legislative Assembly of Rio de Janeiro wrote (in March 1835) of the presence
of "Secret [African] Societies which are laboring to spread insurrection and
the doctrines of Haiti. [These Societies] have funds towards which a great
number of members of color, free as well as slaves, contribute; that from these
funds proceed the subsidies by which emissaries are kept up and maintained,
charged with propagating revolutionary doctrines among the slaves of the different agricultural estates, where they introduce themselves under the color
of selling goods."[67]

The African Society of 1848 was divided into "circles" composed of fifty
slaves, each headed by a chief known as a *Taté* who had six assistants named

Cambondos. The word Taté perhaps has origins in the word *Pajé*, meaning the chief of an indigenous tribe in Brazil. More likely Taté is derived from the Bantu language Kimbundu spoken in the Congo and Angola regions of Africa. Taté is a variant of the word Tateto, which means "father." In African Brazilian religious ceremonies known as *Candomblé*, those influenced by Angolan culture are led by a father of a saint (*pai-de-santo*) who is known as "Tateto ti inkice" or "Tateto t'inkice." In relation to the African Society believed to exist in the province of Rio de Janeiro, Taté would imply a leader or chief.

A Cambondo is most likely a variant of the word "Cambono," a term used to describe a participant at a Candomblé ceremony who provided assistance to persons under the spell of a divine force. This often entailed embracing and protecting the possessed as the *orixá* (divinity) passed through his or her body. The Cambondos included males known as *Filhos do Terreiro* (sons of a house of Candomblé) and three or four African females known as *Mocambas do Anjo.* Sons of a terreiro were men associated with a particular house where Candomblé ceremonies occurred.

Use of the word *Mocamba* perhaps suggested that these African females gained their strength and character from experience in escaped slave communities (*mocambos*). Or it might have its origins in the word *mucamba*, a term used by owners in the nineteenth century to denote a female domestic slave. The investigating committee of the Provincial Assembly of Rio de Janeiro viewed the Mocambas do Anjo (an allusion to female Africans who cared for the children of a master) as particularly dangerous, as they were domestic slaves who resided in close proximity to their owners.

The plan included the poisoning of "masters of whatever sex or age" along with the assassination of "administrators and other free people employed on the estates including those slaves who wished to remain faithful to their masters."[68] Tensions reached such a pitch that slave owners and their families fearful of rebellious slaves abandoned their estates in the interior of São Paulo and fled to towns.

Insecurity among residents of Rio de Janeiro continued over the following months. In the wake of the Malê revolt, significant numbers of Nagô arrived in Rio de Janeiro. Police chief Eusébio de Queiroz requested that ships carrying slaves from Bahia be closely monitored. He did not want dangerous "foreign" Nagôs subverting the slave population of Rio de Janeiro with plans for rebellion.[69] Correspondence from local justices in the province of Rio de Janeiro alluded to Mina slaves as "sons of Bahia," implying special danger.[70] In 1845, slave owners resident in the city of Rio de Janeiro complained that a group of free blacks was stealing slaves and sending them into the interior of the province and nearby Minas Gerais. They charged that blacks of Mina descent had "seduced" unknowing and unprotected slaves as they traveled the streets of the city. The accusation reflected the ongoing tensions provoked by the presence of Minas and Malê Nagôs in Rio.[71]

As late as December 1849, police continued to discuss measures that might thwart a Muslim-led revolt in Rio similar to what had occurred in Salvador in 1835. In the words of historian Beatriz Gallotti Mamigonian, "Rio police took the potential threat represented by the Mina, and particularly the Malês, very seriously, and tried hard to follow their activities closely in the hope of avoiding a repetition of events in Bahia."[72] The chief of police of Rio wrote that,

> . . .some Mina blacks resident in this city gathered in secret associations where, under impenetrable mystery, there were practices and rites that became suspect; they communicated among themselves through ciphered writings, and with blacks of the same nation who reside in Bahia as well as [Mina blacks resident] in São Paulo and Minas [Gerais]. I sent out police to search suspect houses and [ordered that my subordinates] not only arrest individuals but to take possession of all suspicious materials. . . . We confiscated an infinite number of papers written in different colors and in unknown characters, [along with] some books [and] manuscripts. [African] specialists were called [requested] to translate, interpret or decipher these materials, who stated that they [all of the materials] contained nothing more than orations for the most part, taken from the Koran, in basic Arabic with some words mixed in from the language of the Mina-Malê [enchertado de palavras da língua Mina-Malê, meaning Yoruba]. . . . Without giving back the papers and books that had been confiscated, I allowed all those [blacks who had been] detained to go free. . . . However these blacks must continue to be closely watched by the police . . . given that everything that has been found in the recent searches were exactly like those that were found in Bahia when there was an insurrection of slaves in 1835.[73]

These events influenced historian Robert W. Slenes to write that the public anxiety and agitation fomented by the "foreigners from Africa" had as much to do with forcing an end to the transatlantic slave trade to Brazil as British initiatives.[74]

In the Northeast and North of the empire, slave resistance also caused trepidation among planters and provincial authorities alike. In late 1848, an armed rebellion broke out in the province of Pernambuco known as the

Praieira insurrection, forcing provincial governor Antônio Chichorro da Gama the governor to request troops from other provinces to help restore order. (*Praieira* is related to the Portuguese word *praia*, meaning beach. The rebels planned the uprising at a building on Praia Street, Beach Street, in the city of Recife.) Composed of liberals who supported republican reforms and rejected the supremacy of Emperor Pedro II over all branches of Brazil's imperial government, the rebels (known as praieiros) offered to end slavery in return for British recognition. It was no small affair. In spite of its short duration, some five hundred rebels died in the streets of Recife after attacking the city. In the midst of this tumult, rumors again spread (as two years previous) that blacks resident in Recife had joined together in a secret cabal with plans to rebel. The supposed leader of this society was a freed African named Benedito, known as the "governor of the Africans from the [Mina] coast."[75] Further north, governors in the provinces of Maranhão and Pará sent out large parties to hunt down escaped slaves and destroy quilombos.[76]

In a communiqué penned in August 1848, British diplomat James Hudson tried to put a positive spin on the situation. Hudson concluded that the massive disembarkations of African slaves on Brazilian shores had caused a shift in opinion among high-ranking officials in Brazil. "A very satisfactory change appears to be taking place in the mind of the Brazilian government and public, upon the subject of the importation of slaves, due to the effect, I think, of Lord Aberdeen's bill [1845], to the captures made under it [which allowed the British Squadron to seize Brazilian slave vessels wherever encountered]; *to the terror which the late enormous importation of slaves has created in this government, and in the thinking part of the community*; and in the isolated position in which Brazil now stands on this continent and in Europe, where she has lost the hold on both France and Austria."[77]

In spite of a steady stream of warnings, traffickers continued to disembark thousands of African slaves in the cities of Salvador, Rio de Janeiro, and Santos (province of São Paulo) and along nearby beaches. Indeed, the largest number of enslaved Africans to disembark in Brazil or any other region of the Americas in the history of the transatlantic trade occurred in 1848. The peak for two years was 1848–49, and the peak triennium was 1847–49.[78]

In mid-1850, the Municipal Corporation (Council) of Salvador articulated their trepidation concerning these arrivals:

> The traffic in slaves is nowadays tolerated in this second city of Brazil in a most reprehensible manner. There is not one person here, who looking at the

vessels lying at anchor in the port, cannot distinguish those destined to proceed on that piracy; there is not one person here who does not know the Houses, called stations, in which raw (*boçaes*) Africans [meaning newly arrived] are kept for sale, within the limits of this municipality, even in this city. There is not any one person who cannot name those who have taken part in this barbarous and illicit traffic. The Law of 7th November 1831 is therefore disrespected and scorned, and the traffic is carried on with greater ease in as much as it is principally in the hands of strangers, who have come to Brazil to make their fortunes, and to take possession of our national commerce.

No one who seriously reflects upon the future interests of Brazil, in whose veins the blood of free men flows, or whose understanding is acquainted with the sacred tenets of the Christian religion, can be indifferent to this heap of combustibles, which is accumulating against Brazilian society, subjecting us to continual alarm and barbarous insurrections; nor can the Municipal Chamber of Bahia, therefore, view them with indifference.[79]

INSECURITY AT MID-CENTURY

How do we measure the threat posed to "national security" caused by the slave importations from 1835 through 1851? To what extent did fear or terror caused by slave resistance contribute to the decisions of imperial ministers in 1850 to force a permanent halt to the slave traffic to Brazil? Sure answers to these questions are hard to come by. What is clear is that numerous articulate observers remembered well the 1835 slave revolt in Salvador, expressed concern about slave rebellion and resistance, and considered the importations of African slaves after 1835 a real menace to the stability of port cities, rural areas, and even the empire itself. Documents found in Brazilian archives provide further insights in this regard. Three examples are noted.

The first is a slave revolt that occurred in the province of Espírito Santo. In the afternoon of March 19, 1849, a group of thirty or more armed slaves joined together in insurrection in the district of Queimado, situated some three to four *leguas* (twelve miles) outside the capital city of Vitória. In a region where hundreds of slaves labored on coffee and sugar estates, the revolt was led by three male slaves each owned by a different planter. The number of slaves who joined in the rebellion quickly increased to three hundred. Shouting "We demand our Freedom" and "We demand Letters of Manumission" [*carta de manumissão*, an official document that defined one's status as a free person], they also seized arms and ammunition at various estates. The event caused "terror" among the inhabitants around the region and in Vitória. The governor of Espírito Santo warned that without an adequate police presence, similar upheavals could easily spread to other provinces in the empire.[80]

In response, officials sent out twenty men to put down the revolt, this patrol known as the Permanent Company of Hunters (*Companhia Fixa de Caçadores*). Confronted by superior force and a lack of arms, the majority of the escaped slaves fled into nearby forests. Within two days the revolt ended.[81] By the end of the month, thirty of the insurrectionists had been arrested and put in prison to await their fate. Numerous others returned to the properties from which they had fled. In describing this event, the chief of police expressed little surprise at what had occurred. He wrote that "it is generally known that the slaves of our province are in a state of unhappiness [*desmoralização*, meaning that the slaves were resisting the coercion and controls imposed by owners]."[82]

In her description of the "Insurrection at Queimado," Brazilian historian Vilma Paraiso Ferreira de Almada emphasizes that the outbreak was but one example of a long history of slave resistance in the province. During the 1820s and 1830s, slaves showed themselves to be closely attuned to all news related to their condition (for example the illegal enslavement of any African who arrived after the law of November 7, 1831). Quoting Trinidadian historian Eric Williams, Almada agrees that "Not nearly as stupid as his master thought him and later historians have pictured him, the slave was alert to surroundings and keenly interested in discussions about his fate."[83]

Like slaves throughout the Americas, slaves residing in the capital city of Vitória and the interior of the province of Espírito Santo maintained close contact with an Atlantic world that provided them information and inspiration.[84] British actions at sea and debates among planters and officials (discussions at the dinner table, newspaper articles, political discourse, and the like) related to suppression of the slave trade influenced the slaves at Queimado. Officials reacted quickly to ensure the insurrection did not spread. In the words of Professor Almada, "the fear that always existed among the owners shifted into panic [from the late 1840s], given that the slaves, inspired by [this] abolitionist conjuncture, principally those in the plantation regions, refused to remain submissive and became increasingly fearless."[85]

A review of several hundred documents from the period 1835 to 1851 provides numerous descriptions of slave revolts and organized slave resistance, including "tenacious" fighting by escaped slaves hiding in forests. These episodes occurred in the provinces of Maranhão, Pará, Alagoas, Bahia, and Rio de Janeiro (and likely others).[86] Such events further fueled tensions at mid-century.

A second example of insecurity by the end of the 1840s focuses on freed Africans residing in the city of Salvador. These were former slaves (*libertos*) who had gained their freedom, often by saving money from their labor and purchasing a manumission card. Based on investigations carried out in the first months of 1847, police published a list of 2,508 freed Africans residing in the ten parishes of the city. Of these, 993 were male and 1,515 female.[87] Using an estimate for the total population of the city of 54,330, freed Africans made up 4.6 percent of the inhabitants of Salvador, and slaves another 25 percent (or 13,600 persons, a conservative estimate).[88]

Historians have often depicted African freedpersons as having little interest in disrupting the status quo. One historian writes that "Despite the fact of a common white oppression, [in Brazil] Africans and Afro-Brazilians did not rise up [together] along Haitian lines. Those [African freedpersons] whose skills and knowledge were, potentially, the most apt for leadership in a rebellion, were, in reality, the least likely to challenge the established racialized hierarchy."[89] The above list, which noted the home parish and employment of each freed African in Salvador, would appear to confirm such a view. The police official responsible for summing up the findings pointed out that these freed Africans owned at least six hundred slaves, implying that possession of such property made them an unlikely threat to the slave regime.

However, a closer reading of the documents sheds light on the social tensions at mid-century. Freed Africans had played a key role in the Revolt of the Malês in 1835. In the months and years that followed, they suffered systematic reprisals. Several hundred were deported, others departed from Bahia at their own will, and several were thrown into prison on the flimsiest of evidence. By early 1847, fear had mounted dramatically in both city and countryside.

Apprehension is readily evident in a letter penned by the governor of Bahia, Antonio Inácio de Azevedo, soon after the police had concluded their work. "I consider the estimate of 2,508 African *libertos* to be low, given that such records are not always exact. Nevertheless, that number [implying their substantial presence], along with the [high] number of slaves present, justify the fears that now and then surface, and [make understandable] the actions I have taken to bring troops here [to Salvador] capable of putting down any sort of an insurrection which might occur."[90] A survey by police of every freed

African residing in Salvador should be evaluated through the lens of the historical moment. The elite of Bahia had not forgotten the involvement of freed Africans in the Revolt of the Malês, and they remained deeply distrustful of such individuals in their midst.

Strain provoked by the presence of freed Africans in Salvador did not quickly diminish. On May 8, 1853, rumor spread of an impending slave insurrection. Throughout the night, soldiers on horseback patrolled the streets, and the infantry was placed on full alert. British consul James Hudson wrote that

> ... it is reported that arms and ammunition were found secreted in the houses of some liberated Africans [freedmen] of the Nagó or Minas nation, as well as flags and masquerading dresses such as were displayed by them in the last great insurrection in the year 1835.
>
> The jails are full of free Africans and the domiciliary visits of the police are deplorable. I however believe the apprehension entertained by the provincial government is much greater than the facts seem to justify, and that the opportunity is taken to oblige the liberated blacks to return to Africa without their possessing the means of doing so, but which the government by law and by every principle of justice are bound to do at their own expense.
>
> This will only show your Lordship how great the curse is to which all are subjected by the insecurity of life resulting from the awful state of slavery of so many thousands of our fellow creatures in this large slave holding province, where, at stated periods, an insurrection is generally expected.[91]

Although Hudson downplayed the extent of the danger, obviously Bahian police and officials perceived the situation differently. Using force to break into houses, they carried out searches and arrested suspicious Africans. In the weeks that followed, the governor of Bahia demanded that foreign ships departing from Salvador transport these unwanted Africans on board.

A third demonstration of insecurity at mid-century occurred in the city of Recife. In early September 1853, police arrested a Muslim Yoruba *alufá* (priest) named João Rufino. Brought to Bahia as a slave, Rufino had subsequently been sold to new owners in Rio Grande do Sul. After gaining his freedom, he traveled to Rio de Janeiro, where he found employment as a cook on a slave ship named *Ermelinda*. Captured by HMS *Water Witch* off the coast of Angola in October 1841, the ship was taken to Sierra Leone. After a short stay in Freetown, Rufino journeyed to Rio de Janeiro, visited for a short period, and then returned to Sierra Leone. There he studied at a Muslim school for two years.

Returning to Brazil in December 1844, Rufino finally settled in Recife, where he devoted his time to Islamic religious practices.[92]

Besides Rufino, police arrested several other Africans accused of organizing "a new religious sect." Materials confiscated from their homes included a Koran and "many sheets of paper written in Hebraic [Hebrew, but in fact the words were in Arabic]." News of the arrests set off alarms that Muslims were planning a slave revolt. The chief of police in Recife sent one of the Arabic documents to Rio de Janeiro for translation. Preserved at the National Archives of Brazil, the letter proved to be a statement of marriage vows and had nothing to do with rebellion.[93] This episode suggests that police and the upper class of Recife remembered well the events of Salvador in 1835. To prevent the outbreak of another slave insurrection, officials sought to impede the spread of Islamic subversion to Recife.[94]

What did fears of a slave insurrection, the roundup of African slaves and free Africans, and the confiscation of materials in September 1853 have to do with the decision to end the transatlantic slave trade in early 1850? Everything. Events often play out as the result of past history; milieu and experience often shape outcome.

The persecution and arrests of Africans in Salvador and Recife occurred because of continued distrust of free Africans (*Africanos livres*). Fear was further heightened because some free Africans practiced Islam. Such concerns had been articulated on several occasions in the two decades that followed the Revolt of the Malês. Police in Porto Alegre, Rio de Janeiro, Salvador, and Recife (and likely in other locales) confiscated all sorts of documents and materials in their quest to stamp out the perceived threat posed by what two Brazilian historians have termed "Malê contamination."[95] Even though the number of practicing Muslim African slaves and free Africans residing in Brazil had diminished significantly by mid-century, the number of Nagô who arrived from West Africa remained high. Indeed, the Nagô represented "a spectacular presence at mid-century" among the slave population of Salvador.[96] In the minds of the many police, a Nagô African could likely be a Muslim. All of these factors created anxieties that officials throughout the empire hoped might be diminished by means of a halt of slave disembarkations.

Adding to the tensions at mid-century was the historical memory of the Haitian Revolution (1791–1804). Several documents from 1835 through 1850 express concern that if the importations were to continue, "another Haiti" could occur in Brazil. The March 1835 letter sent from the provincial assembly of the province of Rio de Janeiro to imperial ministers (see above) stated:

> These apprehensions, sire, are not groundless. Everyone knows that the doctrines of Hayti are here preached with impunity, that the slaves are allured with the bait of Liberty and urged on by excited spirits, National as well as Foreign, within and without the Empire, to break out into commotions of which those of Bahia are furnishing the most fatal example. . . .
>
> The members of these Societies and their Abettors, National and Foreign, are pointed out by the Public Voice, and yet it would seem that the Administrative Police of the Capital [Rio de Janeiro] either remains ignorant of everything or in an extraordinary manner slumbers carelessly over the crater of the Volcano—and in the meantime the Fire is at the Door.[97]

In speeches on the floor of the imperial Senate in Rio de Janeiro during 1843, Senator Antônio Pedro da Costa Ferreira from the province of Maranhão alluded to Haiti's past. A lawyer and planter, he criticized colleagues uninterested in halting the slave trade. Africans had been transported to Saint-Domingue after the indigenous people had been exterminated. With the Haitian Revolution, "the victimizers [owners] became the victims. . . . Don't you still see the smoke of [rising from] the sacrificed victims in Haiti? Do you consider it possible to conceive of security in Brazil with that [huge] population [of slaves]?"[98] The senator continued: "I have fear with regards to future dangers, and I seek to avoid [*evitar*] them. Far from accepting the erroneous idea that the agricultural sector in Brazil will be destroyed by a lack of African slaves, we must show that a country worked by slaves is never happy. Such a system only brings bad outcomes [*Só acarreta males sobre si*]."[99]

At mid-century, a journalist writing in Recife echoed similar sentiments. During the previous two decades, traffickers had landed at least 55,000 African slaves in the port of Recife or nearby locales.[100] "Let our government hang legally half a dozen of these slave dealers, shame and opprobrium of humanity, let it not permit one more slave to be introduced into our territory, let it make all sacrifices to develop a colonization of free hands, offer to them all the guarantees as is done in the United States, and let it be certain that only in this manner can it avoid that earlier or later we must have in Brazil a new Santo Domingo [another Haitian Revolution]."[101]

Statements by observers, articles written by journalists, the communiqués of provincial officials, and the studies of several historians suggest that fears of slave uprisings and unceasing slave resistance, combined with massive slave disembarkations, influenced imperial officials to put a stop to the transatlantic slave trade in 1850.[102]

THE DEBATES OF 1850

The Enlightenment School affirms that ministers in the cabinet of the imperial government decided to end slave importations in January 1850 based on political considerations. In putting down federalist revolts and consolidating centralized rule under the monarchy, they had gained the confidence of the merchant-planter elite. Astute observers of the world around them, the ministers at mid-century had shown a capacity to lead during the previous two decades. Sensitive to British pressures, they recognized that continued slave importations did not bode well for the empire in terms of international opinion or for maintaining their own positions of authority. This depiction discounts insecurity caused by slave resistance as a motive for their actions.[103]

The above perspective has several flaws. As members or allies of the merchant-planter class, the ministers had dealt for many years with African and creole slaves. They understood that various strategies had to be employed on a daily basis to maintain control over slaves. This included both coercion and negotiation.[104] They knew well that the roots of the Haitian Revolution and the Jamaica Revolt of 1831 could be traced to the tens of thousands of Africans who had been transported to those islands.[105] As angry and rebellious Africans arrived in the cities, towns, and countryside of Brazil during the 1830s and 1840s, these men recognized that their wisest response at least for the short term was to halt importations.

Why would the ministers who attended the closed meeting of the Imperial Council of State that convened in January 1850 not have commented on the insecurities caused by thousands of Africans in their midst? One reason might be traced to their racial biases. These men had little respect for Africa or Africans. They did not believe that Africans and their descendants had mental capacities equal to whites or even persons of mixed race. They scorned the idea that Africans could organize and successfully undermine a slave regime that had flourished for three centuries. In fact, most of them detested the Africans in their midst. They were repulsed by the possibility that Brazil might become "another Africa."[106]

Furthermore, members of the Council of State did not wish to reveal their unquiet to the free underclass. The ministers were part of a male elite determined to maintain its wealth and position. Similar to the obfuscations of modern-day politicians, a suggestion that their political decisions were a response to subaltern pressures was a sign of weakness. British aggressions at sea and along the coast gave added impetus to the cabinet to appear strong and capable.

In the months following passage of the Eusébio de Queiroz Law, several influential observers did comment on the pressures that contributed to political decisions taken in 1850. Minister of Foreign Affairs Paulino José Soares de Sousa stated in May 1851: "50,000, 60,000, or 100,000 Africans had been imported each year to Brazil. Would we not be advised by all moral considerations, by civilization, in our desire to ensure our own security and that of our children, to put an end to the importation of Africans?"[107] Arch-conservative senator Honório Hermeto Carneiro Leão asked of his colleagues in the Senate the same month:

Was not the level of importations of Africans [through 1850] excessive, was it not too much, would it not have brought future dangers to the country [Brazil]? It is in our interest [to support the 1831 Brazilian law ending the slave trade], because the importation of Africans has been excessive, because the provinces from Bahia to the south found themselves overburdened with slaves; their number did not appear to be in proportion to the number of free persons. It was, then, in our interest, and to assure our future security, to take precautions in this respect, thereby halting the traffic, that, while it continued, increased our [internal, domestic] dangers. I think, Mr. President, that the time has come for the government to end this dangerous situation by putting a limit on the trade in slaves; and besides we have accepted this obligation.[108]

Twelve months later, in July 1852, no less a figure than Eusébio de Queiroz, the minister after whom the Brazilian law ending the slave trade was named, left no doubt that importations of the 1840s had been a key variable in shaping his perspectives:

... [I]f [public] opinion ... had brought about this revolution in the country, it was necessary for an occasion to present itself that would allow such a change to make itself known. Some events or, rather, signs of a grave nature, that revealed themselves one after the other in Campos [in the north of the province of Rio de Janeiro], [the province of] Espírito Santo and some other places, such as the important counties of Valença and Vassouras [interior of the province of Rio de Janeiro], produced a terror that I shall call salutary, because it provided the opportunity for that opinion, contrary to the traffic, to develop further and make itself felt.

All who found themselves in Rio de Janeiro at that time and who occupied themselves with this question recognized that it was the same planters who until then had preached the necessity of the traffic who now were the first to contend that the moment for its suppression had arrived.[109]

A FINAL REFLECTION

The differences between the Enlightenment School and the Subaltern School might be characterized as a clash of interpretations. The former offers insights into the worldview and positions of influential politicians. Their actions played a role in the demise of the transatlantic slave trade to Brazil. It is political and institutional history *par excellence*. The historians associated with the Subaltern School suggest that multiple factors caused the end of the slave trade to Brazil. One was the suppression efforts of the British navy.[110] Others included resistance by African slaves and free blacks and the diseases carried to Brazilian shores in slave vessels.

From early 1851, the number of slaves arriving in Brazil dropped off precipitously. At this same juncture, disembarkations at Cuba rose. (See graph.)

Many questions remain. How did the spread of epidemics from slave vessels impact political debates and policy outcomes at mid-century? An influential interpretation is that increased British pressures along the Brazilian coast in the late 1840s turned both elite and popular opinion against the traffic. Yet health conditions in Brazil became of paramount concern. Common folk all along the coast exhibited distress over the landing of sick Africans. The yellow fever epidemic of late 1849 did much to provoke the sudden and widespread popular rejection of continued slave importations at that juncture.[111]

To what extent did slave resistance in other parts of the Atlantic world shape the actions of African slaves, creole slaves, and free blacks in Brazil? To date, no document has surfaced in Brazilian archives showing that the Escalera insurgency in Cuba directly influenced persons or events in Brazil. Yet, it is difficult to believe that news of La Escalera did not filter into Brazil via the hundreds of individuals who partook of the southern triangle trade.

And third, what were the diverse strategies of resistance among the thousands of Africans who labored in ports and along the coast of Brazil? Officials

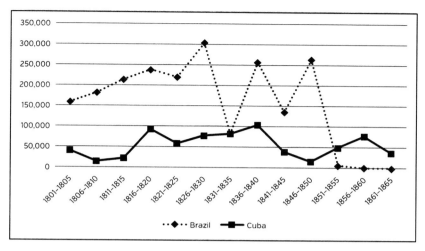

Nineteenth-Century Transatlantic Slave Trade to Brazil and Cuba.
Source: www.slavevoyages.org

in several port cities decried the presence of Africans whom they could not control. In Salvador, the Africans who plied its bay in small boats had organized in the late 1840s. Representatives of these labor groups (known as *cantos*) negotiated wages and defended the interests of the thousand Africans who labored in the port. These workers observed closely the movement of ships and smaller vessels. They witnessed firsthand the scheming of traffickers and the activities of the British Squadron. The Africans who worked in the port of Salvador communicated among themselves, with residents of the city, with the interior of the province, with inhabitants all along the coast, and with the wider Atlantic world. Most likely some of them remembered the Revolt of the Malês, or had learned of it from stories shared. One witness described the Bay of All Saints where Africans (slave and free) ferried goods and persons as "that terrible nucleus of [slave] insurrections."[112] These Africans did not sit idly by when they sensed that a halt in slave importations might be near. Some hoped that the end of the traffic might quickly bring an end to the institution of slavery. Such endeavors merit the closest of scrutiny.

6

INTERPRETERS, TRANSLATORS, AND
THE SPOKEN WORD

———— ∞ ————

Communication played a key role in the transatlantic slave trade to Brazil and Cuba during the nineteenth century. For this commerce to function as an efficient capitalist enterprise, traffickers cultivated contacts throughout the Atlantic world. Through oral communication, such as conversations at taverns or at clandestine meetings, they followed market demand closely in the Americas as well as the availability of slave "cargoes" along the coasts of Africa. Traffickers also shared information by means of written documents, including letters, lease agreements, and bills of sale.

Captains of slave vessels commonly carried written instructions about locales for receiving slaves on the coast of Africa and where to disembark slaves in Brazil and Cuba. Most often such information was penned in code to impede detection. Maps and geographic representations assisted captains in their pursuits. Everyone involved in a slaving venture paid close attention to materials related to their business transactions. If captured by a British cruiser, captains and crews often threw packets of papers into the ocean. In the case of the seizure near Ambriz of the slaver *Martha* from New York by the U.S. brig *Perry* in June 1850, the writing desk of the captain appeared floating nearby. After they pulled it up from the sea, sailors on the *Perry* found papers in drawers that confirmed the captain's identity as a citizen of the United States.[1] In describing the apprehension of the slave ship *Marabout*, British commander Christie wrote that "one of my boats succeeded in picking up a bundle thrown overboard containing a quantity of letters, several of which were directed to some of the principal Slave Dealers in Africa; this alone speaks volumes against her and I strongly suspect that she threw many other things overboard during the night."[2] Aware of such duplicity, the first act of sailors of the British or U.S. Squadron upon boarding a vessel was to demand that the ship's log and documents related to the voyage be handed over.

In one instance, British officials discovered a plan outlined on a sheet of paper to poison crews of the British Squadron. Employed by the Custom House in the port of Rio de Janeiro, the accused plotter was a Brazilian known for his condemnation of slave dealers. The scheme called for a "good dose of *sal amargo* [arsenic or oxalic acid] to be put into a barrel of wine and a barrel of brandy as the captors [British] immediately begin drinking [after taking control over a slave ship], and so they will be done for and you [traffickers] be rid of them."[3]

Intelligence derived from a wide range of sources facilitated British suppression of the transatlantic slave trade. Translators aided the British in learning of the machinations of merchant houses, investors, ship captains, seamen, and government officials. The British Squadron hired interpreters to enable the seizure of slave vessels. Representatives of Mixed Commission Courts (1819–71) commonly questioned African slaves and the crews of slave ships to learn about voyages. For interviews to be carried out and the courts to function, interpreters and translators were needed.

Numerous interpreters and translators were, in the words of historian Ira Berlin, "Atlantic creoles." When used to describe social relations in the British Empire of the seventeenth century, this phrase alludes to African slaves and their descendants who maintained connections "with the ocean that linked Africa, Europe, and the Americas. Atlantic creoles spoke the language of their enslavers and were familiar with the various religions, commercial conventions, and systems of jurisprudence of the Atlantic."[4] These individuals possessed "linguistic dexterity, cultural plasticity, and social agility."[5] They "used their knowledge of the Atlantic world to integrate themselves into European settlements."[6] During the Age of Revolutions (1750 to 1850), the term *Atlantic creole* took on different connotations. In this epoch, such a person could be enslaved or free. To be an Atlantic creole suggested as much a capacity to use knowledge of the Atlantic world as it implied a racial designation or geographic place where one resided.

An Atlantic creole of the British Empire is to be distinguished from a creole (*criollo*) in Spanish America. The latter was commonly understood to be a

Caucasian of primarily Spanish descent born in one of Spain's colonies.[7] Creole dissatisfaction with Spanish colonial structures fueled the wars for independence in Spanish America (1810–25). When employed to describe a slave (*esclavo criollo*) or black (*negro criollo*), "creole" suggested that the individual had been born in Spanish America. An example from Cuba is the former slave Esteban Montejo. Son of a Congo and a Lucumí, Montejo self-identified as a *negro criollo*.[8] In Brazil, colonizers commonly used the Portuguese term *creole* (*crioulo*) to denote a black person born in Brazil. The word was used to distinguish a slave (*escravo crioulo*) from an African (*Africano* or *preto*), a free black (*negro livre*), or a person of mixed race (*pardo* or *moreno*, which denoted the color brown). Seldom was the term *creole* employed in reference to a white individual. In present-day Brazil, the word *crioulo* is a derogatory term used to describe a black person.

Closely attuned to the Atlantic world, Atlantic creoles responded to opportunities created by England's commitment to end the transatlantic slave trade (from 1808) and abolish the institution of slavery throughout the Americas (from 1834). They provided linguistic skills to the British in various endeavors aimed at suppression of the slave trade. Not only did these men and women seek to liberate Africans from the holds of slave vessels, but they also desired to gain their own liberty or to protect hard-won rights.

Residents of Cuba or Brazil who aided the British often faced great risk. Traffickers and the many individuals beholden to them commonly harassed persons who helped the British in capturing ships and convicting those guilty of piratical activities.[9] Intimidation, assassination threats, and physical attacks were made on interpreters, translators, diplomats, judges, and informants.[10]

In this chapter, an "interpreter" is an intermediary who enables face-to-face interaction between persons who speak different languages. A "translator" is someone who translates a written document from one language to another. The "spoken word" is the manner in which one person articulates words to another. It is informed by shared knowledge of a particular culture or region. Evidence is provided of enslaved blacks speaking directly with British and U.S. officials in English in hopes of gaining their freedom.

INTERPRETERS AND THE MIDDLE PASSAGE

From the beginnings of the transatlantic slave trade in the sixteenth century, merchants hired or coerced Africans to act as interpreters.[11] Africans who spoke the mixed pidgin language of Krio facilitated communication among parties engaged in business transactions related to the buying and selling of slaves along African coasts and the interior.[12] Enslaved Africans spoke numerous languages and dialects, including Yoruba, Hausa, Igbo, Ewe, Fon, Alada, Carabalí, Arabic, Akan, Wolof, Fula, Mande, Kikongo, and Kimbundu, among others. Interpreters enabled traffickers to communicate with Africans during all phases of the Middle Passage.

In late July 1836, HMS *Pincher* captured the slave ship *Preciosa* within view of the coast of Cuba with 295 Africans on board.[13] In a deposition before the Anglo-Spanish Mixed Commission Court at Havana, master Santiago Comas stated that the ship had departed from Puerto Rico on December 4, 1835. After taking on slaves at the Pongo River on the coast of West Africa (present-day Guinea), the *Preciosa* sailed on June 12, 1836, with a destination of Matanzas, Cuba. Among the crew of the *Preciosa* were five male African Kru. Inhabitants of Sierra Leone, Liberia, and Ivory Coast, these Kru (also known as Krumen or Kroomen) were "hired as seamen and interpreters" for twelve dollars a month "until they should return to some part of the Coast and that besides some reward should be given to each according to his conduct during the voyage."[14] Comas recalled the names of four of the Krumen as Suma, Cuzimber, Lesandre, and Sias.

To gain information about the voyage of the *Preciosa*, representatives of the Mixed Commission Court interviewed the captain, crewmembers, the five Krumen, and a few of the recaptured Africans. A British official wrote:

> During the examination, it was obvious that these men [the Krumen] had apprehension about their future fate, hence preventing them from making most important disclosures about this slaving voyage and Jousiffe [Edward Jousiffe, a British passenger on board the *Preciosa*, a well-known trafficker in slaves based at Matanzas, Cuba who was believed to be the owner of the *Preciosa*]. One of these men named Alessandro or Lessander [the same Lesandre noted above] feigned a total ignorance of any language but that of his native country [likely the Yoruba-English creole language known as Krio]. [However], when Alessandro had been questioned *alone*, it was discovered he spoke French, English, and Spanish very tolerably, that he was a most intelligent Negro, and that he had made other voyages in the same employ between the Rio Pongo and Matanzas. The other Kroomen were under his charge, and he was evidently the most useful man on board in taking charge of the unhappy beings who composed the cargo.[15]

Jousiffe had been involved in the slave trade between Guinea and Cuba for many years.[16] His ventures brought him influence in both locales. On Africa's west coast, Jousiffe maintained close ties with the widow of a "notorious slave merchant" named John Ormond. The woman had become wealthy running a factory situated on the Pongo River.[17] At the Ormond factory Jousiffe received African slaves and boarded them on vessels. A passenger who journeyed on the *Preciosa* was the woman's fourteen-year-old son, who had the same name of John Ormond and was said to be traveling to Matanzas "to be placed at a school." In Cuba, several associates protested Jousiffe's incarceration aboard the *Pincher* but failed in attempts to free him.

Santiago Comas also had plenty of experience in the traffic. In 1830, the HMS *Primrose* seized the slave vessel *Maria de la Concepción* captained by Comas off the west coast of Africa and condemned the vessel.[18] The capture obviously did little to derail Comas from continuing in his pursuits.

Allesandro's measured responses during the inquiry had much to do with what he knew of Joussiffe and Comas. The latter two had lots of contacts; they had demonstrated a capacity to evade capture by the Royal Navy; both were violent individuals. Allesandro understood that if he accused Joussiffe or Comas of wrongdoing, he or his family might face retribution. Hence his decision to remain silent when questioned in front of others.

During the private discussion, Allesandro's sophistication became evident. Closely linked to maritime activities along the west coast of Africa, he communicated in several languages. Allesandro's linguistic and navigation skills made him an important asset to Jousiffe. Allesandro used his knowledge of sailing routes, personal ties to fellow Krumen, and diplomacy with captured Africans to help guide the ship from Guinea to Cuba as quickly as possible. Although he was residing in an environment full of duplicitous traffickers, Allesandro's abilities enabled him to survive as a free man. Based on the comments of Allesandro and others, the Mixed Commission Court at Havana declared the Africans who had arrived on the *Preciosa* to be liberated and determined that they be sent to the British colony of Honduras to work as "free" workers.

The full history of what had transpired on the *Preciosa* did not surface through the interviews in Havana. Once underway on the Caribbean Middle Passage to Honduras, several spoke about their recent past. "From the account furnished by the mate in charge of the prize [the captured slave ship *Preciosa*], it appears that when he had left Havana and was fairly on his voyage to Belize [his final destination being in fact Honduras], several of the negroes of both sexes spoke to him in English and declared that they had been kidnapped by Jousiffe, that they were British subjects from Sierra Leone, and that fear and menaces of future punishment had kept them silent during their stay in this port [of Havana]."[19]

Africans who had maintained silence in Havana showed themselves to be English speakers. Their comments provided important information to members of the prize crew. A few months later, infantry in Cuba arrested Jousiffe. In early 1837, Lieutenant Byng of the *Pincher* returned to Belize to pick up a couple of the Krumen.[20] These men detailed Jousiffe's actions before the Mixed Commission Court at Havana, providing evidence that was subsequently used by the British to put Jousiffe on trial at Freetown for participation in the traffic.[21]

Once they were landed in Honduras, a manager assured the 193 males and 58 females who arrived from Cuba that they would find future happiness in their new country. Interpreters informed the non-English speakers among the group of their labor responsibilities.[22] For several of the men, this meant cutting down and then hauling mahogany trees to the coast for export. The Africans quickly realized that their "liberated" status required them to labor as indentured workers for three to fourteen years ahead. Indeed, the conditions endured by most Liberated Africans differed little from those of fellow enslaved blacks.[23]

In commenting on the disembarkation of the passengers from the *Preciosa*, the British consul expressed his hope that the Africans would develop their skills and become productive workers, exhibiting none of "the cancer that seems to pervade the mind of the hereditary slave in all countries."[24] The term *hereditary slave* most likely was an allusion to a creole slave, meaning an African descendant who had been born in the Americas. Or (less likely) it implied a free black descended from slaves, given that slavery had been abolished throughout the British empire two years before in 1834. Whichever, the consul echoed the desire of a timber and planter elite that the Africans would become a docile labor force in Honduras and throughout the British Caribbean.

The capture of the Spanish slave ship *La Joven Reyna* off Cuba in March 1835 sheds further light on individuals known as "black interpreters." Captured by H.M. sloop *Arachne* with 254 Congo Africans in its hold some one hundred miles to the west of Havana, *La Joven Reyna* included among its personnel a "Brazilian negro taken on board on the coast of Africa, as an interpreter, at a fixed salary of twenty dollars per month."[25] Known among the crew as Juan Cabinda, this interpreter spoke an African language, Portuguese, and enough Spanish to be understood by the crewmembers from Spain.[26]

Juan Cabinda knew well the perils and profits related to transatlantic slave voyages. Most likely African-born and transported to Brazil on a slave ship, he gained his freedom in Brazil. An Atlantic creole returning to the coast of Africa, Cabinda sought to use his skills to find employment. In seeking interpreters, slave ship captains often contacted a Portuguese merchant named Don Francisco Sousa, who resided at Ouidah [Benin]. Described "as a kind of broker on the coast, to whom all persons engaged in this traffic apply when they have necessity of an interpreter," Sousa could easily have been the intermediary between Miguel Martorell, the captain of the *Joven Reyna*, and Juan Cabinda.[27]

Immediately upon the capture of the *Joven Reyna*, Juan Cabinda requested special treatment, claiming to be not a member of the crew and hence not meriting punishment. British officials disputed Cabinda's claim. Lieutenant James Caldwell of the *Arachne* stated in his deposition before the Mixed Commission Court at Havana that Cabinda's role "had really been to interpret between the bozal negroes and the crew [of the *Joven Reyna*]."[28] British consul Maclean wrote that "although these black interpreters are in fact no other than the person employed by the slave traders on the coast of Africa to procure them these negroes, and consequently little deserving of protection, the Mixed Commission [Court] thought it right to call the Captain General's attention to this man's case in the note which accompanied the copy of the sentence."[29]

Juan Cabinda presented papers that he had kept in his possession during the Middle Passage to Cuba that proved his status as a free man in Brazil (affirming that he had been a slave and gained his emancipation). Cabinda requested of the British captors that he not be imprisoned with the rest of the crew from the *Joven Reyna*. In spite of his plea, Spanish officials at Havana imprisoned him with the others at the Castle de la Fuerza.

INTERPRETERS OF THE MIXED COMMISSION COURTS

One component of British policy to halt the kidnapping and transport of Africans to the Americas was the creation of Mixed Commission Courts. Two of these were established in 1819, one in Rio de Janeiro and the other in Havana, based on bilateral treaties between Great Britain and Portugal, and Great Britain and Spain.[30] In that same year, the British government set up Mixed Commission Courts in Freetown, Sierra Leone and in Paramaribo, Surinam. Subsequent treaties created Mixed Commission Courts in Boa Vista, Cape Verde Islands; Spanish Town, Jamaica; Cape Town, South Africa; Loanda, Angola; and New York City. The Brazilians disbanded the Mixed Commission Court in Rio de Janeiro in 1845. As a result, during the next decade, a British Vice Admiralty Court in Rio de Janeiro determined the fate of captured slave vessels. A Mixed Commission Court at Havana continued to function until 1864 (but with virtually no role after 1845).

The Mixed Commission Courts included a judge representing the nation that signed the treaty along with a British judge, hence the title. If the two judges disagreed on a decision, the vote of an arbitrator appointed by lottery (from two arbitrators present at the court, each representing one of the two nations) determined the outcome of the case. If a vessel was found guilty of involvement in the slave trade, the Mixed Commission Court condemned the ship. Income received from sale of the ship or sale of the materials derived after dismantlement (wood beams, masts, metal, ropes, and so forth) was divided by the two governments or awarded to the British crew who had apprehended the vessel. Described as the first international human rights courts, Mixed Commission Courts heard more than 600 cases and "liberated" some 174,000 Africans taken off captured slave vessels. The largest number of trials before these courts occurred in the 1830s and 1840s.[31]

The Mixed Commission Courts and Vice Admiralty Courts needed interpreters and translators to function. In Rio de Janeiro and Havana, British judges who did not speak Portuguese or Spanish depended on them. Interpreters and translators shared information published in newspapers and picked up informally in the streets with court officials.

As noted previously, in response to extended delays by the Mixed Commission Courts and health conditions on board captured slave vessels, England placed the "receiving ships" *Romney* (1837–45) and the *Crescent* (1840–54) in the ports of Havana and Rio de Janeiro.[32] Numerous Africans died while held on captured prize ships due to the filthy environment, insufficient protection from the sun and heat, infection, and lack of care. Once removed from a slave vessel to the more amenable environment offered by a receiving ship, sick Africans could be treated without being landed in the port city. This policy appealed to Cuban and Brazilian authorities, who feared the spread of epidemics.[33] Besides Liberated Africans, the British commander transferred several

British sailors to the receiving ships. He did this to protect against thugs who on numerous occasions attempted to kidnap Africans domiciled on the receiving ships.

Diversity of language and dialect abounded on the receiving ships. Africans communicated in their native languages. Many spoke the predominant European languages of the transatlantic slave trade, including Portuguese, Spanish, English, Dutch, French, and Italian, along with mixed pidgin languages. Such linguistic skills could be traced to contact with merchants from various countries, European settlers, and traffickers on the African coast.[34]

In such a milieu, interpreters provided their expertise. As representatives of the Mixed Commission Courts, African or African-descendant interpreters asked questions of Africans in their native language about homelands, capture in Africa, and the Middle Passage to Cuba and Brazil. To give an idea of the complexity of this task, from interviews of 392 Africans (257 male, 135 female) on board the captured schooner *Tita* brought to the port of Havana in July 1835, interpreters learned that 333 were of the Lucumí nation. Hence, they spoke Yoruba. Yet, from these 333, the Africans stated that they originated in twenty-three different locales. As such, they spoke dialects of Yoruba. As listed in English in the British documents, these regions included Layi, Llabú, Aivá, Otá, Eyó, Dará, Evá, Otá, Yesa, Labé, Tapa, Yabú, Vacuó, Efú, Llama, Ecua, Ebú, Yebú, Dogú, Lali, Pore, Chavé, and Yacó.[35]

Interpreters conversant in European languages interrogated the captain and crewmembers of the slave ships. From these interviews on board the captured slaver and the receiving ship, judges at the Mixed Commission Courts as well as foreign consuls learned of merchant houses, factories, the operations of traffickers along the coast of Africa, and conditions and treatment during the Middle Passage. Major problems surfaced in finding skilled interpreters to carry out these often difficult and complex tasks.

British consul in Rio de Janeiro Robert Hesketh described such a dilemma (in 1837):

> Another problem that has consumed time at the Mixed Commission [Court] has been the want of a permanent interpreter. . . . It is difficult for the interpreter when there are several cases before the Court. It is the duty of that officer to translate all the documents in the English language [to Portuguese] and the verbal declarations or evidence made in that language. . . . He has also to go on board the vessels to ascertain the exact number and description of the Negroes at the time sentence [by the Mixed Commission Court] is passed; and all such

duties have been found so pressing and the person generally employed so unable to execute them with the requisite expedition, that another part of his Duties, the translations of documents sent to Her Majesty's Secretary of State have been for a long time made by Mr. Grigg, the British Commissioner of Arbitration.

Notwithstanding the duties which an interpreter may be thus called upon to perform, the office is not now a permanent one, and lately a person has been appointed when the court is actively employed, which is a system not likely to promote either zeal or regularity.[36]

In the case of the receiving ship *Romney* at Havana, the British stationed African sailors of the British Royal Navy on board. This decision was motivated by the Africans' capacity "to understand the language and habits of the liberated Africans placed under their charge," who arrived on captured slave vessels.[37] Among these free Africans was George Elder, who became a trusted interpreter for British consul David Turnbull.[38]

INTERPRETERS WHO AIDED THE BRITISH SQUADRON

Interpreters aided in the suppression efforts of the British Squadron. In the case of the schooner *Vencedora*, a free black woman from Havana and a British medical doctor played pivotal roles in determining its complicity in the commerce. The *Vencedora* sailed from the coast of Africa to Cadiz, Spain, and arrived in Puerto Rico on October 6, 1837. After a sojourn of eight days in Puerto Rico, the ship departed with a destination of Cuba. On October 14, crewmembers from HMS *Ringdove* boarded the *Vencedora*. They immediately counted fourteen crewmembers and 49 Spanish passengers. Searching the hold of the *Vencedora*, the British found twenty-six Africans. Of these, we know that nine were adult males, seven were women, seven were boys, and two were girls. In the words of Horatio Stopford Nixon, commander of the *Ringdove*, "the slaves appeared to be of recent importation, had no other clothing than a piece of cloth tied round their loins, their heads shaved, and some of them in a sad state of emaciation."[39] Several had facial scarification, a common practice among the Yoruba of West Africa. W. John Watson, British surgeon on board the *Ringdove*, estimated the age of the children to be "from ten years upwards."

Watson inquired in Spanish about the Africans found below deck on the *Venecedora*. The captain claimed them to be passengers. To support this lie, he exhibited forged passports. Watson requested the captives to state their names in Spanish, but none of the Africans comprehended the question.[40]

One week after the capture of the *Vencedora*, on October 22, British consular officials requested the aid of a "black woman" resident in Havana. As in several port cities in the Atlantic world during the nineteenth century, officials (Mixed Commission Court judges, consuls, police, and personnel at the port) employed Africans and their descendants as interpreters.[41] Speaking in an African language, the woman inquired about the journey of the *Vencedora*. She learned that the ship had departed from Africa "about two moons ago. The men, women, boys and girls had never been in another vessel, [and they] swore to it after the custom of their own country."[42] She then explained in English what she had learned. The responses of the Africans contradicted the captain of the *Vencedora*, who claimed that they had traveled from the west coast of Africa to Cadiz, Spain, on a mail packet and then been transferred to his ship. The descriptions provided critical evidence to British representatives in their investigations.

The willingness to interpret by this unknown woman merits scrutiny. With the disappearance of sugar and coffee production in Saint-Domingue during the Haitian Revolution (1791–1804), cultivation of those crops expanded rapidly in Cuba. To satisfy labor demand, planters imported some 325,000 African slaves from 1790 to 1820, a tripling of imports in thirty years.[43] The arrival of so many Africans quickly transformed Havana and Cuban society.

This was also a period of upheavals in Spanish America (1810–25), which converted four viceroyalties under the direction of the Spanish king into sixteen independent nations. Five decades of political and social instability followed. To retain their status and wealth, the Spaniards who ruled Cuba had no interest in separating from Spain. Given that rebels like Simón Bolívar had close ties to Haiti and had spoken of abolition during the independence wars in Latin America, conservative sectors sought to impede the entrée of what they viewed to be subversive ideas into Cuba.[44]

These events contributed to a hardening of race relations in Havana in the 1830s. The Spanish government made it illegal for persons of color to enter Cuba from Haiti.[45] It also prohibited the import of revolutionary literature from whatever source. Free blacks who had participated in all sectors of Cuban society at the beginning of the nineteenth century faced marginalization at every turn. The black bourgeoisie saw their legal rights erode.

In such an environment, that a black woman agreed to interpret the statements of Africans would appear to be an act of courage. What was she thinking? Most likely she felt a genuine desire to help the Africans who arrived on the *Vencedora*. At the same time, she hoped that British diplomacy and example might help to alleviate the hostility directed at her and fellow free blacks residing in Havana.

African interpreters often participated in patrols of the Royal Navy. In June 1850, Commander Bunce of HMS *Castor* searched for barracoons on the southeast coast of Africa with plans to destroy them and disrupt the traffic in slaves. At Bunce's side was an Arab translator. Five miles up the Mozamba River, Bunce, along with several sailors, went onshore. As they approached the village of Keonga, a chieftain came forward:

> Through the interpreter, I [Bunce] found that he was anxious to make peace. He said the Arabs wanted to be friends with the English, and that the barracoons belonged to the Bunian [people], not to them. I told him we did not want to war with the Arabs, that we would not hurt a hair of their heads. But that I should burn the barracoons to whomsoever belonging. I told him I did not come to destroy his village, but that if an Arab fired a single shot, I would burn it to the ground and shoot every Arab in the place. I then placed the men in position and commenced burning the barracoons, stores, sheds, crawls, and everything connected with them. I had a half dozen men with port fires, whose duty it was to burn, and the whole place was in a blaze in no time.[46]

Commanders of British ships also had to interact with Africans and crews encountered on board slave vessels seized at sea. This occurred with the brig *Aventura* (also known as the *Maria Isabel*), which sailed from Lisbon, Portugal to Rio de Janeiro and then continued to Angola in December 1835. After a voyage from Luanda with 66 slaves on board, a British cruiser captured the *Aventura* near St. Sebastião, Brazil the following April. While the crew was making inquiries with the Africans, one of the women spoke up. "Positive evidence of slave trading by the *Aventura* was taken from one female slave, who, from having been in service in Angola, is perfectly conversant with the Portuguese language." Given that the captain had escaped and the crew denied wrongdoing, the female African who spoke in Portuguese provided key evidence that aided in the Mixed Commission Court's decision to condemn the *Aventura*.[47]

Such episodes occurred throughout the Atlantic world. In waters off the coasts of Africa, African interpreters provided British commanders with geographic information, descriptions of ships, insights about the strategies of traffickers, and critical aid when boarding suspected slaving vessels.[48] In Brazil and Cuba, African and African-descendant interpreters did the same.

They helped the Royal Navy find enclaves used for disembarkations, depots for holding slaves, hidden routes into the interior, and parties alleged to be involved in the trade.

Traffickers in Cuba and Brazil used language as a means to mislead authorities investigating illegal disembarkations of African slaves (those who arrived after the British treaties with Spain of September 23, 1817, and with Brazil of March 13, 1830). If a slave could speak some words in Spanish or Portuguese, he or she could be represented as a creole slave (meaning one who had resided in Brazil or Cuba since birth). To accomplish this task, merchants provided Spanish and Portuguese language instruction to recently landed Africans. In Rio de Janeiro they "established various Deposits for the reception of slaves and the teaching of Portuguese language."[49] The chief of police of Rio de Janeiro wrote that traffickers commonly placed "three or four Africans who can speak a few words of Portuguese in all vessels involved in smuggling [of recently arrived Africans]. They are called 'linguists' but are as much *boçaes* [recently arrived slaves from Africa] as any of the others."[50] One senator lamented that such activities boded ill for the future. "Brazil will be very soon not the initiator and rival of civilized nations, but the imitator and rival of the coast of Africa."[51] In Cuba, traffickers attempted to deceive authorities by including ladino slaves (Africans who had resided in Cuba for an extended period) among recently landed Africans, and having such individuals who could speak at least rudimentary Spanish respond to questions posed.

"THEIR SPEECH BETRAYETH THEM"

An interprovincial slave trade in Brazil expanded from the 1840s between the North and Northeast provinces (for example Pará, Pernambuco, Alagoas, and Bahia) and Center South provinces (Rio de Janeiro, Minas Gerais, and São Paulo). This coastal transfer (and overland to a lesser extent) of some 225,000 slaves occurred for two reasons. One was that as British interventions succeeded in stifling slave disembarkations at and near the port of Rio de Janeiro in the early 1840s, traffickers moved their operations north to Bahia and Pernambuco. With less British presence and a reduced chance of capture, vessels landed thousands of African slaves in those provinces. Merchants then sent them south to the port cities of Rio de Janeiro and Santos.[52] And second, planters in the burgeoning coffee regions of the Central South provinces sent representatives north to purchase slaves. Given the high prices offered and the

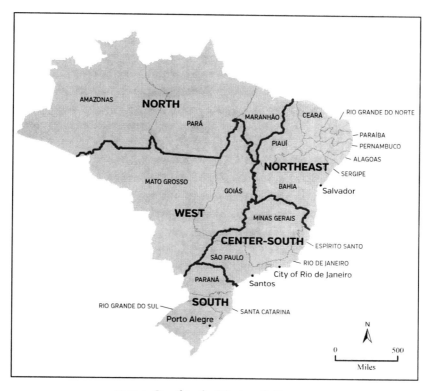

MAP 5. Brazil in the Nineteenth Century

economic difficulties in the North and Northeast provinces, particularly in the sugar sector, planters sold large numbers of their slaves.

The trauma of separation from loved ones and familiar environments caused great suffering among slaves. One observer wrote that "all at once a slave dealer comes into the market [in the north of the empire] from Rio de Janeiro, buys up from the audacious masters all of those slaves he can obtain, and in most cases is the cause of separation of the father from his wife and children and vice versa, the unfortunate African being again perhaps sold at his ulterior destination to some harder master or some unprincipled speculator. This is predominantly carried out by Portuguese. This traffick needs to be suppressed, it is a traffick no less cruel than the African trade itself."[53]

Similar to a transatlantic slave voyage, journeys in a ship along the Brazilian coast became *focos* of resistance.[54] African and Brazilian-born creole slaves conversed during the journey of several days. They discussed the interceptions of the British Squadron and international pressures to end the slave trade. They shared accounts of their experiences in Africa, during the Middle Passage, and in Brazil. As in other regions of the Americas, the pain caused by this dislocation fueled the hostility felt by blacks toward the regime that held them in bondage.[55] Once landed in the Center South, slaves and free blacks who had been deported from the North and Northeast gained notoriety for their resistance.[56] This included work slowdowns, protests, flight, and rebellions.

To impede the movement of *boçaes* into Rio Janeiro and São Paulo, British cruisers detained ships so as to interview slaves and inspect travel documents (such as passports issued by Brazilian port authorities and evidence of provincial export taxes paid). If a slave could speak fluent or passable Portuguese, this would help to confirm that he or she was a creole born in Brazil and therefore could be transferred legally from one province to another if papers were in order. If the slave had difficulty with or could not respond to questions posed in Portuguese, it most often meant that he or she had been born in Africa and landed in Brazil sometime after Brazil's 1831 law that freed all Africans who arrived after that date. Speakers of African languages would then carry out interviews.[57]

What the interpreters learned from the slaves played a key role in determining the response of the authorities. In various instances, British cruisers removed Africans from intercepted vessels sailing along the Brazilian coast. This is exactly what occurred with the British seizure of the ship *Piratinim* in August 1851. Interpreters on board the HMS *Sharpshooter* determined that sixty-six of the ninety-three slaves being transported from Bahia with a destination of São Paulo (all with "legal" passports issued by police in Salvador) were Africans.[58]

The twenty-two African women and forty-one African men (along with three infants) were noted in the record by their "nation" or geographic location of origin. The nations cited included Nagô, Gegé, Tapa, and Ussá (Hausa), and the locations were listed as Mina, Gallinas, Congo, Dahomey (present-day Benin), Angola, or Mozambique. All had resided in Bahia for periods ranging from four months to thirty years. Most of the women had "a very slight knowledge of the Portuguese language." British consul Robert Hesketh questioned how Antonia could be a "Creole Negress" given that she had "no birthplace [as] stated in the passport, and [was] only understood through an interpreter" who determined that she was from Dahomey. The men showed a "knowledge of Portuguese in proportion to the period they stated since arrival [on a slave ship to Brazil]," meaning length of residence in Bahia. Commander Chamberlain of the *Sharpshooter* observed that forty-four of the sixty-three adult Africans could speak no Portuguese whatsoever. Based on the interviews, he placed the sixty-three Africans and three infants onto the receiving ship *Crescent* anchored in the port of Rio de Janeiro. With the *Piratinim* taking on five inches of water an hour, the British commander destroyed it.[59]

The interpreters also provided helpful information about the other blacks encountered on board the *Piratinim*. The "crew" included "nine robust and healthy negroes." Hesketh described them as African slaves. Six were Nagô (Yoruba) and three came from Angola. Their ages ranged from eighteen to twenty-six years. They had landed from seven to sixteen years previous, which meant that they had all arrived after 1831 and hence were legally free.

Among the Brazilian-born creole slaves were four women and twenty-three men and boys. All except one had been born at various locations in the province of Bahia, including the city of Salvador and the interior towns of Santo Amaro, Cachoeira, Maragogipe, São Feliz, and Jacobina. Twelve described themselves as plantation slaves, ten as house servants, two as masons, one as a carpenter, one as a carpenter's apprentice, and one unknown. The ages of the creole slaves ranged from Maria Louisa, "a negress house servant of 8 years," to Ponciano, a house servant aged 32.

It is striking that three of the male Africans had resided in Bahia for longer periods (thirty, twenty, and eighteen years) than several Brazilian-born creoles. It is possible that these men identified more closely with Brazil than Africa (due to family ties, experience, language, and so on) and possessed a more "creolized" view of the world than creole blacks born in Brazil. Instead of emphasizing differences between African and creole slaves (as prevails in the historical literature on this topic), the document provides a glimpse of the origins of an Afro-Brazilian consciousness that surfaced at the turn of the twentieth century.[60]

Similar episodes occurred in Cuba. As British suppression efforts mounted from the 1820s, it became increasingly difficult for a slave vessel to sail into the harbor at Havana and disembark slaves. As a result, traffickers landed Africans at more remote locales, for example on the south side of the island. Planters hoped that Africans could be deposited near their estates. The overland travel, which reduced the distance, also decreased the dangers of something going wrong. Such disembarkations were not always possible, so the Africans could be forced to walk miles to arrive at a private estate.

Soon after arrival at an estate or a depot, traffickers would divide up the Africans and send them to purchasers in various locations on the island.[61] This could mean that the slaves walked overland or were transported by coasting vessels. To accomplish this task, owners employed militias to ensure that the Africans did not escape and that they were not stolen. Owners also forged passports and identity cards (known as *cedulas*) as a way to deceive any authority who might question whether the Africans had recently arrived.[62]

Residents in Cuba easily recognized *bozal* Africans. In comments about the disembarkation of over one thousand Africans on the northwest coast near Havana in early 1842, observers accused merchants Don José Mazorra and Don Julian Zulueta of collusion in the crime. Showing no inhibitions, the traffickers brought the recently landed Africans to barracoons close to the city of Havana with plans to sell them. "The Africans were openly marched [from point of disembarkation to the barracoons] in files through the highways, conspicuous by their scarred faces, their shaven heads and their general appearance."[63]

As in Brazil, language played a critical role in attempts to halt the traffic to Cuba. As one example of many, in late 1846 a British judge at the Anglo-Spanish Mixed Commission Court in Havana received information of a landing of Africans. He learned that

> a number of negroes clad in new dresses and speaking in their native [African] language to one another had been marched along the road with the usual marks of having been recently introduced to the island. [With the help of informants], he had them traced to the house to which they were eventually taken. Upon subsequent investigation, he was satisfied that they had belonged to a coffee estate [that had been] devastated by the late hurricane, and consequently abandoned. The children it proved all spoke Spanish giving proof of their having been born in this island, but their parents spoke their own language among themselves, rather than Spanish, which they had not yet acquired, further than to understand the orders for their usual labors. It appeared that they had been here about seven or eight years and were Lucumís.[64]

Given the lack of evidence, nothing could be done to show that these Lucumí had not resided long on the island. Although it was obvious that the parents had been disembarked illegally (meaning they had arrived after an 1835 law that prohibited the slave trade to Cuba), investigators knew well that the owners would have documents to prove legal ownership and impede any sort of investigation.

In another episode, traffickers landed an estimated 584 Africans in the sheltered bay known as Bahia Honda (translated as Deep Harbor and located forty-three miles west of Havana) by a vessel with no papers on board. Subsequent investigation showed the slaver to be the *Grey Eagle*. Constructed in Robbinston, Maine in 1852 by Zacharia Cutter and Seth G. Low, the ship was enrolled (registered) in the port of Passamaquaddy, Maine. It was purchased by Thomas G. Hollingsworth and others of Philadelphia. The new owners stated that the *Grey Eagle* would be used to fish for pearls off the coast of Venezuela. On September 1, 1853, the *Grey Eagle* sailed for La Guaira, Venezuela and it returned to Philadelphia on December 21, 1853. Most likely this short trip was a voyage to test the vessel's speed and agility for future use as a slave ship. Given the successful interceptions of slavers by the British Squadron, traffickers needed fast-sailing and efficient ships by the 1850s.

In 1854, known trafficker George Marsden of New York City and Rio de Janeiro purchased the *Grey Eagle* and then sold it to Samuel S. Gray of New York. As was common practice, Gray acted as a front for a Spanish entrepreneur named Don Riveiro (perhaps Francisco Riveirosa, who had recently been banished from Rio de Janeiro). Captained by J.G. Darmand, whose real name was Samuel Nicholas, the *Grey Eagle* sailed from New York on March 25, 1854, with a destination of West Africa.[65]

Receiving information of the landing, the lieutenant governor of Bahia Honda Don José de Pavia y Padilla went to the locale of the landing. Arriving at one a.m. with an entourage of armed workers from a nearby sugar plantation, Pavia wrote that "there was heard at a distance a low murmuring of voices."[66] After the men guarding the Africans slipped away into the darkness, Pavia's group successfully recaptured 205 Africans who had recently landed from the *Grey Eagle*. Pavia immediately proceeded to a plantation where he believed other Africans had been moved. To converse with two Africans believed to have arrived on the *Grey Eagle*, Pavia employed "an interpreter, a negro of the Lucumí tribe, who could not write, and who was a slave of Don Luis Castañedo, on whose estate the negroes had been deposited." Imagine the scene! An enslaved Lucumí on a sugar plantation asked to explain the statements of fellow Lucumí who had lately appeared at the estate. The document does not make clear Castañedo's role in the landing. Given Castañedo's position as captain of the port at Bahia Honda, one wonders about his motives.[67]

The interview did not go well. The two Lucumí stated that they had arrived two days previously, which differed from testimony of "authorities and other residents in [local] legal proceedings." They did not know how many fellow Africans perished during the Middle Passage. One stated that "*some of the negroes*" had succumbed and the other stated that "*many died on the pas-sage*."[68] Neither could provide the names of the vessel, master, or crew. One of the Lucumí estimated that they had been on board the ship for two and a half months.

The British consul wrote that "the evidence from [provided by] these two negroes from their extreme ignorance appears to have been of but little impor-tance." Nevertheless, the statements must have been convincing to Lieutenant Governor Pavia. For the following two days, Pavia visited twelve nearby sugar plantations and other estates and inquired about the status of 2,892 slaves, all of whom were determined to be creoles or ladinos. Padilla made arrangements to transport the 205 recaptured Africans from the *Grey Eagle* to Havana on July 2.

Descriptions provided by Africans and articulated by interpreters helped the commanders and crews of the Royal Navy in their quest to put a perma-nent halt to the transatlantic slave trade. Interpreters also provided important information about the interprovincial transport of slaves in Brazil and inter-island movement of slaves in Cuba.

AFRICAN TRANSLATORS

In the wake of the Revolt of the Malês, police hired Africans to aid them in their investigations of Muslim African slaves and free Africans. In Salva-dor, Africans who spoke Arabic, Yoruba, and Portuguese analyzed materials (books, pamphlets, clothing, and metal goods used in religious ceremonies) confiscated from the homes of fellow Africans. Africans translated documents penned in Arabic. Given that several hundred Nagô fled or were deported to Rio de Janeiro, free inhabitants of that city became greatly concerned about the presence of what they perceived to be a foreign threat. In several episodes, police in Rio de Janeiro requested that Nagô translators come to the head-quarters to translate and explain the meaning of written documents confis-cated from Muslim Africans.[69] Fears of rebellion combined with the arrival of thousands of Africans into port cities made African translators important employees of police seeking to maintain public security.[70]

How did African translators view their activities? One view posits that free Africans were conservative in all their activities, particularly after the 1835 Revolt of the Malês. They did not wish to bring attention to themselves or get into trouble.[71] Hence, a translator walked a fine line. On the one hand, he sought to allay the fears of officials suspicious of all things African. On the other, he needed to be forthright in informing police of any and all potential disturbances or threats. This was no easy task, given the widespread distrust of free Africans in the two decades following the revolt.

In one episode in January 1851, four hundred free Congo residents in Rio de Janeiro requested British aid to return to their homelands in Angola and Congo. Leading the group was Joaquim Nicolão de Brito, a native Kikongo (Bantu language) speaker who penned a letter in Portuguese. Brito employed his ability to speak and write in Portuguese to represent his fellow Africans in their quest to depart from Rio de Janeiro. Based on the comments made by a British consul along with a petition submitted by Brito, it is clear these free Africans were Atlantic creoles who understood the rapidly changing political economy of Rio de Janeiro and regions in Africa at mid-century.[72]

In correspondence with his superiors in London, British consul James Hudson emphasized that Brito and his fellow Congo had attained their freedom through committed labor. Many had earned an income as street vendors (*ganhadores*) independent of their owners. Men had found employ in a wide range of jobs, including as porters, boatmen, and canoe men. Women sold fruit, baked goods, and small items. This income enabled them to purchase their emancipation. As slave disembarkations rapidly diminished in late 1850 due to passage of Brazil's anti–slave trade law, white artisans (primarily Europeans) arrived in search of work.[73] As a result, free Africans in Rio de Janeiro found themselves pushed out of the labor market. Not surprisingly, the Africans had little confidence in the majority of the ship owners and captains present in the city. Hence, they turned to the British consul, hoping that he could help the group return to Africa.

The petition translated from the Portuguese into English follows:

Most Illustrious and Most Excellent English Minister, Protector of the Free Africans in This Capital

Joaquim Nicolão de Brito, and many other free Africans, like your petitioner, residing in this capital, having by common accord, among themselves, resolved upon retiring from this capital, solely from motives of their private interests, but being in want of a transport to convey them all together and land them at the port of Ambriz [Angola], where they wish to establish themselves, take the liberty of having recourse to the high protection of Your Excellency, by whom, they confide, they will be well received, and protected by your kindness and phi-

lanthropy, and they most respectfully entreat your Excellency will deign to permit that some English vessel and under your orders may transport them to the
above mentioned port of Ambriz, they your petitioners, subjecting themselves
to defray the expenses of such transport, further hoping that they will be also
protected by Your Excellency with full equity in this respect, in consideration of
the poverty of your petitioners, and of their not being able to bear extraordinary
expenses, and in the hope, from your Excellency's benevolence, that you will
benignly grant the prayer of their petition, they anticipate the assurances of
their most sincere and eternal thanks.

R.M. Rio de Janeiro, January 15, 1851[74]

Seven months later, Brito returned to the British consulate. He explained
that he and the other Congo remained steadfast in their desire to return to
Africa. However, they changed their intended destination from Ambriz to
Cabinda [Angola]. One reason for this shift was that "the nephew of the present Chief of Cabinda, who has passed thirty years in Brazil, had made up his
mind to accompany them." Another motive was that many of the Africans had
relatives and friends in Cabinda who claimed that town superior to Ambriz for
settlement. And third, these Congo "imagine the influence of the slave dealers
[involved in the traffic to Cuba] to be less at Cabinda than at Ambriz, and that
they would be able more easily to deal with it and defeat it."[75]
Joaquim Brito along with a few of his African friends subsequently appeared in several instances at the British consulate inquiring about their proposed journey to Africa. Given that many of the Africans had sold whatever
property they owned in Rio de Janeiro and "terminated engagements" in preparation for what they believed to be an impending departure, their situation
caused the British consul to express regret that the British government had
failed to come to their assistance.[76] The last correspondence relating to this
group of Congo was in June 1853, when British consul Jerningham affirmed
that "if Her Majesty's government be still disposed to lend a favorable ear to
the application of these free Negroes to carry out their wishes for establishing
a colony, it would be a very beneficent and charitable act to afford them the
means of repairing to Africa."[77] If any of the four hundred Congo made it back
to Africa, they did it on their own, without the financial support of the British
government.[78]
African and African-descendant interpreters and translators played multiple roles in cities in Cuba and Brazil in the nineteenth century. They appeared

at police stations and in courts. Interviews they conducted helped determine the fates of Africans brought into the harbors of Havana and Rio de Janeiro on board vessels captured by the British Squadron.[79] Africans translated documents penned in Arabic at the request of police phobic over the presence of African Muslims. Joaquim Brito conversed in Kikongo with compatriots who desired to return to their homelands. He wrote out their statement in Portuguese and then delivered the petition to a British representative residing in the city of Rio de Janeiro. An unknown person, perhaps employed by the consulate, subsequently translated the letter into English. Such endeavors are among the many hidden histories of Atlantic creole interpreters and translators.

SPOKEN WORDS

Africans and their descendants communicated verbally with one another through words. Words provided a way to share stories, personal experiences, history, and cultures. Slaves carefully selected words to express grievances at Mixed Commission Courts and before judges and juries across the Americas in the nineteenth century. In some instances, fluency in a language proved to be of critical importance. Episodes in Brazil and Cuba shed light on the activities of slaves who articulated words in English that enabled them to attain their freedom.

On April 22, 1848, the HMS *Grecian* captured the slave ship *Bella Miquelina* off the coast of Bahia (as described in chapter two). The two ships became separated due to bad weather. In need of provisions, the *Bella Miquelina* entered the port of Salvador on April 29. The *Grecian* sailed into port two days later.

During the short visit of the *Grecian* in the port of Salvador, a black man arrived at the British ship and was allowed to board. Speaking fluent English, he claimed to have been illegally enslaved and wanted to know if the captain could help him. Commander Tindal of the *Grecian* wrote the following:

> A negro who calls himself by the name of John Freeman, native of Sierra Leone and therefore a British subject, and who speaks English perfectly, has come on board H.M. sloop under my command to ask for a passage to his own country.
>
> He states that he was kidnapped about a year ago at Popo [present-day Republic of Benin] to which place he had gone with an Englishman, as servant, when he was seized, put on board a slave vessel, and brought here where he has been for five months.

His master is named San Jardim, a black man, but I cannot find out where he lives [in Salvador]. It is so obvious that he is a British subject that I shall not permit him to leave the *Grecian* until I hear from you, who I request will take the necessary steps to have the case investigated.[80]

The events surrounding John Freeman's escape provide a glimpse into the ties that bound Salvador to the Atlantic world at mid-century. Three days after Freeman gained access to the *Grecian*, the Salvador newspaper *Correio Mercantil* published among its fugitive slave notices a description of great interest to our story about a man known as Manoel.[81] A member of the "nagô nation," this individual "spoke a little bit of English." One of several hundred free and enslaved Africans who sailed small boats in the harbor, Manoel had recently ferried goods and persons to a British ship named *Pilotfish*. He was of "small and regular stature" and "with poor vision" (*pouco enxerga de noite*). Manoel's face was covered with scars left by smallpox (*bastante bexigoso*). As a result, the markings (small cuts) on his face common among the Nagô (*signaes da nação*) were hidden. The last trace of Manoel was that his boat had been seen tied to the stern of the *Pilotfish*. Manoel's owner Gonçalo de Menezes Costa offered a reward for the capture and return of his property.[82]

Although we cannot be absolutely sure that Manoel is John Freeman, it is likely. There could not have been many Africans laboring in the port who spoke English and fled on that May 2. This African employed several names. When Manoel spoke to Commander Tindal, it would appear that he declared himself to be John. Perhaps he took this name to hide his identity and the fact that he had escaped. Manoel did not want to be deposited onshore back into the hands of his owner. Or perhaps Commander Tindal had been informed of the situation from someone on board the *Pilotfish* and purposely used the name John in correspondence. In Salvador, the aggrieved owner Gonçalo Costa and others knew John Freeman as Manoel. Nowhere among the documents (to date) is Manoel's original African name.

The *Grecian* sailed out of Salvador on May 3 destined for Rio de Janeiro with John Freeman on board. For the next six months, Freeman resided in Rio de Janeiro, perhaps on the British receiving ship *Crescent* anchored in the harbor. On November 7, he returned to Salvador on board the *Grecian*. This occurred in response to a request by Bahian officials, to which British consul James Hudson in Rio de Janeiro agreed, that Freeman's fate be determined by the courts of Bahia. What happened to John during this sojourn in Bahia is not known (so far!). At a later date (unknown), he returned to Rio de Janeiro. On

May 27, 1849, John Freeman achieved his goal: he sailed on board the HMS *Adventure* out of Rio de Janeiro destined for Sierra Leone.

John Freeman became an international *cause célèbre*. Brazil's minister of foreign affairs sent a note to the British government protesting what had occurred and demanding reparations (on May 22, 1848). In September, Lord Palmerston responded. He stated that England fully supported the actions of Commander Tindal and that Tindal had acted in accordance with international law. The Brazilian legation in London lodged further protests in subsequent months. In February 1850, almost two years after the short visit of the *Grecian* in the port of Salvador, Minister of Foreign Affairs Paulino José Soares de Souza alluded to John Freeman in a speech before Brazil's Council of Ministers. In it, Soares argued that "the state of liberty of the African [Freeman] who took refuge on the *Grecian* can only be inquired into and decided by the tribunals of the empire. [Hence], British authorities [illegally] constituted themselves judges of the condition of an individual within the proper jurisdiction of the empire."[83]

In venturing into the Bay of All Saints in Salvador to make contact with the British crew of the *Grecian*, John Freeman exhibited the impressive traits of an Atlantic creole. In the five months he resided in Salvador, he learned of the political tensions that simmered in Bahia stirred by the aggressive actions taken by the British Squadron. Laboring independent of his owner, John gained a good grasp of the urban geography of the city and port. The knowledge he acquired enabled him to attain geopolitical literacy.[84]

John showed himself to be closely attuned to the movement of ships and daily bustle of the port. In the hours following the arrival of the *Grecian* he responded quickly, aware that if he failed to do so the British cruiser would be gone and he would miss this opportunity to articulate his grievances. That early morning, John traversed the windy cobblestone roads that led to the docks and embarked in his small boat as usual. He did not want to draw attention to his activities so as not to jeopardize his plan. Similar to numerous Atlantic creoles in the Age of Revolutions portrayed by Professor Jane Landers, John "risked danger, found an opening, seized the moment, and freed himself."[85]

In that same year of 1848, a black man named John Lytle approached the U.S. journalist John L. O'Sullivan, who was touring the countryside of Cuba. Born in Philadelphia, Lytle had endured 11 years as a slave in Cuba. He explained to the visitor that he had been kidnapped on the west coast of Africa and transported to Cuba on a slave ship. John requested that he be able to return to the United States. O'Sullivan, later made famous for coining the phrase "manifest destiny" as editor of the *New York Morning News*, immediately sent a letter to Secretary of State James Buchanan describing the encounter. "He [John] is a dark negro, apparently under thirty years of age, intelligent in appearance, and speaking English perfectly well, without any tinge of Southern accent."[86] O'Sullivan's choice of words sent the message that he was confident that John had never been a slave in the U.S. South. O'Sullivan requested that Buchanan use his office to free John Lytle.

After research confirmed the truth of Lytle's story, the U.S. consul at Havana Robert B. Campbell met with John and penned his "Declaration":

> Says he was born in Philadelphia about the year 1817 in Cane Street and during his early life he lived with Mr. Depejeway who was then a Methodist preacher and that on the removal of Mr. Depejeway he went to sea for some years in the bay trade after which he shipped in the ship *Jupiter* and made two voyages. . . . [On a subsequent voyage] after leaving Montserate [Montserrat, among the Leeward Islands of the Caribbean] the ship [*Jupiter*] was wrecked about the mouth of the Mano River [Mani River, Sierra Leone] and entirely lost but the crew were all saved and made their way to Galenas [at Gallinas River on the border between Sierra Leone and Liberia], a Spanish slave station [factory] on the coast. . . . [A trafficker named] Don Francisco Ramón offered inducements to him to remain under a promise to pay him for his time and services, furnishing him a passage to Havana and a letter which would procure him a passage to the United States, that after remaining about four months and 28 days he was placed on board the slave schooner *Concha* with about 400 slaves and arrived at the out port of Puerto Escondido where Mr. Gaspar Hernández bought 20 negroes and asked me what I was going to do in this country. I answered that I did not know until I saw the American consul. He asked how I would see the consul. I told him I had sent for the consul by one of the crew of the vessel. I saw the consul Mr. Shoemaker at Matanzas who with Mr. Hernández advised me to go to Mr. Hernández's estate [in the summer of 1837] until the consul returned from the United States for which he was soon to sail and that was the last I have seen of him. In all my subsequent efforts to get access to any place where there was a consul I failed until sent for by the present consul at Havana and that during all the intermediate time from 1837 until this month of July [1848] I have been on Mr. Hernández's estate. I reckon the time not from positive recollection but I think I was on the estate about two years before the estate had an engine, and it has had one about nine years. My treatment has always been that of a slave but I have never been punished or cruelly treated. When I left Philadelphia I had a wife and two children.

Signed by John Lytle, July 7, 1848, and co-signed by Robert B. Campbell, U.S. consul at Havana.[87]

As much can be learned from comments not included in John Lytle's "Declaration" as from the description conveyed in the account. From inquiries made by Campbell, it became evident that John put up a fight when he realized that he had been purchased to labor as a slave on the estate of Gaspar Hernández. John forced Hernández to return to the merchant who sold him "in consequence of the defect of title growing out of his [John's] claim to be a free man." In other words, John made it clear that he was a free black man from Philadelphia and demanded his release. Hernández and the merchant paid scant attention to John's protests, but did agree to renegotiate the price to $125, or one-quarter of the original cost of purchase.[88]

John stated that an engine had arrived in 1839, which would have been a steam engine used to crush the sugarcane. He recalled that it had been run by an engineer from the state of Maine, but could not remember his name. Matanzas province produced at least a quarter of Cuba's sugar from the 1820s. To cut the sugarcane, Hernández and other planters purchased increasing numbers of African slaves. In 1827, the population of Matanzas was composed of 16,671 whites, 2,602 free blacks and mixed race mulattoes, and 26,522 black slaves. By 1841, these numbers had increased to 27,148 whites, 4,705 free blacks and mulattoes, and 54,322 slaves. On this latter date, the slave population was double the number of whites in the province.[89]

The slaves of Matanzas gained notoriety for their resistance. Some twenty-two escaped slave communities (*palenques*) sprung up in the mountains of the province in the first half of the century. *Palenqueros* employed guerrilla tactics to attack the coffee and sugar plantations in Matanzas. The Great African Slave Revolt of 1825 left sixteen whites dead and twenty-four estates torched. Resistance continued during the 1830s, culminating in the Escalera insurgency.

John Lytle surely knew about even if he had not personally witnessed the brutal repression in the aftermath of La Escalera while residing at the Hernández estate in Coliseo. Yet he makes no mention of what happened. Why would this be? John knew that Hernández and the planters of Matanzas felt they were under assault from within (African slaves, educated urban free black bourgoisie) and from without (British-led international abolitionism, U.S. desires to purchase Cuba). John did not wish to provoke anyone during the delicate negotiations. All he wanted was to get out of Cuba and back to the United States as soon as possible. Hence, his strategy was to stay mum on any topic that might shed a negative light on the planters of Matanzas or the government of Cuba. Indeed, he emphasized at the conclusion of the Declaration that "my treatment has always been that of a slave but I have never been punished or cruelly treated."

Another example of an Atlantic creole who seized an opportunity to speak out and seek his freedom, John Lytle placed his trust in Robert Campbell. He had little choice. Campbell showed dismay over the injustice suffered by John. However, the moral tenor of the Declaration and the correspondence surrounding it reflected as much Campbell's anti-Spanish bias and political goals as it did his genuine concern for John's plight. This was a precarious moment for U.S. diplomats. Desirous of forging a "New Empire," U.S. elites and their representatives abroad sought to compete with England for economic influence throughout Latin America, push Spain out of the Caribbean, and gain control over Cuba.[90] As the recipient or interpreter of John's story, Campbell determined how the saga would read.

The Campbell-Lytle Declaration compares to a well-known testimony contained in Cuban ethnologist Miguel Barnet's *Biography of a Runaway Slave*. During interviews carried out in 1963, Barnet conversed at length with the last living former slave in Cuba. Esteban Montejo, 103 years old, described life as a slave, a *cimarrón* (escaped slave), and a free man in the years between his birth in 1860 and 1905. In the book, first published in Havana as *Biografía de un cimarrón* (1966), Barnet as listener shaped Esteban's spoken words so as to enhance the appeal of the story to the revolutionary government that attained power in January 1959.[91]

Campbell claimed that John's ordeal "is important to the government of the U.S., and I request that a person be sent by the captain [general] who is fluent in English and Spanish to attend in behalf of John Lytle."[92] Soon after, John gained his freedom. Incredibly, the Cuban government reimbursed John Lytle for his time as a slave. He received $2,211.33, which included $150 for each of the eleven years of his enslavement in Cuba. In late July 1848, John Lytle arrived in New York City, and was immediately embraced by influential African American abolitionists.[93]

English-speaking slaves appeared before British and U.S. representatives stationed in Brazil and Cuba in the hope that their spoken words might bring attention to their condition. Closely attuned to the words and ideas that flowed around them, Atlantic creoles knew about British efforts from the

1780s to halt the transatlantic slave trade, and the abolition of slavery in the British empire in 1834. They heard about blacks calling for an end to slavery in the United States from the late 1820s, knew about the 1831 law that freed all African slaves entering Brazil after that date, and took notice of the French emancipation decree of 1848. They observed closely the activities of the British Squadron and the appearance of captured slave ships in the harbors of Rio de Janeiro and Havana.[94] Such information moved from coasts to interior plantations to Caribbean islands and throughout the Atlantic world.[95] No less an observer than future U.S. president John Adams commented during a visit to South Carolina that "the negroes have a wonderful art of communicating intelligence among themselves; it will run several hundreds of miles in a week or fortnight [two weeks]."[96]

A FINAL REFLECTION

Interpreters, translators, and slaves speaking words all played a part in the transatlantic slave trade to Cuba and Brazil. Some interpreters aided in the kidnapping of Africans, the overland journey of the enslaved to the coasts of Africa, embarkation on slave ships, and the Middle Passage to the Americas.[97] Others joined in British patrols along the coasts of Africa and South America and in the Caribbean Basin. British and U.S. diplomats employed interpreters to help them in investigations of the transatlantic slave trade. Interpreters interviewed coastal residents of Cuba and Brazil to inquire about slave disembarkations, and they conversed with African slaves and ship crews on board captured vessels. Translators read words in one language and then penned them in a second or third language. Mixed Commission Courts could not have functioned without the aid of interpreters and translators. Included among these men and women were Atlantic creoles along with Europeans of diverse origins. A handful of sympathetic officials and foreign diplomats listened closely to the spoken words of slaves. Words articulated in English enabled a few slaves to gain their emancipation. Slaves who witnessed the determination of persons like John Freeman and John Lytle gained inspiration in their quest to be free. Such episodes added to subaltern pressures that pushed forward the international abolitionist movement from the 1770s to 1888.

7

DEMISE

———— ∞ ————

In mid-October 1846, a "sharp-built new Baltimore clipper" sailed into the port of Rio de Janeiro.[1] Originally named the *Rifleman*, it was quickly sold for twelve thousand dollars to an "association" of traffickers and renamed the *Brazil*.[2] This group of investors included New York merchant Jenkins (who described himself as a ship chandler), wealthy British entrepreneur Russell, and Portuguese national Guimarães (most likely Joaquim da Fonseca Guimarães). The three immediately leased the *Brazil* for five months at a cost of one thousand dollars per month to Bernardino de Sá, a renowned trafficker. The latter fitted out the *Brazil* for a slave voyage, and the brig cleared from Rio de Janeiro declaring a false destination. Its real destination was West Central Africa.[3]

Although little is known of this voyage, records show that the *Brazil* received 490 enslaved Africans. In September 1847, it landed 444 survivors of the Middle Passage at an unknown location on the Brazilian coast.[4] Shortly after, the *Brazil* entered the port of Rio de Janeiro in ballast "wearing American colors and well known to belong to notorious slave traders."[5] Pleased by his success, captain David Bevens of New York sailed the *Brazil* back to Africa and returned to Brazil with slaves in the middle of 1848.[6]

After this second journey from Rio de Janeiro to West Central Africa and back, the travels of the *Brazil* become blurred. It is possible that for a year the ship ferried materials between New Orleans and Cuba. More likely the ship sailed on a third slaving venture from Cuba to Africa, organized by de Sá's associate in Havana Pedro Toreado.[7] In September 1849, the *Brazil* appeared in the Bay of All Saints at Salvador, Brazil. Believed to be the source of the yellow fever epidemic that devastated Bahia (described in chapter three), it remained at anchor in the Bay of All Saints for more than three months. In early February 1850 it departed Bahia and journeyed again to West Central Africa. Sailing east under the temporary name *Segunda Melvira*, showing a Brazilian flag and with a crew of forty men, the brig received an estimated six hundred Africans near the mouth of the Congo River.[8] In May 1850, the *Brazil* landed these Africans near Cardenas, Cuba.[9] Abandoned by the crew, local authorities took possession of the ship. Supposedly finding no evidence that the vessel had transported slaves to Cuba, they handed the *Brazil* over to well-known trafficker Pedro Forcade, who declared ownership of the brig. During the next eighteen months, the *Brazil* sailed twice more to Mozambique in East Central Africa and carried an estimated 1,485 Africans to Cuba (of whom 1,287 survived).[10]

How do the six voyages of the *Brazil* reflect the dynamics of the transatlantic slave trade within the international economy at mid-century? First, management and investments made in the *Brazil* remained a transnational enterprise. U.S. citizens, Spaniards, Portuguese, and Brazilians all played prominent roles. Merchant houses in Baltimore, Havana, Salvador, Rio de Janeiro, and most likely Lisbon all profited from transactions related to the voyages of the *Brazil*. Second, as British efforts to suppress the traffic mounted along the Brazilian coast in the final months of the 1840s, traders shifted the *Brazil* out of the south triangle trade and into a slave traffic directed solely to Cuba.[11] Third, U.S. investors continued to play a major role in the slave trade. After building the *Brazil* at a shipyard in Baltimore, merchants sent the clipper to Rio de Janeiro with the clear intention of inserting the ship into the "Rio Trade."[12] One of at least fifteen U.S. ships sold or leased in Rio de Janeiro in 1847, the *Brazil* showed the skillful craftsmanship of U.S. shipbuilders.[13] Eugenio Viñals (also known as Eugenie Vignier), captain of the fifth voyage of the *Brazil* from Cardenas, Cuba to Mozambique and back, boasted that the ship's superior design enabled it to evade British capture.[14]

Although, beginning in the 1820s, U.S. abolitionists criticized the transatlantic slave trade, the U.S. government turned a blind eye to the traffic. Composed of a few ineffective warships, the U.S. Naval Squadron played a minor role in suppressing the traffic. U.S. consuls knowingly signed "sea letters" that enabled U.S. ships to depart from Brazilian and Cuban ports on slaving voyages. Traffickers used U.S. ships to supply factories and facilitate embarkation of slaves on African coasts. Until 1862, they flew the U.S. flag on hundreds of ships as a way to prevent intervention by the British Squadron.[15] Indeed, influential parties in the United States acknowledged the benefits of allowing England to take the lead in chasing down slave vessels. One U.S. diplomat alleged that "we have not exasperated the Brazilian population on the slave trade question. Our government, our treaty, even our minister, are objects of daily reference and eulogy in the debates [in the Brazilian parliament], in the newspapers and in conversation. We have nothing to ask for just now in connection with the treaty making contest. . . . [Hence], we need not be in a hurry. Let Great Britain go before and with her elephantine bulk trample down the obstacles in the path of negotiation. Let us be at hand to profit by her labors. She can obtain nothing but what we shall share."[16] From this perspective, the furor elicited in Brazil by British efforts to suppress the traffic would bring long-term economic benefits to the United States.

DEMISE I: BRAZIL

From mid-1847, the British government intensified assaults on the transatlantic slave trade. Domestic political debates in England, along with evidence of numerous successful disembarkations in Brazil, underpinned this decision. Ship commanders took unprecedented measures at key locales in Africa. David Eltis and David Richardson show that no fewer than one in nine of the 1,575 captures of transatlantic slave ships by the British navy after 1807 occurred in the two years of 1847 and 1848.[17] At Mozambique, British representatives requested that intelligence detailing the sale and transport of slaves from the interior of East Central Africa be furnished by the British explorers Murray, Oswell, and Livingstone.[18] After being fired upon by traffickers, the crew of HMS *Dee* attacked the town of Inhambane, resulting in the death of two hundred defenders and the destruction of its stockade and battery.[19] British cruisers chased suspicious vessels and seized ships in spite of their flying a U.S. flag.[20] British crews destroyed barracoons at the mouth of the Congo River, and at Sherbro island and islands off the Gallinas River south of Freetown, Sierra Leone. In November and December 1851, under the direction of Commander F.E. Forbes, three British ships attacked Lagos, burned down most of the city, and replaced Chief Kosoko with Chief Akitoye, who opposed the slave trade. These actions resulted in the expulsion of numerous traffickers from West Africa, including 34 sent to Salvador on board the U.S. bark *Mary Irvine*.[21]

In Brazil, commanders of the British Squadron paid close attention to the shifting dynamics of the slave trade. Increased surveillance resulted in numerous seizures at the port of Rio de Janeiro. "Wise as serpents," traffickers moved their operations north and south along the coast.[22] Small harbors provided ideal locales to fit ships for voyages, including Angra dos Reis, Mambucada, Mangaratiba, Dois Rios, Armação, and Macahé.

The British Squadron responded to the deceptions of traffickers. In mid-1849, its cruisers intercepted several Brazilian ships along the coast of Bahia, evoking a furor among imperial ministers.[23] In the first half of 1850, Commander Herbert Schomberg seized slaving vessels at Cape Frio (province of Rio de Janeiro, ninety-five miles east of the city of Rio de Janeiro) and Paranaguá (province of Paraná, two hundred miles south of Santos). Among these was the *Chester* (also known as *Paulina*), a 331-ton vessel (which appears to have been U.S.-built), which landed nine hundred Africans on the southeast coast of Brazil in April 1849.[24] The U.S. captain protested the arrest vehemently. Besides encountering evidence of materials to be used for a slaving voyage to Mozambique and sixteen Brazilian seamen hidden in the hold of the vessel, British seamen found twenty-five thousand dollars concealed in casks of wheat flour. Schomberg set fire to several other slaving vessels in front of crowds gathered on beaches.[25]

Schomberg then headed north to Salvador. Upon entering the harbor, he came upon five vessels believed to be preparing to depart on slaving voyages. In a meeting with Governor Martins, Schomberg criticized provincial authorities for failing to search and seize the ships.[26] Burnings of slave vessels in sight of land continued into the fall.[27] These actions contributed to the decision of the imperial government to respond with more aggressive policies of suppression.[28] In September 1850, the Brazilian General Assembly passed the Queiroz Law, which representatives hoped would shut down the traffic to Brazil for good.

Final attempts to land slaves in Brazil in the 1850s involved several U.S.-built ships. On July 9, 1851, the Baltimore-built schooner *Relâmpago* sailed from Salvador destined for West Africa. Owned by the "well-known participator in this iniquitous trade" Geronimo Carlos Salvi, the *Relâmpago* carried a "legal cargo." Soon after arrival at the port of Onim (later Lagos), another trafficker named Marcos Borges Ferraz purchased the vessel. He immediately fitted out the schooner to carry slaves. At Onim, the *Relâmpago* received 820 Africans. During the Middle Passage, 35 perished.[29] On October 29, the Brazilian war schooner *Itapagipe* encountered the suspicious-looking vessel twenty miles south of Salvador. In an attempt to evade capture, Captain Benito Derizanz directed the ship toward the coast.

A posse of thirty armed men appeared to receive the Africans. In a desperate scene that followed, forty of the Africans drowned in the surf trying to get to shore. Another twenty died soon after making it to the beach. In the words of one witness who arrived soon after the landing, "the Africans were forced into the rough water and perished due to their weak condition, being hardly able to stand up from their sufferings during the voyage. Even the mothers were forced, through the application of the lash, to part with their little children, and to see them perish in the sea in which they were thrown by their barbarous executioners! More than forty dead bodies were found on the beach near the disembarkation, some [bodies were found] in the woods through which those Africans who reached the shore in safety had escaped; so that I calculate that no fewer than sixty lost their lives through the covetousness of their executioners."[30] Captain Benito Derizanz and members of the crew survived and fled into the nearby forest.

Alerted by telegraph, chief of police in Salvador João Mauricio Wanderley traveled with forty soldiers of the police corps on board the Brazilian steamship *Catarina*. Arriving on the morning of October 30, Wanderley found forty-nine Africans under the protection of crewmembers from the *Itapagipe*. He soon met up with troops of the local National Guard and headed inland. As the soldiers encountered an escort accompanying the Africans, a firefight ensued. Two of these traffickers died, and one national guardsman was wounded. The soldiers arrested nine creole slaves, recaptured 209 of the recently landed Africans, and took possession of six mules on which the members of the escort had been mounted, along with five guns. Arriving at an abandoned house on the estate "Pontinha," Wanderley discovered food supplies, a "Dictionary on Popular Medicine" by Pedro Luiz Napoleão Chernoviz, and six maps. Each map showed locations throughout the Atlantic world, including (1) the west coast of Africa; (2) the coasts of Africa and Brazil, with disembarkation points highlighted in pen; (3) Caribbean islands; (4) the Gulf of Mexico; (5) the United States, West Europe, and Africa; and (6) the coast of Brazil.[31]

Believing that the traffickers planned to transport a contingent of the Africans to the town of Jequiriçá located six leagues into the interior, Wanderley pressed on. With a force of 140 men, he carried out searches of several plantations, one of which was an estate named Caribé (Caribbean). In spite of discovering hastily constructed huts and the remainders of dried meat and manioc flour near the towns of Caixa Prego, Calabar, Cabrestante, and Estiva, the search party came upon only eighteen more Africans.[32] Inquiries proved fruitless "because the inhabitants of that neighborhood connived at the traffic, or being apprehensive, would not furnish any [exact information]."[33] Wanderley lamented that the traffickers had evaded capture and succeeded in marching many of the Africans to private estates in various parts of Bahia.

On November 5, HMS *Locust* arrived on the scene. Tying ropes to the *Relâmpago*, the British ship successfully pulled the upright slaver off the beach. Boarding 204 of the recaptured Africans onto the *Relâmpago*, the *Locust* towed the vessel to Salvador.[34] Another 59 Africans arrived with Wanderley on November 13.[35] In the weeks that followed, city officials distributed 168 of the Liberated Africans from the *Relâmpago* to labor on public works projects in Salvador. Among these men were Nagó and Hausa. One of the Africans claimed to be of the Ebá nation and to have been enslaved after being captured in battle in Africa. For unknown reasons officials sold this man as a slave.[36]

Seeking to clear his name of accusations of involvement in the traffic, Governor Francisco Gonçalves Martins wrote: "it is clearly seen that the greatest part of this criminal speculation is lost, because those [some 480 Africans not found] who may still escape the search after them by the authorities, will become the prey of robbers, and perhaps of Death occasioned by misery and precipitate marches over almost impracticable places. Would to God such a lesson may put an end to such speculations, contrary as they are to all religious duties, to society, and to the true patriotism which counsels us to be zealous in supporting the dignity of the Nation of which we call ourselves the sons."[37]

Chief of Police Wanderley agreed: "In proportion to the increase of repression, the horrors of the slave trade also increase; the care heretofore taken by the slave dealers of the convenience and health of the passengers has disappeared; it happens that, as in the present instance, hundreds of Africans come huddled together in a small vessel [the *Relâmpago*], in want of provisions and water laying upon the casks, without a platform or a second deck, as was customary. Nothing short of the most severe penalties can counteract so many acts of barbarity."[38]

Wanderley showed an astute capacity to adapt to the changing political winds at mid-century. One of the documents that surfaced during the investigation at the Pontinha estate was a passport signed in January 1851 by Wanderley. It allowed a black Bahian named Manoel Ambrozio da Conceição to travel to West Africa. Wanderley understood that the passport likely enabled this nineteen-year-old tailor (*alfaiate*) to participate in some manner in the slave trade. The determination of the chief of police to investigate "the landing at Pontinha" related to a desire to erase evidence of responsibility or ties to the voyage of the *Relâmpago*.

In the early months of 1852, various officials in Rio de Janeiro took close notice of several U.S. ships present in the harbor. Both the *Mary Adeline* and the *Camargo* raised suspicions. Based on information provided by informants, Minister of Justice (Interior) Eusébio de Queiroz requested that officials investigate the *Mary Adeline* in late April. Accompanied by U.S. Minister Robert Schenk and U.S. Consul Charles Raynsford, Chief of Police Bernardo Augusto Nascentes d'Azambuja visited the ship at anchor in the harbor. Although finding insufficient evidence to seize the *Mary Adeline*, the three agreed that "the cargo [found on board] was precisely calculated for the traffic."

In examining the ship's papers, they learned that a "House that had been notoriously engaged in the traffic" had invested in the voyage. Police and imperial ministers knew well the merchant house of Joaquim da Fonseca Guimarães & Co. The chief of police proceeded to the abode of Guimarães, where he demanded to see documents. "On a glance at the correspondence of the House, it became clear to the chief of police that the charge [of involvement in the planned slave voyage of *Mary Adeline*] was well founded, on which Mr. Guimarães and Mr. Brandão [an associate], who were found concealed in an outhouse, were arrested and taken to prison, where they still remain, until sufficient evidence can be got together to bring them to trial."[39] Subsequent review of the confiscated materials showed that "the House of Guimarães was actively engaged in slave transactions with Lisbon, and had agents for the slave trade in every part of the world. . . . It appears that the documents seized confirm the extensive ramifications of the plan, whose center is Portugal, for supplying Havana with slaves."[40] Three months later, the new minister of justice, José Souza Ramos, expelled Brandão from Brazil, giving him 30 days to return to his home country of Portugal.[41]

After paying a large bond (deposit) to discourage participation in the traffic, the captain of the *Mary Adeline* set sail that same afternoon. Concerned that the legitimate crew on board the vessel at departure was to be substituted offshore with Portuguese sailors (a common practice), Queiroz requested that a Brazilian steamer of war accompany the *Mary Adeline* from the harbor out to sea. Impeded from receiving the replacement sailors, the *Mary Adeline* sailed for Angola.

Soon after arrival off Luanda on June 4, the *Mary Adeline* encountered the British steamship *Fire Fly*. Finding insufficient materials to seize the ship, the British commander allowed the *Mary Adeline* to continue on its journey. On June 17, it entered the mouth of the Congo River. Meeting another British brig named the *Dolphin*, the captain assisted the *Mary Adeline* and enabled it to head upriver. After several attempts to enter the Congo River, the *Mary Adeline* grounded at a shallow locale named Shark's Point. Boats and men from the *Dolphin* attempted to pull the *Mary Adeline* free, but to no avail.

Within hours, an estimated 1,500 to 3,000 Africans attacked the *Mary Adeline*. They used muskets, spears, oars, and cutlasses as weapons, along with hooks and poles to climb the side of the ship. The small crew of the *Mary Adeline* fought back by shooting a six-pound cannon lent by the *Dolphin* that killed several of the Africans. In spite of aid from the steamship *Fire Fly*, the *Mary Adeline* remained beached for three days. After some two-thirds of the cargo from the *Mary Adeline* was transferred to the *Dolphin*, the former set off and was moved to deep water offcoast (on June 22). Sailing from near the Congo River, the *Mary Adeline* arrived in Salvador on July 21 after a quick voyage of twenty-one days.[42] On August 9, the *Mary Adeline* returned to Rio de Janeiro in ballast, the port from where it had hastily departed the previous April.[43]

News of what happened to the *Mary Adeline* at the Congo River spread quickly in Salvador and Rio de Janeiro. A planned attack by Africans on a slaving vessel helped to convince Brazilians and foreigners that a resumption of the slave trade posed significant and unwanted risks. The notion that ship crews would have to fight armed warriors when trying to load Africans on slaving vessels appealed to no one.[44] Furthermore, the Africans who participated in violent confrontations on the coasts of Africa surely gained confidence from these episodes. Such individuals would not be easily enslaved or coerced onto a slave ship.

Another U.S. ship anchored in the port of Rio de Janeiro in spring 1852 raised the suspicions of port officials. The *Camargo* arrived at Rio from California in October 1851 with a cargo of hides. On April 12, it sailed out of the harbor under the direction of a twenty-six-year-old captain from Portland, Maine named Nathaniel Gordon. With a declared destination of the Cape of Good Hope, Gordon stated that he planned to pick up cattle and horses from South Africa and then return to Rio de Janeiro to sell them. A British consul who had been watching the *Camargo* closely complained that "this is a species of commerce which from requiring the same supplies and accommodations for the live cargo which would serve for slaves, lends itself to the purposes of fraud."[45] Henry Southern also reiterated that U.S. citizen Robert Marsden, a broker long resident in Rio de Janeiro and known to have invested in the voyage of the *Mary Adeline*, had been "actively interested in getting up and aiding this speculation [meaning the *Camargo*'s journey to Africa]."[46]

Following a short visit to Cape Town, the Camargo continued up the southeast coast to Quelimane (Mozambique). After final preparations, it received 550 Africans on board.[47] Fifty of the Africans perished during the Middle Passage. The *Camargo* arrived on December 12 at a beach at the entrance of the Bracuhy River, located close to the town of Angra dos Reis, some one hundred miles southwest of the city of Rio de Janeiro. After landing the five hundred Africans, the crew set fire to the vessel. An "armed force" of men received Captain Gordon, his wife, and the fourteen crewmembers and directed them to houses nearby. A hidden trail was cut through the forest to transfer the Africans inland without being seen. It led to the estate of José Breves, "one of the wealthiest and most extensive proprietors of slaves in Brazil."[48] Alerted to the disembarkation two weeks after the event, the minister of justice sent the chief of police of the province of Rio de Janeiro to Bracuhy. With the aid of fifty to sixty officers, they found thirty-eight of the *Camargo* Africans and sent them to Rio de Janeiro.

The landing outraged British and U.S. representatives in Rio de Janeiro, who sought to suppress the traffic. "All the facts related to the *Camargo* case, the false information, the difficulties of extracting information from the arrested, the slowness of communication, the difficulty of finding out about the landed blacks: All these facts clearly demonstrate that the slave dealers in the country have not relinquished their evil practices, and that deeply organized schemes must still exist and will, if not discovered and frustrated, give rise to fresh complication of difficulties."[49] The representatives judged Minister of Justice Souza Ramos to be "very deficient both in sagacity and vigor" and the imperial government incapable of decisive action. They recommended that England take more aggressive actions to suppress the traffic. Suggestions included sending British steamers to patrol along the coast and mounting more aggressive expeditions on land to search for recently landed Africans.[50]

The *Camargo* landing caused a major stir. By the first week of January 1853, police in Rio de Janeiro arrested four of the crew of the *Camargo* who had returned to the city. During an examination with a Brazilian judge, they admitted to having sailed on the *Camargo* and been on board when the ship returned to Brazil with the 550 enslaved Africans. They claimed that when departing from Rio de Janeiro the previous April, they had no idea that the captain of the *Camargo* had plans for a slave voyage. The judge belittled this defense as carrying little weight, given that the sailors did not report what had occurred to the police or the U.S. consulate upon their arrival in Rio de Janeiro. In fact, the arrests thwarted their attempt to escape from Rio de Janeiro. Among their possessions was money that they received for participation in the voyage.[51]

Police in Rio de Janeiro also arrested George Marsden for his alleged connection to the outbound and inbound voyages of the *Camargo*. Upon his release, he fled from Rio de Janeiro to New York City, where he resumed dealing in the traffic of Africans to Cuba. Captain Gordon also escaped prosecution in Brazil. Nine years later, he would be the first and only U.S. citizen executed for his attempt to transport 897 Africans from Shark's Point at the Congo River to Cuba. The ship he captained on that voyage was the *Erie*, a three-mast vessel of 477 tons constructed in Swansea, Massachusetts.[52]

Searches for the Africans from the *Camargo* continued through the spring. Suspecting that many had been moved to regions of coffee cultivation in the interior of Rio de Janeiro province and nearby São Paulo province, police "rigorously searched the estates and farms of wealthy individuals."[53] This did not go unnoticed by the slaves. Like urban blacks who witnessed the arrival of captured slave ships, so did rural slaves and free blacks pay close attention to officials carrying out searches. They understood that those Africans (the majority) who had arrived after the law of November 7, 1831, were legally free. The investigations represented a possible avenue to liberation. Planters in the region of Bananal, São Paulo decried heightened tensions in the region in a communiqué sent to the Ministry of Justice: "The fears of the community are therein stated to have been aroused by a spirit of insurrection which has shown itself in some plantations; that planters have not been able to check the partial insubordination of some of the Negroes. That others are suffering from the fact of their slaves absconding in whom they had placed confidence. And that these dangers and agitations appear to have been created simply by the *presence* of an armed force sent to apprehend the newly imported Africans, who were supposed to be concealed in the vicinity."[54] Although Minister of Foreign Affairs Paulino Souza downplayed the published accounts of "insubordination" among the slaves at Bananal as an exaggeration, nevertheless he did acknowledge "lots of bad spirit in that quarter."[55]

The imperial government instituted legal proceedings against the planter

José de Sousa Breves, on whose property the Africans of the *Camargo* had been disembarked. Acquitted by the unanimous vote of a jury at Angra dos Reis, "supporters set off rockets and fireworks to celebrate" the decision.[56]

In the wake of the *Camargo* landing, U.S. representatives in Rio de Janeiro called for greater controls over U.S. vessels. These proposals included (1) prohibition of all trade in U.S. vessels between Brazil and the coast of Africa; (2) prohibition of the export in U.S. vessels of all articles employed in the slave trade; (3) prohibition of the sale of U.S. vessels at Brazilian ports, even if sanctioned by the U.S. consul; and (4) immediate reorganization of the U.S. Squadron, providing it with fast-sailing and light vessels capable of chasing slavers to small bays, coves, and rivers along the coast of Brazil.[57]

Although the U.S. government failed to implement these reforms, officials in several Brazilian ports commenced more thorough investigations of ships suspected of preparing for illegal voyages to Africa.[58] They also hired informants to follow obfuscating traffickers. The latter included U.S. citizens at Rio de Janeiro Robert C. Wright, William S. Maris, John W. Disney, and Jacintho Derizanz (Venezuelan by birth, he claimed to be a U.S. citizen).[59] Journalists also played an important role by denouncing the incompetence and corruption of authorities.[60] After the acquittal at a provincial court of a captain and crew arrested while disembarking three hundred Africans, one Bahian beseeched, "Oh God! What does this mean? There were books without leaves, machinery without use, crimes without criminals—Might there not also have been Bribes, Family Connections, Deception, Substitutions, Simulations? Where, where are we? Are we in Negrita, Abyssinia, or in Hell? Tell us—are we in Bahia? There is a screw loose somewhere . . . the Africanites [traffickers] vitiated the process, they paid for proofs, [and] they nullified justice."[61]

The last ship captured when transporting Africans to Brazil was the U.S. schooner *Mary E. Smith*. Weighing 122 tons, the vessel was built for $15,000 in Essex, Massachusetts specifically for the slave trade.[62] Previous to its departure from Boston on August 25, 1855, the ship raised the suspicions of U.S. and British authorities due to materials taken on board known to be used on slaving vessels (extra wood planks to construct a slave deck, metal shackles, a large number of water casks, and the like). Fending off arrest by a U.S. deputy marshal and a handful of men in his employ who boarded the *Mary E. Smith* as it was pulled out of Boston harbor by a tugboat, Captain Vincent D. Cranotick forced the intruders off and set sail.[63]

Based on documents seized by police in Rio de Janeiro in early December, the *Mary E. Smith* sailed from Boston directly to southeast Africa. Several Portuguese investors were involved, including Guilherme da Silva Correa, who maintained barracoons near the mouth of the Congo River.[64] Other parties included the house "Figaniere & Irmãos" and "Spencer and Buddens," both of New York City.[65] Port officials in Rio de Janeiro alerted Brazilian, British, and U.S. naval forces of the impending arrival of the *Mary E. Smith*. Few vessels in the history of the transatlantic slave trade garnered such notice with regard to their impending arrival.

After sailing to the Congo region of Africa, where it took on an estimated 400 to 450 Africans between the ages of fifteen and twenty, the *Mary E. Smith* arrived near São Mateus (on the northern coast of the province of Espírito Santo) in January 1856. Informed of a possible attempt to leave African slaves on the coast, the Brazilian steamship *Olinda* seized the vessel and escorted it to Salvador. Port authorities there estimated that at least seventy-one Africans died from sickness between the time of interception off the Brazilian coast on January 20 and arrival in Salvador on January 31.

Bahian officials condemned the *Mary E. Smith* and brought the surviving Africans into the city. This act "caused terror among the population of the city," spurred by the belief that the presence of ill Africans would exacerbate the cholera epidemic that had devastated Bahia since the previous August. Bahian doctors and health officials offered medical care and provided food. Observers claimed optimistically that these actions improved the Africans' health. In spite of such measures, one hundred more of the blacks who had arrived on the ship perished during the following two weeks. By February 14, out of 213 Africans who survived, 88 remained desperately ill, suffering from a variety of sicknesses, including cholera morbus. Incidents of infections markedly increased in the city in February. Inhabitants attributed the spread of cholera during that month to the Africans from the *Mary E. Smith* and the decision to allow them to disembark.

Accused of illegal trafficking of slaves based on Brazilian laws passed in 1831 and 1850, ten crewmembers stood trial on June 30, 1856 (the captain died soon after the *Mary E. Smith* landed in Salvador). Of the ten, five were U.S. citizens. Attempts to explain their innocence proved futile. "We had no one to speak a good word for us. Police concluded that we knew everything and would tell nothing." Nathaniel Stanton, Joseph Sisson, and William Blake (born in England) received sentences of three years in prison, along with the requirement to pay a huge fine of two hundred *mil-reis* (U.S. $112.00) for each

African brought into Brazil. The judge also required that they pay expenses for the reexportation of the Africans back to Africa. For whatever reason, Dumblemont Eugene (born in France) and William Bussley received reduced prison terms of two years, along with similar monetary fines.

Nearly two years after entering prison at the San Antonio Fort in Salvador, the five North Americans wrote to U.S. consul in Rio de Janeiro Richard K. Meade.[66] They complained about their imprisonment, lamenting that they had no knowledge upon departure from Boston that the captain of the *Mary E. Smith* planned to sail the ship to the coast of Africa to pick up slaves. Once the ship was at sea, unknown individuals appeared on board, men who "behaved treacherous to us and we believe knew all about it [plans to embark Africans] from the time we left Boston." Once on the coast of Africa, they estimated that in two hours 526 Africans were forced into the hold of the *Mary E. Smith*. Captain Cranotick prodded the five to get off the ship and remain onshore, an offer that the five refused. "The passage across to this coast was full of suffering, and misery to us, and of horrible cruelty to the slaves."

Various individuals visited the five North Americans at the prison. British chaplain Edge and British merchant Hogg both offered solace. Reminded of their predicament by U.S. consul John Gilmer, governor of Bahia João Lins Vieira Cansanção de Sinimbú stopped by in spring 1857. Conversing with the prisoners in English, the president assured them that they would be pardoned. Unfortunately, nothing changed between the time of his visit and the penning of the letter. The five decried their imprisonment and treatment as a "*queer way of doing justice*."[67]

After U.S. consul Meade wrote several letters to Brazil's minister of foreign affairs on behalf of the five North Americans, and met personally with Pedro II, the elderly Nathaniel Stanton received an official pardon on September 29, 1858. This shortened Stanton's term by nine months. To their dismay, the other North Americans failed to be granted a similar pardon. At that moment in late September, Eugene and Bussley had lingered in the prison three months beyond their sentence of two years, while Sisson and Blake hoped to be released nine months later in June 1859. Indeed, the plight of the four looked bleak. The documents do not tell us when the sailors exited from San Antonio prison.

Two individuals who surfaced in the trial of the *Mary E. Smith* never endured incarceration. Based on evidence seized from the captured U.S. ship, the court in Salvador found José Maria Junqueira and J.M. Pamplona guilty of participation in the traffic. At decade's end, they continued as key figures in the slave trade at Luanda. Accused of "sinister machinations" and "extraordinary activity," the two supplied vessels destined for Cuba with slaves and materials.[68]

Rumors swirled through the early 1860s of planned slave voyages to the Brazilian coast. In January 1857, the governor of the province of Rio de Janeiro Luiz Antonio Barbosa received notice from Minister of Justice José Thomaz Nabuco de Araújo of the imminent arrival of an armed slave vessel. The brig *Barca* had departed from New York the previous October (1856) and sailed to Africa, where it supposedly embarked between five hundred and six hundred Africans. Nabuco requested that police be vigilant all along the coast of that province to impede a landing. In October 1857, Nabuco learned via a communiqué from the island of Madeira that the U.S. ship *M.M. Standard* was preparing to transport Africans to Brazil. The minister sent out another warning to police along the coast requesting that they be on full alert. On February 18, 1861, the minister of justice sent a "Confidential Notice" (*Circular Reservada*) to chiefs of police in several provinces saying that slaves had been boarded on slaving vessels at Benguela and at the Cuanza River in the south of Angola. The Circular ascertained that the trafficker involved was "an individual [named] Oliveira Botelho, who had previously invested in the voyages of the slave vessels *Orytra* and *Pedreira*, which had sailed to this Empire [Brazil] and to Havana." The minister recommended that police investigate all persons who might have been acquainted with Botelho. In this way, they could learn if the unknown ships might soon arrive on Brazilian shores.[69] All of these warnings proved to be without merit; none of the vessels arrived in Brazil (that is, evidence has not surfaced to confirm such arrivals). If any of these vessels did succeed in boarding slaves, most likely they sailed to Cuba.

Several factors contributed to the demise of the traffic to Brazil. British suppression played a prominent role. Even a cursory review of correspondence found in archives throughout the Atlantic world cannot but impress one of the extraordinary endeavors of Great Britain. In the words of one distinguished scholar, "there is still much to be said for the historian W.E.H. Lecky's famous conclusion, following the American Civil War, that England's crusade against slavery 'may probably be regarded as among the three or four perfectly virtuous acts recorded in the history of nations.'"[70]

Such virtue and heroism should not obfuscate the fact that financial incentives gave impetus to suppression efforts. Captains and crews of the British West Africa Squadron received payments for every vessel found guilty of complicity at Mixed Commission Courts and for every Liberated African freed from captured slavers.[71] Critics of British suppression accused English commanders of purposely delaying seizure of slavers until after they had departed from African coasts with slaves on board so as to earn extra income. Critics also suggested that English sailors allowed captains and crews of captured slave vessels to go free in the belief that the latter would continue in the traffic and therefore increase the chances of future seizure of prizes by the British Squadron.[72]

As shown in the preceding chapters, other factors also played a role in ending the slave trade to Brazil. These included slave resistance on the coasts of Africa and Brazil, slave revolts on board slave vessels, fear of infectious diseases being transmitted by disembarked Africans, popular revulsion over continued importations, widening sentiments in favor of free labor, international pressures exerted by visits from representatives of the Society of Friends (Quakers), and actions taken by imperial and provincial officials.[73] Although the head of the serpent—the slave trade to Brazil—was cut off, the body of the snake—the slave trade to Cuba—remained alive. It would take another 16 years (after 1851) to halt the traffic in Africans to Cuba.

DEMISE II: CUBA

Several ships that landed slaves in Cuba from mid-century had previously transported slaves to Brazil. Some of these vessels departed from the African coast with a destination of Brazil but were forced to redirect their voyage to Cuba due to enhanced vigilance and seizures of slavers along the Brazilian coast. Traffickers expelled from Rio de Janeiro and Bahia joined up with existing enterprises in Havana. British consul John Morgan, stationed at Salvador, Brazil wrote (in mid-1853) that a "great deal of activity here [has been observed] in dispatching and taking up vessels for the coast of Africa. I have been informed that the slave dealers of this city, undeceived at last as to the danger of continuing their nefarious practices on this coast [of Brazil], have turned their attention to the Cuba markets, and hence therefore, the unusual quantity of rum [cachaça] and tobacco that is now being shipped for the [Africa] Coast in partnership with the Cuba dealers, and for the purpose of slave trading."[74] It is during this period in the early 1850s when U.S. involvement in the traffic shifted from the south triangle (1830–51) back to the north triangle (1850–67) once again.

The final journey of the *Brazil* (noted above) tells us much about the traffic to Cuba at mid-century. The ship departed from Bahia Honda, Cuba sometime after late February 1851, traveled to Mozambique, and returned with 741 Africans on board. During the Middle Passage, 124 Africans perished. Arriving at Cardenas, the crew landed the 617 survivors. Of these, police took control over 414. "They were in the most miserable state of emaciation from ship fever, scurvy, and dysentery." A great number of the recaptured Africans died from their illnesses.[75] Well-known slave merchants Pedro Forcade and Julian Zulueta succeeded in absconding with 203 survivors. The captain of the *Brazil* proceeded to Havana where he was seen enjoying himself in public. This landing, along with countless others, exposed the continued incapacity and unwillingness of Spanish administrators and local authorities to intervene against powerful traffickers.

The captain general of Cuba deemed the recaptured Africans from the *Brazil* to be Liberated Africans (*emancipados*) and placed under the guidance of private owners. Different from slaves who could save money and purchase their freedom, Liberated Africans could only attain full freedom by a decision of the colonial government. Offended by these schemes, opponents of the traffic lamented that "money constantly procures his reassignment for new periods of slavery and degradation, but it cannot purchase his [or her] freedom. The emancipado amongst other things is exposed to be substituted for the slave in which case he [the latter] is reported to be Dead!"[76]

The Africans from the *Brazil* who ended up enslaved on estates around Cardenas faced a desperate situation. After surviving the trauma of the Middle Passage during which many fell sick, they were forced to reside in unhealthy rural environments. Cholera had raged in the western part of the island since mid-1850. On one estate owned by Julian Zulueta located near Matanzas, an estimated three hundred to four hundred out of eight hundred to nine hundred slaves died from cholera. On another sugar plantation near Guines, 152 slaves out of 220 succumbed to cholera in two weeks, forcing production to a halt.[77] Some sixteen thousand slaves perished from cholera in the jurisdiction of Matanzas from June 1853 to June 1854.[78] Another fourteen thousand died in other parts of the island. Yellow fever was also prevalent in Havana and in the nearby countryside during these years.[79] To add to this misery, smallpox took the lives of numerous slaves.[80]

Why did such insalubrious conditions not result in a termination of the slave traffic to Cuba, as had occurred in Brazil? The situation from mid-1850 to mid-1854 made planters wary about introducing recently landed *bozales* to their estates. They did not want Africans to transmit or pick up infectious disease after arrival in Cuba. In spite of the deaths of several thousand blacks (slaves and free) during these months, merchants and planters continued with importations. Estimates of disembarkations shed light on their lack of concern. In 1859, Cuba received over 26,000 African slaves, the largest number imported in a single year since the first slaves arrived (officially in 1674) on board a slaving vessel directly from Africa to the island. From 1856 through 1860, ships landed 77,400 Africans, the third largest number of disembarkations for a five-year period in the history of the slave trade to Cuba.[81] The demand for labor on rural estates and the lure of profits overrode concerns related to public health.

Historians have minimized the role of slave resistance in Cuba between the Escalera insurgency (final trials in December 1844) and the outbreak of the independence war in 1868. Cuban scholar Manuel Barcia affirms that "after La Escalera, slaves' involvement in Cuba's social movements fell off, returning to its previous levels only at the start of the Ten Years' War in 1868."[82] Gabino La Rosa Corzo echoes this perspective, writing that "1848 marked the high point in the system of active [slave] resistance, whose main form in the eastern region of Cuba was the creation of runaway slave settlements. At the same time, the specialized repressive system achieved its most polished form. That year also saw the largest number of attacks on runaway slave settlements and the most alarming incidents." Corzo contends that after 1848 slave resistance and repression by authorities diminished. "The process of decline could be observed in both systems."[83]

Residents of Cuba during this interlude echo such views. Writing a short five years after La Escalera, British consul James Kennedy claimed that "these slaves speak different languages, have often national differences, are kept far from each other without any arms or resources so that even if their number doubled or trebled, the whites could have no well founded reason to fear the increase, being as they are well armed and with a large number of troops in the island. As it has long been the policy of dealers to bring few or no females, there are very few half castes here, and none to form a class. Consequently the colored people are without those leaders, whom they have had in other countries to make any insurrection really to be dreaded, as of themselves neither have they any union or intelligence to do more than temporary damages at most."[84]

Historians have questioned just about every assertion of Mr. Kenne⊏ slaved Africans in Cuba forged alliances with fellow Africans in spite guistic and ethnic differences. They also joined with free blacks and persons of color in several instances to resist the slave regime from the 1790s. And as the documents have shown, whites had exhibited lots of distress due to the steady arrival of Africans on Cuban shores.

Contemporaries showed far less confidence than Mr. Kennedy that all was calm. Noting that slaves on the island had heard that emancipation had been decreed from Madrid, resident of Cuba Juan Martínez lamented (in 1854) that "from every direction symptoms of an early uprising of the African race are beginning to be felt. Abolitionists of the Northern States of the Union [United States] preach loudly in favor of *black slaves* of Cuba. Would it not be more becoming, more useful to civilization and more noble in the sight of God that they should say something first for the *white slaves* it holds?" [In other words Martínez is distraught that whites composed a minority of the population and they remained subservient to the Spanish Crown.][85]

Several sources offer evidence of widespread disquiet provoked by slaves during these years. In April 1854, a black member of Havana's Navy Department stayed overnight at Caymito, some nineteen miles southwest of Havana. During a conversation with a journalist, he spoke of a *palenque* that existed in the district of Mayarí near Santiago (eastern end of Cuba). A relative had been a captain of Mayarí in former years and had led an expedition to destroy the *palenque* in 1836. With a posse of 160, his uncle had "reached the top of a mountain and there saw a large village and cultivated land to the extent of three miles or more, planted with all classes of roots or vegetables, and very well stocked with bee hives. The negroes, on perceiving the party, blew their horns, which resounded throughout the mountain, and assembling in a force at least of 3,500 (rather more than fewer), rushed on the whites who defended themselves but were obliged to retreat in great haste, leaving more than half their number dead and wounded in the hands of the negroes. The captain escaped with four of his men, one of them a colored man who was very courageous and never left his side—but this poor fellow was shot down in flight."[86]

The unidentified black lodger had been sent by Spanish officials to investigate the dangers posed by escaped slaves around Santiago. Based on more recent descriptions, the sailor estimated that the population of the *palenque* had doubled in size.[87] That military attacks on runaway slave settlements diminished in the 1850s (Corzo's description) in no way meant that the *palenques* had disappeared. Indeed, it would appear that the captain general shifted military patrols to the sugar regions of the west of Cuba in his attempt to maintain vigilance over thousands of recently landed Africans.[88]

Numerous episodes during the Middle Passage and disembarkations during this period provide glimpses of slave resistance. Informants described a landing of at least 1,100 Africans "at or near Cardenas" in March 1853. Within hours the crew torched the vessel at a location known as Cape Piedra. Many Africans had perished during the transatlantic voyage: "there were 200 more bozal negroes on board the slaver when she left the coast of Africa, that on more than one occasion [they] attempted to rise and take the vessel, as many as the number last mentioned were killed in suppressing said mutinies."[89] Eleven years later the ship *Huntress* sailed from Matanzas to New York City and then on to the Congo River and back to Cuba. The ship carried 350 female and 400 male African slaves. In the words of one of the crew, "during our long voyage from the coast of Africa we lost about 250 negroes by death, who were thrown overboard. The voyage was full of hardship and suffering and there was a great scarcity of water."[90] In early January 1862, U.S. and British officials learned of another landing at Cardenas. The "cargo consisted of 150 Caffres from the east coast of Africa. These negroes were so unruly that *forty* of them were *shot* in their transportation inland."[91] Certainly these experiences and events were never forgotten by the survivors.

Several incidents within and outside Cuba added to the tensions of the early 1850s. In defiance of treaty stipulations (1835, 1845) between England and Spain, Captain General Valentin Cañedo sent troops to search private estates for recently landed *bozales* in mid-1853. This disrupted decades-long collusion between Spain's colonial representatives and traffickers. During one such sweep, officials secured 173 Africans from a property owned by the trafficker Don Julien Zulueta. "Publicly were the negroes drawn from the estates and paraded the whole length of the railroad, and the imprisonment of the wealthy proprietor Don Julian Zulueta was conducted with equally ostentatious and wanton show of power." Although such actions did little to disrupt disembarkations and resulted soon after in the crown recalling Cañedo to Spain, they did not go unnoticed by slaves. In the words of the U.S. representative Christopher Madan, the decision "to make searches in the interior not warranted by laws [has caused] a state of confusion to ensue in which actual fights have taken place, armed robbers of slaves have appeared, and a general feeling of insecurity has been sown."[92]

Historians have also minimized the resistance of free blacks in the wake of La Escalera. Matthias Röhrig Assunção and Michael Zeuske portray the 1850s as a time of relative peace. "Only twenty years later [from the late 1840s] did the first War of Independence [1868] create new space for the affirmation of non-white pan-Cuban identity for blacks and mulattoes."[93] A close analysis of this period demonstrates lots of struggle to defend personal rights and create space. In spite of suffering the brutalities inflicted during 1844–45 and enduring steady harassment in the years that followed, free blacks exhibited multiple levels of agency. Tens of free blacks who had been expelled during the repression of La Escalera returned to the island. Foreign-born free blacks successfully protested orders of expulsion. Numerous free blacks appeared in courts to demand that occupational bans that had been imposed be lifted. Black workers in Havana joined several recently established Abakuá mutual aid societies founded on Carabalí ideals and philosophy.[94] Free blacks pursued educational opportunities and strategized on ways to elude recruitment into militias by officials in need of troops. In the words of historian Michele Reid-Vasquez, "despite the deliberate and violent ways colonial officials and elites reinforced political authority and white supremacy [between 1846 and 1868], free *pardos* and *morenos* continued to seek out avenues for self-preservation, community survival, and economic stability."[95]

Slave and free black resistance contributed to fears of "Africanization" of the island. This term had three meanings. First, it was invoked to accuse Madrid of pursuing a deliberate policy of allowing continued slave importations. In this view, Spanish ministers desired an African majority residing on the island to inhibit creole support for independence.[96] These men knew well of precedents on nearby Jamaica and other British Caribbean islands, where planters had remained loyal to England during the North American independence war for fear of losing control over their slaves.[97] One U.S. representative went so far as to claim that allowing slaves to cultivate small plots and sell the products at local markets strengthened bonds between master and slave, thereby enhancing Spain's capacity to rule. "Though this has been well covered under the pretense of guarding against fires [purposely set on plantations by slaves], it is another link in the Africanization chain."[98] If the Africanization strategy failed and a war for independence erupted, then Madrid would emancipate slaves as a way to gain their loyalty, receive approval from England, and retain imperial discipline over the island (similar to what had occurred after emancipation in the British and French Caribbean islands).

Second, U.S. expansionists trumpeted the Africanization of Cuba in hopes of garnering support in Washington for the annexation of Cuba. Increased ties between Cuba and the United States in the first half of the nineteenth century brought all sorts of new technology to the island, including railroads, telegraph lines, and steam-powered engines.[99] Supporters of slavery in the United States and Cuba desired that the United States annex Cuba so as to integrate the island into the rapidly expanding U.S. economy while assuring the preservation of the slave regime. U.S. pro-annexationists distrusted British and French motives in the Caribbean. They did not want Cuba "to become another Jamaica [meaning an island inhabited primarily by former slaves and free blacks and that remained part of the British empire]. Cuba must become African [an unacceptable outcome] or American."[100] Such critics further accused England of a plan to introduce 70,000 to 100,000 African apprentices to the island as a way to assure a sufficient labor force and friendly relations with Spain.[101]

A third prism through which to interpret "Africanization" was when it was employed by white creoles residing in Cuba to decry the incessant arrivals of African slaves.[102] Reflecting this sentiment, one witness in the mid-1850s besmirched disembarkations as "continuing to an extent revolting to the civilization of the age."[103] Planters had faced unceasing slave resistance and they distrusted free blacks. They did not want to see the outbreak of another Haitian Revolution. They feared violent acts of retribution from free Africans and dreaded the thought that they would become subservient subjects of a large population of African descendants.

For light-skinned Cuban creoles and Spaniards, a specter of Africa certainly existed in Cuba. The composition of two estates provides evidence of a robust African presence.[104] At the Campana coffee estate, a scribe registered eighty-seven slaves on the property in 1835. Of these, forty-two had been born in Africa, and they represented seven different ethnic groups. At the sugar plantation El Dorado near Sagua (north coast in Villa Clara province) in 1854, of a total of 265 slaves, ninety-six were African (36 percent). Of the males, twelve were described as Congo, twenty-two Lucumí, three Mandinga, ten Mina, two Carabalí, one Macua, and fourteen Ganga (most likely from the present-day Central African Republic), for a total of sixty-four African males. These men labored alongside eighty-two creole slaves who had been born in Cuba, which meant that Africans composed 44 percent of the male workforce. Among the women, thirty-two were African and eighty-seven creole; hence 26 percent of the female slaves had been born in Africa. These females included five Mina, five Congas, nine Ganga, four Carabalí, and nine Lucumí.[105] Due to disembarkations of 164,000 slaves between 1850 and 1867, Africans represented an important segment of the population in Cuba until well after slavery ended in 1886.[106]

As in Brazil between 1830 and 1850, U.S. slave vessels played a major role in the slave trade to Cuba in the two decades after mid-century. The journey of the slave ship *Esperanza* and two of its American crew tell us much about the epoch.

In late August 1854, U.S. consul Savage received the news of a recent landing of Africans. He wrote: "Several seamen with about 170 bozal negroes had been captured in the vicinity of Guines [parish], about thirty-six or forty miles from this City [Havana], and that two of the seamen were apparently Americans. It was corroborated on the 31st when I learned that the men had been brought here by the railroad on the day before. Presuming that they were in the Public Jail I called there on the same day and found eight men, six of them Portuguese, and two evidently native Americans. I conversed with these two, who gave me their names as Mark Chauncey of Philadelphia and William Winn of Maine. I judge that they are Americans from their appearance, language and manners."[107]

From the interviews, Savage learned that the U.S.-built schooner *Mary Reed* had departed on a "lawful trading voyage" the previous March from New York City with a destination of the Cape of Good Hope.[108] Chauncey and Winn both claimed ignorance that the ship would be used to transport Africans to Cuba. Nor could the two Americans recall the name of the captain or mate, except "that they were both Portuguese to judge from their accent, but spoke the English language fluently, and must be naturalized American citizens." After a voyage of sixty-seven days to Africa, they arrived "at a place without houses," a sailor erased the name *Mary Reed* from the stern, and the new name *Esperanza* was painted on. There they "witnessed the hatches taken off and discovered that she had nothing but provisions and other articles for the slave trade."[109] Small boats carried some 450 Africans to the *Esperanza*, and the schooner set sail for Cuba. During a Middle Passage of forty-eight days westward, 41 Africans perished.

Arriving on the south side of the Isle of Pines on July 3, the sailors and Africans on the *Esperanza* came onshore. The crew set fire to the ship. For the next twenty days, the group languished at that beach. "Provisions were very scarce, and the negroes would go into the bushes and get poisonous beans, snakes, etc., and eat them, which caused the death of a very large number, so that there were only about 335 left." Word of their presence spread, and soon there appeared two small schooners. Dividing into two groups, the survivors boarded the coasting vessels. After being separated off the coast, the second boat was forced to put in near the town of Rosario. For another ten days, 170 Africans and several crewmembers camped in a forest. Troops appeared, the lieutenant governor arrested everyone, and subsequently the group was sent to Havana.

While under arrest at Rosario, U.S. citizen Mark Chauncey penned a letter to U.S. consul Savage informing him of his predicament and providing further details of the voyage of the *Esperanza*.

> When we made the coast of Africa, the Captain called all hands aft and said he intended to alter the voyage and take on board negroes. All hands immediately refused, upon which he stated we had our choice, either to go ashore on a barren and rocky coast or consent to remain on his terms, which were a large sum of money each and a passport through Cuba to the United States. Not knowing what course to pursue he gave us until Meridian to consider upon it. At that time four launches came alongside loaded with negroes who threatened putting us on shore as there were more men ashore who had been captured and put ashore on the coast and would be happy to get on board. Upon which course to take it was hard to decide, cannibals and starvation on one side, and the other a shade better or worse.

In seeking the sympathy of Consul Savage, Chauncey provided some details about his experiences: "There are but two natives of America among us, but all have sailed a long time in American vessels, and I presume are considered as Americans. Our clothes and everything appertaining to us I suppose are lost or taken by the Authorities. We have heard it stated here that we would have no opportunity of writing or seeing you. And therefore [we have] availed ourselves of the kindness of an American lady (resident here) who has kindly tendered to us her services in transmitting this letter to Havana and also to contribute everything in her power to ameliorate our condition here."[110]

After eight days in a large cell at the Havana prison, Chauncey and his shipmates were transferred to another "more comfortable [cell], apart from the mass of prisoners." Savage queried about why the move. He learned that a Portuguese subject residing in Havana agreed to pay the added rent and food costs of the incarcerated. "I naturally suspect that this person must be either a party concerned in the cargo of slaves that the seamen brought in the *Esperanza*, or an agent of the owners."[111]

Mark Chauncey wrote further communiqués to the U.S. consul during September. Optimistic that he would be freed in the near future, Chauncey alternately expressed buoyancy and distress.

Sir.

I hope you will pardon the long delay I have caused you, but I can assure you I have been very sick, but am now recovering rapidly, and through the means of a gentleman here who kindly furnished me with medicine, which I think has completely eradicated the fever [perhaps yellow fever].

I presume you are aware that we have changed quarters twice since I saw you and furnished with provisions from outside. All of which has been done by some secret agency of the owners, we suppose. It has been stated to us that we are to receive a *part* of the money which they said we were to receive had all the negroes been saved. Who these persons are, it is impossible to find out, but two or three prisoners here appear to do their business for them. Since here we have received a sum of money from them to purchase clothes. [We were] compelled to leave the apartment where the Portuguese are confined as we found it impossible to live with them, without fighting—they are, sir, without exception, the most infernal cowardly set of cutthroats that ever went unhung. They were so much afraid we [Chauncey and Winn] should have something done for us by you [Savage] that it was almost impossible to prevent them from abusing the shipping master every time he came. We at length spoke to the Alcalde [superintendent] who had us removed to better quarters. When we were removed their anger knew no bounds, but it was soon tempered by the simple word "stocks" [meaning when we get our hands on you we are going to put you in stocks!]. I have now sir to beg your indulgence for a few more days before I make out my statement, as I wish first to receive this money. And besides you will have a very different statement from that contained in my [previous] letter to you from Guines [Rosario], which letter was written at the *instigation* and by the *dictation* of the Portuguese, who when they found out here that the owner would do something for them were most venomous against you, and the shipping master in particular, as they were afraid we would say something to him which they would not hear, but thank Heaven we are now clear of them.

For the articles which you so kindly furnished us we will repay you, so that some poor cast away or sick and penniless American may be benefited by the sum. To us it was a perfect Godsend. And sir, be pleased now to accept our thanks not only for the kindness you have shown us but also for the promptitude in which you attended our case.

Mark Chauncey[112]

Mark Chauncey's story raised suspicions for Savage. During a visit at the Havana prison cell, the U.S. consul learned that Chauncey's fellow American William Winn in fact had been the captain of the *Esperanza*. During his interview of Winn, Chauncey alluded to three Portuguese merchants residing in New York City as being part of a Brazilian company that organized slave voyages. These included Antonio Rodrigo Abreo, Antonio Deverino de Avillar, and Joaquim Gaspar de Motta. As part of a crackdown on traffickers, Captain General Pezuela had "requested" that the latter two depart from Havana the previous February or face expulsion.[113] Avillar and Motta sailed directly for New York City on board the ship *Black Warrior* and resumed their operations.

Seeking the release of Chauncey and Winn, U.S. consul William H. Robertson met with the captain general in late October. He explained that the two North Americans knew much of the dealings of traffickers based in the United States. Hence, if they could be turned over to Robertson he would transfer them to New York City, where they could provide evidence to U.S. authorities seeking the suppression of the traffic. The captain general expressed appreciation for the diplomat's interest and concern, but explained that he could not intervene in the case.[114]

As the weeks passed at the Havana jail, Chauncey became increasingly desperate.

Sir.

I have thus far found it impossible to ascertain in full the names of the Portuguese. I have endeavored to come at it by as circumlocutory a manner as possible but they are suspicious of me, their first names I can give you, with bare exception of the Brazilian negro. The sailors' names viz. Sebastian, Pauline, Antonio, Jack, Andres and Lyons. These are the names by which they call each other. The four first [hail] from Lisbon, the fifth [is] a Chilean, and the sixth is from the Island of Madeira and shipped as a cook in New York, the African negro is from St. Paul de Loanda where he has been a slave, was brought to Cuba as such by the same captain last year, but for some deed or other was liberated by his master here and went to New York and was taken by the captain as cabin boy. He did not sign the articles. The Brazilian negro (the largest of the two) came on board in Africa whilst embarking the negroes, he had been taken prisoner in a slaver and been put ashore by the American war brig *Perry* and came on board for a passage, he was made cook in place of Lyons who knew nothing of the business. I am a favorite of his and could obtain from him anything which you should desire, but for the talking part of it, as I fear an interpreter would expose him and myself both and perhaps be the means of making the sailors worse against me. At present they appear friendly, but I presume you know the Portuguese character. The only way I know of to obtain their names is either from the Alcalde of the prison or the shipping masters in New York, Woodward, Royberg, and Pentz, South Street near the Burling Slip. They invariably keep a copy of all shipping articles.

The clouds are darkening over my head, for not hearing any reliable news from you and knowing there are several persons here sentenced to the chain gang for being caught with negroes both on shore and at sea. I am beginning to think my case a desperate one. My whole confidence rests in you and I am very anxious to know if there is a possibility of my having to perambulate this country in chains, doing their public work and exposed to the brutal treatment which an American would be made to suffer from the overseers. However, I shall give them some trouble if such should be the case, I feel myself too much of a freeman to submit tamely to such a disgraceful punishment.

I am aware your attention is much engaged by your many duties and at every opportunity you are doing all in your power for me but these *chain gang* sentences terrify me.

Mark Chauncey[115]

Things did not go as planned for Chauncey and Winn in the months that followed. In early April, they believed that they would be freed within ten days. This did not occur. In late June, U.S. consul Robertson brought up the continued imprisonment of the two Americans in a meeting with the captain general. In response, "His Excellency in my presence directed his Secretary to address the President of the Court to bring their trial to a final issue which may be done."[116] Again, the men were not let go. By September, Chauncey and Winn showed "very depressed spirits." In November, the court decided the case. Chauncey and Winn were sentenced to three years of hard labor on a chain gang along with the five other imprisoned crewmembers from the *Esperanza*.

Although the lives of the imprisoned crew of the *Esperanza* faded from the historical record, we do know that they exited the Havana Jail (date not determined). Similar to so many slave vessels that reentered the traffic through auction after having been captured and penalized, Mark Chauncey showed himself to be undeterred by the imprisonment in Havana. In February 1862 the U.S. barque *Ocilla* built in Mystic, Connecticut departed Havana with a declared destination of Havre, France, having been sold by its North American owners to an unknown purchaser at Havre. Mark Chauncey took command of the *Ocilla* and sailed south from France to the Congo River. There the vessel received 1,500 Africans. The *Ocilla* continued on to Cuba, where it landed 1,200 survivors at Bahia Honda in December 1862. The documents note that "a Spanish captain brought the ship [*Ocilla*] to Cuba. Chauncey was left ill at the coast of Africa," his final fate not known.[117]

Every one of the estimated 43,000 slave voyages of the transatlantic slave trade possesses its own history.[118] Various documents, particularly depositions of crews before British and U.S. consuls or Mixed Commission Courts, provide descriptions of the traffic. More hidden are the voices of Africans who survived the Middle Passage.[119]

Fifty of the fifty-nine vessels that departed Cuba for Africa between January 1857 and July 1858 were listed as American. (See Table 5, Appendix.) The others included seven Spanish ships, one Peruvian vessel, and one Norwegian brig. During the next two years (September 30, 1858, to September 30, 1860), British officials at Havana noted seventy-three vessels that departed for Africa or were fitting out for the traffic. Of these, thirty-four were American, twenty-eight Spanish, five Mexican, four Chilean, one French, and one Uruguayan. Although other vessels certainly set out from Havana and Cuba undetected, the numbers provide evidence of the magnitude of the U.S. presence in the slave trade to Cuba at this juncture.[120]

Under the list of departures for 1857 shown in Table 5 appears the *James Buchanan*. Sailing out of Havana with a declared destination of Boston, the schooner journeyed to Ouidah, where it received three hundred Africans. Of these, 260 survived the Middle Passage and landed in western Cuba.[121]

In an article first published in the *Philadelphia Monitor* and days later in *The New Orleans Delta*, a journalist affirmed that the *James Buchanan* had been constructed and fitted out along the Delaware River. The article estimated that its owners, having transported Africans on four voyages since 1856, "had cleared $400,000" in profit. Pointing to the close ties between investors from the U.S. North, planters in the U.S. South, and the slave trade to Cuba, the author explained:

This is highly collaborative of the opinion we have frequently expressed of the existence of a strong, practical, though latent disposition in the North to encourage and sustain slavery and the slave trade. We now repeat that, if the South should ever manifest the insane purpose to do away with negro slavery, we would not be at all surprised to hear a furious clamor raised among the Northern people against the project. And, truly, they would have a right, in common with the civilized world, to protest against an act that would be so disastrous to commerce and repugnant to wholesome principles of civilization.

But, for immediate practical purposes, the pocket argument is strongest, of course, with Northern commercialists. If Northern ship owners have realized immense profits by conveying European emigrants, and Northern capitalists incalculably benefitted by the cheap and abundant labor thus acquired, still greater would be the gains derived from both resources, if African slave importation were opened as a legitimate branch of the American shipping business, and if an unrestricted supply of that kind of labor, to meet a natural demand, were permitted to swell those productions that are the materials of the richest commerce in the world.[122]

Such views motivated a gathering of New York's "merchant princes" in December 1861 to contemplate aligning themselves with the recently formed Confederate States of America by seceding from the Union.[123]

Profits derived from the slave trade to Cuba at this juncture are striking. In one analysis from early 1861, British consul Joseph Crawford (with nineteen years experience) estimated $1,200.00 paid by planters for each Lucumí landed. Expenses for the voyage included:

Cost for vessel and provisions: $25,000.00

Cost of 500 Africans at $50.00 each: $25,000.00

Ten percent mortality: $2,500.00

Wages and gratifications to master and crew: $30,000.00

Bribe paid for 450 slaves at $120.00 each = $54,000.00

One year interest paid at 10 percent per annum: $13,650.00

Total: $150,150.00

Sale of 450 slaves at $1,200 each = $540,000.00

Profit on the adventure is $389,850.00[124]

If we use an estimate of $1.00 in 1860 being worth $40.00 in 2013, one gets a sense of the enormity of the wealth derived from a successful slave voyage.[125]

Why did suppression fail until the early 1860s? A British consul at Madrid pointed to two key reasons. In contrast to what had occurred in Brazil, the Spanish government never declared the slave trade as piracy. Hence traffickers felt little concern that capture would lead to severe punishment. Second, the powerful slave trade bloc impeded at every turn the "more efficient discovery and punishment of offenders who had actually landed slaves and introduced them into the interior of the country" (based on the 9th article of Cuba's 1845 Penal Laws).[126] Again, this contrasted with the situation in Brazil, where police and troops successfully pursued disembarked Africans and militias as they journeyed inland and investigated private estates during the 1850s.

Several other factors impeded suppression of the traffic to Cuba. Corruption prevailed at all levels and in all regions of the island. Prices rose significantly for slaves over the 1850s. In the early years of the decade, planters paid $300 to $400 for a male slave. By 1859, this rose to $1,200–$1,300 for a "good field hand." The price of a female domestic slave increased to $1,200–$1,800, and a recently landed female African was purchased for $850.[127] With this spike in prices, bribes paid to Spanish officials for each African disembarked increased from $68 (mid-1850s) to $153 (1859).[128] Commanding officers, captains, collectors at ports, and tide surveyors, to name a few, all willingly accepted ounces of gold to facilitate entry of Africans. Merchants and planters bribed local officials to produce forged registrations (cedulas), baptismal records, and passes as a way to hide evidence of recent disembarkations and to move African bozales around the island legally as if they were creoles who had been born in Cuba.

The British, Cuban, and American Squadrons that appeared in the Caribbean during these years never acted with a tenacity equal to that exhibited by Commander Schomberg along the coasts of Brazil. Aware of the connivance of captain generals and an "inert mass of passive resistance clothed in the garb of official routine," naval commanders had little incentive to intercept a slaver.[129] More importantly, the brig sloops of these Squadrons proved inadequate in pursuing slavers.[130] Purchased cheaply at U.S. ports or in Cuba, U.S.-built clippers and yachts traveled at a high rate of speed and proved adept at avoiding detection. Improved technology, including ships powered by steam engines, enhanced versatility at sea.

Traffickers resident in Cuba had easy access to coasting schooners and small launches that enabled them to offload Africans quickly from large barques and then transport them to remote locales around the island. To avoid detection, crews commonly burned slave ships after disembarkations. Men willing to sail as part of a crew were abundant. Tips provided by informants to critics of the traffic became scarce.[131]

What caused the halt in the slave traffic to Cuba? One key cause related to a shift in diplomacy by the U.S. government. From 1808, England forged treaties with several nations that enabled the British Squadron to seize slaving vessels. Due to the influence of southern planters in Congress, the United States refused to sign such agreements. It claimed that only vessels belonging to the American Squadron, a force never larger than six warships, could detain a U.S.-flagged ship. As a result, several hundred vessels of diverse origins transported African slaves under the protection of the U.S. flag with little fear of interception.

With the election of Abraham Lincoln in 1860, federal policy changed. Tensions that had mounted for decades exploded into the Civil War. Southern representatives who had been so influential in forging national policy during the antebellum era joined the Confederacy. Wary of England aligning itself with the Confederacy, Lincoln signed a treaty with Great Britain in 1862 that allowed for mutual right of search at sea. Traffickers throughout the Atlantic world took note. Enhanced patrols by the British and U.S. Squadrons along the coasts of Africa proved successful in increasing the number of captures. Professors Eltis and Richardson show that after passage of the 1862 treaty, only three other slave vessels sailed under the U.S. flag. This number contrasted to the 123 voyages that had sailed under the U.S. flag during the previous five years (1857–62).[132]

As with other key moments in the nineteenth century related to suppression of the slave trade, the turnaround in policy by the United States is only part of the story. Indeed, the Trans-Atlantic Slave Trade Database shows that between 1862 and 1866, 73 slave vessels traversed the Atlantic in search of slaves. Many of these had been constructed in the United States and looked to transport Africans to Cuba. Hence, we need to consider other variables within Cuba that came into play in causing the demise of the traffic.

As support for annexation by the United States evaporated in Cuba by the late 1850s, several wealthy sugar planters joined together to advocate reforms of the colonial system of Cuba. This group included José Morales Lemus, José Manuel Mester, José Antonio Echeverría, and the wealthy entrepreneur Miguel Aldama. For the first time in Cuban history, a Reformist Party (*Partido Reformista*) appeared that was recognized by the Spanish government. The party built on ideas from earlier in the century. During the first reform movement of the 1790s to 1820s, Arango e Parreño had defended the slave trade to Cuba until his abrupt shift in 1825. Antonio Saco played an important role in the second reform movement of the 1830s. He called for the prohibition of the slave trade while allowing that slavery to be continued on the island. The Reformist Party of the early 1860s went the furthest in demanding an end to the slave trade to Cuba and gradual abolition in the near future.

Swept up by the turbulence caused by the American Civil War, creole reformers in Cuba paid close attention to the shifting winds of abolitionist thought. With Lincoln's executive order proclaiming emancipation of all slaves in Confederate territory in January 1863 and Confederate surrender at Appomattox in April 1865, private and public protests against the slave trade in Cuba widened. In mid-1865, a young Havana lawyer named Antonio González de Mendoza organized the Association Against the Slave Trade (*Asociación contra la trata*). Supported by several creole intellectuals and a few Spaniards resident in Cuba, the Association called for a ban on the purchase of any African disembarked after November 19, 1865. Although Spain refused to acknowledge this Association, its presence reflected anxiety in influential circles over the continuation of the traffic in Africans. Within a year, the reformers of Cuba succeeded in pressuring the Cortes in Madrid to pass the "Law for the Suppression and Punishment of the Slave Trade." Carrying harsh penalties and enhanced restrictions on slave owners in Cuba, this law of July 1866 contributed much to the downturn in the number of slaves disembarked in Cuba.[133]

Infectious disease added to the tensions caused by slave disembarkations from the late 1850s. For residents of Havana, yellow fever remained "most malignant. Indeed, every year that terrible malady is worse and worse."[134] Outbreaks of smallpox caused havoc for traffickers in Cuba and throughout the South Atlantic.[135] Smallpox "raged with great violence in the city and province of Luanda" in May and June 1864.[136] Between July and October, the "black population of São Tomé experienced frightful mortality from smallpox."[137] Smallpox broke out on a British ship patrolling in the waters along the coast of Angola while it was investigating the presence of barracoons.[138] After several successful interceptions in 1862 and 1863, the South Division of the British Squadron was reduced to three ships due to the high number of sailors taken ill.[139] Captured slavers destined for Sierra Leone continued to experience high mortality rates.[140] Outbreaks of infection caused severe conditions on several transatlantic voyages to Cuba after 1862 and the arrival in Cuba of numerous ill African men, women, and children.

Resistance by slaves and free blacks continued. In late July 1864, U.S. consul Thomas Savage wrote that

> a plot amongst the colored population at Santiago de Cuba, having for its object the attainment of freedom to their race, was denounced by the authorities on or about the 21st June, by a negro slave on one of the coffee plantations in that neighborhood. It is reported and believed that over 2,000 colored persons and a few whites are implicated. They are charged with intent to revolt, destroy the public property at Santiago and even to murder all the whites. The scheme having been discovered, is nipped in the bud for the present, but there can be no doubt that the seed has been sown [and] broadcast and that the spirit of discontent amongst the negroes is universal and will sooner or later break out with terrible effect. It is said that a large quantity of arms had been found concealed. The rising was to take place on the 24th or 28th June [hence during annual celebrations in praise of the Catholic saint John the Baptist, Peter and Paul].[141]

In his description of this plot, Savage lamented that "I fear that the horrors of 1844 will be reproduced unless the Captain General should adopt a different course from that pursued by his predecessor, General O'Donnell, at that time."[142] Savage was writing exactly two decades after the Escalera insurrection. His career as a U.S. diplomat in Havana spanned twenty-one years. Clearly the historical memory of that event remained vivid for this Cuban-born and fluent Spanish speaker. Unfortunately, Savage provided no further analysis of what occurred in the aftermath of the plot being exposed.

News of the Civil War that raged in the United States filtered into the slave quarters of Cuba. U.S. consul general Robert Schufeldt wrote that "among the negroes themselves I have no doubt the effect of the war is well canvassed [known] and I am told that they already mingle within their songs the significant refrain '*Avanza a Lincoln, Avanza! Tu eres nuestra Esperanza!*' [Advance Lincoln, Advance! You are our Hope!]"[143] U.S. consul Savage concurred: "the colored population are certainly somewhat agitated, the words 'Lincoln advances' are often heard in their songs and conversations among themselves."[144] It is likely that slaves and free blacks of Cuba heard of black soldiers fighting for the Union and fugitive slaves aiding the Northern army. It would only be a matter of months before slaves joined in Cuba's war for independence from Spain. In so doing, they too would ultimately gain their liberation.[145]

CONCLUSION

———— ∞ ————

In October 1836, British consul to Havana Edward Schenley penned a letter to Foreign Minister Lord Palmerston in London. Schenley wrote that six schooners recently constructed in the United States had arrived in Havana during the preceding two months. These included the *Emanuel, Dolores, Fanny Butler, Rosanna, Viper,* and *Anaconda*. Varying in size between 50 and 150 tons, their "light draught of water" aided them in "escaping from and deceiving His Majesty's cruisers." Aware that U.S. presidents had refused to sign a treaty with England with regard to suppression of the slave trade, Schenley alleged that "American citizens had built and fitted out in their own ports vessels only calculated for piracy or the slave trade. [They then] entered this harbor and in concert with the Havana slave traders, took on board a prohibited cargo, manacles, etc, and proceeded openly to that most notorious depot for this iniquitous traffic, the Cape Verde islands, under the shelter of their national flag." After picking up slaves along the coast of Africa, they departed in convoys of three or four vessels. If "being hard pressed by chase [by the British Squadron]," they would "sacrifice one of their number for the purpose of securing, if possible, the safety of others."[1]

Writing twelve years later from Rio de Janeiro, British consul James Hudson echoed the comments of his colleague Schenley. "United States ships not only bring slaves to Brazil, but they are sold, fitted and armed for the slave trade in this port. The purpose of the armament, as it is publicly stated, is to sink the boats of those British cruisers which may venture to overhaul them on the coast [of Africa]. . . . It used to be said by citizens of the United States that they were a law abiding people. [Our correspondence] shows their utter contempt for their own law; its weakness and inefficiency; and the timidity of their own government when opposed by kidnappers and the very scum of society will go far to destroy this legitimate source of satisfaction."[2]

Moving ahead another twelve years to 1860, British consul to Havana John Crawford penned an account that compared to those of Misters Schenley and Hudson. "There never was a time since the treaty with Spain [signed in 1835] when the preparations for the traffic were more formidable. There are numerous joint stock companies around the island with immense capital and with extensive ramifications in the United States and Europe. They can count on three in every twelve slave ships safely landing African slaves in Cuba, the proceeds of which cover all of the other and bring in a handsome profit."[3] Crawford pronounced further that "the slave trade continues at a torrid pace. The vessels employed in carrying on the slave trade are mostly American built . . . [they] fit out and sail from the United States and such has been the impunity enjoyed by the slave traders that the American masters and crews no longer hesitate to continue on board [for a transatlantic journey to Africa and return to Cuba] and have brought all of their energies and cunning into operation to avoid their own Government cruisers, as well on the coast of Africa as in the waters of Cuba."[4]

During these same four decades between the 1830s and 1860s, U.S. representatives also condemned the participation of U.S. merchants and citizens in the traffic. In the midst of a deluge of African slaves disembarked at Rio de Janeiro, U.S. consul Henry Wise lamented (in 1845) that the "African slave trade thickens around us, and we are treading on its dragons' teeth." Wise condemned the leading role of U.S. capital and expertise in this traffic:

Our flag alone gives the requisite protection against the right of visit, search and seizure; and our citizens, in all the characters of *owners*, of *consignees*, of *agents*, and of *masters and crews of our vessels*, are concerning in the business and partake of the profits of the African slave trade, *to and from the ports of Brazil*, as fully as the Brazilians themselves and others, in conjunction with whom they carry it on. In fact, without the aid of our citizens and our flag, it could not be carried out with success at all. They furnish the protection; they are the common carriers; they sail over and deliver up to the trade, *vessels* as well as *cargoes*; they transport the *supplies* of slave factories, the food and raiment of the slave trade agents, and the goods which constitute the *purchase-money* of the slave trade's victims; they carry the *arms* and the *ardent spirits* which are the hellish agents and instruments of the savage wars of African captivity; they afford *safe passage* to Brazilian masters and crews intended for the slaver vessels when sold, and for the American masters and crews who have manned those vessels over to the coast; and they realize a profit in proportion to the risks of a contraband trade. In one word, the sacred principle of the inviolability of the protection of our flag, is perverted in the ports of Brazil into a perfect monopoly of the unhallowed gains of the navigation of the African slave trade. And for the reason of this inviolability, our flag and vessels are sought and bought, and our citizens at home and here, *sail* them and *sell* them in the African slave trade to and from all ports of Brazil. And in all those ports, and in the metropolitan port of Rio de Janeiro, especially, our vessels are fitted out for the slave trade, and the most of the crimes of that trade, in violation of the laws of the United States, openly have their inception under the very eye of the Imperial Government, and in them all, and in this port especially, *the consummation of these crimes is sheltered, as of right, by the sovereign jurisdiction of this Empire.*[5]

Writing in April 1852, seventeen months after passage of the Eusébio de Queiroz law, U.S. consul at Rio de Janeiro Edward Kent praised the actions of the British and Brazilians in halting the traffic. Yet, he distrusted the slave bloc resident in the city and expressed uneasiness about the future:

It is true that there is a large party composed principally of native Brazilians who are earnestly opposed to the traffic, but there is on the other hand a very powerful and influential body composed of men of wealth and enterprise, who have apparently no conscientious scruples on the subject, who would I have no doubt enter again into the trade as soon as the chances of success outweigh the chances of capture. It is generally conceded that if one cargo out of three comes safely over from Africa, a decided profit will ensue to the owners although two of the vessels with their cargoes may be captured or lost. A slave costs on the Coast from 20 to 40 dollars, and is worth when landed from two to three hundred dollars. This profit is so great that it is in vain to hope that "moral suasion" alone will deter those who have no conscientious scruples on the subject.

A system so long established enlisting in its support not merely reckless adventurers, outcasts and pirates but many men of wealth, intelligence, and station who do not yet see or will not admit the moral iniquity of this traffic, which offers such overpowering temptations to cupidity and such excitement to gamblers in the human flesh, and meets in some degree the demand for laborers on immense tracts of uncultivated lands, cannot be finally suppressed by a few captures and by temporary measures of active interposition on the high seas.

Candor compels me to add that I fear that upon demand and with suffi-
ciently tempting offers, our own vessels and some of our Citizens would be
found again prostituting the honored flag of our nation, by participation in this
disgraceful commerce in human beings.[6]

In evaluating "this relic of barbarism," Kent suggested strategies to prevent
a resurgence of the slave trade to Brazil. "[We need] suppression in interior
and coast of Africa, destruction of the barracoons and trading stations, enlist-
ment of native princes and other men of influence and power against the wars
and barbarous customs of other years; [this can be accomplished] by extending schemes of colonization, introduction of civilization and Christian religion
into Africa. [In this way] the evil will be reached at its fountain head." Kent
also called for more stringent measures to impede U.S. ships from participating in the slave trade. This included thorough inspections of vessels previous
to departure and the requirement that bonds be posted worth two to three
times the cost of the vessel to ensure its return to the United States within
a specified time. A functionary who had astutely carried out duties at Rio de
Janeiro since 1849, it was Kent who warned that "in their business, the slave
traders are wise as serpents." Furthermore, he had little confidence in legal
measures, eliciting an opinion that "*oaths are often cobwebs.*" Hence, "physical
force would [continue to] be necessary along the coasts of Africa and Brazil
and [on the] high seas."[7]

In the half century previous to prohibition of the slave trade to the United
States (in 1808), U.S. merchants invested their income derived from slaving
ventures in a diverse portfolio of businesses and institutions. These included
banks, distilleries, insurance companies, shipyards, foundries, and universities, among others.[8]

From 1808 to 1868, U.S. merchants continued to play a central role in
the "illegal" transatlantic slave trade to Brazil and Cuba. They built efficient
sailing ships; established and aided enterprises at Rio de Janeiro, Salvador,
Havana, and Matanzas mired in the slave trade; shared information; paid captains and crews; and facilitated the use of the U.S. flag on slave vessels to avoid
capture by the British Squadron.[9] U.S. merchants supplied factories on the
coast of Africa with an array of goods. A partial list includes U.S.-produced
rum, ale, porter, cider, jerked beef, pork, mackerel, biscuit, wheat flour, salt,
tobacco, refined and brown sugar, cornmeal, rice, beans, butter, lard, sperm
candles, soap, cheese, raisins, bread, wine, bees, trumpets, beads, rope, oakum,

bricks, cables, brass wash basins, brass pots, brass pans, mugs, jugs, boilers, water casks capable of holding 687 gallons of water, wood planks, wood spoons, wooden buckets, tin pans, tin buckets, tin tubes used as straws to suck water from casks, blank books, paper, ink, quills, paint oil, lamp oil, shackles (forged in Providence, R.I.), spikes, crow bars, shovels, cutlasses, axes, cross-cut saws, knives, cutlery, locks, hinges, nails, barrels, gold coins, coarse cloth, flannels, cotton textiles, woolen caps, muskets, gunpowder in ten- and twenty-pound kegs, swan shot; and foreign goods such as Birmingham shackles and muskets, British textiles, Brazilian manioc, coffee, and cachaça, and Spanish brandy.[10] Before setting fire to the village of Monega situated along the Tejungo river (also known as the Monega River, located ninety miles north of Quelimane) in early January 1851, Commander Bunce of H.M.S. *Castor* "found empty powder-barrels bearing date 'Boston-1850,' which [he believed] very probably had been recently bartered for slaves."[11]

A debate exists over the extent to which U.S. traffickers invested their profits into the U.S. economy during the era of the illegal slave trade. Professor David Eltis believes such investments to be minimal.[12] This book suggests otherwise. Shipyards located at coastal port cities were centers of economic growth in the nineteenth century. Construction of sea vessels provided significant trickle-down income into numerous sectors of local and regional economies. Farmers who supplied slave voyages and slave factories on the coast of Africa gained disposable income that they invested into various endeavors. Captains and crews of slave ships used their profits to purchase goods and property.

One approximation of the income derived from U.S. involvement in the traffic to Cuba in the mid-1850s was provided by British consul Francis Lousada. Lousada estimated that forty U.S. ships sailed from Cuba to Africa in search of slaves each year during that period. The majority were constructed in Boston, New York, and Baltimore. They weighed between 150 and 250 tons. The cost for provisions and "every equipment for a successful trip" was $8,000 per ship, or $320,000 invested in 40 slave vessels. Lousada's overview of costs and profits is as follows:

Expenses at the port for brokerage and commission, at $3,000 per vessel = $120,000 for 40 voyages

Captain's and seamen's wages for one voyage of $160, or $6,400 for 40 voyages

Amount paid for slaves on the coast of Africa at $15 per head, allowing 600 for each vessel: $360,000 for 40 voyages

Port money and secret money paid at landing place in Cuba, which he estimated
at $100 per head, allowing a diminution of 100 to each vessel by death in
passage: $2,000,000

Total: $2,806,400

From this estimate it will be seen that the amount of capital in use was, in
round numbers, 2.8 million dollars, upon which the profits were immense.
In a single voyage of this fleet, 24,000 human beings were carried off from
different points on the coast of Africa, and of these no fewer than 4,000, or
one-sixth of the total number, became victims of the horrors of the Middle
Passage. That left some 20,000 fit for market. For each of these the trader
earned an average of $500, making a total of 10 million dollars. Hence, we
have an estimate of 7.2 million dollars in profit on a capital investment of 2.8
million dollars in forty completed transatlantic voyages.[13]

Given the investments of "American capitalists" in numerous slaving voyages out of Havana and previously from Brazil (1820s–1850s), a portion of
these enormous profits flowed into the economies of the United States, Brazil,
and Cuba.[14] This ranged from purchasing basic consumer goods to facilitating
the expansion of plantation agriculture to investments in businesses. Wealth
and knowledge derived from the many sectors of the transatlantic slave trade
contributed to the impressive industrial revolution of New England in the first
two-thirds of the nineteenth century.[15]

Comparisons abound in analysis of the histories of Brazil and Cuba in the
nineteenth century. Both countries strengthened their ties to international
markets through the export of commodities (particularly sugar, coffee, and
tobacco). To satisfy the demand for labor, planters and merchants purchased
tens of thousands of African slaves. U.S. ships and capital played an integral
role in a transnational enterprise that linked Brazil, Cuba, and Africa. Many
of the enslaved Africans who ended up in the cities and countryside of both
countries had their origins in the same regions of Africa. In both Brazil and
Cuba, a cycle of revolts and conspiracies caused huge problems for the authorities. In particular, the Revolt of the Malês and the Escalera insurgency
showed the determination and capacity of Africans to resist their enslavement.
Both events provoked a severe backlash. For at least two decades following
(1835–55 in Brazil, 1845–65 in Cuba), slaves and free blacks remembered well
these tumultuous events.[16]

International events played a decisive role in ending the traffic to Brazil and Cuba. From early 1848, the aggressive actions by the British Squadron made boarding slaves in Africa and then landing them on Brazilian shores increasingly difficult. Passage of the Eusébio de Queiroz law in late 1850 and the enforcement of that legislation by the imperial government helped to bring a halt to disembarkations of African slaves. British patrols and interceptions of slave vessels destined for Cuba continued for the next two decades, although with less effect. With the outbreak of the American Civil War and the Union blockade of the U.S. South, traffickers faced mounting pressures on their business. The decision by Abraham Lincoln, a man with an impressive grasp of the Atlantic world, to allow British cruisers to seize U.S. vessels, added to the difficulties faced by slave merchants in the early 1860s.

As *Disease, Resistance, and Lies* has shown, the demise of the transatlantic slave trade was a more complex process than simply policies implemented by British and U.S. leaders. The spread of sickness from infected Africans caused protests in Brazil and Cuba. Yellow fever and cholera plagued both countries. Common folk in port cities and in the countryside associated disembarkations with the spread of epidemics. Other threats arose from African slaves. These individuals had survived the Middle Passage. They participated in revolts at sea and on land led by fellow Africans. They observed closely the actions of the British Squadron and they listened closely to the words of abolitionists transmitted swiftly around the Atlantic world. Their actions played a decisive role in forcing the end of the transatlantic slave trade.

APPENDIX

TABLE 1. List of Vessels That Sailed from the Port of Havana for the Coast of Africa during the Year 1839

No.	Date	Nation	Class	Vessel	Destination	Remarks
1	Jan. 23	American	Schooner	Rebecca	Gallinas	Captured [STDB # 2596]
2	Jan. 26	American	Brig	Oriental	Lagos	Returned Oct. 24 & sailed Oct. 26 for New Orleans
3	Jan. 28	Portuguese	Brig	Fortuna	Lagos	Returned July 19 see no. 40
4	Feb. 8	American	Schooner	William Bayard	Cape Verde	
5	Feb. 19	Spanish	Schooner	Nuestra Snra del Rosaria	Cape Verde	
6	Feb. 19	Portuguese	Schooner	Montaña	San Pablo de Loanda	Returned Oct. 5 [landed 277 slaves Oct. 5, 1839, STDB # 1867]
7	Feb. 19	American	Brig	Morris Cooper	Lagos	Returned as Casualidad [landed 489 slaves at Guanimar, STDB # 1874]
8	Feb. 21	American	Schooner	Perry Spencer	Gallinas	[STDB # 2665]
9	March 6	American	Brig	Wyoming	Pitavasa	Captured [STDB # 2644]
10	March 6	American	Schooner	Octavia	Costa de Oro	Returned Sept. 2 [landed 423 slaves, STDB # 1864]
11	March 12	Portuguese	Schooner	Josefna	San Tomé	Returned June 14 [landed 240 slaves, STDB # 1858]
12	March 21	Portuguese	Schooner	Constitucion	San Tomé	Captured
13	March 21	American	Schooner	Joseph Wilding	Cape de Verde	Captured
14	April 12	Portuguese	Brig	Matilde	Prince's Island	Captured [condemned at Sierra Leone, STDB # 2679]
15	April 22	Portuguese	Brig	Elisa	Rio Pongo	Returned Oct. 11 [landed 119 slaves, STDB # 1869]
16	May 7	Portuguese	Schooner	Josefna	Loanda	
17	May 7	Portuguese	Schooner	Victoria	Cape Mesurado	
18	May 7	Portuguese	Ship	Amalia	Madagascar	Returned Nov. 20 [landed 840 slaves, STDB # 1937]
19	May 16	Oriental	Brig	Primogenitor	San Pablo de Loanda	

	Date	Nationality	Type	Vessel	Location	Outcome
20	May 16	Portuguese	Schooner	*Liberal*	Loanda	Captured [condemned at Sierra Leone, STDB # 2635]
21	May 29	Hamburg	Brig	*Margaret*	Isla del Principe	
22	June 5	Portuguese	Ship	*Maria Segunda Socorro*	Mozambique	Returned Dec. 6 [landed 580 slaves, STDB # 1941]
23	June 5	Portuguese	Brig	*Ulises*	Prince's Island	Captured as *Manso*
24	June 5	Portuguese	Schooner	*Ligera*	Loanda	Captured
25	June 17	Portuguese	Brig	*Duquesa de Braganza, also known as Venus*	Goa	Returned [landed 720 slaves, STDB # 1943]
26	June 17	American	Schooner	*Hound*	Lagos	Returned to Puerto Rico
27	June 19	American	Brig	*Mary*	Gallinas	Returned Nov. 12 [landed 465 slaves, STDB # 1939]
28	June 25	American	Schooner	*Catherine*	Gallinas & Bonny	Captured & carried to the United States [STDB # 2627]
29	June 26	American	Schooner	*Elvira*	Prince's Island	Returned as Portuguese *Porto Formoso* [landed 307 slaves, STDB # 1865]
30	July 1	Portuguese	Schooner	*Dois Amigos*	San Tomé	Captured [condemned at Sierra Leone, STDB # 2639]
31	July 2	American	Schooner	*Butterfly*	Isla del Principe	Captured & carried to the United States
32	July 5	Portuguese	Brig	*Triunfo de Loanda*	Mozambique	
33	July 8	Portuguese	Brig	*Felicidad*	Lagos	Returned Oct. 7 [landed 444 slaves, STDB # 1868]
34	July 20	Spanish	Brig	*Ensayador*	Cape Verde	
35	July 26	Portuguese	Schooner	*Victoria*	Rio Congo	Captured
36	July 27	Portuguese	Schooner	*Josefina*	San Tomé	Captured [landed 277 slaves, STDB # 1940]
37	August 1	American	Brig	*Douglas*	Bonny	
38	August 2	Spanish	Schooner	*Iberia*	San Tomé	
39	August 5	Portuguese	Schooner	*Magdalena*	Gallinas	Captured
40	August 5	Portuguese	Brig	*Fortuna (a) Llobregat*	Lagos	Captured

TABLE 1, continued

No.	Date	Nation	Class	Vessel	Destination	Remarks
41	August 24	Spanish	Schooner	*Numantina*	Cape de Verde	Returned [landed 277 slaves, STDB # 1944]
42	Sept. 10	American	Schooner	*Lark*	Isla del Principe	[condemned at Sierra Leone, STDB # 2664]
43	Sept. 10	Portuguese	Schooner	*Savaderra*	San Tomé	Captured
44	Sept. 19	Spanish	Schooner	*Mercedita*	Cape Lopez	Captured
45	Sept. 22	American	Schooner	*Hound*	Cape Mesurado & Gallinas	
46	Sept. 26	American	Schooner	*Cutter Campbell*	Gallinas	
47	Oct. 12	American	Schooner	*Nymph*	Rio Braza	
48	Oct. 23	American	Ship	*John*	Gold Coast	
49	Oct. 23	Spanish	Brig	*Joven Emeline*	Gold Coast	
50	Nov. 5	Portuguese	Schooner	*Astrea*	San Pablo de Loanda	
51	Nov. 13	Spanish	Pailebot	*Margarita*	Gallinas	
52	Nov. 16	American	Schooner	*Asp*	Rio Braza	[condemned at Sierra Leone, STDB # 2663]
53	Nov. 19	Portuguese	Schooner	*Elvira*	Cape Verde	
54	Dec. 11	American	Schooner	*Hanna*	Isla del Principe	
55	Dec. 15	Spanish	Schooner	*Montaña*	Cape Verde	
56	Dec. 16	American	Schooner	*Centipede*	San Tomé	
57	Dec. 22	Portuguese	Brig	*Dos Hermanos*	San Tomé	
58	Dec. 23	American	Schooner	*Hyperion*	San Tomé	
59	Dec. 25	Portuguese	Schooner	*Veloz*	Santiago de Praya	

Source: Kennedy and Dalrymple to Palmerston, Havana, January 1, 1841, FO 84:348. Information derived from Trans-Atlantic Slave Trade Database is noted as STDB and voyage number.

TABLE 2. List of U.S. Vessels Cleared from the Port of Rio de Janeiro for the Coast of Africa from July 1, 1844, to September 30, 1849

Dates	Rig	Names	Captains	Where Belonging
11/17/1844	Brig	*Sterling*	Gallop	Beverly, MA
11/21/1844	Brig	*Susan & Mary*	B. Connor	Baltimore
12/4/1844	Brig	*Sea Eagle*	Smith	Boston
1/24/1845	Brig	*Arctic*	Pascal	Baltimore
2/18/1845	Bark	*Herschell*	Adams	New York
2/28/1845	Brig	*Janet*	Burk	Not listed
3/22/1845	Bark	*Pons*	Graham	Philadelphia
4/19/1845	Bark	*Pilot*	Swift	Boston
5/17/1845	Bark	*Madeline*	Shanklaw	Not listed
7/19/1845	Bark	*Pons*	Graham	Philadelphia
8/4/1845	Ship	*Panther*	Clapp	Providence
8/11/1845	Bark	*Pilot*	Swift	Boston
10/11/1845	Schooner	*Enterprise*	Nicholson	Boston
10/30/1845	Brig	*Harriet*	Jarvis	Baltimore
11/?/1845	Bark	*L.D.*	Bascett	Boston
11/18/1845	Bark	*Cuba*	Blanchard	Boston
12/3/1845	Brig	*Benlak*	Merrill	Portland, ME
12/13/1845	Brig	*Roaver*	Auchinslost	New York
12/20/1845	Bark	*Lucy Penniman*	Reddell	New York
12/31/1845	Bark	*Pilot*	Swift	Boston
2/13/1846	Bark	*Laida*	Chapman	Wiscasset, MA
3/7/1846	Brig	*Vintago*	Flory	Salem, MA
3/11/1846	Brig	*Francis Ann*	Tate	New York
5/20/1846	Brig	*Casket*	Woodberry	Beverly, MA
7/28/1846	Brig	*Chipola*	Neuman ?	Baltimore
8/11/1846	Brig	*Francis Ann*	Tate	New York
8/24/1846	Brig	*Benlak*	Merrill	Portland, ME
8/29/1846	Brig	*Vintage*	Edwards	Salem, MA
9/15/1846	Brig	*Forest*	Altridge	New York
9/30/1846	Schooner	*Dover*	Illegible	New York
11/26/1846	Brig	*Francis Ann*	Tate	New York
12/?/1846	Brig	*Sterling*	Gallop	Beverly, MA
12/19/1846	Brig	*Frederica*	Ranier ?	Key West, FL

TABLE 2, *continued*

Dates	Rig	Names	Captains	Where Belonging
12/31/1846	Brig	*Senator*	Kelley	Boston
12/31/1846	Bark	*Fame*	Marks	New London, CT
2/27/1847	Bark	*Josephine*	Jones	New York
3/23/1847	Brig	*Casket*	Woodberry	Beverly, MA
3/27/1847	Brig	*Forest*	Altridge	New York
4/24/1847	Brig	*Malaga*	Lovett	Not listed
7/10/1847	Brig	*Don Juan*	Maris	Not listed
7/16/1847	Brig	*Illegible*	Russell	Providence, RI
8/4/1847	Brig	*Casket*	Woodberry	Beverly, MA
9/30/1847	Brig	*Malaga*	Lovett	Not listed
10/28/1847	Schooner	*Alicia*	Jones	Not listed
11/6/1847	Bark	*Canes*	Harvis	Not listed
11/8/1847	Bark	*Camilla*	Not known	Not listed
12/29/1847	Brig	*W. Huntington*	Illegible	Not listed
1/5/1848	Brig	*Whig*	Brand	Not listed
1/21/1848	Brig	*Brazil*	Bevans	Not listed
3/3/1848	Bark	*California*	Pednick	Not listed
3/18/1848	Brig	*Caracas*	Littlefield	Not listed
3/18/1848	Schooner	*Morris*	Curvier	Not listed
3/23/1848	Schooner	*M.L. Smith*	Smith	Not listed
4/1/1848	Brig	*Frederica*	Faulkner	Not listed
4/12/1848	Brig	*C.K. Rogers*	Rauch	Not listed
5/6/1848	Ship	*Herald*	Barken	Not listed
5/23/1848	Brig	*Gregory*	Ayres	Not listed
5/27/1848	Bark	*Louisa*	Sonder	Not listed
6/8/1848	Schooner	*Juliet*	Gordon Jr.	Not listed
7/15/1848	Schooner	*Morris*	Jones	Not listed
7/17/1848	Schooner	*Lenovia*	Belton	Not listed
8/16/1848	Brig	*J.W.Huntington*	Roberts	Not listed
8/28/1848	Bark	*Globe*	Bevans	Not listed
9/15/1848	Schooner	*Mary Catherine*	W. Griffin	Baltimore
9/25/1848	Schooner	*Marion*	W.J. Rogers	Sag Harbor, NY
9/26/1848	Brig	*Venus*	Adams	Gloucester, MA

TABLE 2, *continued*

Dates	Rig	Names	Captains	Where Belonging
10/31/1848	Schooner	*Henrietta*	Otis Rinco ?	Not listed
11/4/1848	Bark	*Camilla*	Forsyth	Not listed
11/8/1848	Brig	*Caracas*	Shavis ?	Not listed
11/10/1848	Brig	*Albertina*	Montgomery	New York
11/14/1848	Schooner	*Morris*	Jones	Not listed
11/14/1848	Bark	*Illegible*	Appleton	Salem, MA
11/18/1848	Ship	*France*	Corning	Not listed
11/28/1848	Brig	*Snow*	Washburn	Not listed
11/30/1848	Bark	*Louisa*	Rauch	Not listed
12/11/1848	Bark	*A.D.Richardson*	Stoner	Not listed
12/13/1848	Brig	*Independence*	Burns	Not listed
12/19/1848	Brig	*Flora*	Clapp	Not listed
1/16/1849	Schooner	*Lenovia*	Belton	Not listed
2/7/1849	Brig	*Illegible*	Nickols	Philadelphia
2/12/1849	Brig	*Whig*	Wrippy	New York
2/27/1849	Brig	*Depolet*	Clark	Boston
3/?/1849	Bark	*Quincy*	Myers	Boston
3/24/1849	Schooner	*Morris*	Jones	Not listed
6/11/1849	Brig	*Rowena ?*	Not listed	Not listed
6/30/1849	Brig	*W. Thomas*	Not listed	Not listed
7/7/1849	Brig	*Caracas*	Not listed	Not listed
8/3/1849	Brig	*Das Laras ?*	Not listed	Not listed
8/6/1849	Ship	*Illegible*	Belton	Not listed
8/25/1849	Bark	*Christie ?*	Nickols	Not listed
9/1/1849	Brig	*Snow*	Washburn	Not listed
9/30/1849	Brig	*Casco*	Kinney	Not listed
9/30/1849	Brig	*Swan*	Walford	Not listed

? = word or letters are not clearly legible

Source: Former U.S. consul Gorham Parks to David Tod, Rio de Janeiro, January 29, 1850, U.S. Department of State Records, National Archives Record Group 59, Diplomatic Dispatches from Brazil, M-121:20.

TABLE 3. List of Vessels Reported to Be from the Coast of Africa That Arrived in Cuba in the Year 1843

No.	Date	Nation	Class	Vessel	Remarks
1	Jan. 6	Spanish	Brig	Roldau	Said to have landed 300 Negroes, but doubtful
2	February	Spanish	Brig	Name Unknown	Said to have landed 600 Negroes on the South side of the Island
3	March	Spanish	Brig	Huracán	Landed 230 at Santiago [STDB # 2223]
4	March	Spanish	Brig	Constancia	Landed 510 near Trinidad [STDB # 2269]
5	April	Spanish	Brig	Segunda Palmyra	Landed 800 at Matanzas [STDB # 2224]
6	April	Spanish	Brig	Volador	Brought 600 to Matanzas
7	April	Spanish	Brig	Venganza	Came to Matanzas [landed 250 slaves at Matanzas on 5/24/1843; STDB # 2253]
8	June	American	Brig	Cyrus	In ballast [captured in June 1844 with 336 slaves on board; condemned at Sierra Leone by Mixed Commission Court, STDB # 3855]
9	July	Spanish	Schooner	Mariana	Brought 260 to Matanzas
10	July	Spanish	Schooner	Name Unknown	Brought 320 to Matanzas
11	August	Spanish	Schooner	Name Unknown	Reported landing at Trinidad
12	Sept. 18	Spanish	Brig	Segunda Palmyra	Brought about 900 to Matanzas of whom 93 were seized [landed 700 slaves, STDB # 2228]
13	November	Spanish	Bark	Name Unknown	Brought 130 to Matanzas
14	November	Portuguese	Schooner	Name Unknown	Brought 350 to Matanzas
15	Nov. 16	American	Brig	Uncas	In ballast, 500 Negroes [believed to have been landed]
16	December	Spanish	Brig	Jacinto	Landed cargo at Cuba [landed 444 slaves at Cabañas, STDB # 2270]
17	December	Spanish	Felucca	Name Unknown	Landed cargo, came to Pedro Martínez [number not known]

No.	Date	Nation	Class	Vessel	Remarks
18	December	Spanish	Brig	*Escorpión*	Landed 560 slaves, landed at Trinidad de Cuba [STDB # 2272]
19	December	Spanish	Brig	*Maria*	Landed 89 slaves, landed at Trinidad de Cuba [also known as *Maria Forcade*, STDB # 2273]

TOTAL: 2 American; 16 Spanish; 1 Portuguese = 19 vessels

List of Vessels Dispatched from Cuba during the Year of 1843 Suspected of Being Intended for Slave Trade

No.	Date	Nation	Class	Vessel	Destination	Remarks
1	January 1	American	Brig	*Angelina*	Rio Pongo	
2	January 1	Spanish	Brig	*Oriental*	Montevideo	
3	February	Spanish	Brig	*Jacinto*		Returned [landed 300 slaves at Trinidad de Cuba in 1844, STDB # 3913]
4	June 22	Spanish	Brig	*Segunda Palmyra*		From Matanzas [landed 700 slaves at Matanzas, Sept. 19, 1843, STDB # 2228]
5	June 22	American	Brig	*Uncas*	Loanda	Captured by United States before slaves embarked, STDB # 4940
6	July 14	American	Schooner	*Hannah*	Isla de Principe	
7	July 21	American	Brig	*Elsanor*	Sierra Leone	
8	October 8	Spanish	Ship	*Zafiro*	Cadiz	By Pedro Martinez
9	October	Spanish	Schooner	*Estrella*	Cadiz	By Pedro Martinez
10	October 17	Spanish	Bark	*Terrible*	Cadiz	By Pedro Martinez

TABLE 3, continued

No.	Date	Nation	Class	Vessel	Destination	Remarks
11	October	Spanish	Brig	Carmen	Montevideo	
12	October 30	Spanish	Felucca	Huracán	Buenos Ayres	From Matanzas [possibly landed 369 slaves at unknown location just before this departure, STDB # 46669]
13	Nov. 12	Spanish	Brig	Emprendidor	Barcelona	
14	Nov. 15	Spanish	Brig	Salindor	Barcelona	
15	Nov. 19	American	Ship	Chester	New York	Chartered for the Coast
16	Nov. 29	American	Brig	America	San Tomé	
17	Nov. 30	Spanish	Ship	Manuelita	Montevideo	
18	November	Spanish	Ship	Segunda Palmyra		From Matanzas [most likely landed 1,114 slaves at Bahia Honda, Feb. 8, 1844, STDB # 3896]
19.	Dec. 11	American	Brig	Uncas	Monrovia	[captured in April 1845, condemned at Sierra Leone; owned by Manoel Pinto da Fonseca, STDB # 3484]
20	Dec. 12	Spanish	Ship	Andaluza	Buenos Ayres	[landed 750 slaves at Guanimar on April 24,1844, STDB # 3900]
21	Dec. 18	American	Brig	Cybele	Cape Verde	
22	Dec. 20	American	Brig	Daniel Webster	Rio Nunez	
23	Dec. 26	Spanish	Schooner	Mariana		From Matanzas [landed 277 slaves at Matanzas in 1844, STDB # 3902]

TOTAL: 9 American; 14 Spanish = 23 vessels

Source: Kennedy and Dalrymple to Aberdeen, Havana, January 1, 1844, FO 84;508

TABLE 4. Slave Expeditions and Disembarkations in Cuba, 1821–67

Year	Number of Expeditions	Number of Slaves Landed
1821–31	300	60,000*
1832	27	8,200
1833	27	9,000
1834	33	11,400
1835	50	24,959
1836	43	23,414
1837	51	20,545
1838	50	22,582
1839	47	19,834
1840	44	17,739
1841	27	14,124
1842	9	4,739
1843	19	8,012
1844	25	9,897
1845	6	2,865
1846	4	432
1847	4	1,510
1848	5	2,010
1849	20	7,621
1850	7	3,098
1851	7	7,820
1852	12	8,098
1853	17	15,455
1854	19	12,706
1855	13	5,343
1856	14	7,008
1857	23	10,448
1858	19	15,396
1859	39	26,290
1860	21	18,260
1861	34	14,621
1862	14	10,382
1863	not reported	5,649
1864	not reported	3,895
1865	1	1,855
1866	3	722
1867	1	0

Sources: The estimates for 1821–31 (*) are from Louis A. Pérez Jr., *Cuba: Between Reform and Revolution*, 4th ed. (New York: Oxford University Press, 2011), 79. Other expeditions are listed in D.R. Murray, "Statistics of the Slave Trade to Cuba, 1790–1867," *Journal of Latin American Studies* 3:2 (November 1971), 142, 144, 147; the estimates on number of Africans disembarked in Cuba are from The Trans-Atlantic Slave Trade Database. The estimated number of expeditions does not include numerous clandestine landings at remote locations in Cuba.

TABLE 5. List of Vessels Reported to Have Sailed for the Coast of Africa to Be Employed in the Slave Trade to Cuba, January 1857 to July 1858

Date of Sailing	Class	Vessel	Tons	Cleared for	Remarks
1857					
Jan. 10	American brig	Adam Cray	138	New Orleans	Captured in April by HMS Prometheus
Jan. 31	American brig	Crimea	237	Cienfuegos	Landed 514 slaves at Guanimar [STDB # 4276]
Feb. 12	American bark	Panchita	NA		Fitted at Newport, R.I. Captured in May by HMS Sappho [STDB # 4877]
Feb. 12	American bark	Splendid	270	Cuba from New York	Captured in July by Portuguese schooner Cabo Verde [STDB # 4426]
—	American schooner	Jupiter	227		Captured in June by Antelope with 70 slaves [STDB # 4246]
—	American brig	Elisa Jane	307		Captured in August by Alecto in Cabinda Bay [STDB # 4249]
—	American brig	William Clark	149	Cleared from New Orleans	Captured in August by Firefly near Little Popo [STDB # 4255]
—	American schooner	Onward	265		Captured in September by Myrmidon [STDB # 4251]
—	Spanish bark	Conchita	287		Captured in August by Firefly near Whydah [STDB # 4261]
—	American ship	Charles	NA	Cleared from New Orleans	Captured near Annobon [STDB # 4252]
March 4	American brig	W.D. Miller	128	Montevideo	Landed 15 slaves near Sierra Morena in July and was then burnt [real number landed was 412, STDB # 4232]
April 4	American bark	Minnetonka	320	Madagascar	Landed 10 slaves at Remedios in November, returned to the Coast on second slaving expedition and is said to have been captured [STDB # 4266 and # 4272]
April 4	Spanish schooner	Mercedita	NA	Remedios	Landed 23 slaves on September 18 at Havana. Owner Duranona [STDB # 4237]

Date	Ship type	Ship name	Number	Port	Notes
April 7	Spanish bark	Restauración	354	Batavia	Sailed from Matanzas and is said to have landed a cargo of slaves in Cuba. Then returned to the Coast and was captured December 2 by Alecto [STDB # 4259]
April 16	American ship	Hydra	499	Buenos Aires	[STDB # 4278 notes the landing of 560 Africans in Cuba in 1858 from a bark named Venus]
April 29	Spanish ship	Venus	419		
May 6	American schooner	Jos. A. Record	109	Montevideo	Captured in September with 191 slaves in the Bight of Benin [STDB # 4254]
May 9	American schooner	Abbott Devereux	113	Monrovia	Captured in August with 270 slaves near Whydah by Fearer [STDB # 4247]
May 16	American brig	R.B. Lawton	198	Boston	Supposed to have landed 450 slaves at Sierra Morena [STDB # 4235]
June 3	American bark	C.B. Williams	331	Callao	Said to have been captured at the River Congo [STDB # 4258]
June 23	American schooner	James Buchanan	164	Boston	Landed 50 slaves near the Isle of Pines, went to Yucatan and was . . . [illegible] [STDB # 4242 notes 260 Africans landed]
July 13	American brig	Windward	177	United States	Captured in November with 630 slaves near the River Congo by Alecto [STDB # 4874]
July 13	Spanish bark	Eloisa 3 Hermanas	110	Antwerp	[STDB # 4330 and 4358 show voyages of ship Eloisa in 1859 and 1860]
July 27	American brig	Telegraph	185	United States	Landed cargo of slaves in Cuba [STDB # 4274 shows Telegraph landed 500 Africans at Sagua, Cuba]
Aug. 1	American brig	Braman	185	Key West	Captured by HMS Vesuvius
Aug. 4	Spanish bark	Primero de Cardenas	116	Montevideo	
Aug. 19	American schooner	Niagra	72	United States	Said to have been captured and destroyed

TABLE 5, continued

Date of Sailing	Class	Vessel	Tons	Cleared for	Remarks
Aug. 20	Peruvian ship	Architect	520	Buenos Aires	
Nov. 25	American brig	C. Perkins	176	St. Thomas	Landed slaves near Mariel. Went to Sisal, Yucatan and returned to Havana May 30, 1858. Was fitting out for another slave voyage when seized by the authorities and was under detention [STDB # 4277 notes that C. Perkins landed 400 Africans at Mariel]
Dec. 18	American schooner	Wintermoyeh	109	Boston	Captured by Conflict
Dec. 18	American bark	Paez (a) Mazappa	236	Philadelphia	Captured in September with 385 slaves onboard by Spanish schooner Christina [STDB # 4236]
Dec. 18	American bark	Petrel	381	Mobile	Captured Oct. 15 with 537 slaves onboard by Spanish steamer Neptuno [STDB # 4239]
Dec. 18	American bark	Vesta	NA	Boston	Captured Oct. 23 with 169 slaves onboard by Spanish schooner Isabel Second [STDB # 4241]
Dec. 18	American bark	Lexington	NA	NA	Captured in October with 497 slaves onboard by Spanish steamer Vendito [STDB # 4245]
1858					
Jan. 5	American bark	Almeida	327	NA	Sailed from St. Jago, Cuba and was captured April 26 by Conflict [STDB # 4269]
Jan. 5	American brig	R.M. Charlton	147	NA	[STDB # 4271]
Feb. 9	American brig	General Scott	148	St. Thomas	[STDB # 4273]

Date	Vessel type	Ship name	Number	Port	Notes
Feb. 9	American brig	Henry Cole	191	NA	[STDB # 4214 notes the schooner C.F.A. Cole from Baltimore that landed 300 Africans at Sagua, Cuba in 1856]
Feb. 9	American brig	Putnam (a) Echo	197	New Orleans	Captured August 1 with 328 slaves by U.S. brig Dolphin off Double Head [STDB #4284]
Feb. 11	American bark	E.A. Rawlins	273	New Orleans	Sailed from New Orleans for 4 days and landed 650 slaves at Punta de la Feja after which it went to Savannah where it was fined $500 for irregularity of papers [STDB # 4286]
Feb. 14	American schooner	Angeline	149	Boston	Supposed to have landed 300 slaves at Punta Gorda near Matanzas on June 26 [STDB # 4792]
Feb. 16	Norwegian brig	St. Olof	150	Buenos Aires	
Feb. 25	American bark	Governor Parris	275	Portland	[STDB # 4795]
March 14	American schooner	Lydia Gibbs	114	Annobon	Captured May 29 near Whydah by Trident [STDB # 4264]
March 21	Spanish ship	Emilia	590	Marseilles	Captured March 22 by Styx [STDB # 4972]
March 27	American brig	St. Andrew	147	Charleston	Captured with over 300 slaves and sent to St. Helena. Crew arrived there in Dutch coolie ship on August 3 [STDB # 4793]
April 15	American schooner	Cortez	315	Annobon	Captured by Forward off Cayo Piedra [STDB # 4878]
April 19	American brig	Mary Elisabeth	124	St. Thomas	
April 22	American bark	Venus	240	Annobon	STDB # 42789 and 4290 show two voyages of the Venus in 1858
May	American brig	Huntress	NA		Sailed from Matanzas, taken into Key West by the Styx and seized there by American authorities [STDB # 4973]
May	American schooner	Kate Helen	180		Sailed from Matanzas [STDB # 4265]
June 16	American schooner	Austin	132	Mosquito	
June 19	American bark	General Green	242	Charleston	

TABLE 5, *continued*

Date of Sailing	Class	Vessel	Tons	Cleared for	Remarks
June 25	American brig	*Juliet*	NA		Cleared for Macao from St. Jago, Cuba and is owned by the Portuguese named Bautista [most likely STDB # 4975]
June 30	American ketch	*Brothers*	142	Charleston	[STDB # 4919]
July 5	American bark	*Lyra*	207	Key West	Seized by American authorities [STDB # 4910]
July 6	American brig	*Rufus Soule*	173	Liberia	Seized at Matanzas [STDB # 4796]
July 19	American bark	*L.W. Reid*	150		Sailed from St. Jago, Cuba and fitted out by the same party who owned the *Almeida*
July 19	American brig	*Nancy*	219		Landed a cargo of slaves in Cuba, went to Laguna from where it arrived at Havana on April 11 and was fitting on for another expedition to Africa when seized on July 17 by the Spanish authorities and was under detention [STDB # 4280 notes 520 Africans landed at south coast of Cuba]

Source: Crawford to Malmesbury, Havana, September 3, 1858, FO 84:1042.
NA means tonnage estimate was not available.

NOTES

---∞---

INTRODUCTION

1. A few examples include Bernard Bailyn, *The New England Merchants in the Seventeenth Century* (Cambridge, Mass.: Harvard University Press, 1955); Charles Boxer, *Salvador de Sá and the Struggle for Brazil and Angola, 1602–1686* (London: University of London Press, 1952); Charles Boxer, *The Dutch in Brazil, 1624–1654* (Oxford: Clarendon Press, 1957); Charles Boxer, *The Portuguese Seaborne Empire, 1415–1825* (New York: Alfred Knopf, 1969); C.H. Haring, *The Spanish Empire in America* (New York: Oxford University Press, 1947); Basil Davidson, *Black Mother* (Boston: Little, Brown, 1961); Herbert S. Klein, *Slavery in the Americas: A Comparative Study of Virginia and Cuba* (Chicago: University of Chicago Press, 1967); Pierre Verger, *Flux et reflux de la traite des negres entre le Golfe de Bénin et Bahia de todos os Santos, du XVIIe au XIXe siècle* (Paris: Mouton & Co., 1968), translated as *Trade Relations Between the Bight of Bénin and Bahia from the Seventeenth to Nineteenth Century* (Ibadan, Nigeria: Ibadan University Press, 1976).

2. See Alison Games, "Atlantic History: Definitions, Challenges, and Opportunities," *American Historical Review* 111:3 (June 2006), 741–57. Helpful studies include Immanuel Wallerstein, *The Modern World-System III: The Second Era of Great Expansion of the Capitalist World-Economy, 1730–1840s* (New York: Academic Press, 1989); Jorge Cañizares-Esguerra and Erik R. Seeman, eds., *The Atlantic in Global History, 1500–2000* (Upper Saddle River, NJ: Pearson Prentice Hall, 2007); Bernard Bailyn, *Atlantic History: Concepts and Contours* (Cambridge, Mass.: Harvard University Press, 2005); Alison F. Games and Adam Rothman, eds., *Major Problems in Atlantic History* (Boston: Houghton Mifflin, 2008); Jack P. Greene and Philip D. Morgan, eds., *Atlantic History: A Critical Appraisal* (New York: Oxford University Press, 2009); Thomas Benjamin, *The Atlantic World: Europeans, Africans, Indians and Their Shared History, 1400–1900* (Cambridge: Cambridge University Press, 2009); Beatriz G. Mamigonian and Karen Racine, eds., *The Human Tradition in the Black Atlantic, 1500–2000* (Lanham, Md.: Rowman and Littlefield, 2010); Karen Racine and Beatriz G. Mamigonian, eds., *The Human Tradition in the Atlantic World, 1500–1850* (Lanham, Md.: Rowman and Littlefield, 2010); James H. Sweet, *Domingos Álvares, African Healing, and the Intellectual History of the Atlantic World* (Chapel Hill: University of North Carolina Press, 2010);

João José Reis, Flávio dos Santos Gomes, and Marcus J.M. de Carvalho, *O alufá Rufino: tráfico, escravidão e liberdade no Atlântico Negro (c.1822–c.1853)* (São Paulo: Companhia das Letras, 2010); Roquinaldo Ferreira, *Cross-Cultural Exchange in the Atlantic World: Angola and Brazil during the Era of the Slave Trade* (Cambridge: Cambridge University Press, 2012); Karen Ordahl Kupperman, *The Atlantic in World History* (New York: Oxford University Press, 2012); John K. Thornton, *A Cultural History of the Atlantic World, 1250–1820* (Cambridge: Cambridge University Press, 2012).

3. Anne Farrow, Joel Lang, and Jenifer Frank, *Complicity: How the North Promoted, Prolonged, and Profited from Slavery* (New York: Ballantine Books, 2005), 6–10; Gene Dattel, *Cotton and Race in the Making of America: The Human Costs of Economic Power* (Lanham, Md.: Ivan R. Dee, 2011).

4. Márcia Berbel, Rafael Marques, and Tâmis Parron, *Escravidâo e política: Brasil e Cuba, c. 1790–1850* (São Paulo: Editora Hucitec, 2010), 183.

5. George Reid Andrews, *Afro-Latin America, 1800–2000* (New York: Oxford University Press, 2004), 69, 106; Richard Graham, *Britain and the Onset of Modernization in Brazil, 1850–1914* (Cambridge: Cambridge University Press, 1968).

6. Louis A. Pérez Jr., *Cuba: Between Reform and Revolution*, 4th ed. (New York: Oxford University Press, 2011), 59.

7. Ibid., 59–60. See also Manuel Moreno Fraginals, *The Sugarmill: The Socioeconomic Complex of Sugar in Cuba, 1760–1860* (New York: Monthly Review Press, 1976); Fernando Ortiz, *Cuban Counterpoint: Tobacco and Sugar* (Durham, N.C.: Duke University Press, 1995; 1st ed. 1940); Pablo Tornero Tinajero, *Crecimiento económico y transformaciones sociales. Esclavos, hacendados y comerciantes en la Cuba colonial (1760–1840)* (Madrid: Ministerio de Trabajo y Seguridad Social, 1996).

8. The bibliography related to the U.S. economy in the nineteenth century is extensive. A place to start is Richard D. Brown, *Modernization: The Transformation of American Life, 1600–1865* (New York: Hill and Wang, 1976), and Thomas Bender, *A Nation Among Nations: America's Place in World History* (New York: Hill and Wang, 2006).

9. Kent to Webster, Rio de Janeiro, February 8, 1851, United States National Archives, Record Group 59 (hereafter USNA, RG 59), Consular Dispatches from Rio de Janeiro, T-172:15.

10. Pérez, *Between Reform and Revolution*, 61–62.

11. David Eltis and David Richardson, "The Transatlantic Slave Trade and the Civil War," *The New York Times*, January 12, 2011.

12. Colin A. Palmer, "The Middle Passage," in *Captive Passage: The Transatlantic Slave Trade and the Making of the Americas* (Washington, D.C.: The Smithsonian Institution Press, 2002), 54; David Brion Davis, "Foreword," in David Eltis and David Richardson, *Atlas of the Transatlantic Slave Trade* (New Haven, Conn.: Yale University Press, 2010), xvii–xxvi.

13. Eltis and Richardson, *Atlas of the Transatlantic Slave Trade*, 17. Works describing the transatlantic slave trade to Cuba include David R. Murray, *Odious Commerce: Britain, Spain and the Abolition of the Slave Trade* (Cambridge: Cambridge University Press, 1980); Arthur F. Corwin, *Spain and the Abolition of Slavery in Cuba, 1817–1886* (Austin: University of Texas Press, 1967); Tinajero, *Crecimiento económico*; José Luciano Franco, *Comercio clandestino de esclavos* (La Habana: Editorial de Ciencias Sociales, 1996); José Guadalupe Ortega, "From Obscurity to Notoriety: Cuban Slave Merchants and the Atlantic World," in *The Changing Worlds of Atlantic Africa: Essays in Honor of Robin Law*, ed. Toyin Falola and Matt D. Childs (Durham, NC: Carolina Academic Press, 2009), 287–304. For the transatlantic slave trade to Brazil, see Leslie Bethell, *The Abolition of the Brazilian Slave Trade: Brazil and the Slave Trade Question (1807–1869)* (Cambridge: Cambridge

University Press, 1970); Verger, *Flux et reflux*; Robert Edgar Conrad, *World of Sorrow: The African Slave Trade to Brazil* (Baton Rouge: Louisiana State University Press, 1986); Manolo Florentino, *Em costas negras: uma história do tráfico de escravos entre a África e o Rio de Janeiro (Séculos XVIII–XIX)* (São Paulo: Companhia das Letras, 1997); Jaime Rodrigues, *O infame comércio: propostas e experiências no final do tráfico de africanos para o Brasil, 1800–1850* (Campinas, SP: UNICAMP, 2000); Jaime Rodrigues, *De costa a costa: escravos, marinheiros e intermediários do tráfico negreiro de Angola ao Rio de Janeiro, 1780–1860* (São Paulo: Companhia das Letras, 2005); Walter Hawthorne, *From Africa to Brazil: Culture, Identity, and an Atlantic Slave Trade, 1600–1830* (Cambridge: Cambridge University Press, 2010).

14. Robin Blackburn, *The Overthrow of Colonial Slavery, 1776–1848* (London: Verso, 1988), 7.

15. See Richard Graham's pathbreaking essay "Slavery and Economic Development: Brazil and the United States South in the Nineteenth Century," *Comparative Studies in Society and History* 23:4 (October 1981), 620–55. Also see Michael Zeuske, "Comparing or Interlinking? Economic Comparisons of Early Nineteenth-Century Slave Systems in the Americas in Historical Perspective," in *Slave Systems: Ancient and Modern*, ed. Enrico Dal Lago and Constantina Katsari (Cambridge: Cambridge University Press, 2008), 148–83; and Laird W. Bergad, *The Comparative Histories of Slavery in Brazil, Cuba and the United States* (Cambridge: Cambridge University Press, 2007).

16. Sidney Chalhoub, *A força da escravidão: ilegalidade e costume no Brasil oitocentista* (São Paulo: Companhia das Letras, 2012), 35.

17. Cited in Conrad, *World of Sorrow*, 62.

18. There is an extensive bibliography describing the major contours of the transatlantic slave trade. Insightful studies include Philip D. Curtin, *The Atlantic Slave Trade: A Census* (Madison: University of Wisconsin Press, 1969); David Eltis, *Economic Growth and the Ending of the Transatlantic Slave Trade* (New York: Oxford University Press, 1987); Hugh Thomas, *The Slave Trade: The Story of the Atlantic Slave Trade, 1440–1870* (New York: Simon & Schuster, 1997); Emma Christopher, *Slave Ship Sailors and Their Captive Cargoes, 1730–1807* (New York: Cambridge University Press, 2006); Lisa A. Lindsay, *Captives as Commodities: The Transatlantic Slave Trade* (Upper Saddle River, NJ: Pearson Education Publishers, 2007); Herbert S. Klein, *The Atlantic Slave Trade*, 2nd ed. (Cambridge: Cambridge University Press, 2010).

19. Eltis and Richardson, *Atlas of the Transatlantic Slave Trade*, 17, 265.

20. See Linda Heywood, "Introduction," in *Central Africans and Cultural Transformations in the American Diaspora*, ed. Linda Heywood (Cambridge: Cambridge University Press, 2002); Joseph Miller, "Central Africa During the Era of the Slave Trade, c.1490s–1850s," in Heywood, ed., *Central Africans*, 21–69; Mary C. Karasch, "Central Africans in Central Brazil, 1780–1835," in Heywood, ed., *Central Africans*, 117–51; Elizabeth W. Kiddy, "Who is the King of the Congo? A New Look at African and Afro-Brazilian Kings in Brazil," in Heywood, ed., *Central Africans*, 153–82; Robert W. Slenes, "The Great Porpoise-Skull Strike: Central African Water Spirits and Slave Identity in Early-Nineteenth-Century Rio de Janeiro," in Heywood, ed., *Central Africans*, 183–208; James H. Sweet, *Recreating Africa: Culture, Kinship, and Religion in the African-Portuguese World, 1441–1770* (Chapel Hill: University of North Carolina Press, 2003).

21. Ferreira, *Cross-Cultural Exchange*, 203–41; José C. Curto, *Enslaving Spirits: The Portuguese-Brazilian Alcohol Trade at Luanda and Its Hinterland, c.1550–1830* (Leiden and Boston: Brill Publishers, 2004).

22. Heywood, "Introduction," 13. See also Ferreira, *Cross-Cultural Exchange*, and David Northrup, *Africa's Discovery of Europe, 1450–1850*, 2nd ed. (New York: Oxford University Press, 2009), 38–43.

23. Juliana Barreto Farias, Flávio dos Santos Gomes, Carlos Eugênio Líbano Soares, and Carlos Eduardo de Araújo Moreira, *Cidades negras: africanos, crioulos e espaços urbanos no Brasil escravista do século xix* (São Paulo: Alameda, 2006), 13.

24. Alison Games, "Adaptation and Survival," in Games and Rothman, eds., *Major Problems*, 177. See also John K. Thornton, "'I Am the Subject of the King of Congo': African Political Ideology and the Haitian Revolution," *Journal of World History* 4:2 (1993), 181–214.

25. Kelly E. Hayes, "Black Magic and the Academy: Macumba and Afro-Brazilian 'Orthodoxies,'" *History of Religions* 46:4 (May 2007), 283–315.

26. Eltis and Richardson, *Atlas of the Transatlantic Slave Trade*, 267.

27. Mariana P. Candido, "Trans-Atlantic Links: The Benguela-Bahia Connections, 1700–1850," in *Paths of the Atlantic Slave Trade: Interactions, Identities, and Images*, ed. Ana Lucia Araujo (Amherst, N.Y.: Cambria Press, 2011), 239–72.

28. See Kristin Mann, "Shifting Paradigms in the Study of the African Diaspora and of Atlantic History and Culture," in *Rethinking the African Diaspora: The Making of a Black Atlantic World in the Bight of Benin and Brazil*, ed. Kristin Mann and Edna G. Bay (London: Frank Cass Publishers, 2001), 3–21; Robin Law, "Ethnicities of Enslaved Africans in the Diaspora: On the Meanings of 'Mina' (Again)," *History of Africa* 32 (2005), 247–67; João José Reis and Beatriz Gallotti Mamigonian, "Nagô and Mina: The Yoruba Diaspora in Brazil," in *The Yoruba Diaspora in the Atlantic World*, ed. Toyin Falola and Matt D. Childs (Bloomington: Indiana University Press, 2004), 77–110; Sandra Lauderdale Graham, "Being Yoruba in Nineteenth-Century Rio de Janeiro," *Slavery and Abolition* 32:1 (March 2011), 1–26.

29. There is a rich bibliography on this topic. A good place to start is Lisa A. Lindsay, "'To Return to the Bosom of Their Fatherland': Brazilian Immigrants in Nineteenth-Century Lagos," *Slavery and Abolition* 15:1 (April 1994), 22–50; Robin Law, "The Evolution of the Brazilian Community in Ouidah," in Mann and Bay, eds., *Rethinking the African Diaspora*, 22–41; and Alberto da Costa e Silva, *Francisco Félix de Souza, mercador de escravos* (Rio de Janeiro: Nova Fronteira, EdUERJ, 2004).

30. Miller, "Central Africa," 33.

31. Matt D. Childs and Toyin Falola, "The Yoruba Diaspora in the Atlantic World: Methodology and Research," in Falola and Childs, eds., *The Yoruba Diaspora*, 4.

32. See Ortiz, *Cuban Counterpoint* (first published in 1940); Sidney Mintz, *Sweetness and Power: The Place of Sugar in Modern History* (New York: Penguin Books, 1985).

33. Trans-Atlantic Slave Trade Database, http://www.slavevoyages.org/. Hereafter in these notes, all Trans-Atlantic Slave Trade voyage numbers are derived from this URL.

34. "Fragments of a conference that Dr. Ortiz presented at the Club Atenas in Havana on December 12, 1942." These are reflections by Ortiz with regard to *Hampa afrocubana: los negros brujos* (Miami: New House Publishers, 1973; 1st ed. 1906), xvii.

35. Miguel Barnet, *Biography of a Runaway Slave*, trans. W. Nick Hill (Willimantic, Conn.: Curbstone Press, 1994), 17–43.

36. See Farias, Gomes, Soares, and Moreira, *Cidades negras*.

37. Ivor L. Miller, *Voice of the Leopard: African Secret Societies and Cuba* (Jackson: University Press of Mississippi, 2012), 75.

38. Thanks to Manuel Barcia for noting these towns.

39. Miller, *Voice of the Leopard*, 85.

40. Representatives of the Religious Society of Friends, *An Exposition of the African Slave Trade from the Year 1840 to 1850, Inclusive, Prepared from Official Documents* (Philadelphia: J. Rakestraw, Printer, 1851); Reverend Rufus W. Clark, *The African Slave Trade* (Boston: American Tract Society, 1860); Robert Wilson Schufeldt, "Secret History of the Slave Trade to Cuba Written by an American Naval Officer," *The Journal of Negro History* 55:3 (July 1970), 218–35 (written 1861); W.E.B. DuBois, *The Suppression of the African Slave-Trade to the United States of America, 1638–1870* (New York: Longmans, Green, and Co., 1896); James R. Spears, *The American Slave-Trade: An Account of Its Origin, Growth and Suppression* (New York: Charles Scribner's Sons, 1900); Luís Henrique Dias Tavares, *Comércio proibido de escravos* (São Paulo: Editora Ática, 1988); Conrad, *World of Sorrow*, 133–53; Gerald Horne, *The Deepest South: The United States, Brazil, and the African Slave Trade* (New York: New York University Press, 2007); Dale T. Graden, "O envolvimento dos Estados Unidos no comércio transatlântico de escravos para o Brasil, 1840–1858," *Afro-Ásia* 35 (2007), 9–35; David Eltis, "The U.S. Transatlantic Slave Trade, 1644–1867: An Assessment," *Civil War History* 44:4 (2008), 347–78; Leonardo Marques, "A participação norte-americana no tráfico transatlântico de escravos para os Estados Unidos, Cuba e Brasil," *História: Questões e Debates* (Curitiba) 52 (jan./jun. 2010), 91–117; Leonardo Marques, "Slave Trading in a New World: The Strategies of North American Slave Traders in the Age of Abolition," *Journal of the Early Republic* 32 (Summer 2012), 233–60.

41. The best historical overview and bibliography of the north and south triangle trades is Berbel, Marquese, and Parron, *Escravidão e política*. For analysis of the north triangle trade, see D. Armitage and M.J. Braddick, eds., *The British Atlantic World, 1500–1800* (New York: Palgrave Macmillan, 2002), and Benjamin, *The Atlantic World*, 326–419. For the southern triangle and bilateral trades, see Luis Felipe de Alencastro, *O trato dos viventes: formação do Brasil no Atlântico sul, séculos XVI e XVII* (São Paulo: Companhia das Letras, 2000); Florentino, *Em costas negras*; Rodrigues, *De costa a costa*; José C. Curto and Paul E. Lovejoy, eds., *Enslaving Connections: Changing Cultures of Africa and Brazil during the Era of Slavery* (Amherst, N.Y.: Humanity Books, 2004); and Ferreira, *Cross-Cultural Exchange*.

42. Seymour Drescher, *Capitalism and Antislavery: British Mobilization in Comparative Perspective* (New York: Oxford University Press, 1987); Seymour Drescher, *Abolition: A History of Slavery and Antislavery* (Cambridge: Cambridge University Press, 2009).

43. David Brion Davis, *The Problem of Slavery in the Age of Revolution, 1770–1823* (Ithaca, N.Y.: Cornell University Press, 1975); Christopher Leslie Brown, *Moral Capital: Foundations of British Abolitionism* (Chapel Hill: University of North Carolina Press, 2006).

44. Eltis, *Economic Growth*; Thomas Bender, ed., *The Antislavery Debate: Capitalism and Abolitionism as a Problem in Historical Interpretation* (Berkeley: University of California Press, 1992).

45. See Beatriz G. Mamigonian, "In the Name of Freedom: Slave Trade Abolition, the Law and the Brazilian Branch of the African Emigration Scheme (Brazil-British West Indies, 1830s–1850s)," *Slavery and Abolition* 30:1 (March 2009), 41–66; Luis Martínez-Fernández, "The Havana Anglo-Spanish Mixed Commission for the Suppression of the Slave Trade and Cuba's Emancipados," *Slavery and Abolition* 16:2 (August 1995), 205–25; Jenny S. Martinez, "Anti-Slavery Courts and the Dawn of International Human Rights Law," *Yale Law Journal* 117:4 (January 2008), 550–641; Jenny S. Martinez, "The Slave Trade on Trial: Lessons of a Great Human Rights Law Success," *Boston Review* (Sept./Oct. 2007), 12–17.

46. Foundational works on the spread of infections to the Americas include Alfred W. Crosby, *Ecological Imperialism: The Biological Expansion of Europe, 900–1900*, 2nd ed. (Cambridge: Cambridge University Press, 2004); John E. Kicza, "Patterns in Early Spanish Overseas Expansion," *William and Mary Quarterly* 49:2 (April 1992), 229–53; and John E. Kicza, *Resilient Cultures: America's Native Peoples Confront European Colonization, 1500–1800* (Upper Saddle River, N.J.: Prentice Hall, 2003).

47. Tensions caused by the spread of infectious diseases and their ties to the transatlantic slave trade are analyzed in Sidney Chalhoub, *Cidade febril: cortiços e epidemias na corte imperial* (São Paulo: Companhia das Letras, 1996), and Kaori Kodama, "Os debates pelo fim do tráfico no periódico *O Philantropo* (1849–1852) e a formação do povo: doenças, raça e escravidão," *Revista Brasileira de História* (São Paulo) 28:56 (2008), 407–30. See also Arthur Vianna, *As epidemias no Pará* (Belem: Editora Universidade Federal do Pará, 1975; 1st ed. 1906).

48. A few sources to begin a review include João José Reis, "Slaves as Agents of History: A Note on the New Historiography of Slavery in Brazil," *Society and History* 51:5–6 (Sept./Dec. 1999), 437–45; Matthias Röhrig Assunção, "A resistência escrava nas Américas: Algumas considerações comparativas," in *Trabalho livre, trabalho escravo: Brasil e Europa, séculos XVII e XIX*, org. Douglass Cole Libby and Júnia Ferreira Furtado (São Paulo: Annablume, 2006), 335–60; Dale T. Graden, "Slave Resistance and the End of the Transatlantic Slave Trade to Brazil in 1850," *História Unisinos* (Rio Grande do Sul) 14:3 (set./dez. 2010), 283–94; Robert W. Slenes, "Malungu Ngoma vem: África coberta e descoberta no Brasil," in *Mostra do redescobrimento: negro de corpo e alma*, org. Nelson Aguilar (São Paulo: Associação Brasil 500 Anos Artes Visuais, 2000), 212–33; Farias, Gomes, Soares, and Moreira, *Cidades negras*; Eric Robert Taylor, *If We Must Die: Shipboard Insurrections in the Era of the Atlantic Slave Trade* (Baton Rouge: Louisiana State University Press, 2006); Pedro Deschamps Chapeaux, *Los cimarrones urbanos* (Havana: Editorial de ciencias sociales, 1983); Francisco de Solano y Augustín Guimerá, eds., *Esclavitud y derechos humanos: la lucha por la libertad del negro en el siglo XIX* (Madrid: Consejo Superior de Investigaciones Científicos, 1990); M. Dolores González-Ripoll, C. Naranjo, A. Ferrer, G. Garcia, and J. Opatrny, *El rumor de Haití en Cuba: temor, raza y rebeldía, 1789–1844* (Madrid: Consejo Superior de Investigaciones Científicos, 2004); Ada Ferrer, "Speaking of Haiti: Slavery, Revolution, and Freedom in Cuban Slave Testimony," in *The World of the Haitian Revolution*, ed. David P. Geggus and Norman Fiering (Bloomington: Indiana University Press, 2009), 223–47; Manuel Barcia, *Seeds of Insurrection: Domination and Resistance on Western Cuban Plantations, 1808–1848* (Baton Rouge: Louisiana State University Press, 2008). For comparative perspectives, see Andrews, *Afro-Latin America*; Peter Blanchard, *Under the Flags of Freedom: Slave Soldiers and the Wars of Independence in Spanish South America* (Pittsburgh: University of Pittsburgh Press, 2008); David Brion Davis, "Looking at Slavery from Broader Perspectives," *American Historical Review* 105:2 (April 2000), 452–66; Seymour Drescher and Pieter C. Emmer, eds., *Who Abolished Slavery? Slave Revolts and Abolitionism: A Debate with João Pedro Marques* (New York: Berghahn Books, 2010).

49. See Bethell, *The Abolition of the Brazilian Slave Trade*; Murray, *Odious Commerce*; Kenneth Morgan, *Slavery and the British Empire: From Africa to America* (New York: Oxford University Press, 2007); Thomas, *The Slave Trade*.

50. Games, "Atlantic History," 754.

51. Steve J. Stern, "Feudalism, Capitalism, and the World-System in the Perspective of Latin America and the Caribbean," *American Historical Review* 93:4 (October 1988), 871.

CHAPTER ONE

1. For analysis of the various laws, see W.E.B. DuBois, *The Suppression of the African Slave Trade* (New York: Library of America, 1987; originally published in 1896 with the title *The Suppression of the African Slave-Trade to the United States of America, 1638–1870*).

2. David Eltis and David Richardson, "The Transatlantic Slave Trade and the Civil War," *The New York Times*, January 13, 2011; David Eltis, "The U.S. Transatlantic Slave Trade, 1644–1867: An Assessment," *Civil War History* 54:4 (2008), 372. See Wise to Buchanan, Rio de Janeiro, March 6, 1846, USNA, RG 59, Consular Dispatches from Brazil, M-121:17.

3. Bernard Bailyn, *The New England Merchants in the Seventeenth Century* (Cambridge, Mass.: Harvard University Press, 1955); Margaret Ellen Newell, "The Birth of New England in the Atlantic Economy: From Its Beginnings to 1770," in *Engines of Enterprise: An Economic History of New England*, ed. Peter Temin (Cambridge, Mass.: Harvard University Press, 2000), 11–68. For the eighteenth century, see Linda K. Salvucci, "Atlantic Intersections: Early American Commerce and the Rise of the Spanish West Indies (Cuba)," *Business History Review* 79:4 (Winter 2005), 781–809.

4. Ronald Bailey, "The Slave(ry) Trade and the Development of Capitalism in the United States: The Textile Industry of New England," in *The Atlantic Slave Trade: Effects on Economies, Societies, and Peoples in Africa, the Americas, and Europe*, ed. Joseph E. Inikori and Stanley L. Engerman (Durham, N.C.: Duke University Press, 1992), 214; Philip S. Foner, *A History of Cuba and Its Relations with the United States: 1492–1845*, vol. 1 (New York: International Publishers, 1962), 65–72; Jennifer L. Anderson, "New England Merchants and the Circum-Caribbean Slave Trade," in *Paths of the Slave Trade: Interactions, Identities, and Images*, ed. Ana Lucia Araujo (Amherst, N.Y.: Cambria Press, 2011), 21–48.

5. Anne Farrow, Joel Lang, and Jenifer Frank, *Complicity: How the North Promoted, Prolonged, and Profited from Slavery* (New York: Ballantine Books, 2005), 53.

6. Eltis, "The U.S. Transatlantic Slave Trade," 363, 368–70.

7. Jay Coughtry, *The Notorious Triangle: Rhode Island and the African Slave Trade, 1700–1807* (Philadelphia: Temple University Press, 1981), 27–28, 6. See also Rachel Chernos Lin, "The Rhode Island Slave-Traders: Butchers, Bakers, and Candlestick-Makers," *Slavery and Abolition* 23:3 (December 2002), 21–38, and George Francis Dow, *Slave Ships and Slaving* (Salem, Mass.: Marine Research Society, 1927), 255–65.

8. José Luciano Franco, *Comercio clandestino de esclavos* (Havana: Ciencias Sociales, 1980), 110–22; Norman R. Bennett and George E. Brooks Jr., eds., *New England Merchants in Africa: A History through Documents, 1802 to 1865* (Boston, Mass.: Boston University Press, 1965); and George E. Brooks Jr., *Yankee Traders, Old Coasters and African Middlemen: A History of American Legitimate Trade with West Africa in the Nineteenth Century* (Boston, Mass.: Boston University Press, 1970).

9. See Alejandro de la Fuente, *Havana and the Atlantic in the Sixteenth Century* (Chapel Hill: University of North Carolina Press, 2011).

10. William McNeill, *Plagues and Peoples* (Garden City, N.Y.: Anchor Press, 1976), 166–70.

11. Michele Reid, "The Yoruba in Cuba: Origins, Identities, and Transformations," in *The Yoruba Diaspora in the Atlantic World*, ed. Toyin Falola and Matt D. Childs (Bloomington: Indiana University Press, 2004), 113.

12. Sherry S. Johnson, *The Social Transformation of Eighteenth-Century Cuba* (Gainesville: University Press of Florida, 2001), and Guadalupe Garcia, "'Nuestra patria La Habana': Reading the

1762 British Occupation of the City," *Nuevo Mundo, Mundos nuevos: Debates* (2011), http://nuevo-mundo.revues.org/61119.

13. Adrian Lopez Denis, "Disease and Society in Colonial Cuba, 1790–1840." PhD diss., UCLA, 2007, 45.

14. José Guadalupe Ortega, "Cuban Merchants, Slave Trade Knowledge, and the Atlantic World, 1790s–1820s," *Colonial Latin American Historical Review* 15:3 (2006), 225–51.

15. Salvucci, "Atlantic Intersections," 805–06; Javier Cuenca Esteban, "Trends and Cycles in U.S. Trade with Spain and the Spanish Empire, 1790–1819," *Journal of Economic History* 44 (1984), 540–41. See also John H. Coatsworth, "American Trade with European Colonies and the Caribbean and South America, 1790–1812," *William and Mary Quarterly*, 3rd ser., 24 (1967), 243–66.

16. *Slavery and Justice: Report of the Brown University Steering Committee on Slavery and Justice* (Providence, R.I.: Brown University Press, 2007), 22. See also Charles Rappleye, *Sons of Providence: The Brown Brothers, the Slave Trade, and the American Revolution* (New York: Simon & Schuster, 2006).

17. *Slavery and Justice*, 22.

18. Coughtry, *The Notorious Triangle*, 28. See also Paul Davis, *Unrighteous Traffick: Rhode Island's Slave History*, http://www.providencejournal.com/.

19. Katrina Browne, *Traces of the Trade: A Story from the Deep North*, PBS documentary, http://www.tracesofthetrade.org/. See also Leonardo Marques, "A participação norte-americano tráfico transatlântico de escravos para os Estados Unidos, Cuba e Brasil," *História: Questões & Debates* (Curitiba) 52 (jan/jun 2010), 111–17.

20. Hugh Thomas, *The Slave Trade: The Story of the Atlantic Slave Trade, 1440–1870* (New York: Simon & Schuster, 1997), 545.

21. Farrow, Lang, and Frank, *Complicity*, 53.

22. Melville and Hook to Aberdeen, Sierra Leone, December 31, 1844, Foreign Office Records of Great Britain Number 84: Slave Trade Department and Successors: General Correspondence before 1906, microfilm roll 507 (hereafter FO 84); Eric Anderson, "Yankee Blackbirds: Northern Entrepreneurs and the Illegal International Slave Trade, 1815–1865," Master's thesis, University of Idaho, 1999, 25–26; Eltis, "The U.S. Transatlantic Slave Trade," 364–65.

23. Anderson, "Yankee Blackbirds," 123.

24. Trist to Forsyth, Havana, December 13, 1834, USNA, RG 59, Consular Dispatches from Cuba, T-20:6.

25. Kennedy to Everett, Havana, May 28, 1840, FO 84:312; Everett to Forsyth, Washington, D.C., July 21, 1840, USNA, RG 59, Consular Dispatches from Cuba, T-20:14. See also David R. Murray, *Odious Commerce: Britain, Spain, and the Abolition of the Cuban Slave Trade* (Cambridge: Cambridge University Press, 1980), 100–06.

26. Trist to Forsyth, Havana, January 20, 1839, USNA, RG 59, Consular Dispatches from Cuba, T-20:9. Trans-Atlantic Slave Trade Database, Voyage number 1783.

27. Trans-Atlantic Slave Trade Database.

28. Nelville and Hook to Aberdeen, Sierra Leone, December 31, 1844, FO 84:507.

29. Nelville and Hook, "Report on the Mixed Commissions," Sierra Leone, December 31, 1845, FO 84:560.

30. Louis A. Pérez Jr., *Cuba: Between Reform and Revolution*, 4th ed. (New York: Oxford University Press, 2011), 56–59.

31. Macleay to Aberdeen, Havana, January 1, 1829, FO 84:91; Franco, *Comercio clandestino de esclavos*.

32. Schenley to Palmerston, Havana, April 15, 1835, FO 84:216; Kennedy to Palmerston, Havana, August 22, 1838, FO 84:240; Kennedy and Dalrymple to Trist, Havana, January 8, 1839, USNA, RG 59, Consular Dispatches from Cuba, T-20:9; Melville and Hook to Aberdeen, Sierra Leone, December 31, 1842, FO 84:393; Kennedy and Dalrymple to Aberdeen, Havana, September 27, 1842, FO 84:396; Kennedy and Dalrymple to Aberdeen, Havana, April 26, 1843, FO 84:451; Kennedy to Aberdeen, Havana, August 7, 1844, FO 84:509. See also Louis A. Pérez Jr., "Cuba and the United States: Origins and Antecedents of Relations, 1760s–1860s," *Cuban Studies* 21 (1997), 71–73, 77–80.

33. William R. Swagerty, *The Indianization of Lewis and Clark*, vol. 1 (Norman: Arthur H. Clark Co., 2012), 165.

34. Deposition of Gilbert Smith before U.S. consul George William Gordon, Rio de Janeiro, May 9, 1845, USNA, RG 59, Consular Dispatches from Rio de Janeiro, T-172:11.

35. Deposition of Zebomar H. Small Jr. [from Harwich, Mass.] before U.S. consul George W. Gordon, Rio de Janeiro, November 30, 1844, USNA, RG 59, Consular Dispatches from Rio de Janeiro, T-172:8.

36. Deposition of Gilbert Smith before U.S. consul George William Gordon, Rio de Janeiro, May 9, 1845, USNA, RG 59, Consular Dispatches from Rio de Janeiro, T-172:11. For an in-depth description of a factory at Inhambane, Mozambique, see Deposition of "the colored seaman" Peter Johnson from Kingston, New York, Johnson to Gordon, Rio de Janeiro, January 13, 1845, USNA, RG 59, Consular Dispatches from Brazil, M-121:15. See also Maria Cristina Cortez Wissenbach, "As feitorias de Urzela e o tráfico de escravos: Georg Tams, José Ribeiro dos Santos e os negócios da África Centro-Occidental na década de 1840," *Afro-Ásia* 43 (2011), 43–90; Frederick E. Forbes, *Six Months' Service in the African Blockade, from April to October, 1848, in command of HMS Bonetta* (London: R. Bentley, 1849), 75–84; and Dow, *Slave Ships*, 58–60, 211–36.

37. Ibid.

38. Trist to Kennedy and Dalrymple, Havana, January 8, 1839, USNA, RG 59, Consular Dispatches from Cuba, T-20:9.

39. Kennedy and Dalrymple to Aberdeen, Havana, January 2, 1843, FO 84:451.

40. Schenley and Madden to Trist, Havana, October 17, 1836, USNA, RG 59, Consular Dispatches from Cuba, T-20:7; Kennedy and Dalrymple to Aberdeen, Havana, September 27, 1842, FO 84:396. Underlined in original.

41. Schenley and Madden to Palmerston, Havana, March 3, 1837, FO 84:216. See also Ouseley to Palmerston, Rio de Janeiro, October 16, 1840, FO 84:325, and Wise to Hamilton, Rio de Janeiro, December 1, 1844, USNA, RG 59, Consular Dispatches from Brazil, M-121:15.

42. Kennedy and Dalrymple to Aberdeen, Havana, January 19, 1843, FO 84:451.

43. Gregory to Castlerough, Sierra Leone, February 25, 1820, FO 84:4.

44. Deposition of George Gardner to Edward Gregory and Edward Fitzgerald, HBM commissioners, Sierra Leone, May 15, 1821, FO 84:11.

45. George Collier to the Registrar of the Court of the British and Spanish Mixed Commission at Sierra Leone, on board the *Tartar* off the Bonny River, March 26, 1821, FO 84:11.

46. Trist to Forsyth, Havana, May 22, 1848, USNA, RG 59, Consular Dispatches from Cuba, T-20:7.

47. Schenley to Strangways, Havana, February 24, 1837, FO 84:216.

48. Jameson, "Statement respecting the illicit slave trade of the island of Cuba," September 1, 1821, FO 84:13.

49. Kennedy and Dalrymple to Aberdeen, Havana, June 9, 1846, FO 84:620.

50. Ibid. See also Pérez, "Cuba and the United States," 71.

51. Trist to Forsyth, Havana, June 2, 1838, USNA, RG 59, Consular Dispatches from Cuba, T-20:7.

52. Louis A. Pérez Jr., *Hurricanes and the Transformation of Nineteenth Century Cuba* (Chapel Hill: University of North Carolina Press, 2001); Manuel Barcia, *Seeds of Insurrection: Domination and Resistance on Western Cuban Plantations, 1808–1848* (Baton Rouge: Louisiana State University Press, 2008); Robert L. Paquette, *Sugar Is Made With Blood: The Conspiracy of La Escalera and the Conflict Between Empires Over Slavery in Cuba* (Middletown, Conn.: Wesleyan University Press, 1990, reprint ed.); Murray, *Odious Commerce*, 185–86; Melville and Hook to Aberdeen, Sierra Leone, December 31, 1842, FO 84:393; Melville and Hook to Aberdeen, Sierra Leone, December 31, 1844, FO 84:507; Kennedy and Dalrymple to Aberdeen, Havana, January 1, 1846, FO 84:620. The downturn was evidenced by a decrease in sugar output from 170,000 tons in 1844 to 73,000 tons in 1845, and from 18.5 million pounds of coffee produced in 1844 to 4.25 million pounds in 1846.

53. Gordon to Monteiro, Rio de Janeiro, June 26, 1838, FO 84:253.

54. Macleay to Aberdeen, Havana, January 18, 1831, FO 84:119.

55. W.G. Ouseley, "Notes on the Subject of the Slave Trade in the Province and City of Bahia, September 1835," letter included in Ouseley to Fox, Rio de Janeiro, October 27, 1835, FO 84:179. Emphasis and underlining in the original. See also Whately to Palmerston, Bahia, October 24, 1839, FO 84:289; Porter to Aberdeen, Bahia, May 30, 1843, FO 84:470; Hesketh and Grigg to Aberdeen, Rio de Janeiro, March 21, 1845, FO 84:563; Howden to Palmerston, Rio de Janeiro, November 12, 1847, FO 84:678; Hudson to Palmerston, Rio de Janeiro, November 13, 1849, FO 84:766; Hesketh to Palmerston, Rio de Janeiro, March 14, 1850, FO 84:808; Jerningham to Clarendon, Rio de Janeiro, June 11, 1853, FO 84:911.

56. Macleay to Palmerston, Havana, February 13, 1831, FO 84:119. See Trans-Atlantic Slave Trade Database, Voyage numbers 2396 and 1203.

57. Vives to the British-Spanish Mixed Commission Court, Havana, February 9, 1831, FO 84:119.

58. Smith to Trist, Havana, August 21, 1838, USNA, RG 59, Consular Dispatches from Cuba, T-20:13.

59. "Proceedings of the year 1844 of the British and Spanish Mixed Court of Justice at Sierra Leone," as found in Melville and Hook to Aberdeen, Sierra Leone, December 31, 1844, FO 84:507.

60. Kennedy and Dalrymple to Aberdeen, Havana, November 8, 1845, FO 84:562; Whately to Palmerston, Bahia, October 24, 1839, FO 84:289. For another description of slave vessels traveling from Havana to West Africa to Brazil under the direction of the Havana merchant house Sama y Hermano, see Kennedy to Aberdeen, Havana, February 7, 1845, FO 84:561.

61. Macleay to Aberdeen, Havana, January 18, 1831, FO 84:119. See also Whately to Palmerston, Salvador, October 24, 1839, FO 84:289.

62. Crusoe deposition to C.D. Tolmé, Havana, August 5, 1839, USNA, RG 59, Consular Dispatches from Cuba, T-20:11.

63. Kennedy to Everett, Havana, May 28, 1840, FO 84:312.

64. Ibid.

65. By a Calm Observer [Nicholas Trist], "Letter to WM.E. Channing, D.D., in reply to one addressed to him by R.R. Madden, on the Abuse of the Flag of the United States in the Island of Cuba, for Promoting the Slave Trade" (Boston: Published by William Ticknor, 1840).

66. Everett to Forsyth, Washington, D.C., July 21, 1840, USNA, RG 59, Consular Dispatches from Cuba, T-20:14.

67. Ibid. Other traffickers who had been based in Rio de Janeiro and then sent to Havana to expand operations included Rodrigo José Abreu and José Gonçalves Moreira, "a well known slave merchant" in Rio, as noted in Southern to Malmesbury, Rio de Janeiro, April 8, 1852, FO 84:878. See also David Eltis, *Economic Growth and the Ending of the Transatlantic Slave Trade* (New York: Oxford University Press, 1987), 156–59.

68. Kennedy to Everett, Havana, June 9, 1840, FO 84:312.

69. Kennedy and Dalrymple to Aberdeen, Havana, August 21, 1843, FO 84:452.

70. At least 1,250 U.S. citizens resided in Cuba in 1845, and their presence rose to 2,500 by 1862. Although this is not a large number, these individuals controlled strategic sectors of the economy and the slave trade. See Louis A. Pérez Jr., *Cuba and the United States: Ties of Singular Intimacy* (Athens: University of Georgia Press, 1988), 17–24; Marques, "A participação," 161.

71. U.S. consul George W. Gordon to Secretary of State James Buchanan, Rio de Janeiro, September 18, 1845, USNA, RG 59, Consular Dispatches from Rio de Janeiro, T-172:11; Luís Henrique Dias Tavares, *Comércio proibido de escravos* (São Paulo: Editora Ática, 1988); Dale T. Graden, "O envolvimento dos Estados Unidos no comércio transatlantic de escravos para o Brasil, 1840–1856," *Afro-Ásia* 35 (2007), 9–35; Gerald Horne, *The Deepest South: The United States, Brazil, and the African Slave Trade* (New York: New York University Press, 2007).

72. Maxwell Wright and Co. to U.S. consul R.K. Meade, Rio de Janeiro, January 19, 1859, USNA, RG 59, Consular Dispatches from Brazil, M-121:27; Deposition of William Applegarth, merchant of city of Baltimore, before Notary Public H. Ballard Johnson, April 25, 1854, Baltimore, Maryland, included in USNA, RG 59, Consular Dispatches from Brazil, M-121:27.

73. Representatives of the Religious Society of Friends, *An Exposition of the African Slave Trade from the Year 1840 to 1850, Inclusive, Prepared from Official Documents* (Philadelphia: J. Rakestraw, Printer, 1851), 37–47.

74. Deposition of William E. Anderson before U.S. consul Edward Kent, Rio de Janeiro, June 11, 1851, USNA, RG 59, Consular Dispatches from Brazil, M-121:20.

75. Depositions of Joshua Clapp before U.S. consul Gorham Parks, Rio de Janeiro, November 14 and 24, 1847, USNA, RG 59, Consular Dispatches from Rio de Janeiro, T-172:12; Parks to Clayton, Rio de Janeiro, July 20, 1849, USNA, RG 59, Consular Dispatches from Rio de Janeiro, T-172:14. For the *Panther*, see Trans-Atlantic Slave Trade Database, Voyage number 4926.

76. Deposition of William E. Anderson before U.S. consul Edward Kent, Rio de Janeiro, June 11, 1851, USNA, RG 59, Consular Dispatches from Brazil, M-121:20.

77. Ibid.

78. Frere and Surtees to Palmerston, Cape Town, South Africa, April 23, 1850, FO 84:790. The British commissioners understood the vessel to be named *Deliberação*.

79. Ibid. For a description of the capture of the Brazilian slave vessel *Progresso* off of Mozambique and a desperate voyage to the Cape of Good Hope, see Pascoe Grenfell Hill, *Fifty Days on Board a Slave Vessel, in the Mozambique Channel, April and May 1843* (Baltimore: Black Classic Press, 1993; originally published, London: J. Murray, 1844).

80. Deposition of William E. Anderson before U.S. consul Edward Kent, Rio de Janeiro, June 11, 1851, USNA, RG 59, Consular Dispatches from Brazil, M-121:20.

81. Grigg and Jackson to Palmerston, Rio de Janeiro, July 9, 1838, FO 84:241; Ouseley to Palmerston, Rio de Janeiro, April 13, 1840, FO 84:324; Ouseley to Palmerston, Rio de Janeiro, October 16, 1840, FO 84:325; Hesketh to Aberdeen, Rio de Janeiro, April 23, 1842, FO 84:411; Hesketh to Aberdeen, Rio de Janeiro, July 3, 1843, FO 84:470; Porter to Aberdeen, Salvador, July 20, 1843, FO 84:470; Hesketh and Grigg to Aberdeen, Rio de Janeiro, March 21, 1845, FO 84:563.

82. Slacum to Webster, Rio de Janeiro, July 1, 1843, USNA, RG 59, Consular Dispatches from Rio de Janeiro, T-172:8.

83. Wise to Calhoun, Rio de Janeiro, November 1, 1844, USNA, RG 59, Consular Dispatches from Brazil, M-121:15. For Wise's description of the ports of origin of U.S.-built slave vessels present at Rio de Janeiro in early 1846, see Wise to Buchanan, Rio de Janeiro, March 6, 1846, USNA, RG 59, Consular Dispatches from Brazil, M-121:17. These included five ships from Boston, four from Baltimore, three from New York, three from Philadelphia, two from Beverly, Mass. and one each from Providence, R.I. and Portland, Maine.

84. Wise to Maxwell Wright and Co., Rio de Janeiro, December 9, 1844, USNA, RG 59, Consular Dispatches from Brazil, M-121:15, underlined in the original. See also Wise to Hamilton, Rio de Janeiro, December 1, 1844, and Wise to Calhoun, Rio de Janeiro, February 18, 1845, both at USNA, RG 59, Consular Dispatches from Brazil, M-121:15.

85. State Executive Committee of the National American Party, *The Record of George W.M. Gordon* (Boston: J.E. Farwell and Company, 1856), 5.

86. Gordon to Calhoun [James Buchanan], Rio de Janeiro, April 22, 1845, USNA, RG 59, Consular Dispatches from Rio de Janeiro, T-172:10.

87. John Gilmer to Buchanan, Salvador, May 10, 1845, USNA, RG 59, Consular Dispatches from Salvador, T-432:4.

88. Gilmer to Buchanan, Salvador, May 10, 1845, USNA, RG 59, Consular Dispatches from Salvador, T-432:4.

89. See Gilmer to Gordon, Salvador, July 24, 1845; Gordon to Gilmer, Rio de Janeiro, August 5, 1845; Gilmer to Gordon, Salvador, August 27, 1845; and Gilmer to Buchanan, Salvador, September 3, 1845, all found in USNA, RG 59, Consular Dispatches from Rio de Janeiro, T-172:12.

90. Thomas Wilson to Seward, Salvador, July 14, 1862, USNA, RG 59, Consular Dispatches from Bahia, T-331:2.

91. Joao José Reis, Flávio dos Santos Gomes, and Marcus J.M. de Carvalho, *O alufá Rufino: tráfico, escravidão e liberdade no Atlântico negro (c. 1822–c. 1853)* (São Paulo: Companhia das Letras, 2010), 267–68.

92. Anderson, "Yankee Blackbirds," 49, 281.

93. Ibid., 34.

94. Leonardo Marques, "The United States and the Transatlantic Slave Trade to the Americas." PhD. diss., Emory University, 2013.

CHAPTER TWO

1. Eric Anderson, "Yankee Blackbirds: Northern Entrepreneurs and the Illegal International Slave Trade, 1815–1865," Master's thesis, University of Idaho, 1999, 169–72; R. Hoeppli, *Parasitic*

Diseases in West Africa and the Western Hemisphere: Early Documentation and Transmission by the Slave Trade (Basel, Switzerland: Verlag Fur Recht und Gesellschaft Ag. Basel, 1969); José Moreira, "Memoria sobre as molestias endemicas da costa occidental d'Africa," *Jornal da sociedade das ciencias médicas da Lisboa* 15:1 (1842), 121–52; Kenneth F. Kiple, *Another Dimension to the Black Diaspora: Diet, Disease, and Racism* (New York: Cambridge University Press, 1981), 12–14. Recent research has shown that other variables determined the seasonality of the slave trade on the coasts of Africa, including African crop harvests during the dry months. See Stephen D. Behrendt, "Seasonality in the Trans-Atlantic Slave Trade," The Trans-Atlantic Slave Trade Database.

2. See Marcus Rediker, *The Slave Ship: A Human History* (New York: Penguin, 2007), 73–131; David Northrup, *Africa's Discovery of Europe, 1450–1850*, 2nd ed. (New York: Oxford University Press, 2008), 158–65.

3. Judith A. Carney and Richard Nicholas Rosomoff, *In the Shadow of Slavery: Africa's Botanical Legacy in the Atlantic World* (Berkeley: University of California Press, 2009), 46–72.

4. David Eltis and David Richardson, *Atlas of the Transatlantic Slave Trade* (New Haven, Conn.: Yale University Press, 2010), 284–85.

5. Ibid., 18–19; David Eltis and Olatunji Ojo, "The Diaspora of Africans Liberated from Slave Ships in the Nineteenth Century," forthcoming essay.

6. Smith to Aberdeen, Sierra Leone, May 12, 1830, FO 84:104. See also Sylvianne A. Diouf, ed., *Fighting the Slave Trade: West African Strategies* (Athens: Ohio University Press, 2003).

7. Alberto da Costa e Silva, *Francisco Felix de Souza: mercador de escravos* (Rio de Janeiro: Editora Nova Fronteira, 2004); Ana Lucia Araujo, *Public Memory of Slavery: Victims and Perpetrators in the South Atlantic* (Amherst, N.Y.: Cambria Press, 2010), 279–347; David Ross, "The First Chacha of Whydah, Francisco Felix De Souza," *Odu* 1:2 (1969), 19–28; Robin Law, "Francisco Felix de Souza in West Africa, 1820–1849," in *Enslaving Connections: Changing Cultures of Africa and Brazil during the Era of Slavery*, ed. José C. Curto and Paul E. Lovejoy (New York: Humanity Books, 2004), 187–211.

8. Findlay and Smith to Aberdeen, Sierra Leone, October 18, 1830, FO 84:104.

9. Williams and Kendall to Canning, Sierra Leone, "Report of the Case of the Spanish schooner *Iberia*," March 25, 1826, FO 84:50.

10. Ibid.

11. Trans-Atlantic Slave Trade Database, Voyage number 3022.

12. Ricketts and Smith to Aberdeen, Sierra Leone, September 26, 1829, FO 84:90.

13. Trans-Atlantic Slave Trade Database, Voyage number 2387.

14. Ricketts and Smith to Aberdeen, Sierra Leone, September 26, 1829, FO 84:90.

15. Ricketts and Smith to Aberdeen, Sierra Leone, "Report of the case of the Brazilian schooner *Mensageira*," June 26, 1829, FO 84:90.

16. Ricketts and Smith to Aberdeen, Sierra Leone, "Report on the case of the Brazilian schooner *Santo Jago*," October 10, 1829, FO 84:90.

17. Brazil and British Mixed Commission Court at Sierra Leone, Proceedings for the year January 1, 1830 to January 1, 1831, FO 84:118.

18. Shelton to Clarendon, Sierra Leone, February 15, 1858, FO 84:1041.

19. George Francis Dow, *Slave Ships and Slaving* (Salem, Mass.: Marine Research Society, 1927), 274–76. Trans-Atlantic Slave Trade Database, Voyage number 4955. For the remarkable history of finding and preserving the sole remaining figurehead from a clipper ship, that being

the figurehead of Jenny Lind from the *Nightingale*, see Karl Eric Svärdskog, *Jenny Lind and the Clipper Nightingale Figurehead* (Portsmouth, N.H.: Portsmouth Marine Society, 2001), and Karl Eric Svärdskog, "Jenny Lind: The Mystery of *Nightingale's* Figurehead," http://www.swedishnightingale.com/artikel.htm.

20. Smith to Aberdeen, Sierra Leone, May 12, 1830, FO 84:104. The *Altimara* was captured on March 27 and arrived at Freetown harbor on April 25, 1830. See F. Harrison Rankin, *The White Man's Grave: A Visit to Sierra Leone in 1834*, 2 vols. (London: Richard Bentley Publisher, 1836).

21. Alexander Bryson, *An Account of the Origin, Spread, and Decline of the Epidemic Fevers of Sierra Leone with Observations of Sir William Pym's Review of the "Report on the Climate and Diseases of the African Station"* (London: Henry Renshaw Publishers, 1849).

22. Herbert S. Klein, *The Atlantic Slave Trade*, 2nd ed. (New York: Cambridge University Press, 2010), 146.

23. Ibid., 160.

24. Macleay to Aberdeen, Havana, July 17, 1829, FO 84:92.

25. Ibid.; Kennedy and Dalrymple to Aberdeen, Havana, May 18, 1844, FO 84:508.

26. Macleay to Aberdeen, Havana, July 31, 1829, FO 84:92.

27. Schenley to Palmerston, Havana, September 13, 1836, FO 84:197.

28. Ricafort to Mixed Commission Court, Havana, November 20, 1833, FO 84:137.

29. *Diário de la Habana*, April 13 and 26, 1833. See also Macleay and MacKenzie to Palmerston, Havana, April 27, 1833, FO 84:136.

30. *Diário de la Habana*, April 26, 1833.

31. Macleay and MacKenzie to Grant, Havana, April 14, 1833, FO 84:136.

32. Ricafort to Mixed Commission Court at Havana, Havana, November 20, 1833, FO 84:137.

33. Kennedy and Dalrymple to Palmerston, Havana, June 18, 1841, FO 84:349. See Rosanne Marion Adderley, *New Negroes from Africa: Slave Trade Abolition and Free African Settlement in the Nineteenth-Century Caribbean* (Bloomington: Indiana University Press, 2006), 63–71.

34. Macleay to Wellington, Havana, April 29, 1835, FO 84:171.

35. Anonymous to Kennedy, Havana, November 30, 1839, included in Kennedy and Dalrymple to Palmerston, Havana, January 1, 1840, FO 84:312, underlined in the original.

36. Kennedy and Dalrymple to Palmerston, Havana, January 1, 1840, FO 84:312.

37. Tacón to British Commissioners, Havana, June 20, 1837, FO 84:216, underlined in the original.

38. Trist to Webster, Havana, June 12, 1841, USNA, RG 59, Consular Dispatches from Cuba, T-20:16.

39. Tacón to British Commissioners, Havana, May 20, 1835, FO 84:171; Tacón to First Secretary of State (in Madrid), Havana, November 7, 1836, FO 84:221.

40. Memorial signed by 248 inhabitants of Belize (woodcutters of mahogany) to Francis Cockburn, Honduras, January 30, 1835, FO 84:171.

41. Kennedy and Dalrymple to Strangways, Havana, April 29, 1840, FO 84:312.

42. Turnbull to H.M. Commissioners, Havana, January 12, 1841, FO 84:347. See also Edward E. Baptist, "'Cuffy,' 'Fancy Maids,' and 'One-Eyed Men': Rape, Commodification, and the Domestic Slave Trade in the United States," *American Historical Review* 106:5 (2001), 1619–50.

43. Kennedy and Dalrymple to James Bandenel, Havana, January 25, 1841, FO 84:347.

44. Kennedy and Dalrymple to Palmerston, Havana, Feb 20, 1841, FO 84:348.

45. See Adrián López-Denis, "Melancholia, Slavery, and Racial Pathology in Eighteenth-Century Cuba," *Science in Context* 18:2 (2005), 179–99. The book was not published until 1953 when an "obscure publishing house issued a very small edition in Havana," as noted in Adrián López-Denis, "Disease and Society in Colonial Cuba, 1790–1840." PhD diss., UCLA, 2007, 74.

46. Matt D. Childs, *The 1812 Aponte Rebellion in Cuba and the Struggle Against Atlantic Slavery* (Chapel Hill: University of North Carolina Press, 2006), 53; López-Denis, "Disease and Society," 122–31.

47. J.L.F. Madrid, "Memoria sobre la disentería en general, y en particular sobre disentería de los barracones," *Memorias de la Real Sociedad Económica de la Habana* 11 (November 30, 1817), 381–89, cited in Childs, *The 1812 Aponte Rebellion*, 53.

48. David E. Stannard, *American Holocaust: The Conquest of the New World* (New York: Oxford University Press, 1992); Robin Blackburn, *The Making of New World Slavery: From the Baroque to the Modern, 1492–1800* (London: Verso, 1997).

49. Kenneth F. Kiple and Brian T. Higgins, "Yellow Fever and the Africanization of the Caribbean," in *Disease and Demography in the Americas*, ed. John W. Verano and Douglas H. Ubelaker (Washington: Smithsonian Press, 1992), 237–48.

50. J.R. McNeill, "Yellow Jack and Geopolitics: Environment, Epidemics, and the Struggles for Empire in the American Tropics, 1650–1825," *OAH Magazine of History* 18:3 (April 2004), 11.

51. John Robert McNeill, *Mosquito Empires: Ecology and War in the Greater Caribbean, 1620–1914* (Cambridge: Cambridge University Press, 2010); Katherine Arner, "Making Yellow Fever American: The Early American Republic, the British Empire and the Geopolitics of Disease in the Atlantic World," *Atlantic Studies* 7:4 (2010), 447–71.

52. For a list of yellow fever epidemics in the United States, see K. David Patterson, "Yellow Fever Epidemics and Mortality in the United States, 1693–1905," *Social Science and Medicine* 34:8 (1992), 855–65; and PBS documentary "American Experience: The Great Fever."

53. Jonathan Curry-Machado, *Cuban Sugar Industry: Transnational Networks and Engineering Migrants in Mid-Nineteenth Century Cuba* (New York: Palgrave Macmillan, 2011), 64.

54. Schenley to Strangways, Havana, July 31, 1837, FO 84:217; Campbell to Upshaw, Havana, October 6, 1843, USNA, RG 59, Consular Dispatches from Cuba, T-20:19; Campbell to Clayton, Havana, June 30, 1849, USNA, RG 59, Consular Dispatches from Cuba, T-20:22.

55. Curry-Machado, *Cuban Sugar Industry*, 65.

56. Robertson to Marcy, Havana, May 22, 1855, USNA, RG 59, Consular Dispatches from Cuba, T-20:29. See "Whole Mortality in the City of Havana in 1857" and "Returns of Military Hospitals in Havana, 1854 to July 1858" provided by Vice Consul Thomas Savage, Havana, September 1, 1858, USNA, RG 59, Consular Dispatches from Cuba, T-20:39; Savage to Seward, Havana, July 1, 1867, USNA, RG 59, Consular Dispatches from Cuba, T-20:49. For an insightful analysis of yellow fever in Cuba for a later period, see Mariola Espinosa, *Epidemic Invasions: Yellow Fever and the Limits of Cuban Independence, 1878–1930* (Chicago: University of Chicago Press, 2009).

57. Kiple and Higgins, "Yellow Fever and the Africanization of the Caribbean."

58. Macleay to Bart, Havana, February 23, 1835, FO 84:171, and López-Denis, "Disease and Society," 151–215.

59. López-Denis, "Disease and Society."

60. Macleay and MacKenzie to Palmerston, Havana, September 12, 1833, FO 84:137.

61. Macleay and MacKenzie to Palmerston, Havana, September 12, 1833, FO 84:137.

62. For a description of the 1833 revolt that focuses on Lucumí resistance but with no comment on recent landings of Africans, see Manuel Barcia, *Seeds of Insurrection: Domination and Resistance on Western Cuban Plantations, 1808–1848* (Baton Rouge: Louisiana State University Press, 2008), 37.

63. Kennedy and Dalrymple to Valdes, Havana, August 9, 1841, FO 84:349; Kennedy and Dalrymple to Palmerston, January 1, 1841, FO 84:348.

64. Consul James Kennedy estimated that thirty thousand slaves had died in the northern part of Cuba by mid-1850. Kennedy to Palmerston, Havana, August 24, 1850, FO 84:789. Kennedy wrote several letters to Palmerston in spring 1850 describing the ties between the spread of the cholera and the slave trade, all found in FO 84:789.

65. Savage to Seward, Havana, November 11, 1867, USNA, RG 59, Consular Dispatches from Cuba, T-20:49. See Kenneth F. Kiple, "Cholera and Race in the Caribbean," *Journal of Latin American Studies* 17:1 (May 1985), 157–77. For comparative perspectives, see Charles E. Rosenberg, *The Cholera Years: The United States in 1832, 1849, and 1866* (Chicago: University of Chicago Press, 1962).

66. Kennedy to Palmerston, Havana, January 1, 1850, FO 84:789.

67. Turnbull to British Commissioners, Havana, May 18, 1841, FO 84:348; Kennedy to Palmerston, Havana, June 19, 1838, FO 84:240.

68. Schenley and Madden to Tacón, Havana, June 16, 1837, FO 84:216.

69. Kennedy to Palmerston, Havana, January 1, 1850, FO 84:789.

70. Kennedy to Palmerston, Havana, August 22, 1838, FO 84:240.

71. Kennedy and Dalrymple to Palmerston, Havana, March 5, 1841, FO 84:348.

72. Kennedy and Dalrymple to Aberdeen, Havana, January 17, 1842, FO 84:395.

73. Kennedy to Palmerston, Havana, January 1, 1850, FO 84:789.

74. Tacón to First Secretary, Havana, August 31, 1836, FO 84:221.

75. Macleay and MacKenzie to Captain General, Havana, September 12, 1833, FO 84:137.

76. Kennedy to Palmerston, Havana, January 1, 1850, FO 84:789.

77. Kennedy to Palmerston, Havana, July 17, 1838, FO 84:240; Kennedy to Palmerston, Havana, August 24, 1850, FO 84:789.

78. "Report of the Board for the Promotion of Agriculture and Commerce in the Island of Cuba *(Junta de Fomento)*" as it appears in Kennedy and Dalrymple to Palmerston, Havana, October 27, 1841, FO 84:349.

79. George Reid Andrews, *Afro-Latin America, 1800–2000* (New York: Oxford University Press, 2004), 69–73.

80. Robertson to Marcy, Havana, February 7, March 20, May 7, 1854, USNA, RG 59, Consular Dispatches from Cuba, T-20:27; Davis to Marcy, Washington, D.C., May 22, 1854, USNA, RG 59, Consular Dispatches from Cuba, T-20:29.

81. Cited in Childs, *The 1812 Aponte Rebellion*, 39.

82. See M. Dolores González-Ripoll, C. Naranjo, A. Ferrer, G. Garcia, and J. Opatrny, *El rumor de Haití en Cuba: temor, raza y rebeldía, 1789–1844* (Madrid: Consejo Superior de Investigaciones Científicos, 2004).

83. David R. Murray, *Odious Commerce: Britain, Spain, and the Abolition of the Cuban Slave Trade* (Cambridge: Cambridge University Press, 1980), 114–15.

84. "Memorial of the Junta de Fomento," in Kennedy and Dalrymple to Palmerston, Havana, June 3, 1841, FO 84:349, hereafter described as the Society for Progress.

85. Tacón to British Commissioners, Havana, August 26, 1837, FO 84:217, emphasis in the original; Trist to Forsyth, Havana, September 14, 1837, USNA, RG 59, Consular Dispatches from Cuba, T-20:7.

86. Kennedy and Dalrymple to Palmerston, Havana, November 7, 1840, FO 84:312.

87. Ibid.

88. Schenley and Madden to Captain General, Havana, October 26, 1836, FO 84:197.

89. Kennedy and Dalrymple to Aberdeen, Havana, December 19, 1842, FO 84:396.

90. Barcia, *Seeds of Insurrection*, 34–39.

91. Letter from City Corporation of Havana to the Provisional Regency, Havana, approximately March 1841, included in Kennedy and Dalrymple to Palmerston, Havana, June 3, 1841, FO 84:349.

92. Andrews, *Afro-Latin America*, 107–08.

93. Matthias Röhrig Assunção and Michael Zeuske, "'Race,' Ethnicity and Social Structure in 19th Century Brazil and Cuba," *Ibero-Amerikanishes Archiv* 24:3–4 (1998), 391.

94. Madan to Pierce, Havana, October 4, 1853, USNA, RG 59, Consular Dispatches from Cuba, T-20:27.

CHAPTER THREE

1. Stevenson to Hamilton, Rio de Janeiro, February 1, 1837, FO 84:222. See also Trans-Atlantic Slave Trade Database description of the *Leão*, Voyage number 1586.

2. Howden to Palmerston, Rio de Janeiro, February 9, 1848, FO 84:725.

3. Ouseley to Monteiro, Rio de Janeiro, July 17, 1838, FO 84:253.

4. Ouseley to Herbert, Rio de Janeiro, January 29, 1839, FO 84:285.

5. Hesketh to Ouseley, Rio de Janeiro, May 31, 1839, FO 84:286.

6. Ibid.

7. Ouseley to Palmerston, Rio de Janeiro, September 24, 1840, FO 84:325.

8. *Contemporaneo* (Rio de Janeiro), July 21, 1848, found in Hudson to Palmerston, Rio de Janeiro, August 5, 1848, FO 84:726. Underlined in the original.

9. Howden to Palmerston, Rio de Janeiro, February 9, 1848, FO 84:725.

10. "Report of the Minister of the Marine," as found in Jackson to Palmerston, Rio de Janeiro, June 17, 1833, FO 84:138. Underlined in original document. One definition of *Cordon Sanitaire* is "a barrier designed to prevent a disease or other undesirable condition from spreading."

11. Hesketh and Grigg to Palmerston, Rio de Janeiro, October 4, 1837, FO 84: 219; Juliana Barreto Farias, Flávio dos Santos Gomes, Carlos Eugênio Líbano Soares, and Carlos Eduardo de Araújo Moreira, *Cidades negras: africanos, crioulos e espaços urbanos no Brasil escravista do século XIX* (São Paulo: Alameda, 2006), 18.

12. Goring to Palmerston, Recife, October 24, 1840, FO 84:326.

13. Cowper to Aberdeen, Recife, January 1, 1844, FO 84:526. See Dauril Alden and Joseph C. Miller, "Out of Africa: The Slave Trade and the Transmission of Smallpox to Brazil, 1560–1831," *Journal of Interdisciplinary History* 18:2 (1987), 195–224.

14. "Correspondencia," *Diario de Pernambuco*, June 21, 1841, p. 2, as found in Late acting consul [illegible] to Palmerston, Recife, July 26, 1841, FO 84:368.

15. Cowper to Aberdeen, Recife, January 1, 1844, FO 84:526. "The Medical Association of Pernambuco" is the title of this entity in the documents.

16. Luiz dos Santos Vilhena, *A Bahia no século XVIII* (Salvador: Editôra Itapuã, 1969), vol. I, 156.

17. Ibid. See Alexandre Vieira Ribeiro, "The Transatlantic Slave Trade to Bahia, 1582–1851," in *Extending the Frontiers: Essays on the New Transatlantic Slave Trade Database*, ed. David Eltis and David Richardson (New Haven, Conn.: Yale University Press, 2008), 147.

18. Porter to Palmerston, Bahia, October 18, 1847, FO 84:679.

19. Tindal to Porter, Bahia, April 30, 1848, FO 84:725. It appears that one African female died between seizure of the *Bella Miquelina* and arrival in Sierra Leone, where British officials listed the names and ages of the survivors. This information is provided at the African Origins Project site, http://www.african-origins.org/african-data/.

20. D'Aguilar to Porter, Bahia, April 30, 1848, FO 84:725.

21. Porter to Hudson, Bahia, May 5, 1848, FO 84:725.

22. Baron Cayrú's Report to the General Legislative Assembly, Rio de Janeiro, May 4, 1846, Foreign Office Record Group 13: General Correspondence from Brazil, Roll 235 (hereafter FO 13); Whitaker to Hamilton, Santos, January 7, 1844, FO 13:210; Sullivan to Ouseley, Rio de Janeiro, April 24, 1839, FO 13:153.

23. Howden to Palmerston, Salvador, May 5, 1848, FO 84:725.

24. D'Aguilar to Porter, Salvador, April 30, 1848, FO 84:725.

25. D'Aguilar to Tindal, Salvador, May 1, 1848, FO 84:725.

26. Leão to Porter, Salvador, May 1, 1848, FO 84:725.

27. Hudson to Palmerston, Rio de Janeiro, September 2, 1850, FO 84:806. The Trans-Atlantic Slave Trade Database lists a ship named the *Brazil* landing slaves on the Brazilian coast in 1848 with subsequent landings in Cuba. See voyage identification numbers 900228, 4425, 4430, and 4435.

28. Campbell to Clayton, Havana, June 30, 1849, USNA, RG 59, Consular Dispatches from Cuba, T-20:22.

29. John L. Paterson, Esquire, M.D. Physician to the British Hospital at Bahia, "Report on Yellow Fever," 133–34, as found in Porter to Palmerston, Salvador, August 19, 1850, FO 13:277.

30. J.O. M'William, *Some Account of The Yellow Fever Epidemy by Which Brazil was Invaded in the Latter Part of the Year 1849* (London: William Tyler, printer, 1851), 8–9.

31. Hudson to Palmerston, Rio de Janeiro, September 2, 1850, FO 84:806.

32. Interview of Consul Porter with Governor Francisco Gonçalves Martins on December 13, 1849, included in Porter to Palmerston, Salvador, December 21, 1849, FO 13:268; Hudson to Palmerston, Rio de Janeiro, March (n.d.), 1850, FO 13:274.

33. Speech of President Francisco Gonçalves Martins at the opening of the Provincial Assembly, March 1, 1850, as printed in *Correio Mercantil* (Salvador), March 7, 1850, FO 84:806; Porter to Palmerston, Salvador, December 21, 1849, FO 13:268; Paterson, "Report on Yellow Fever," p. 135, FO 13:277.

34. Donald B. Cooper, "Brazil's Long Fight Against Epidemic Disease, 1849–1917, With Special Emphasis on Yellow Fever," *Bulletin of the New York Academy of Medicine* 51:5 (May 1975), 676.

35. "Report of the Council of Health," Salvador, June 30, 1853, FO 13:308.

36. Paterson, "Report on Yellow Fever," Porter to Palmerston, Salvador, August 19, 1850, FO 13:277. For comments on race and immunity to yellow fever, see Kenneth F. Kiple, "Response to Sheldon Watts, 'Yellow Fever Immunities in West Africa and the Americas in the Age of Slavery and Beyond: A Reappraisal,'" *Journal of Social History* 34:4 (2001), 969–74.

37. "The Epidemic and the Traffic in Africans," *Itamontano* (Ouro Preto, Minas Gerais), April 3, 1850, as preserved and translated in FO 84:806. See statements by Francisco Gonçalves Martins in this regard derived from his speech at the opening of the Provincial Assembly, March 1, 1850, as printed in *Correio Mercantil* (Salvador), March 7, 1850, FO 84:806.

38. "The Epidemic and the Traffic in Africans," *Itamontano*, April 3, 1850.

39. J.O. M'William, *Some Account of The Yellow Fever Epidemy*, pp. 10–12, as found in Christophers to Palmerston, Recife, January 29, 1851, FO 13:287.

40. *Itamontano*, April 3, 1850, as noted in Hudson to Palmerston, Rio de Janeiro, September 2, 1850, FO 84:806.

41. Sidney Chalhoub, *Cidade febril: cortiços e epidemias na corte imperial* (São Paulo: Companhia das Letras, 1996), 60–78; Hudson to Palmerston, Rio de Janeiro, February 21, 1850, FO 13:274.

42. Chalhoub, *Cidade febril*, 61; Cooper, "Brazil's Long Fight Against Epidemic Disease," 679.

43. Cowper to Palmerston, Recife, December 21, 1849, FO 13:269; Newcomen to Palmerston, Paraíba, January 21, 1850, FO 13:277; M'William, *Some Account of The Yellow Fever Epidemy*, 9–19.

44. *Itamontano* (Ouro Preto), April 3, 1850, as found in FO 84:806.

45. "The Traffickers in Human Flesh and the Reigning Epidemy," *O Philanthropo* (Rio de Janeiro), March 29, 1850, as found in FO 84:806. Underlined in the original.

46. "Report of the Council of Health of Bahia," Salvador, December 12, 1849. This document is included in Morgan to Clarendon, Salvador, December 17, 1853, FO 13:308. Author's emphasis.

47. Porter to Palmerston, Salvador, April 24, 1849, FO 84:767.

48. Porter to Palmerston, Salvador, December 31, 1849, FO 84:767.

49. Porter to Palmerston, Salvador, July 13, 1850, FO 84:808; João Carneiro da Silva Rego, "Letter from the Municipal Corporation of the City of Bahia to the Chamber of Deputies," published in *Correio Mercantil*, August 19, 1850, translation in Hudson to Palmerston, Rio de Janeiro, September 2, 1850, FO 84:808; Porter to Palmerston, Salvador, November 18, 1850, FO 84:808.

50. "Report of the Council of Health of Bahia," Salvador, June 29, 1853, FO 13:308.

51. Souto to Moncorvo e Lima, Salvador, June 30, 1853, FO 13:308.

52. Martins to President of the Board of Health, Rio de Janeiro, January 3, 1853, FO 13:302.

53. Lecointe-Marsillac, *Le More-Lack, ou Essai sur les moyens le plus doux et les plus équitables d'abolir la traite et l'esclavage des Nègres d'Afrique* (Paris: n.p., 1789), 45–46, 61, 63, as cited in Sean Quinlan, "Colonial Encounters: Colonial Bodies, Hygiene and Abolitionist Politics in Eighteenth-Century France," *History Workshop Journal* no. 42 (1996), 119–21. For descriptions of yellow fever from the late eighteenth century, see Kenneth F. Kiple and Virginia H. King, *Another Dimension to the Black Diaspora: Diet, Disease, and Racism* (New York: Cambridge University Press, 1978); Kenneth F. Kiple, *The Caribbean Slave: A Biological History* (New York: Cambridge University Press, 1984); J.H. Powell, *Bring Out Your Dead: The Great Plague of Yellow Fever in Philadelphia in 1793* (Philadelphia: University of Pennsylvania Press, 1949; reprint ed. 1993); Debbie Lee, "Yellow Fever and the Slave Trade: Coleridge's 'The Rime of the Ancient Mariner,'" *ELH (English Literary History)* 65:3 (Fall 1998), 675–700.

54. Manuel Vieira da Silva, *Reflexões sobre alguns dos meios propostas por mais conducentes para melhorar o clima da cidade do Rio de Janeiro* (Rio de Janeiro: Impressão Régia, 1808), 17–20.

55. Jean Baptiste Alban Imbert, *Manual do fazendeiro ou tratado doméstico sobre as enfermidades dos negros* (Rio de Janeiro: Tipografica Nacional, 1839), xiii. See the insightful article of Alisson Eugênio, "Reflexões médicas sobre as condições de saúde da população escrava no Brasil no século XIX," *Afro-Ásia* 42 (2010), 125–55.

56. José Martins da Cruz Jobim, *Discurso sobre as moléstias que mais afligem a classe pobre do Rio de Janeiro* (Rio de Janeiro: Tipografia Fluminense de Brito e Cia., 1835); David Gomes Jardim, "Algumas considerações sobre a higiene dos escravos." Tese apresentada à Faculdade de Medicina do Rio de Janeiro, 1847; José Rodrigues de Lima Duarte, "A higiene da escravatura no Brasil." Tese apresentada à Faculdade de Medicina do Rio de Janeiro, 1849; Augusto César Ernesto de Moura, "Algumas proposições de higiene." Tese apresentada à Faculdade de Medicina do Rio de Janeiro, 1849; Pedro Dornellas Pessoa, *Anais da Sociedade de Medicina Pernumbucana* 1:1 (1842). For an overview of these contributions, see Alisson Eugênio, "A reforma dos costumes no Brasil do século XIX," PhD thesis, Universidade de São Paulo, 2008.

57. William Pym, *Observations upon the Bulam Fever* (London: J. Callow, 1815).

58. William Pym, *Observations on Bulam, Vomito-negro, or Yellow Fever* (London: J. Churchill, 1848).

59. See Chalhoub, *Cidade febril*, 74–75; Kaori Kodama, "Os debates pelo fim do tráfico no periódico O Philantropo (1849–1852) e a formação do povo: doenças, raça e escravidão," *Revista Brasileira de História* (São Paulo) 28:56 (2008), 419–22.

60. For the sharing of information throughout the Atlantic Basin, see Peter Linebaugh and Marcus Rediker, *The Many-Headed Hydra: Sailors, Slaves, Commoners, and the Hidden History of the Revolutionary Atlantic* (Boston: Beacon Press, 2000).

61. Souto to Moncorvo e Lima, Salvador, June 30, 1853, FO 13:308; M'William, *Some Account of the Yellow Fever Epidemy*, 8–19.

62. Jeffrey D. Needell, *The Party of Order: The Conservatives, the State, and Slavery in the Brazilian Monarchy, 1831–1871* (Stanford, Calif.: Stanford University Press, 2006), 149–55.

63. Ibid., 141.

64. "Sessão em 13 de Maio de 1850," *Annais do senado do império do Brasil* (Rio de Janeiro: Senado Federal, 1978) (hereafter cited as ASIB), pp. 16–17. Batista de Oliveira had previously expressed his desire to end the slave traffic and the institution of slavery in his publication *A escravatura no Brasil e a época provável de extinção* (St. Petersburg: n.p., 1842).

65. "Sessão em 23 de Maio de 1850," ASIB, pp. 38–39; "Sessão em 9 de Setembro de 1850," ASIB, pp. 518–19.

66. Hudson to Palmerston, Rio de Janeiro, July 27, 1850, FO 84:805. Author's emphasis.

67. Hudson to Palmerston, Rio de Janeiro, May 12, 1850, FO 13:275. See also Hudson to Palmerston, Rio de Janeiro, February 3, 1850, FO 84:801.

CHAPTER FOUR

1. David Barry Gaspar, "Antigua Slaves and Their Struggle to Survive," in *Seeds of Change: A Quincentennial Commemoration*, ed. Herman J. Viola and Carolyn Margolis (Washington, D.C.: Smithsonian Institution Press, 1991), 131. See David P. Geggus, ed., *The Impact of the Haitian*

Revolution in the Atlantic World (Columbia: University of South Carolina Press, 2002); João José Reis and Flávio dos Santos Gomes, *Liberdade por um fio: história dos quilombos no Brasil* (São Paulo: Companhia das Letras, 1996); Flávio dos Santos Gomes, *A hidra e os pântanos: mocambos, quilombos e comunidades de fugitivos no Brasil (Séculos XVII–XIX)* (São Paulo: Ed. UNESP, 2005); Sidney Chalhoub, *Visões da liberdade: uma história das últimas décadas da escravidão na corte* (São Paulo: Companhia das Letras, 1990); José Luciano Franco, *Los palenques de los negros cimarrones* (Havana: Colección historia, 1973); Pedro Deschamps Chapeaux, *Los cimarrones urbanos* (Havana: Editorial de ciencias sociales, 1983); Michel-Rolph Trouillot, *Silencing the Past: Power and the Production of History* (Boston: Beacon Press, 1995).

2. The historiography is rich. A few examples include Robin Blackburn, *The Overthrow of Colonial Slavery, 1776–1848* (London: Verso, 1988); Seymour Drescher, *Abolition: A History of Slavery and Antislavery* (New York: Cambridge University Press, 2009); Seymour Drescher and Pieter C. Emmer, eds., *Who Abolished Slavery: Slave Revolts and Abolitionism: A Debate with João Pedro Marques* (New York: Berghahn Books, 2010); Gloria García Rodríguez, *Conspiraciones y revueltas: la actividad política de los negros en Cuba (1790–1845)* (Santiago de Cuba: Editorial Oriente, 2003); Gelien Matthews, *Caribbean Slave Revolts and the British Abolitionist Movement* (Baton Rouge: Louisiana State University Press, 2008); Laird W. Bergad, *The Comparative Histories of Slavery in Brazil, Cuba, and the United States* (Cambridge: Cambridge University Press, 2007), 165–250; George Reid Andrews, *Afro-Latin America, 1800–2000* (New York: Oxford University Press, 2004).

3. Manuel Barcia, *Seeds of Insurrection: Domination and Resistance on Western Cuban Plantations, 1808–1848* (Baton Rouge: Louisiana State University Press, 2008), 28.

4. Manuel Barcia, *The Great African Slave Revolt of 1825: Cuba and the Fight for Freedom in Matanzas* (Baton Rouge: Louisiana State University Press, 2012), 4.

5. Ibid., 51–55.

6. Barcia, *Seeds of Insurrection*, 31–34.

7. Matt D. Childs, *The 1812 Aponte Rebellion in Cuba and the Struggle Against Atlantic Slavery* (Chapel Hill: University of North Carolina Press, 2006), 33.

8. Ibid., 122–23.

9. Ibid., 127–33.

10. Ibid., 138.

11. Michele Reid, "The Yoruba in Cuba: Origins, Identities, and Transformations," in *The Yoruba Diaspora in the Atlantic World*, ed. Toyin Falola and Matt D. Childs (Bloomington: Indiana University Press, 2004), 116.

12. Childs, *The 1812 Aponte Rebellion*, 3.

13. Ibid., 54.

14. Ibid.

15. Ibid., 52–53.

16. David Murray, "The Slave Trade, Slavery and Cuban Independence," *Slavery and Abolition* 20:3 (1999), 113–15. For an insightful analysis of the influence of the Haitian Revolution in Cuba during this period, see Ada Ferrer, "Speaking of Haiti: Slavery, Revolution, and Freedom in Cuban Slave Testimony," in *The World of the Haitian Revolution*, ed. David Patrick Geggus and Norman Fiering (Bloomington: Indiana University Press, 2009), 223–47.

17. Childs, *The 1812 Aponte Rebellion*, 176.

18. Barcia, *The Great African Slave Revolt*, 97–101, 130.

19. Ibid., 36.

20. Michele Reid-Vazquez, *The Year of the Lash: Free People of Color in Cuba and the Nineteenth-Century Atlantic World* (Athens: University of Georgia Press, 2011), 39.

21. Barcia, *Seeds of Insurrection*, 37.

22. Childs, *The 1812 Aponte Rebellion*, 176.

23. Reid-Vazquez, *The Year of the Lash*, 45–46.

24. Tacón to First Secretary of State in Madrid, Havana, August 31, 1836, FO 84:221.

25. Jonathan Curry-Machado, *Cuban Sugar Industry: Transnational Networks and Engineering Migrants in Mid-Nineteenth Century Cuba* (New York: Palgrave Macmillan, 2011), 176.

26. Barcia, *Seeds of Insurrection*, 25–26.

27. Ibid., 39.

28. Aisha K. Finch. "Insurgency at the Crossroads: Cuban Slaves and the Conspiracy of La Escalera, 1841–1844." PhD diss., New York University, 2007, 192–93.

29. Barcia, *Seeds of Insurrection*, 40.

30. Kennedy and Dalrymple to Aberdeen, Havana, April 18, 1843, FO 84:451; Reid-Vazquez, *The Year of the Lash*, 47–48.

31. Curry-Machado, *Cuban Sugar Industry*, 177.

32. Kennedy and Dalrymple to Aberdeen, Havana, September 8, 1843, FO 84:452.

33. Kennedy and Dalrymple to Aberdeen, Havana, November 8, 1843, FO 84:452.

34. Curry-Machado, *Cuban Sugar Industry*, 178.

35. Fernando Ortiz, *Los negros esclavos* (Havana: Editorial de Ciencias Sociales, 1975; originally published 1916); Manuel Moreno Fraginals, *The Sugarmill: The Socioeconomic Complex of Sugar in Cuba, 1760–1860*, trans. by Cedric Belfrage (New York: Monthly Review Press, 1976; originally published in Spanish in 1964); José Luciano Franco, *La gesta heroica del triunvirato* (Havana: Editorial de Ciencias Sociales, 1978); García Rodríguez, *Conspiraciones y revueltas.*

36. Finch, "Insurgency at the Crossroads," 1, 213–14. For an interpretation of La Escalera that places free blacks at the center of the story, see Reid-Vazquez, *The Year of the Lash*.

37. Finch, "Insurgency at the Crossroads," 19–20.

38. Ibid., 17.

39. Laird W. Bergad, Fe Iglesias García, and María del Carmen Barcia, *The Cuban Slave Market, 1790–1880* (Cambridge: Cambridge University Press, 1995), 16, 29, 34.

40. Finch, "Insurgency at the Crossroads," 101.

41. Ibid., 103.

42. Robert L. Paquette, *Sugar Is Made with Blood: The Conspiracy of La Escalera and the Conflict Between Empires over Slavery in Cuba* (Middletown, Conn.: Wesleyan University Press, 1988); David R. Murray, *Odious Commerce: Britain, Spain and the Abolition of the Cuban Slave Trade* (Cambridge: Cambridge University Press, 1980), 159–80; Barcia, *Seeds of Insurrection*, 46; Rodolfo Sarracino, *Inglaterra: sus dos caras en la lucha cubana por la abolición* (Havana: Letras Cubanas, 1989).

43. Barcia, *Seeds of Insurrection*, 28.

44. Kennedy and Dalrymple to Aberdeen, Havana, May 8, 1844, FO 84:508.

45. Kennedy to Aberdeen, Havana, October 4, 1844, FO 84:509. This information was taken from an account published in the *Diario de la Habana*, September 26, 1844.

46. Kennedy to Aberdeen, Havana, October 4, 1844, FO 84:509. This information was taken from an account published in the *Diario de la Habana*, September 28, 1844.

47. Decision taken against the "free Negress" Rita Dominguez, published in *Diario de la Habana*, September 27, 1844.

48. As cited in Curry-Machado, *Cuban Sugar Industry*, 178. See also Manuel Barcia, "Exorcising the Storm: Revisiting the Origins of the Repression of La Escalera Conspiracy in Cuba, 1843–1844," *Colonial Latin America Historical Review* 15:3 (2006), 311–26.

49. Finch, "Insurgency at the Crossroads," 298.

50. Ibid., 300–01.

51. Ibid., 303–04.

52. Reid-Vazquez, *The Year of the Lash*, 68–97.

53. Finch, "Insurgency at the Crossroads," 362–63.

54. Kennedy and Dalrymple to Aberdeen, Havana, June 8, 1844, FO 84:508.

55. Ibid.

56. Barcia, *The Great African Slave Revolt*, 145–47.

57. Curry-Machado, *Cuban Sugar Industry*, 175–93.

58. Gera Burton, "Liberty's Call: Richard Robert Madden's Voice in the Anti-Slavery Movement (1833–1842)," *Irish Migration Studies in Latin America* 5:3 (November 2007), 199–206.

59. El Conde de Villanueva and members of the *Junta de Fomento*, Memorial "To the Provisional Regency of the Kingdom," February 27, 1841, found in Kennedy and Dalrymple to Palmerston, Havana, June 3, 1841, FO 84:349. In the British correspondence, *Junta de Fomento* is translated as "Board for the Promotion of Agriculture and Commerce."

60. David Eltis and Olatunji Ojo, "The Diaspora of Africans Liberated from Slave Ships in the Nineteenth Century," forthcoming essay.

61. Macleay and Schenley to Wellington, Havana, May 13, 1835, FO 84:171; Trans-Atlantic Slave Trade Database, Voyage number 1372.

62. Murray, *Odious Commerce*, 277.

63. Tacón to First Secretary of State in Madrid, Havana, November 7, 1836, FO 84:221.

64. Kennedy and Dalrymple to Aberdeen, Havana, October 31, 1845, FO 84:562.

65. Kennedy and Dalrymple to Captain General, Havana, March 9, 1844, FO 84:508. See Oscar Grandio Moraguez, "Dobo: A Liberated African in Nineteenth-Century Havana," The Trans-Atlantic Slave Trade Database.

66. Kennedy and Dalrmyple to Aberdeen, Havana, January 1, 1844, FO 84:508.

67. Kennedy and Dalrymple to Aberdeen, Havana, May 8, 1844, FO 84:508.

68. Kennedy and Dalrymple to Aberdeen, Havana, July 4, 1844, FO 84:508.

69. Backhouse to Clarendon, Havana, October 10, 1853, FO 84:898.

70. Trans-Atlantic Slave Trade Database, Voyage number 1266.

71. Backhouse to Clarendon, Havana, October 10, 1853, FO 84:898.

72. Tacón to British commissioners, Havana, June 20, 1837, FO 84:216.

73. Ortiz, *Los negros esclavos*, 298.

74. Madan to Pierce, Havana, October 4, 1853, USNA, RG 59, Consular Dispatches from Cuba, T-20:27.

75. Rosanne Marion Adderley, *"New Negroes from Africa": Slave Trade Abolition and Free African Settlement in the Nineteenth-Century Caribbean* (Bloomington: Indiana University Press, 2006), 50–51.

76. Childs, *The 1812 Aponte Rebellion*, 178.

77. Ibid.

78. Dale Tomich, "The Wealth of Empire: Francisco Arango y Parreño, Political Economy, and the Second Slavery in Cuba," *Comparative Studies in Society and History* 45:1 (2003), 5.

79. Childs, *The 1812 Aponte Rebellion*, 90; Arango y Parreño, "Discurso sobre la agricultura de la Habana y medios de fomentarla," in Francisco Arango y Parreño, *De la factoría a la colonia* (Havana: Publicaciones de la Secretaría de Educación, 1936; originally published 1793), 88–89.

80. Murray, *Odious Commerce*, 86–87.

81. Ibid., 87.

82. Philip S. Foner, *A History of Cuba and Its Relations with the United States: From the Conquest of Cuba to La Escalera*, vol. 1 (New York: International Publishers, 1962), 174.

83. Trans-Atlantic Slave Trade Database.

84. Childs, *The 1812 Aponte Rebellion*, 63, 186.

85. Ibid., 90.

86. Ibid., 17.

87. Ibid., 90.

88. Ibid., 91.

89. Foner, *A History of Cuba*, vol. 1, 173.

90. Ibid., 173; Christopher Schmidt-Nowara, *Empire and Antislavery: Spain, Cuba, and Puerto Rico, 1833–1874* (Pittsburgh: University of Pittsburgh Press, 1999), 14–36.

91. Foner, *A History of Cuba*, vol. 1, 174.

92. Márcia Berbel, Rafael Marquese, and Tâmis Parron, *Escravidão e política: Brasil e Cuba, c. 1790–1850* (São Paulo: Editora Hucitec, 2010), 212–13.

93. Murray, *Odious Commerce*, 128–29.

94. Graciella Cruz-Taura, "Annexation and National Identity: Cuba's Mid-Nineteenth-Century Debate," *Cuban Studies* 27 (1997), 94.

95. José Antonio Saco, *Mi primera pregunta. La abolición del comercio de esclavos africanos arruinará ó atrasará la agricultura cubana?* (Madrid: Imprensa de M. Calero, 1837).

96. Foner, *A History of Cuba*, vol. 1, 174–78; Murray, *Odious Commerce*, 130–31.

97. José María Auilera-Manzano, *The Informal Communication Network Built by Domingo del Monte from Havana between 1824 and 1845* (San Domenico de Fiesole: European University Institute/Max Weber Program, Working Paper 2007/16, 2007), 3.

98. Finch, "Insurgency at the Crossroads," 417–18, notes 276 and 277; Ivan A. Schulman, "Introduction," in Juan Francisco Manzano, *The Autobiography of a Slave*, trans. Evelyn Picon Garfield (Detroit: Wayne State University Press, 1996), 5–37.

99. Cited in Schulman, "Introduction," 16–17.

100. Murray, *Odious Commerce*, 149.

101. Ibid.

102. Finch, "Insurgency at the Crossroads," 144. An insightful essay analyzing the fears about the underclass during the Age of Revolutions is George Reid Andrews, "Spanish American Independence: A Structural Analysis," *Latin American Perspectives* 12:1 (1985), 105–32.

103. Cited in Murray, *Odious Commerce*, 179.

104. Bill J. Karras, "Alexander Everett and Domingo Delmonte: A Literary Friendship, 1840–1845," *Caribbean Studies* 18:1–2 (April–July 1978), 137–48.

105. El Conde de Villanueva and members of the *Junta de Fomento*, Memorial "To the Provisional Regency of the Kingdom," February 27, 1841, found in Kennedy and Dalrymple to Palmerston, Havana, June 3, 1841, FO 84:349.

106. Ibid.

107. Members of the *Ayuntamiento* of the city of Havana to the Provisional Regency, Havana, no date, found in Kennedy and Dalrymple to Palmerston, Havana, June 3, 1841, FO 84:349.

108. Ibid.

109. Merchants, Proprietors and Occupiers of the District of Matanzas to Captain General O'Donnell, Matanzas, November 29, 1843, found in Kennedy and Dalrymple to Aberdeen, February 20, 1844, FO 84:508.

110. Kennedy and Dalrymple to Aberdeen, Havana, February 20, 1844, FO 84:508.

111. Benigno Gener to Captain General O'Donnell, Matanzas, December 8, 1843, found in Kennedy and Dalrymple to Aberdeen, Havana, February 20, 1844, FO 84:508.

112. Proprietors of estates of Havana to Captain General O'Donnell, Havana, no date (sometime between December 8, 1843, and early February 1844), found in Kennedy and Dalrymple to Aberdeen, Havana, February 20, 1844, FO 84:508.

113. Kennedy to Aberdeen, Havana, September 5, 1844, FO 84:509.

114. Ibid.

115. See "Report of the Junta de Fomento and Royal Patriotic Society," Havana, no date (between March and November 1841), as found in Kennedy and Dalrymple to Palmerston, Havana, December 10, 1841; Kennedy and Dalrymple to Palmerston, Havana, March 10, 1841, FO 84:348.

116. Kennedy to Aberdeen, Havana, November 7, 1844, FO 84:509. See Curry-Machado, *Cuban Sugar Industry*, 189–90, for a description of repression directed at well-off owners of property.

117. Murray, *Odious Commerce*, 244. The estimate by the British commissioners for 1840 to 1843 was 35,246 landed. More recent analysis derived from the Trans-Atlantic Slave Trade Database provides a total of 44,614 Africans landed in Cuba during this four-year period.

118. Kennedy and Dalrymple to Aberdeen, Havana, November 8, 1843, FO 84:452.

119. Kennedy and Dalrymple to Aberdeen, Havana, September 8, 1843, FO 84:452; Kennedy to Aberdeen, Havana, January 1, 1845, FO 84:561.

120. *La Scorpion* is most likely the *Escorpion*, which landed 560 Africans at Trinidad, Cuba in early 1843. Trans-Atlantic Slave Trade Database, Voyage number 2272.

121. Trans-Atlantic Slave Trade Database, Voyage number 2269.

122. Kennedy and Dalrymple to Aberdeen, Havana, April 26, 1843, FO 84:451. Underlined in the original.

123. Kennedy and Dalrymple to Aberdeen, Havana, December 8, 1843, FO 84:452; Melville and Hook to Aberdeen, Sierra Leone, December 31, 1844, FO 84:507.

124. Melville and Hook to Aberdeen, Sierra Leone, December 31, 1844, FO 84:507.

125. Kennedy and Dalrymple to Aberdeen, Havana, January 1, 1844, FO 84:508. See also Gabino La Rosa Corzo, *Runaway Slave Settlements in Cuba: Resistance and Repression*, trans. Mary Todd (Chapel Hill: University of North Carolina Press, 2003), 218.

126. Kennedy and Dalrymple to Aberdeen, Havana, April 8, 1844, FO 84:508.

127. Melville and Hook to Aberdeen, December 31, 1844, FO 84:507.

128. Ibid.

129. Kennedy and Dalrymple to Aberdeen, Havana, January 1, 1846, FO 84:620. The shift of slaves from failed coffee estates into sugar had been going on for at least 15 years. See Maclean to Aberdeen, Havana, January 1, 1830, FO 84:107.

130. Kennedy and Dalrymple to Aberdeen, Havana, June 10, 1845, FO 84:561; Kennedy to Aberdeen, Havana, February 7, 1845, FO 84:561; Kennedy and Dalrymple to Aberdeen, Havana, September 9, 1846, FO 84:621. For earlier descriptions of the Cuba-Brazil connection, see Macleay and MacKenzie to Palmerston, Havana, January 1, 1834, FO 84:150.

131. Melville and Hook to Aberdeen, Sierra Leone, December 31, 1844, FO 84:507.

132. See Gerald Horne, *The Deepest South: The United States, Brazil, and the African Slave Trade* (New York: New York University Press, 2007).

133. See Crawford to Palmerston, Havana, January 1, 1852, FO 84:870; Southern to Malmesbury, Rio de Janeiro, April 8, 1852, FO 84:878; Jerningham to Russell, Rio de Janeiro, April 2, 1853, FO 84:911.

134. An extended analysis that renders the "seditious acts" of Liberated Africans and slaves as being inspired by "Methodist Societies" based in Europe, and particularly England, is included in Tacón to Secretary of State (in Madrid), Havana, August 31, 1836, FO 84:221.

135. Andrews, *Afro-Latin America*, 74–75; Corzo, *Runaway Slave Settlements*, 200.

136. Foner, *A History of Cuba*, vol. 1, 228; Barcia, *Seeds of Insurrection*, 28.

CHAPTER FIVE

1. Jeffrey D. Needell, *The Party of Order: The Conservatives, the State, and Slavery in the Brazilian Monarchy, 1831–1871* (Stanford, Calif.: Stanford University Press, 2006), 138–55. Brazilian historians who could be included in this school include Lilia Moritz Schwarcz, *As barbas do imperador: D. Pedro II, um monarca nos trópicos*, 2nd ed. (São Paulo: Companhia das Letras, 1998), 297; and Emilia Viotti da Costa, *The Brazilian Empire: Myths and Histories* (Chapel Hill: University of North Carolina Press, 2000), 128–32. Historians of the nineteenth century whose contributions align with the Enlightenment School include David Brion Davis, *The Problem of Slavery in the Age of Revolution, 1770–1823* (New York: Oxford University Press, 1999); Adam Hochschild, *Bury the Chains: Prophets and Rebels in the Fight to Free an Empire's Slaves* (Boston: Houghton Mifflin, 2005); Seymour Drescher, *Capitalism and Antislavery: British Mobilization in Comparative Perspective* (New York: Oxford University Press, 1987).

2. Leslie Bethell, *The Abolition of the Brazilian Slave Trade: Britain, Brazil and the Slave Trade Question, 1807–1869* (Cambridge: Cambridge University Press, 1970). A more recent study that follows Bethell's lead and is based solely on British sources is Hugh Thomas, *The Slave Trade: The Story of the Atlantic Slave Trade, 1440–1870* (New York: Simon & Schuster, 1997).

3. Needell, *The Party of Order*, 146; Katia M. de Queirós Mattoso, *Bahia, século XIX: uma província no império*, trans. Yedda de Macedo Soares (Rio de Janeiro: Editora Nova Fronteira, 1992), 542.

4. Needell, *The Party of Order*, 149.

5. João José Reis, *Rebelião escrava no Brasil: a história do levante dos Malês em 1835*, edição revista e ampliada (São Paulo: Companhia das Letras, 2003), 509, 517. Historians of the "Subaltern School" include Sidney Chalhoub, Robert Slenes, Flávio Gomes, and José Maia Bezerra Neto. For

perspectives on the debate described above, see Sidney Chalhoub, "Os conservadores no Brasil Império," *Afro-Ásia* no. 35 (2007), 317–26. Historians of international abolition in the nineteenth century whose interpretations align with this group's include Robin Blackburn, *The Overthrow of Colonial Slavery, 1776–1848* (London: Verso, 1988). I would suggest that Seymour Drescher has a foot in both schools. After decades of research on a wide range of themes, Professor Drescher has embraced slave resistance as a key variable in antislavery debates of the nineteenth century. See *Abolition: A History of Slavery and Antislavery* (New York: Cambridge University Press, 2009).

6. João José Reis, *Slave Rebellion in Brazil: The Muslim Uprising of 1835 in Bahia*, trans. Arthur Brakel (Baltimore: Johns Hopkins University Press, 1993), 40–41.

7. Ibid., 50.

8. Ibid., 67.

9. Ibid., 141–46. It should be noted that creole slaves revolted outside of the Recôncavo from the end of the eighteenth century. At the Santana sugar *engenho* (plantation) in Ilhéus, south of Bahia, creole slaves killed their overseer in mid-1789, fled into a nearby forest, and established a *mocambo* (escaped slave community). A few months later, the slaves offered a treaty of peace with their former master. The Santana creole slaves revolted again in 1821–24 and 1828. See Stuart B. Schwartz, "Resistance and Accommodation in Eighteenth-Century Brazil: The Slaves' View of Slavery," *Hispanic American Historical Review* 57:1 (February 1977), 69–81, and Stuart B. Schwartz, *Slaves, Peasants, and Rebels: Reconsidering Brazilian Slavery* (Urbana: University of Illinois Press, 1992), 50–63. Creole slaves also joined in revolts by free people and the Bahian war for independence against the Portuguese during this period. Thanks to João Reis for his comments in this regard.

10. See João José Reis and Beatriz Gallotti Mamigonian, "Nagô and Mina: The Yoruba Diaspora in Brazil," in *The Yoruba Diaspora in the Atlantic World*, ed. Toyin Falola and Matt D. Childs (Bloomington: Indiana University Press, 2004), 77–110; and J. Lorand Matory, "The English Professors of Brazil: On the diasporic roots of the Yoruba nation," *Comparative Studies in Society and History* 41:1 (1999), 72–103.

11. João José Reis, "Domingos Pereira Sodré, a Nagô Priest in Nineteenth-Century Bahia," in *The Changing Worlds of Atlantic Africa: Essays in Honor of Robin Law*, ed. Toyin Falola and Matt D. Childs (Durham, N.C.: Carolina Academic Press, 2009), 387–407.

12. João José Reis, "Um balanço dos estudos sobre as revoltas escravas da Bahia," in *Escravidão e invenção da liberdade: estudos sobre o negro no Brasil*, org. João José Reis (São Paulo: Editora Brasiliense/Conselho Nacional de Desenvolvimiento Científico e Tecnológico, 1988), 87–140; Paul Lovejoy, "Background to Rebellion: The Origins of Muslim Slaves in Bahia," *Slavery and Abolition* 15:2 (1994), 151–80; Alberto da Costa e Silva, "Sobre a rebelião de 1835 na Bahia," *Revista Brasileira* 8:31 (2002), 9–33.

13. Parkinson to Wellington, Salvador, January 29, 1835, FO 13:121.

14. Reis, *Rebelião escrava no Brasil*, 151–57.

15. Ibid., 333–34.

16. Ibid., 177.

17. Ibid., 335.

18. Parkinson to Wellington, Salvador, February 2, 1835, FO 13:121.

19. Ibid.

20. Parkinson to Wellington, Salvador, March 3, 1835, FO 13:121.

21. "Extract of the speech of the President of Bahia at the opening of the Provincial Assembly [in early March 1836]," included in Jackson to Palmerston, Rio de Janeiro, March 5, 1836, FO 84:198.

22. Ibid.; Reis, *Rebelião escrava no Brasil,* 482–83, 491–92. Vessels that transported free Africans back to Africa included the Brazilian schooner *Maria Dorniana* and the Brazilian brigs *Annibal* and *Oriento,* as described in Parkinson to Palmerston, no date (most likely late January 1836), Salvador, FO 13:141.

23. *Jornal do Commercio* no. 37, February 17, 1835, cited in Reis, *Rebelião escrava,* 517.

24. *Aurora Fluminense* (Rio de Janeiro), March 20, 1835, p. 3818. The Assembly convened on March 1, 1835.

25. Message from the Provincial Assembly of Rio de Janeiro to the Central Government, Rio de Janeiro, March 17, 1835, as found in Jackson and Grigg to Wellington, Rio de Janeiro, March 23, 1835, FO 84:174.

26. Fox to Wellington, Rio de Janeiro, March 25, 1835, FO 84:179.

27. Fox to Wellington, Rio de Janeiro, May 30, 1835, FO 13:117.

28. Representation of the Provincial Assembly of Bahia to the General Legislative Assembly in Rio de Janeiro, Salvador, May 11, 1835, FO 84:175. See also Miguel Calmon du Pin e Almeida, *Memória sobre o estabelecimento d'uma companhia de colonização nesta província* (Salvador: Centro de Estudos Baianos/UFBa, 1985; originally published in 1835).

29. "Extract of the speech of the President of Bahia at the opening of the Provincial Assembly [in early March 1836]," included in Jackson to Palmerston, Rio de Janeiro, March 5, 1836, FO 84:198.

30. Ibid.

31. Francisco de Souza Martins to Frederick Robilliand, Salvador, March 28, 1835, FO 13:121.

32. Marcus J.M. de Carvalho, "'Que crime é ser cismático?': As transgressões de um pastor negro no Recife patriarchal, 1846," *Estudos Afro-Asiáticos* 36 (Dezembro 1999), 97–122. See also Marcus J.M. de Carvalho, "Agostinho José Pereira: The Divine Teacher," in *The Human Tradition in Modern Brazil,* ed. Peter M. Beattie (Wilmington, Del.: Scholarly Resources, 2004), 23–42.

33. Marcus Joaquim M. de Carvalho, "Q quilombo de Malunguinho, o rei das matas de Pernambuco," in *Liberdade por um fio: história dos quilombos no Brasil,* org. João José Reis and Flávio dos Santos Gomes (São Paulo: Companhia das Letras, 1996), 407–32.

34. Carvalho, "Que crime é ser cismático," 114.

35. Cowper to Palmerston, Recife, September 30, 1847, FO 84:679.

36. Juliana Barreto Farias, Carlos Eugênio Líbano Soares, and Flávio dos Santos Gomes, *No labirinto das nações: africanos e identidades no Rio de Janeiro* (Rio de Janeiro: Arquivo Nacional, 2005), 23. See also Juliana Barreto Farias, Flávio dos Santos Gomes, Carlos Eugênio Líbano Soares, and Carlos Eduardo de Araújo Moreira, *Cidades negras: africanos, crioulos e espaços urbanos no Brasil escravista do século XIX* (São Paulo: Alameda, 2006).

37. Sandra Lauderdale Graham, "Being Yoruba in Nineteenth-Century Rio de Janeiro," *Slavery and Abolition* 32:1 (2011), 6.

38. See Beatriz Gallotti Mamigonian, "José Majojo e Francisco Moçambique, marinheiros das rotas Atlânticas: Notas sobre a reconstituição de trajetórias da era da abolição," *Topoi* 11:20 (jan.–jun. 2010), 75–91.

39. Jaime Rodrigues, *De costa a costa: escravos, marinheiros e intermediarios do tráfico negreiro de Angola ao Rio de Janeiro (1780–1860)* (São Paulo: Companhia das Letras, 2005), 186–87.

40. Farias, Gomes, Soares, *No labirinto*, 87.

41. Thomas H. Holloway, *Policing Rio de Janeiro: Repression and Resistance in a Nineteenth-Century City* (Stanford, Calif.: Stanford University Press, 1993), 223–28; Thomas H. Holloway, "'A Healthy Terror': Police Repression of Capoeiras in Nineteenth Century Rio de Janeiro," *Hispanic American Historical Review* 69:4 (November 1989), 637–76; Carlos Eugênio Líbano Soares, *A capoeira escrava e outras tradições rebeldes no Rio de Janeiro, 1808–1850* (São Paulo: Editora da Unicamp/Cecult, 2001).

42. Holloway, *Policing Rio de Janeiro*, 176–79.

43. Robert W. Slenes, "A ávore de *Nsanda* transplantada: Cultos *Kongo* de aflição e identidade escrava no sudeste brasileiro (século XIX)," in *Trabalho livre, trabalho escravo: Brasil e Europa, séculos XVII e XIX*, org. Douglas Cole Libby and Júnia Ferreira Furtado (São Paulo: Annablume, 2006), 280. See also Robert W. Slenes, "The Great Porpoise-Skull Strike: Central African Water Spirits and Slave Identity in Early-Nineteenth-Century Rio de Janeiro," in *Central Africans and Cultural Transformations in the American Diaspora*, ed. Linda M. Heywood (Cambridge: Cambridge University Press, 2002), 183–208.

44. *Aurora Fluminense* (Rio de Janeiro), November 30, 1831.

45. Marcos Ferreira de Andrade, "Rebelião escrava na Comarca do Rio das Mortes, Minas Gerais: o caso Carrancas," *Afro-Asia* 21–22 (1998–1999), 45–82.

46. Basil Gerson, *A escravidão no Império* (Rio de Janeiro: Pallas, 1975), 50; Márcia Berbel, Rafael Marquese, and Tâmis Parron, *Escravidao e política: Brasil e Cuba, c.1790–1850* (São Paulo: Editora Hucitec, 2010), 194–95.

47. Mary C. Karasch, *Slave Life in Rio de Janeiro, 1808–1850* (Princeton, N.J.: Princeton University Press, 1987), 324.

48. Holloway, *Policing Rio de Janeiro*, 121; João José Reis, Flávio dos Santos Gomes, and Marcus J.M. de Carvalho, *O alufá Rufino: tráfico, escravidão e liberdade no Atlântico negro (c.1822–c.1853)* (São Paulo: Companhia das Letras, 2010), 83–96.

49. Holloway, *Policing Rio de Janeiro*, 164.

50. David Eltis, *Economic Growth and the Ending of the Transatlantic Slave Trade* (New York: Oxford University Press, 1987), 244.

51. Karasch, *Slave Life*, 313.

52. President of the province Manuel José de Oliveira to Minister of Justice Bernardo Pereira da Vasconcellos, Rio de Janeiro, May 4, 1838, National Archives of Brazil in Rio de Janeiro: Section of Executive Powers, IJ 1 860 (hereafter ANRJ/SPE). See also Alaôr Eduardo Scisinio, *Escravidão e a saga de Manuel Congo* (Rio de Janeiro: Achiamé, 1988), and João Luiz D. Pinaud and Carlos Otávio de Andrade, *Insurreição negra e justiça* (Rio de Janeiro: Expressão e Cultura, 1987).

53. See the court proceedings for the slave José Lisboa, accused of killing an overseer on a plantation in the interior of Rio de Janeiro province. The overseer was the fourth assassinated "in the recent past." Interim judge João José Coutinho to Pedro II, Itaguahy, Angra, Rio de Janeiro, November 22, 1845, ANRJ/SPE, IJ 1 863.

54. Chief of Police Queiroz to Minister of Justice Soares de Souza, Rio de Janeiro, August 26, 1842, National Archives of Brazil in Rio de Janeiro, Secretary of Police, IJ 6 199 (hereafter ANRJ/Polícia). See the important analyses of Flávio dos Santos Gomes, *Histórias de quilombolas: mocambos e comunidades de senzalas no Rio de Janeiro, século XIX* (Rio de Janeiro: Arquivo Nacional, 1995), and "Quilombos do Rio de Janeiro no século XIX," in *Liberdade por um fio: história dos*

quilombos no Brasil, org. João José Reis and Flávio dos Santos Gomes (São Paulo: Companhia das Letras, 1996), 276–81.

55. Parkinson to Wellington, Salvador, January 29, 1835, FO 13:121.

56. Needell, *The Party of Order*, 148.

57. Parkinson to Wellington, Salvador, January 29, 1835, FO 13:121; W.G. Ouseley, "Notes on the subject of the slave trade in the province and city of Bahia, September 1835," sent from Ouseley to Fox, Rio, October 27, 1835, FO 84:179. See "The Yacht *Maria Até Ver*," *O Século*, October 3, 1850, translated in Porter to Hudson, Salvador, October 9, 1850, FO 84:807. See also Ubiritan Castro de Araújo, "1846: um ano a rota Bahia-Lagos; negócios, negociantes e outros parceiros," *Afro-Ásia* 21–22 (1998–1999), 83–110; Manolo Florentino, *Em costas negras: uma história do tráfico de escravos entre a África e o Rio de Janeiro (séculos XVIII e XIX)* (São Paulo: Companhia das Letras, 1997); and Manolo Florentino, "Slave Trading and Slave Traders in Rio de Janeiro, 1790–1830," in *Enslaving Connections: Changing Cultures of Africa and Brazil during the Era of Slavery*, ed. José C. Curto and Paul E. Lovejoy (New York: Humanity Books, 2004), 57–79.

58. Magalhães to minister of justice, Salvador, February 9, 1848, ANRJ/SPE, IJ 1 710.

59. Cowper to Palmerston, Recife, February 19, 1848, FO 84:727.

60. Ari Oro, "Religiões Afro-Brasileiros do Rio Grande do Sul: Passado e Presente," *Estudos Afro-Asiáticos* 24:2 (2002), 348.

61. Reis, Gomes, and Carvalho, *O alufá Rufino*, 53–59.

62. Morgan to Howden, Pelotas, February 9, 1848, FO 84:727.

63. Morgan to Palmerston, Rio Grande do Sul, February 15, 1848, FO 84:727.

64. Morgan to Howden, Pelotas, February 9, 1848, FO 84:727.

65. Howden to Palmerston, Rio de Janeiro, March 20, 1848, FO 84:725. For a description of supposed Mina superiority to "tribes further north" in Africa, see Webb to Seward, Petropolis, May 20, 1862, USNA, RG 59, Consular Dispatches from Brazil, M-121:29.

66. Carlos Eugênio Libano Soares and Flávio dos Santos Gomes, "'Com o pé sobre um vulcão': Africanos Minas, identidades e a repressão antiafricano no Rio de Janeiro (1830–1840)," *Estudos Afro-Asiáticos* 23:2 (2001), 346.

67. Message from the Provincial Assembly of Rio de Janeiro to the Imperial Government, March 17, 1835, as found in Jackson and Grigg to Wellington, Rio de Janeiro, March 23, 1835, FO 84:174. See also Jackson and Grigg to Wellington, Rio de Janeiro, April 13, 1835, FO 84:174.

68. F.S. Dias da Motta and José Alves Carneiro Montezuma, Rio de Janeiro, July 8, 1848: "Secret Report of the Select Committee of the Provincial Assembly of Rio de Janeiro on Secret Societies of Africans in the Province of Rio de Janeiro," July 8, 1848 [Assembly House in Secret Session, July 8, 1848]. This document is translated in Hudson to Palmerston, Rio de Janeiro, February 20, 1850, FO 84:802.

69. Chief of Police Queiroz to Minister of Justice Branco, Rio de Janeiro, May 22, 1835, ANRJ/Polícia, IJ 6 171.

70. Judge João Carneiro de Campos to Chief of Police Queiroz, Cabo Frio, Rio de Janeiro, January 13, 1836, Public Archive of the State of Rio de Janeiro, PPs, collection 5, maço 2. See also Alberto da Costa e Silva, "Buying and Selling Korans in Nineteenth Century Rio de Janeiro," *Slavery and Abolition* 22:1 (2001), 83–90.

71. Luiz Fortunato to Minister of Justice José Carlos Pereira Torres, Rio de Janeiro, June 12, 1845, ANRJ/Polícia, IJ 6 204; Farias, Gomes, and Soares, *No labirinto*, 73–78.

72. Reis and Mamigonian, "Nagô and Mina," 100.

73. Chief of Police Simões da Silva to Minister of Justice Eusébio de Queiroz, Rio de Janeiro, December 2, 1849, ANRJ/Polícia, IJ 6 212.

74. Robert W. Slenes, "'*Malungu, ngoma* vêm!': África coberta e descoberta no Brasil," in *Mostra do Redescobrimento: Negro de Corpo e Alma—Black in Body and Soul*, ed. Nelson Aguilar (São Paulo: Fundação Bienal de São Paulo, 2000), 218–19. See also Robert W. Slenes, "A ávore de *Nsanda*," 301–06, and Gomes, *Histórias de quilombolas*, 262.

75. Marcus J.M. de Carvalho, "A 'revolução de novembro,' a 'populaça' do Recife e suas lideranças em 1848," in Libby and Furtado, org., *Trabalho livre, trabalho escravo*, 445.

76. Flávio dos Santos Gomes, *A hidra e os pântanos: mocambos, quilombos e comunidades de fugitivos no Brasil (Séculos XVII–XIX)* (São Paulo: Ed. UNESP, 2005), 141.

77. Hudson to Palmerston, Rio de Janeiro, August 5, 1848, FO 84:726. Author's emphasis.

78. Seymour Drescher, *Abolition: A History of Slavery and Antislavery* (Cambridge: Cambridge University Press, 2009), 291.

79. "Representação sobre o tráfico," from the Municipal Corporation of the city of Salvador to the General Assembly in Rio de Janeiro, published in *Correio Mercantil* (Rio de Janeiro), August 3, 1850, FO 84:806.

80. Antonio Joaquim de Siqueira to Minister of Interior Visconde de Monte Alegre, Victoria, March 20, 1849, ANRJ/SPE, IJJ 9 362.

81. Siqueira to Alegre, Vitória, March 24, 1849, ANRJ/SPE, IJJ 9 362.

82. Chief of Police José Ignácio Accioli de Vasconcellos to President Siqueira, Vitória, March 23, 1849, ANRJ/SPE, IJJ 9 362.

83. Vilma Paraíso Ferreira de Almada, *Escravismo e transição: O Espirito Santo (1850–1888)* (Rio de Janeiro: Edições Graal, 1984), 168; Eric Williams, *Capitalism and Slavery* (New York: Putnam, 1980; originally published 1944), 202.

84. Comment about the spread of information from coast to plantations is in Simon Schama, *Rough Crossings: Britain, The Slaves and the American Revolution* (New York: HarperCollins, 2006), 66. See also Jane G. Landers, *Atlantic Creoles in the Age of Revolutions* (Cambridge, Mass.: Harvard University Press, 2010), 5.

85. Almada, *Escravismo e transição*, 172–73.

86. President of Maranhão (illegible) to Minister of Interior Manoel Antonio Galvão, Maranhão, December 30, 1839, ANRJ/SPE, IJJ 9 133; President of Pará Manoel Paranhos da Silva Vellozo to Minister of Justice, Pará, January 28, 1846, ANRJ/SPE, IJ 1 202; President of Alagoas Bernardo de Sousa Franco to Galvão, Alagoas, November 19, 1844, ANRJ/SPE, IJ 1 357; President of Bahia Joaquim Vasconcelos to Minister of Justice, Bahia, December 14, 1841, ANRJ/SPE, IJ 1 399; Comandante das Armas José Joaquim Coelho to president Francisco Martins, Salvador, October 23, 1848, ANRJ/SPE, IG 1 119; Francisco Pereira de Vasconcellos to Minister of Justice Eusébio de Queiroz, Rio de Janeiro, December 16, 1851, ANRJ/Policia, IJ 6 215; police delegate Roberto Jorge Haddock to Chief of Police Antonio Simoens da Silva, Rio de Janeiro, June 13 and June 15, 1849, ANRJ/Polícia, IJ 6 212.

87. "Mappa demonstrativo do numero de Africanos libertos n'esta cidade com declaração do negocio em que se empregão." Salvador, March 20, 1847, ANRJ/SPE, IJ 1 403.

88. Anna Amélia Vieira Nascimento, *Dez freguesias da cidade do Salvador* (Salvador: Fundação Cultural do Estado da Bahia, 1986), 65. The 1855 census notes a total population in Salvador

of 56,000, with 68.9 percent free (38,584), 27.5 percent slave (15,400), and 3.5 percent liberto (2,016), as noted on p. 97.

89. Needell, *The Party of Order*, 143. For an alternative perspective, see Manuel Barcia, "'A Not-So-Common Wind': Slave Revolts in the Age of Revolutions in Cuba and Brazil," *Review-Fernand Braudel Center for the Study of Economies, Historical Systems, and Civilizations* 31:2 (2008), 169–94.

90. President of Bahia Antonio Inácio de Azevedo to Minister of Justice Joaquim Fernando Torres, Salvador, April 6, 1847, ANRJ/SPE, IJ 1 403.

91. Morgan to Clarendon, Salvador, May 13, 1853, FO 84:912.

92. See Reis, Gomes, and Carvalho, *O alufá Rufino*; João José Reis, Flávio dos Santos Gomes, and Marcus J.M. de Carvalho, "Rufino José Maria (1820s–1850s): A Muslim in the Nineteenth-Century Brazilian Slave Trade Circuit," in *The Black Atlantic: 1500–2000*, ed. Beatriz G. Mamigonian and Karen Racine (Lanham, Md.: Rowman & Littlefield Publishers, 2010), 65–75.

93. Alexander Joaquim (illegible) to Minister of Justice, Recife, Pernambuco, October 5, 1853, ANRJ/Polícia, IJ 6 216; Reis, Gomes, and Carvalho, *O alufá Rufino*, 313–19.

94. Soares and Gomes, "Com o pé sobre um vulcão," 346. This description and a picture of the Arabic document are found in Dale T. Graden, *From Slavery to Freedom in Brazil: Bahia, 1835–1900* (Albuquerque: University of New Mexico Press, 2006), 29.

95. Chief of Police Evaristo Fernando d'Argollo to President Tomás Xavier Garcia de Almeida, Salvador, July 26, 1839, Public Archive of the State of Bahia: Colonial and Provincial Section, maço 2949; Chief of Police Antonio Simões da Silva to Minister of Justice Eusébio de Quieroz, Rio de Janeiro, March 26, 1849, ANRJ/Polícia, IJ 6 212.

96. Reis, *Rebelião escrava*, 334.

97. Message from the Provincial Assembly of Rio de Janeiro to the Imperial Government, Rio de Janeiro, as found in Jackson and Grigg to Wellington, Rio de Janeiro, March 17, 1835, FO 84:174. See also Fox to Wellington, Rio de Janeiro, April 13, 1835, FO 13:117; Parkinson to Wellington, Salvador, January 26, 1835, FO 13:121.

98. "Sessão em 27 de Março de 1843," *Annais do senado do império do Brasil* (Rio de Janeiro: Senado Federal, 1978) (hereafter cited as ASIB), pp. 411–13; "Sessão em 10 de Junho de 1843," ASIB, p. 105.

99. "Sessão em 27 de Março de 1843," ASIB, p. 413.

100. Trans-Atlantic Slave Trade Database.

101. *Commercial* (Recife), May 31, 1850, as found in FO 84:809. See also Carlos Eugênio Libano Soares and Flávio dos Santos Gomes, "Sedições, haitianismo e conexões no Brasil: outras margens do Atlântico negro," *Novos Estudos CEBRAP*, 63 (Julho 2002), 131–44; Flávio dos Santos Gomes, "Experiências transatlânticos e significados locais: idéias, temores e narrativas em torno do Haiti no Brasil escravista," *Revista Tempo* (Rio de Janeiro), 7:13 (2002), 209–46; and João José Reis and Flávio dos Santos Gomes, "Repercussions of the Haitian Revolution in Brazil, 1791–1850," in *The World of the Haitian Revolution*, ed. David Patrick Geggus and Norman Fiering (Bloomington: Indiana University Press, 2009), 284–313.

102. For a discussion of tensions that surfaced during the following decade, see José Maia Bezerra Neto, "O Africano indesejado: combate ao tráfico, segurança pública e reforma civilizador (Grão-Pará, 1850–1860)," *Afro-Ásia* 44 (2011), 171–217.

103. Needell, *The Party of Order*, 139–49.

104. João José Reis and Eduardo Silva, *Negociação e conflito* (São Paulo: Companhia das Letras, 1989).

105. Carolyn E. Fick, *The Making of Haiti: The Saint Domingue Revolution from Below* (Knoxville: University of Tennessee Press, 1990); Laurent DuBois, *Avengers of the New World: The Story of the Haitian Revolution* (Cambridge, Mass.: Harvard University Press, 2004); Mary Turner, *Slaves and Missionaries: The Disintegration of Jamaican Slave Society, 1787–1834* (Urbana: University of Illinois Press, 1984); Michael Craton, *Testing the Chains: Resistance to Slavery in the British West Indies* (Ithaca, N.Y.: Cornell University Press, 1982), 294–96; Gelien Matthews, *Caribbean Slave Revolts and the British Abolitionist Movement* (Baton Rouge: Louisiana State University Press, 2006).

106. See Célia Maria Marinho de Azevedo, *Onda negra, medo branco: o negro no imaginário das elites–século XIX* (Rio de Janeiro: Paz e Terra, 1987).

107. "Sessão em 24 de Maio de 1851," ASIB, p. 320.

108. "Sessão em 27de Maio em 1851," ASIB, pp. 387–88.

109. Eusébio de Queiroz Coutinho Mattoso Camara, speech to Chamber of Deputies on July 16, 1852, reproduced in Agostinho Marques Perdigão Malheiro, *A escravidão no Brasil: ensaio histórico, jurídico, social* (originally published 1867), 3rd ed., 2 vols. (Petrópolis: Editora Vozes, 1976), Vol. II, p. 210.

110. Bethell, *The Abolition of the Brazilian Slave Trade*; Thomas, *The Slave Trade*; Graden, *From Slavery to Freedom*.

111. See, for example, Walter Fraga Filho, *Mendigos, moleques e vadios na Bahia do século XIX* (Salvador: Edufba, 1996), 144–49.

112. "A indústria de saveiros," *O Argos Cachoeirano*, October 1, 1850, p. 1.

CHAPTER SIX

1. George Francis Dow, *Slave Ships and Slaving* (Salem, Mass.: Marine Research Society, 1927), 274.

2. Christie to Porter, Salvador, October 13, 1841, FO 84:367. See also Melville and Hook to Aberdeen, Sierra Leone, December 31, 1844, FO 84:507.

3. Antonio José Mesquita to Senhor Gaspar, Rio de Janeiro, April 20, 1839, included among papers taken from either the *Maria Carlota* or *Recuperadora*, captured by HMS *Grecian* on May 28, 1839, found in Ouseley to Palmerston, Rio de Janeiro, July 18, 1839, FO 84:287.

4. Ira Berlin, "African Immigration to Colonial America," *History Now* no. 3 (March 2005), http://www.gilderlehrman.org/historynow/03_2005/historian3.php.

5. Ira Berlin, *Many Thousands Gone: The First Two Centuries of Slavery in North America* (Cambridge, Mass.: Harvard University Press, 2000), 24; Ira Berlin, "From Creole to African: Atlantic Creoles and the Origins of African-American Society in Mainland North America," *William and Mary Quarterly* 53:2 (April 1996), 251–88. See also Jane G. Landers, *Atlantic Creoles in the Age of Revolutions* (Cambridge, Mass.: Harvard University Press, 2010), 1–14.

6. Berlin, "African Immigration."

7. Carlos Fuentes, *The Buried Mirror: Reflections on Spain and the New World* (New York: Houghton Mifflin, 1992), 138.

8. Matthias Röhrig Assunção and Michael Zeuske, "Race, Ethnicity and Social Structure in 19th Century Brazil and Cuba," *Ibero-Amerikanishes Archiv* 24:3–4 (1998), 426. See also Miguel

Barnet, *Biography of a Runaway Slave*, trans. W. Nick Hill (Willimantic, Conn.: Curbstone Press, 1994).

9. Fox to Wellington, Rio de Janeiro, June 1, 1835, FO 84:179; Ouseley to Palmerston, Rio de Janeiro, December 15, 1838, FO 84:254; Cowper to Aberdeen, Recife, September 30, 1843, FO 84:470.

10. Hudson to Palmerston, Rio de Janeiro, August 14, 1851, FO 13:285.

11. Joan M. Fayer, "African Interpreters in the Atlantic Slave Trade," *Anthropological Linguistics* 45:3 (Fall 2003), 281–95.

12. Marcus Rediker, *The Slave Ship: A Human History* (New York: Penguin, 2007), 117–18, 206; Peter Linebaugh and Marcus Rediker, *The Many-Headed Hydra: Sailors, Slaves, Commoners, and the Hidden History of the Revolutionary Atlantic* (Boston: Beacon Press, 2000), 154. See also José C. Curto and Renée Soulodre-La France, "Introduction: Interconnections between Africa and the Americas during the Era of the Slave Trade," in *Africa and the Americas: Interconnections During the Slave Trade*, ed. José C. Curto and Renée Soulodre-La France (Trenton, N.J.: Africa World Press, 2005), 1–11, and the documentary directed by Alvaro Toepke and Angel Serrano, *The Language You Cry In*, and review by Jane Collings, "The Language You Cry In: Story of Mende Song," *Oral History Review* 28:1 (Winter/Spring 2001), 115–18.

13. Trans-Atlantic Slave Trade Database, Voyage number 1479.

14. Schenley to Palmerston, Havana, date not known, approximately August 1, 1836, FO 84:197. The captor's declaration was taken on July 30, 1836. For descriptions of Krumen and African interpreters involved in the traffic, see Dow, *Slave Ships and Slaving*, 116, 122–23, 295–96.

15. Schenley to Halkett, Havana, July 28, 1836, FO 84:197; Schenley to Commissioners at Sierra Leone, Havana, July 28, 1836, FO 84:197. Underlined in the original.

16. See Macleay and MacKenzie to Palmerston, Havana, March 31, 1834, FO 84:150; Schenley to Palmerston, Havana, July 30, 1836, FO 84:197. John Ormond and Edward Joussiffe invested in the Portuguese slave schooner *Nympha*, captured near the Pongas River in November 1830. See Finley and Smith to Aberdeen, Sierra Leone, December 20, 1830, FO 84:103.

17. For comments about John Ormond, see Macleay to Aberdeen, Havana, December 2, 1829, FO 84:92, and José Luciano Franco, *Comercio clandestino de esclavos* (Havana: Ciencias Sociales, 1980), 185–89.

18. Trans-Atlantic Slave Trade Database, Voyage number 2406.

19. Schenley to Palmerston, Havana, August 24, 1836, FO 84:197.

20. Schenley and Madden to Palmerston, Havana, January 6, 1837, FO 84:216. See also Macleay and MacKenzie to Palmerston, Havana, March 31, 1834, FO 84:150.

21. See Kennedy to Aberdeen, Havana, October 30, 1844, FO 84:562. English-speaking Krumen aided British investigations of clandestine disembarkations right until the last months of the traffic to Cuba. See Crawford to Russell, Havana, February 19, 1864, FO 84:1215.

22. Anderson to Schenley, Honduras, August 10, 1836, FO 84:197.

23. Robert Edgar Conrad, *World of Sorrow: The African Slave Trade to Brazil* (Baton Rouge: Louisiana State University Press, 1986), 154–70; Hesketh to Hudson, Rio de Janeiro, September 30, 1851, FO 84:847; Luis Martínez-Fernández, *Fighting Slavery in the Caribbean: The Life and Times of a British Family in Nineteenth-Century Havana* (Armonk, N.Y.: M.E. Sharpe, 1998), 50–58.

24. Schenley to Palmerston, Havana, August 24, 1836, FO 84:197.

25. Macleay to Wellington, Havana, April 11, 1835, FO 84:171.

26. Deposition of José Cerda before British and Spanish Mixed Commission at Havana, April 6, 1835, in Macleay to Wellington, Havana, April 11, 1835, FO 84:171.

27. Deposition of Juan Costa before British and Spanish Mixed Commission at Havana, July 10, 1835, in Macleay and Schenley to Palmerston, Havana, July 19, 1835, FO 84:172.

28. Deposition of James Caldwell before British and Spanish Mixed Commission at Havana, April 6, 1835, in Macleay to Wellington, Havana, April 11, 1835, FO 84:171.

29. Macleay to Wellington, Havana, April 11, 1835, FO 84:171. For another description of an interpreter seeking special treatment after capture by a British cruiser, see Macleay and Schenley to Palmerston, Havana, July 19, 1835, FO 84:172.

30. An overview is provided in Leslie Bethell, "The Mixed Commissions for the Suppression of the Transatlantic Slave Trade in the Nineteenth Century," *The Journal of African History* 7:1 (1966), 79–93. Descriptions of the Havana Mixed Commission Court are found in David R. Murray, *Odious Commerce: Britain, Spain and the Abolition of the Cuban Slave Trade* (New York: Cambridge University Press, 1980), 75–77, 101–03; and Martínez-Fernández, *Fighting Slavery in the Caribbean*, 41–50. For the Mixed Commission Court at Rio de Janeiro, see Leslie Bethell, *The Abolition of the Brazilian Slave Trade: Britain, Brazil and the Slave Trade Question* (New York: Cambridge University Press, 1970), 122–50.

31. Jenny S. Martinez, "Anti-Slavery Courts and the Dawn of International Human Rights Law," *Yale Law Journal* 117:4 (January 2008), 550–641; Jenny S. Martinez, "The Slave Trade on Trial: Lessons of a Great Human-Rights Law Success," *Boston Review* (Sept./Oct. 2007), 12–17; Marion Adderley, *New Negroes from Africa: Slave Trade Abolition and Free African Settlement in the Nineteenth-Century Caribbean* (Bloomington: Indiana University Press, 2006), 3; David Eltis and Olatunji Ojo, "The Diaspora of Africans Liberated from Slave Ships in the Nineteenth Century," forthcoming article.

32. Hesketh to Ouseley, Rio de Janeiro, May 31, 1837, FO 84:286; Martinez, "Anti-Slavery Courts," 584–85.

33. There are numerous descriptions of the spread of infections from ports to cities to countryside in Foreign Office Record Group 84 and in the diplomatic correspondence from U.S. consuls contained in U.S. National Archives Record Group 59. For example, see Hesketh and Grigg to Palmerston, Rio de Janeiro, October 4, 1837, FO 84: 219; Campbell to Clayton, Havana, June 30, 1849, USNA, RG 59, Consular Dispatches from Cuba, T-20:22.

34. Rediker, *The Slave Ship*, 276–78; David Northrup, *Africa's Discovery of Europe, 1450–1850*, 2nd ed. (New York: Oxford University Press, 2008, 64–69.

35. Macleay and Schenley to Palmerston, Havana, December 31, 1835, FO 84:172. See African Origins Project for information describing the Africans of the captured slave ship *Tita*.

36. Hesketh to Ouseley, Rio de Janeiro, May 31, 1837, FO 84:286.

37. Villiers to Don Eusebio de Bardaji y Azara, Madrid, December 2, 1837, FO 84:221; Turnbull to H.M. Commissioners, Havana, January 11, 1841, FO 84:347.

38. Turnbull to H.M. Commissioners, Havana, January 12, 1841, FO 84:347.

39. Kennedy and Schenley to Palmerston, Havana, November 22, 1837, FO 84:217.

40. Kennedy and Schenley to Palmerston, Havana, November 22, 1837, FO 84:217.

41. Jerningham to Clarendon, Rio de Janeiro, April 9, 1856, FO 84:993.

42. Nixon to Commissioners of Mixed Court, Havana, October 24, 1837, FO 84:217.

43. Robertson to Marcy, Havana, February 7, 1854, USNA, RG 59, Consular Dispatches from Cuba, T-20:27.

44. Piero Gleijeses, "Haiti's Contribution to the Independence of Spanish America: A Forgotten Chapter," *Revista/Review Interamericana* 9:4 (Winter 1979–1980), 511–28.

45. Landers, *Atlantic Creoles*, 174; George Reid Andrews, *Afro-Latin America, 1800–2000* (New York: Oxford University Press, 2004), 68–69.

46. Bunce to Wyvill, Tenghy Bay, June 8, 1850, FO 84:868; Frere and Surtees to Palmerston, Cape Town, March 1, 1851, Accounts and Papers of Parliament: Slave Trade, 47:1, document no. 44.

47. Jackson and Grigg to Palmerston, Rio de Janeiro, July 31, 1835, FO 84:175.

48. The "intelligent interpreter" Tom Reed is described in Gregory to Castlerough, Sierra Leone, February 25, 1820, FO 84:4; the African interpreter Ogoo is noted in Jackson and Ricketts to Aberdeen, Sierra Leone, February 26, 1829, FO 84:90; "a Native of the Gold Coast" interpreted the statements of enslaved Africans after the capture of the Brazilian slave brig *Felicidade* by HMS *Syhynx* in Hayne to Backhouse, Under Secretary of State for Foreign Affairs in London, on board H.M. brig *Sphynx*, at sea off West Africa, November 12, 1829, FO 84:93; the interpreter Juan Cabinda is described in Macleay to Wellington, Havana, April 11, 1835, FO 84:171; inquiries related to the self-proclaimed interpreter Manuel are found in Macleay and Schenley to Palmerston, Havana, July 19, 1835, FO 84:172; the African sailor George Elder, a member of the West India Regiment stationed on board the *Romney*, interpreted the statements of recaptured Africans from the Spanish slave schooner *Jesus Maria* after it arrived at the port of Havana, as noted in Turnbull to H.M. Commissioners, Havana, January 12, 1841, FO 84:347; the African named Thomas Pilot interpreted the words of the female Assatu, a Liberated African from the captured slave ship *Tobasco*, as found in the "Interrogation of various Liberated Africans before Robert Lawson Esquire, Police Magistrate, and John McCormack," Freetown, October 9 and 11, 1847, FO 84:665; the Kruman Mark Antony interpreted on behalf of Lieutenant F.M. Campbell of HMS *Castor* along the Monega (or Tejungo) River, as described in Campbell to Wyvill, on board the *Castor*, January 4, 1851, Accounts and Papers of Parliament: Slave Trade, 47:1, Reports from Naval Officers, Document 131, Enclosure 2; the Malay African named Margan interpreted the words of "the Negro boy José" from the Portuguese brig *Eolo* at the Mixed British and Portuguese Commission Court at Cape Town, as noted in Frere and Surtees to Palmerston, Cape Town, June 15, 1851, Accounts and Papers of Parliament: Slave Trade, 47:1, Document No. 46, Enclosure 6; and Jim Johnson, "a native of the Cossoo country," interpreted for the workers named Sesah and Bye at the Police Court of Freetown, Examination before Robert Armstrong, Police Magistrate for the colony, as found in McDonald to Malmesbury, Freetown, July 5, 1852, FO 84:868. For the critical role of the African interpreters James Ferry (Kissi who spoke Vai), Charles Pratt, and James Covey (both Mende speakers) during the famous trial of the *Amistad* Africans at New Haven, Connecticut, see Marcus Rediker, *The Amistad Rebellion: An Atlantic Odyssey of Slavery and Freedom* (New York: Viking Penguin, 2012), 124–26, 136–37.

49. Senate speech of Marques of Barbacena, Rio de Janeiro, June 30, 1837, FO 84:218.

50. Bernardo Augusto Nascentes D'Azambuja, "Affairs at Marambaia," *Jornal do Commercio*, Feb. 21, 1851. For descriptions of the critical role of speech and vocabulary to determine whether an African had been "recently landed" or could communicate in "the Brazilian language," meaning that they had been born in Brazil or had resided in Brazil for an extended period, see Sidney

Chalhoub, *A força da escravidão: ilegalidade e costume no Brasil oitocentista* (São Paulo: Companhia das Letras, 2012), 83–91, 103–04, 137–40.

51. Senate speech of Marques of Barbacena, Rio de Janeiro, June 30, 1837, FO 84:218. See Robert W. Slenes, "The Brazilian Internal Slave Trade, 1850–1888: Regional Economies, Slave Experience, and the Politics of a Peculiar Market," in *The Chattel Principle: Internal Slave Trades in the Americas*, ed. Walter Johnson (New Haven, Conn.: Yale University Press, 2004), 325–70; and Richard Graham, "*Another Middle Passage?*: The Internal Slave Trade in Brazil," in Johnson, ed., *The Chattel Principle*, 291–324.

52. Hamilton to Coutinho, Rio de Janeiro, October 21, 1841, FO 84:367.

53. Howard to Abreo, Rio de Janeiro, April 8, 1854, FO 84:942; Cowper to Malmsbury, Recife, May 6, 1852, FO 84:880.

54. See Maggie Montesinos Sale, *The Slumbering Volcano: American Slave Ship Revolts and the Production of Rebellious Masculinity* (Durham, N.C.: Duke University Press, 1997); and Phillip Troutman, "*Grapevine in the Slave Market*: African American Geopolitical Literacy and the 1841 *Creole* Revolt," in Johnson, ed., *The Chattel Principle*, 203–33.

55. Edward E. Baptist, "'*Cuffy*,' '*Fancy Maids*,' and '*One-Eyed Men*': Rape, Commodification, and the Domestic Slave Trade in the United States," *American Historical Review* 106:5 (2001), 1619–50.

56. "Message from the Provincial Assembly of Rio de Janeiro to the Imperial Government," Rio de Janeiro, March 17, 1835, FO 84:174; Beatriz Gallotti Mamigonian, "Do que 'o preto mina' é capaz: etnia e resistência entre africanos livres," *Afro-Ásia* 24 (2000), 77–80; Celia Maria Marinho de Azevedo, *Onda negra, medo branco: o negro no imaginário das elites, século xix* (Rio de Janeiro: Paz e Terra, 1987), 112–23; Maria Helena Machado, *O plano e o pânico: os movimentos sociais na década da abolição* (São Paulo: Editora UFRJ/EDUSP, 1994).

57. Kent to Webster, Rio de Janeiro, April 10, 1852, USNA, RG 59, Consular Dispatches from Rio de Janeiro, T-172:15. This letter includes the observation that interviews enabled authorities to determine whether a slave was a "new black" because "their speech betrayeth them." In other words, a recently landed African could not speak Portuguese or Spanish. See also comments of Lieutenant Charles Wake, commander of the HMS *Bonetta* to Southern, Salvador, Feburary 19, 1852, FO 84:878.

58. Hudson to Palmerston, Rio de Janeiro, August 14, 1851, FO 84:846; Hesketh to Hudson, Rio de Janeiro, August 1, 1851, FO 84:846.

59. Commander Chamberlain on board HMS *Sharpshooter*, Rio de Janeiro, July 26, 1851, FO 84:846; Hudson to Palmerston, Rio de Janeiro, August 14, 1851, FO 84:846. See also Beatriz G. Mamigonian, "In the Name of Freedom: Slave Trade Abolition, the Law and the Brazilian Branch of the African Emigration Scheme (Brazil-British West Indies, 1830s–1850s)," *Slavery and Abolition* 30:1 (March 2009), 41–66.

60. Andrews, *Afro-Latin America*, 143–44; George Reid Andrews, *Blacks and Whites in São Paulo, Brazil, 1888–1988* (Madison: University of Wisconsin Press, 1991); Florestan Fernandes, *A integração do negro na sociedade de classes*, vol. 2 (São Paulo: Editora Ática, 1978), 7–115.

61. Macleay to Aberdeen, Havana, January 1, 1831, FO 84:119.

62. Crawford and Lousada to Clarendon, Havana, October 30, 1856, FO 84:984.

63. Kennedy and Dalrymple to Aberdeen, Havana, January 17, 1842, FO 84:395.

64. Kennedy and Dalrymple to Palmerston, Havana, November 6, 1846, FO 84:621.

65. Backhouse to Clarendon, Havana, June [a mistake, in fact July] 18, 1855, FO 84:959. See also Crawford to Clarendon, Havana, January 14, 1856, FO 84:984.

66. José Pavia to Captain General, Entrance of Ortigosa, June 27, 1854, FO 84:930.

67. Ibid.

68. Crawford to Clarendon, Havana, January 14, 1856, FO 84:984, underlined in the original. The Trans-Atlantic Slave Trade Database notes that 600 slaves departed from Ouidah and that 584 were disembarked at Bahia Honda, Voyage number 4190.

69. Chief of Police Eusébio de Queiroz to Minister of Justice Manoel Alves Branco, Rio de Janeiro, Feb. 27, 1835, ANRJ/SPE, IJ 6 170; Chief of Police Antonio Simoens da Silva to Minister of Justice Eusébio de Queiroz, Rio de Janeiro, December 2, 1849, ANRJ/SPE, IJ 6 212.

70. Dale T. Graden, "Slave Resistance and the Abolition of the Trans-Atlantic Slave Trade to Brazil in 1850," *Revista História Unisinos* 14:3 (September/December 2010), 283–94.

71. Jeffrey D. Needell, *The Party of Order: The Conservatives, the State, and Slavery in the Brazilian Monarchy, 1831–1871* (Stanford, Calif.: Stanford University Press, 2006), 143.

72. For communication through the port cities of the Atlantic basin, see Linebaugh and Rediker, *The Many-Headed Hydra*, and W. Jeffrey Bolster, *Black Jacks: African American Seamen in the Age of Sail* (Cambridge, Mass.: Harvard University Press, 1997).

73. Disembarkations in Brazil dropped rapidly from thirty thousand Africans in 1850 to five thousand in 1851 to zero in 1853 (as listed in official British Foreign Office records). Clandestine disembarkations continued for at least a decade, but the number of arrivals is not known. Bethell, *The Abolition of the Brazilian Slave Trade*, 313–15.

74. Hudson to Palmerston, Rio de Janeiro, February 11, 1851, FO 84:843.

75. Hudson to Palmerston, Rio de Janeiro, August 14, 1851, FO 84:846.

76. Southern to Granville, Rio de Janeiro, March 11, 1852, FO 84:878.

77. Jerningham to Clarendon, Rio de Janeiro, June 11, 1853, FO 84:911. See Mônica Lima e Souza, "Entre margens: O retorno à África de libertos no Brasil, 1830–1870," PhD thesis, Universidade Federal Fluminense, 2008; Mamigonian, "Do que 'o preto mina' é capaz"; Beatriz Gallotti Mamigonian, "Conflicts over the Meaning of Freedom: The Liberated Africans' Struggle for Final Emancipation in Brazil, 1840s–1860s," in *Paths to Freedom: Manumission in the Atlantic World*, ed. Rosemary Brana-Shute and Randy J. Sparks (Columbia: University of South Carolina Press, 2009), 235–64.

78. Manuela Carneiro da Cunha, *Negros, estrangeiros: os escravos libertos e sua volta à África* (São Paulo: Brasiliense, 1985), and Marianno Carneiro da Cunha, *From Slave Quarters to Town Houses: Brazilian Architecture in Nigeria and the People's Republic of Benin* (São Paulo: Livraria Nobel-Edusp, 1985).

79. Conrad, *World of Sorrow*, 154–70; Martínez-Fernández, *Fighting Slavery in the Caribbean*, 50–58.

80. Tindal to Porter, Salvador, Bahia, May 2, 1848, FO 84:725.

81. See Gilberto Freyre, *O escravo nos anúncios de jornais brasileiros do século XIX* (Recife: Imprensa Universitária, 1963).

82. "Fugidas," *Correio Mercantil*, May 5, 1848. Thanks to Paulo Cesar de Oliveira for pointing out the notice. See Dale T. Graden and Paulo Cesar Oliveira de Jesus, "*Bella Miquelina*: tráfico de africanos, tensões, medos e luta por liberdade nas águas da Baia de Todos os Santos em 1848," in *Escravidão e invenção da liberdade*, vol. 2, ed. Lisa Earl Castillo (Salvador: Editora Universidade Federal da Bahia, 2014).

83. Report from Paulino José Soares de Souza to Chamber of Deputies, Session of February 1, 1850 (Rio de Janeiro: Typographia Imperial e Constitucional, 1850), as found in Hudson to Palmerston, Rio de Janeiro, February 18, 1850, FO 13:274.

84. Troutman, "*Grapevine in the Slave Market*," 206–07.

85. Landers, *Atlantic Creoles*, 13.

86. O'Sullivan to Buchanan, Havana, April 28, 1848, USNA, RG 59, Consular Dispatches from Cuba, T-20:21.

87. Campbell to Buchanan, Havana, July 7, 1848, USNA, RG 59, Consular Dispatches from Cuba, T-20:22.

88. O'Sullivan to Buchanan, Havana, April 28, 1848, USNA, RG 59, Consular Dispatches from Cuba, T-20:21.

89. My description is based on Landers, *Atlantic Creoles*, 204–30.

90. Walter LaFeber, *The New Empire: An Interpretation of American Expansion, 1860–1898* (Ithaca, NY: Cornell University Press, 1963); Robert E. May, *Manifest Destiny's Underworld: Filibustering in Antebellum America* (Durham: University of North Carolina Press, 2002).

91. Barnet, *Biography of a Runaway Slave*; Dale T. Graden, "*Biography of a Runaway Slave*: Testimonial Literature as History," H-Ethnic, Reviews in the Humanities and Social Sciences (October 1996), http://www.h-net.org/reviews/showpdf.php?id=650; Michael Zeuske, "The *Cimarrón* in the Archives: A Re-Reading of Miguel Barnet's Biography of Esteban Montejo," *New West Indian Guide/Nieuwe West Indische Gids* 71:3–4 (1997), 265–79.

92. Campbell to Alcoy, Havana, June 19, 1848, USNA, RG 59, Consular Dispatches from Cuba, T-20:22.

93. Buchanan to O'Sullivan, Washington, July 27, 1848, USNA, RG 59, Consular Dispatches from Cuba, T-20:22. See R.M. Blackett, *Building an Antislavery Wall: Black Americans in the Atlantic Abolitionist Movement, 1831–1860* (Baton Rouge: Louisiana State University Press, 1983).

94. Macleay to Aberdeen, Havana, January 1, 1829, FO 84:91.

95. See Mamigonian, "Do que 'o preto mina' é capaz," 71–95.

96. Cited in Simon Schama, *Rough Crossings: The Slaves, the British, and the American Revolution* (New York: HarperCollins, 2006), 66.

97. Dow, *Slave Ships and Slaving*, 122–23.

CHAPTER SEVEN

1. Parks to Buchanan, Rio de Janeiro, November 14, 1846, USNA, RG 59, Consular Dispatches from Rio de Janeiro, T-172:12.

2. Hesketh to Palmerston, Rio de Janeiro, February 19, 1847, FO 84:679. See also deposition of J. David Clement Bevans at U.S. consulate, Rio de Janeiro, November 14, 1846, USNA, RG 59, Consular Dispatches from Rio de Janeiro, T-172:12.

3. Parks to Buchanan, Rio de Janeiro, November 14, 1846, and August 20, 1847, USNA, RG 59, Consular Dispatches from Rio de Janeiro, T-172:12. See Mary Karasch, "The Brazilian Slavers and the Illegal Slave Trade, 1836–1851," Master's thesis, University of Wisconsin, 1967, 15–17.

4. Trans-Atlantic Slave Trade Database, Voyage number 900221.

5. Westwood to Palmerston, Rio de Janeiro, February 17, 1848, FO 84:727.

6. Trans-Atlantic Slave Trade Database, Voyage number 900228. Given that the same number of slaves embarked and disembarked as listed in note 4 above (voyage number 900221), it would appear that more research needs to be done on the second voyage of the *Brazil*. See also Parks to Buchanan, Rio de Janeiro, December 4, 1848, USNA, RG 59, Consular Dispatches from Rio de Janeiro, T-172:12.

7. Hudson to Palmerston, Rio de Janeiro, September 2, 1850, FO 84:806, and Porter to Palmerston, Salvador, August 19, 1850, FO 13:277. For a convoluted description of the travels of the *Brazil*, see the deposition of Lewis Kraft at the U.S. consulate in Rio de Janeiro on September 14, 1848, as contained in Parks to Buchanan, Rio de Janeiro, December 4, 1848, USNA, RG 59, Consular Dispatches from Rio de Janeiro, T-172:12. It appears that Kraft had a financial stake in the *Brazil*, as noted in Karasch, "The Brazilian Slavers," 17.

8. Porter to Fanshawe, Salvador, May 4, 1850, FO 84:808; Porter to Palmerston, Salvador, May 13, 1850, FO 84:808.

9. Kennedy to Palmerston, Havana, January 1, 1851, FO 84:832. Trans-Atlantic Slave Trade Database, Voyage number 4425.

10. Trans-Atlantic Slave Trade Database, Voyage numbers 4430 and 4435. For a description of another slaving vessel named the *San José* that sailed from Brazil to Africa and landed 419 Africans at Cabañas, Cuba in February 1846, see Dalrymple to Palmerston, Havana, June 7, 1847, FO 84:667, and Trans-Atlantic Slave Trade Database, Voyage number 4403.

11. Crawford to Palmerston, Havana, November 12, 1851, FO 84: 832. See Robin Law, "A communidade brasileira de Uidá e os últimos anos do tráfico Atlântico de escravos, 1850–66," *Afro-Ásia* 27 (2002), 41–77, and Luiz Alberto Couceiro, "Acusações atlânticos: o caso dos escravos num navio fantasma—Rio de Janeiro, 1861," *Revista de História* 152 (2005), 71–74.

12. Depositions of Joshua Clapp to Gorham Parks, Rio de Janeiro, November 14 and 24, 1847, USNA, RG 59, Consular Dispatches from Rio de Janeiro, T-172:12. See Robin Blackburn, *The American Crucible: Slavery, Emancipation and Human Rights* (London: Verso, 2011), 294; Robert Edgar Conrad, *World of Sorrow: The African Slave Trade to Brazil* (Baton Rouge: Louisiana State University Press, 1986), 133–53; Seymour Drescher, *Abolition: A History of Slavery and Antislavery* (New York: Cambridge University Press, 2009), 316; Gerald Horne, *The Deepest South: The United States, Brazil and the African Slave Trade* (New York: New York University Press, 2007).

13. Westwood to Palmerston, Rio de Janeiro, February 17, 1848, FO 84:727. See also Tod to Buchanan, Rio de Janeiro, October 16, 1847, USNA, RG 59, Consular Dispatches from Brazil, M-121:19.

14. Kennedy to Palmerston, Havana, January 1, 1851, FO 84:832. Trans-Atlantic Slave Trade Database, Voyage number 4430.

15. Hesketh to Palmerston, Rio de Janeiro, March 14, 1850, FO 84:808. See also Blackburn, *The American Crucible*, 232, and Warren S. Howard, *American Slavers and the Federal Law, 1837–1862* (Berkeley: University of California Press, 1963).

16. Hunter to Webster, Rio de Janeiro, Rio de Janeiro, January 31, 1843, USNA, RG 59, Consular Dispatches from Brazil, M-121:14.

17. David Eltis and David Richardson, *Atlas of the Transatlantic Slave Trade* (New Haven, Conn.: Yale University Press, 2010), 285.

18. Surtees to Palmerston, Cape Town, South Africa, January 23, 1850, FO 84:790.

19. Ibid. See also Bunce to Hamerton, on board HMS *Castor* near Zanzibar, May 27, 1850, FO 84:868; Bunce to Wyvill, Tenghy Bay, June 8, 1850, FO 84:868.

20. Frere and Surtees to Palmerston, Cape Town, January 30 and April 23, 1850, FO 84:790.

21. McDonald to Porter, Sierra Leone, December 1849, FO 84:803; Porter to Hudson, Salvador, January 22, 1850, FO 84:803.

22. Porter to Hudson, Salvador, October 31, 1850, FO 84:807; Hudson to Souza, Rio de Janeiro, November 6, 1850, FO 84:807; Christophers to Palmerston, Recife, December 21, 1850, FO 84:809; Kent to Webster, Rio de Janeiro, April 10, 1852, USNA, RG 59, Consular Dispatches from Rio de Janeiro, T-172:15.

23. Olinda to Hudson, Rio de Janeiro, September 3, 1849, FO 84:766; Paulino to Hudson, Rio de Janeiro, June 14, 1850, FO 84:804.

24. Schomberg to Hudson, Rio de Janeiro, February 8, 1850, FO 84:802; Trans-Atlantic Slave Trade Database, Voyage number 4100. The *Paulina* departed Africa with 1,094 Africans in its hold. Hence, 194 Africans perished in the Middle Passage.

25. Schomberg to Reynolds, Rio de Janeiro, July 5, 1850, FO 84:804.

26. Schomberg to Martins, Salvador, October 5, 1850, and Schomberg to Reynolds, Salvador, October 10, 1850, FO 84:807. See also Porter to Hudson, Salvador, January 11, 1851, FO 84:843.

27. "The English Blockade," *O século*, October 8, 1850.

28. Palmerston to Lisboa, London, October 10, 1851, FO 84:842.

29. Trans-Atlantic Slave Trade Database, Voyage number 4786.

30. Wanderley to Martins, Salvador, November 18, 1851, FO 84:878.

31. Luís Henrique Dias Tavares, *O desembarque da Pontinha* (Salvador: Centro de Estudos Baianos, UFBA, 1971), 5. The book was most likely the recently published *Dicionário de medicina popular*, 2nd ed. (Rio de Janeiro: Tipografia Laemmert, 1851). See M.R.C. Guimarães, "Chernoviz e os manuais de medicina popular no Império," *História, Ciências, Saúde-Manguinhos* (Rio de Janeiro) 12:2 (maio/ago. 2005), 501–14.

32. Tavares, *O desembarque*, 6.

33. Wanderley to Martins, Salvador, November 18, 1851, FO 84:878.

34. Wetherell to Hudson, Salvador, November 7, 1851, FO 84:847; Wetherell to Palmerston, Salvador, November 11, 1851, FO 84:848.

35. Wanderley to Martins, Salvador, November 18, 1851, FO 84:878; Martins to Queiroz, Salvador, November 29, 1851, FO 84:878.

36. Tavares, *O desembarque*, 6.

37. Martins to Wanderley, Salvador, November 5, 1851, FO 84:847.

38. Wanderley to Martins, Salvador, November 18, 1851, FO 84:878. See also Jaime Rodrigues, *O infame comércio: propostas e experiências no final do tráfico de africanos para o Brasil (1800–1850)* (Campinas, SP: Unicamp/Cecult, 2000), 188–91.

39. Southern to Malmesbury, Rio de Janeiro, May 1, 1852, FO 84:878.

40. Southern to Malmesbury, Rio de Janeiro, May 1, 1852, FO 84:878 (separate document from above). Key figures in this "association of slave dealers" included Antonio Pinto da Fonseca, José Rodrigues Bernardino Ferreira, and the U.S. citizen George Marsden at Rio de Janeiro, along with a Brazilian named Leandro Rodrigues Chaves at Porto Alegre. Individuals at Lisbon and Porto, Portugal included Manoel Pinto da Fonseca (brother of Antonio), Thomas Domingo

da Costa Ramos, José de Sá Miranda, João Pedro da Costa Coimbra, and Francisco Riveirosa, all of whom had fled or been banished from Brazil. Traffickers along the coast of Africa included Fernando (also known as Francisco) Antonio Flores at Ambriz, Angola; Manoel Domingues Dias Pereira at Luanda, Angola; João José de Lima at Lomé, Togo; Domingos José Martínez at Porto Novo, Benin; and Joaquim de Almedia, an African who had been enslaved at Salvador, gained his freedom, and then went to Agué, Central African Republic. In Havana, key figures included Rodrigo José de Abreu, Antonio Augusto Botelho, Francisco dos Santos Tavares, and Manoel Joaquim Teixeira, and in the Azores, Antonio Severino de Avellar. See Southern to Malmesbury, Rio de Janeiro, April 8 and May 21, 1852, FO 84:878; Southern to Paulino, Rio de Janeiro, June 24 and October 27, 1852, FO 84:879; Morgan to Southern, Salvador, December 29, 1852, FO 84:911; Jerningham to Clarendon, Rio de Janeiro, October 1, 1853, FO 84:911; Jerningham to Paranhos, Rio de Janeiro, September 20, 1855, FO 84:968; Jerningham to Clarendon, Rio de Janeiro, March 8, 1856, FO 84:993.

41. Southern to Malmesbury, Rio de Janeiro, August 13, 1852, FO 84:879.

42. Kent to Southern, Rio de Janeiro, August 27, 1852, FO 84:879; A. Oaksmith to U.S. consul John Gillmer, Salvador, July 26, 1852, USNA, RG 59, Consular Dispatches from Bahia, T-172:11.

43. Southern to Paulino, Rio de Janeiro, August 16, 1852, FO 84:879.

44. See Winston McGowan, "African Resistance to the Atlantic Slave Trade in West Africa," *Slavery and Abolition* 11:1 (May 1990), 5–29.

45. Southern to Malmesbury, Rio de Janeiro, May 1, 1852, FO 84:878.

46. Ibid.

47. Trans-Atlantic Slave Trade Database, Voyage number 4154.

48. Southern to Malmesbury, Rio de Janeiro, January 4, 1853, FO 84:911. See Martha Abreu, "O caso do Bracuhy," in *Resgate: uma janela para o oitocentos*, org. Hebe Maria Mattos de Castro and Eduardo Schnoor (Rio de Janeiro: Topbooks, 1995), 166–95.

49. Jerningham to Malmsebury, Rio de Janeiro, February 7, 1853, FO 84:911.

50. Jerningham to Malmesbury, Rio de Janeiro, February 7, 1853, FO 84:911; Kent to Everett, Rio de Janeiro, January 22, 1853, USNA, RG 59, Consular Dispatches from Rio de Janeiro, T-172:15.

51. Kent to Everett, Rio de Janeiro, January 22, 1853, USNA, RG 59, Consular Dispatches from Rio de Janeiro, T-172:15; Francisco Pereira de Vasconcellos to José Sousa Ramos, Rio de Janeiro, January 8, 1853, ANRJ/SPE, IJ 6 468.

52. Kent to Everett, Rio de Janeiro, January 22, 1853, USNA, RG 59, Consular Dispatches from Rio de Janeiro, T-172:15; Helm to Cass, Havana, April 11, 1860, USNA, RG 59, Consular Dispatches from Cuba, T-20:40. See also Ron Soodalter, *Hanging Captain Gordon: The Life and Trial of an American Slave Trader* (New York: Atria Publishers, 2006), 24; Adam Goodheart, "A Slave Ship in New York," *The New York Times*, November 3, 2010, http://opinionator.blogs.nytimes.com/2010/11/03/a-slave-ship-in-new-york/.

53. Jerningham to Malmesbury, Rio de Janeiro, February 7, 1853, FO 84:911.

54. Jerningham to Russell, Rio de Janeiro, March 4, 1853, FO 84:911, underlined in the original; Abreu, "O caso do Bracuhy," 186–89.

55. Jerningham to Russell, Rio de Janeiro, April 2, 1853, FO 84:911; Jerningham to Clarendon, Rio de Janeiro, June 11, 1853, FO 84:911; *Jornal do Commercio* (Rio de Janeiro), May 18 and 19, 1853.

56. Jerningham to Clarendon, Rio de Janeiro, August 27, 1853, FO 84:911. See also Thiago Campos Pessoa, "O comércio negreiro na clandestinidade: as fazendas de recepção de africanos da família Souza Breves e seus cativos," *Afro-Ásia* 47 (2013), 43–78.

57. Kent to Webster, Rio de Janeiro, April 10, 1852, USNA, RG 59, Consular Dispatches from Rio de Janeiro, T-172:15; Jerningham to Clarendon, Rio de Janeiro, June 11, 1853, FO 84:911.

58. Howard to Clarendon, Rio de Janeiro, August 28, 1854, FO 84:943; Cowper to Clarendon, Recife, April 13, 1855, FO 84:969; Morgan to Clarendon, Salvador, January 2, 1854, FO 84:944; Morgan to Clarendon, Salvador, March 17, 1855, FO 84:969.

59. Howard to Clarendon, Rio de Janeiro, June 10, 1854, FO 84:943.

60. See as examples *Philanthopo* (Rio de Janeiro), February 1, 1850, and *Grito Nacional* (Rio de Janeiro), November 3, 1855; *O século* (Salvador), July 9, 1850, and *A Justiça: Periódico Politico e Litterário* (Salvador), January 25, 1851; *Diário de Pernambuco* (Recife), October 17, 1855.

61. "The Yacht *Maria Até Ver*," *O século* (Salvador), October 3, 1850.

62. "Trial and condemnation of the *Mary E. Smith*," Ministry of Justice, signed by Marques de Abrantes, April 17, 1856, Rio de Janeiro. This document is contained in FO 84:994. Also see "Deposition of Vincent Daniel Cranatich before chief of police of Bahia," February 4, 1856, as found in Jerningham to Clarendon, Rio de Janeiro, June 12, 1856, FO 84:994.

63. Howard, *American Slavers*, 124–26; Gilmer to Secretary of State William Marcy, Salvador, February 1, 1856, USNA, RG 59, Consular Dispatches from Bahia, T-331:1.

64. Howard to Marquis de Soulé, Lisbon, December 3, 1856, FO 84:992.

65. Jerningham to Clarendon, Rio de Janeiro, December 14, 1855, FO 84:968.

66. William Blake et al. to U.S. consul R.K. Meade, Salvador, May 27, 1858, USNA, RG 59, Consular Dispatches from Brazil, M-121:27.

67. Ibid., author's emphasis.

68. Gabriel to Captain General José Rodrigues Coelho do Amaral, Loanda, May 14, 1859, FO 84:1075.

69. Couceiro, "Acusações atlânticos," 70–73.

70. David Brion Davis, "Foreword," in Eltis and Richardson, *Atlas of the Transatlantic Slave Trade*, xxii. For a good overview of British suppression strategies from 1826 to 1852, read Cowper to Malmesbury, Recife, May 6, 1852, FO 84:880.

71. See João José Reis, Flávio dos Santos Gomes, and Marcus J.M. de Carvalho, *O alufá Rufino: tráfico, escravidão e liberdade no Atlântico negro (c.1822–c.1853)* (São Paulo: Companhia das Letras, 2010), 255–57.

72. Wise to Calhoun, Rio de Janeiro, October 11, 1844, USNA, RG 59, Consular Dispatches from Brazil, M-121:15; William Gore Ouseley, *Notes on the Slave-Trade with Remarks on the Measures Adopted for its Suppression* (London: John Rodwell Publisher, 1850), 61–62.

73. For a description of a slave revolt on board the *Santa Cruz* in December 1849 near the coast of Brazil, see José Santos to Leopoldo Camara Lima, Santos, January 6, 1850, FO 84:802, and Hudson to Palmerston, Rio de Janeiro, February 20, 1850, FO 84:802. The successful interceptions of landings along the coast of São Paulo by Brazilian magistrates Motta and Xavier are described in Hudson to Palmerston, Rio de Janeiro, May 12, 1850, FO 84:803. The visit of the Quakers named Chandler and Burgess, which included a meeting with Pedro II, is described in Southern to Malmesbury, Rio de Janeiro, November 13, 1852, FO 84:879. See also The Religious

Society of Friends, *Facts and Observations Relative to the Participation of American Citizens in the African Slave Trade* (Whitefish, Mont.: Kessinger Publishers, 2010; originally published in 1841); Philadelphia Yearly Meeting of the Religious Society of Friends, *An Exposition of the African Slave Trade, from the year 1840 to 1850, inclusive* (Philadelphia: J. Rakestraw, printer, 1851); Howard Temperley, *British Antislavery, 1833–1870* (London: Longman, 1972).

74. Morgan to Clarendon, Salvador, August 18, 1853, FO 84:912. For an in-depth description of the resurgence of the north triangle and some of the principal traffickers after mid-century, see Southern to Malmesbury, Rio de Janeiro, April 8, 1852, FO 84:878. See also Kennedy to Palmerston, Havana, January 1, 1850, FO 84:789. For an earlier description of such a voyage, see Dalrymple to Palmerston, Havana, June 7, 1847, FO 84:667.

75. Crawford to Palmerston, Havana, January 1, 1852, FO 84:870. Trans-Atlantic Slave Trade Database, Voyage number 4435.

76. Ibid. The FO 84 series has numerous comments about the terrible treatment inflicted on Liberated Africans. Andres Carabalí is described in Crawford to Palmerston, Havana, October 8, 1847, FO 84:668; Angela Lucumí in Backhouse to Clarendon, Havana, February 7, 1855, FO 84:959; and the African named Trinidad in Crawford and Lousada to Clarendon, Havana, May 25, 1857, FO 84:1012.

77. Kennedy to Palmerston, Havana, May 27, 1850, FO 84:789; Backhouse to Clarendon, Havana, January 1, 1853, and October 10, 1853, FO 84:898.

78. Backhouse to Clarendon, Havana, January 1, 1855, FO 84:959.

79. Campbell to Clayton, Havana, June 30, 1849, USNA, RG 59, Consular Dispatches from Cuba, T-20:22; Clayton to Marcy, New York, July 17, 1853, USNA, RG 59, Consular Dispatches from Cuba, T-20:26.

80. Backhouse to Clarendon, Havana, October 10, 1853, FO 84:898; Robertson to Marcy, Havana, June 22, 1855, USNA, RG 59, Consular Dispatches from Cuba, T-20:29.

81. Trans-Atlantic Slave Trade Database.

82. Manuel Barcia, *Seeds of Insurrection: Domination and Resistance on Western Cuban Plantations, 1808–1848* (Baton Rouge: Louisiana State University Press, 2008), 28.

83. Gabino La Rosa Corzo, *Runaway Slave Settlements in Cuba: Resistance and Repression*, trans. Mary Todd (Chapel Hill: University of North Carolina Press, 1988), 200.

84. Kennedy to Palmerston, Havana, January 1, 1850, FO 84:789. See Luis Martínez-Fernández, *Fighting Slavery in the Caribbean: The Life and Times of a British Family in Nineteenth-Century Havana* (Armonk, N.Y.: M.E. Sharpe, 1998).

85. Martínez to Davis, Havana, May 14, 1854, USNA, RG 59, Consular Dispatches from Cuba, T-20:29. Underlined in the original.

86. Robertson to Marcy, Havana, May 18, 1854, USNA, RG 59, Consular Dispatches from Cuba, T-20:27.

87. Ibid.

88. For comments on the existence of palenques composed of "disaffected gangs of slaves in the eastern part of the island," see Schufeldt to Seward, Havana, October 12, 1862, USNA, RG 59, Consular Dispatches from Cuba, T-20:45.

89. Crawford to Captain General Cañedo, Havana, March 23, 1853, FO 84:898. The impact of ship revolts on worldview is analyzed in Maggie Montesinos Sale, *The Slumbering Volcano:*

American Slave Ship Revolts and the Production of Rebellious Masculinity (Durham, N.C.: Duke University Press, 1997), and Eric Robert Taylor, *If We Must Die: Shipboard Insurrections in the Era of the Atlantic Slave Trade* (Baton Rouge: Louisiana State University Press, 2006).

90. Deposition of John McCarthy, Savage to Seward, Havana, May 14, 1864, USNA, RG 59, Consular Dispatches from Cuba, T-20:47.

91. Schufeldt to Seward, Havana, Havana, January 14, 1862, USNA, RG 59, Consular Dispatches from Cuba, T-20:45. Underlined in the original.

92. Madan to Pierce, Havana, October 4, 1853, USNA, RG 59, Consular Dispatches from Cuba, T-20:27.

93. Matthias Röhrig Assunçao and Michael Zeuske, "Race, Ethnicity and Social Structure in 19th Century Brazil and Cuba," *Ibero-Amerikanishes Archiv* 24:3–4 (1998), 430.

94. Ivor L. Miller, *Voice of the Leopard: African Secret Societies and Cuba* (Jackson: University Press of Mississippi, 2009), 89–102.

95. Michele Reid-Vazquez, *The Year of the Lash: Free People of Color in Cuba and the Nineteenth-Century Atlantic World* (Athens: University of Georgia Press, 2011), 175; see also 146–79.

96. Davis to Marcy, Washington, D.C., May 22, 1854, USNA, RG 59, Consular Dispatches from Cuba, T-20:29.

97. Andrew Jackson O'Shaughnessy, *An Empire Divided: The American Revolution and the British Caribbean* (Philadelphia: University of Pennsylvania Press, 2000), 147–59.

98. Robertson to Marcy, Havana, February 7, 1854, USNA, RG 59, Consular Dispatches from Cuba, T-20:27.

99. Louis A. Pérez, ed., *Impressions of Cuba in the Nineteenth Century: The Travel Diary of Joseph J. Dimock* (Wilmington, Del.: Scholarly Resources, 1998), ix–xvi.

100. Clayton to Marcy, Havana, December 12, 1853, USNA, RG 59, Consular Dispatches from Cuba, T-20:26; Robertson to Marcy, Havana, March 20, 1854, USNA, RG 59, Consular Dispatches from Cuba, T-20:27. See also Graciella Cruz-Taura, "Annexation and National Identity: Cuba's Mid-Nineteenth-Century Debate," *Cuban Studies* 27 (1997), 90–109, and Tom Chaffin, "'Sons of Washington': Narciso López, Filibustering, and U.S. Nationalism, 1848–1851," *Journal of the Early Republic* 15:1 (Spring 1995), 79–108.

101. Robertson to Marcy, Havana, January 26, 1856, USNA, RG 59, Consular Dispatches from Cuba, T-20:33.

102. C. Stanley Urban, "The Africanization of Cuba Scare, 1853–1855," *Hispanic American Historical Review* 37:1 (February 1957), 30.

103. Campbell to Buchanan, Havana, April 8, 1845, USNA, RG 59, Consular Dispatches from Cuba, T-20:21.

104. William C. van Norman, "The Process of Cultural Change among Cuban Bozales during the Nineteenth Century," *The Americas* 62:2 (October 2005), 200–01.

105. Robertson to Marcy, Havana, May 7, 1854, USNA, RG 59, Consular Dispatches from Cuba, T-20:27.

106. Leslie Bethell, *The Abolition of the Brazilian Slave Trade: Britain, Brazil and the Slave Trade Question, 1807–1869* (Cambridge: Cambridge University Press, 1970), 287, 385; David R. Murray, *Odious Commerce: Britain, Spain and the Abolition of the Cuba Slave Trade* (Cambridge: Cambridge University Press, 1980), 248, 268. See also Crawford to Clarendon, Havana, January 14, 1856,

FO 84:984, and Blythe to Appleton, Havana, March 9, 1858, USNA, RG 59, Consular Dispatches from Cuba, T-20:39.

107. Savage to Marcy, Havana, September 7, 1854, USNA, RG 59, Consular Dispatches from Cuba, T-20:28.

108. Trans-Atlantic Slave Trade Database, Voyage number 4192. With regards to New York's involvement in the slave trade and the politics of suppression there, see Sharla M. Fett, "'The Ship of Slavery': Atlantic Slave Trade Suppression, Liberated Africans, and Black Abolition Politics in Antebellum New York," in *Paths of the Slave Trade: Interactions, Identities and Images*, ed. Ana Lucia Araujo (Amherst, N.Y.: Cambria Press, 2011), 131–59. Fett writes (p. 134) that between spring of 1859 and summer of 1860, traffickers outfitted at least 85 slave vessels at New York.

109. Savage to Marcy, Havana, September 7, 1854, USNA, RG 59, Consular Dispatches from Cuba, T-20:28.

110. Chauncy's written deposition on behalf of himself and seven others imprisoned at Güines (a town located thirty miles southeast of Havana), penned on August 28, 1854, as included in Savage to Marcy, Havana, September 7, 1854, USNA, RG 59, Consular Dispatches from Cuba, T-20:28.

111. Savage to Marcy, Havana, September 11, 1854, USNA, RG 59, Consular Dispatches from Cuba, T-20:28.

112. Chauncey to Savage, Havana Prison, September 19, 1854, USNA, RG 59, Consular Dispatches from Cuba, T-20:28. Underlined in the original.

113. Robertson to Marcy, Havana, October 7, 1854, USNA, RG 59, Consular Dispatches from Cuba, T-20:28.

114. Robertson to Marcy, Havana, October 22, 1854, USNA, RG 59, Consular Dispatches from Cuba, T-20:28.

115. Chauncey to Savage, Havana prison, November 18, 1854, USNA, RG 59, Consular Dispatches from Cuba, T-20:28. Underlined in the original.

116. Robertson to Marcy, Havana, June 22, 1855, USNA, RG 59, Consular Dispatches from Cuba, T-20:29.

117. Schufeldt to Seward, Havana, December 11, 1862, USNA, RG 59, Consular Dispatches from Cuba, T-20:45. Trans-Atlantic Slave Trade Database, Voyage number 4867.

118. The 34,934 documented slave voyages are estimated to be "just over 80 percent of all of the slave ventures that ever set out for Africa to obtain slaves from all locations around the Atlantic," as noted in Eltis and Richardson, *Atlas of the Transatlantic Slave Trade*, xxv.

119. Useful sources include Philip D. Curtin, ed., *Africa Remembered: Narratives by West Africans from the Era of the Slave Trade* (Long Grove, Ill.: Waveland Press, 1997; originally published in 1967), and Anne C. Bailey, *African Voices of the Atlantic Slave Trade: Beyond the Silence and the Shame* (Boston: Beacon Press, 2005).

120. Crawford to Russell, Havana, September 30, 1860, FO 84:1106.

121. Trans-Atlantic Slave Trade Database, Voyage Number 4242.

122. *Philadelphia Monitor*, September 11, 1857, as found in Crawford to Malmesbury, Havana, October 1, 1858, FO 84:1042.

123. Anne Farrow, Joel Lang, and Jenifer Frank, *Complicity: How the North Promoted, Prolonged, and Profited from Slavery* (New York: Ballantine Books, 2005), 10–23.

124. Crawford to Russell, Havana, February 5, 1861, FO 84:1106.

125. One dollar from 1860 could be worth anywhere from $30 to $60 in 2013. Based on the Consumer Price Index, $1 in 1913 would be worth $22 in 2013. If we take into account inflation from the late nineteenth century, an estimate of $40 appears reasonable. Thanks to University of Idaho professor Eric Stuen for helpful estimates. Professor Rediker has estimated a lower amount of inflation, with one dollar in 1839 being worth $24 in 2012, in Marcus Rediker, *The* Amistad *Rebellion: An Atlantic Odyssey of Slavery and Freedom* (New York: Viking Penguin, 2012), 111.

126. Crampton to Russell, Madrid, January 20, 1865, FO 84:1239.

127. Lousada to Clarendon, Havana, May 8, 1856, FO 84:984; Ryder to Malmsebury, Havana, June 24, 1859, FO 84:1073.

128. Crawford and Ryder to Russell, Havana, December 5, 1859, FO 84:1073.

129. Lousada to Clarendon, Havana, April 5, 1857, FO 84:1012.

130. Crawford to Lousada, Havana, January 31, 1857, FO 84:1012.

131. Crawford and Lousada to Clarendon, Havana, January 26, 1858, FO 84:1042.

132. David Eltis and David Richardson, "The Transatlantic Slave Trade and the Civil War," *The New York Times*, January 13, 2011, http://opinionator.blogs.nytimes.com/2011/01/13/the-transatlantic-slave-trade-and-the-civil-war/.

133. For an overview of the political debates of this period, see Philip S. Foner, *A History of Cuba and Its Relations with the United States, 1845–1895: From the Era of Annexation to the Outbreak of the Second War for Independence*, vol. II (New York: International Publishers, 1963), 125–61. Cuban scholars have estimated that traffickers landed twenty thousand African slaves on the island from 1868 through 1873. See Corzo, *Runaway Slave Settlements*, 273, note 20.

134. Savage to Cass, Havana, October 13, 1857, USNA, RG 59, Consular Dispatches from Cuba, T-20:36; Shelton to Clarendon, Sierra Leone, February 15, 1858, FO 84:1041; Crawford to Malmsebury, Havana, July 1, 1858, FO 84:1042.

135. Savage to Cass, Havana, October 13, 1857, USNA, RG 59, Consular Dispatches from Cuba, T-20:36.

136. Vredenbury to Russell, Loanda, June 30, 1864, FO 84:1214

137. Vredenbury to Russell, Loanda, October 25, 1864, FO 84:1214.

138. Vredenbury to Russell, Loanda, September 20, 1864, FO 84:1214.

139. Ibid.

140. Shelton to Clarendon, Sierra Leone, February 15, 1858, FO 84:1041.

141. Savage to Seward, Havana, July 2, 1864, USNA, RG 59, Consular Dispatches from Cuba, T-20:47.

142. Ibid.

143. Schufeldt to Seward, Havana, January 14, 1862, USNA, RG 59, Consular Dispatches from Cuba, T-20:45 (confidential).

144. Savage to Seward, Havana, October 3, 1863, USNA, RG 59, Consular Dispatches from Cuba, T-20:46. See also Matthew J. Clavin, *Toussaint Louverture and the American Civil War: The Promise and Peril of a Second Haitian Revolution* (Philadelphia: University of Pennsylvania Press, 2010).

145. Ada Ferrer, *Insurgent Cuba: Race, Nation, and Revolution, 1868–1878* (Chapel Hill: University of North Carolina Press, 1999); George Reid Andrews, *Afro-Latin America, 1800–2000* (New York: Oxford University Press, 2004), 77–80; Teresa Prados-Torreira, *Mambisas: Rebel Women in Nineteenth-Century Cuba* (Gainesville: University Press of Florida, 2005), 48–75.

CONCLUSION

1. Schenley to Palmerston, Havana, October 25, 1836, FO 84:197. Underlined in the original.

2. Hudson to Palmerston, Rio de Janeiro, November 16 and December 16, 1848, FO 84:726.

3. Crawford to Russell, Havana, September 30, 1860, FO 84:1106.

4. Crawford to Russell, Havana, February 5, 1861, FO 84:1135.

5. Wise to Calhoun, Rio de Janeiro, February 18, 1845, USNA, RG 59, Consular Dispatches from Brazil, M-121:15. Underlined in the original.

6. Kent to Webster, Rio de Janeiro, April 10, 1852, USNA, RG 59, Consular Dispatches from Rio de Janeiro, T-172:15.

7. Ibid. Author's emphasis.

8. See Craig Steven Wilder, *Ebony and Ivy: Race, Slavery, and the Troubled History of America's Universities* (New York: Bloomsbury, 2013).

9. Macleay to Aberdeen, Havana, January 1, 1829, FO 84:91; Melville and Hook to Aberdeen, Sierra Leone, December 31, 1844, FO 84:507; Wise to Hamilton, Rio de Janeiro, December 1, 1844, USNA, RG 59, Consular Dispatches from Brazil, M-121:15; Tod to Buchanan, Rio de Janeiro, October 16, 1847, USNA, RG 59, Consular Dispatches from Brazil, M-121:19; Tod to Clayton, Rio de Janeiro, October 17, 1849, USNA, RG 59, Consular Dispatches from Brazil, M-121:19; Hamilton to Cooke, Montevideo, January 16, 1849, USNA, RG 59, Consular Dispatches from Brazil, M-121:19.

10. Ouesley to Backhouse, Rio de Janeiro, April 13, 1835, FO 84:179; Moon to Gordon, São Luis, Maranhão, May 26, 1838, FO 84:255; Slacum to Upshur, Rio de Janeiro, September 10, 1843, USNA, RG 59, Consular Dispatches from Rio de Janeiro, T-172:8; Ouseley to Palmerston, Rio de Janeiro, October 16, 1840, FO 84:325; Melville and Hook to Aberdeen, Sierra Leone, December 6, 1844, FO 84:507; John R. Spears, *The American Slave-Trade: An Account of Its Origins, Growth and Suppression* (New York: Charles Scribner's Sons, 1900), 42–43. For transatlantic perspectives on this topic, see Barbara L. Solow, ed., *Slavery and the Rise of the Atlantic System* (Cambridge: Cambridge University Press, 1991), and Joseph E. Inikori, *Africans and the Industrial Revolution in England: A Study in International Trade and Economic Development* (Cambridge: Cambridge University Press, 2002).

11. Bunce to Wyvill, on board the *Castor* off Cape Fitzwilliam, January 7, 1851, Accounts and Papers of Parliament: Slave Trade, 47:1, Reports from Naval Officers, Document 131, Enclosure 1.

12. David Eltis, "The U.S. Transatlantic Slave Trade, 1644–1867: An Assessment," *Civil War History* 54:4 (2008), 361, 372.

13. Lousada to Clarendon, Havana, April 5, 1857, FO 84:1012. Note that these estimates do not include the profits derived from construction of the ships.

14. Crawford and Ryder to Russell, Havana, December 5, 1859, FO 84:1073. See also Wise to Buchanan, Rio de Janeiro, May 1, 1845, USNA, RG 59, Consular Dispatches from Brazil, M-121:15; Parkes to Tod, Rio de Janeiro, January 29, 1850, USNA, RG 59, Consular Dispatches from Brazil, M-121:20.

15. See Winifred Barr Rothenberg, "The Invention of American Capitalism: The Economy of New England in the Federal Period," in *Engines of Enterprise: An Economic History of New England*, ed. Peter Temin (Cambridge, Mass.: Harvard University Press, 2000), 93, and Peter Temin, "The Industrialization of New England, 1830–1880," in *Engines of Enterprise*, 109–52.

16. Another book can focus on the historical memory of slave revolts and slave resistance among African slaves, creole slaves, and free blacks in nineteenth-century Brazil and Cuba. I would note that in attempting to comprehend the past, the present often provides insights. U.S. participation in the Vietnam War ended in 1975. In the U.S. presidential elections of 2004 (Bush-Kerry) and 2008 (Obama-McCain), historical memory of the war and its legacies was an important topic, if not the central issue, for the candidates and many citizens. Vivid and frequent reminders of it suggest that individuals of diverse ethnic and class backgrounds do not quickly forget the past.

INDEX

CPSIA information can be obtained at www.ICGtesting.com
Printed in the USA
LVOW11s1824111016

508326LV00002B/262/P